W9-ABZ-619

HELL
under fire

MODERN SCHOLARSHIP REINVENTS
ETERNAL PUNISHMENT

HELL
UNDER fire

Christopher W. Morgan ✦ *Robert A. Peterson*
General Editors

GRAND RAPIDS, MICHIGAN 49530 USA

We affectionately dedicate this book to our students, at
California Baptist University and Covenant Theological Seminary,
respectively, who have helped us grapple with issues
concerning heaven and hell.

CHRISTOPHER W. MORGAN AND ROBERT A. PETERSON

ZONDERVAN™

Hell under Fire
Copyright © 2004 by Christopher W. Morgan and Robert A. Peterson

Requests for information should be addressed to:
Zondervan, *Grand Rapids, Michigan 49530*

Library of Congress Cataloging-in-Publication Data

Hell under fire / Christopher W. Morgan and Robert A. Peterson, general editors—1st ed.
  p. cm.
  Includes bibliographical references and index.
  ISBN 0-310-24041-7
  1. Hell—Christianity. 2. Hell—Biblical teaching. I. Morgan, Christopher W. 1971–II. Peterson,
Robert A., 1948–.
  BT836.3.H45 2004
  236'.25—dc22   2004006766
                                                                          CIP

This edition printed on acid-free paper.

All Scripture quotations, unless otherwise indicated, are taken from the *Holy Bible: New International Version*®. NIV®. Copyright © 1973, 1978, 1984 by International Bible Society. Used by permission of Zondervan. All rights reserved.

The website addresses recommended throughout this book are offered as a resource to you. These websites are not intended in any way to be or imply an endorsement on the part of Zondervan, nor do we vouch for their content for the life of this book.

Interior design by Nancy Wilson

Printed in the United States of America

04 05 06 07 08 09 10 /❖ DC/ 10 9 8 7 6 5 4 3 2 1

CONTENTS

CONTRIBUTORS   7

ABBREVIATIONS   9

INTRODUCTION   11
CHRISTOPHER W. MORGAN AND ROBERT A. PETERSON

1. MODERN THEOLOGY:
THE DISAPPEARANCE OF HELL   15
R. ALBERT MOHLER JR.

2. THE OLD TESTAMENT ON HELL   43
DANIEL I. BLOCK

3. JESUS ON HELL   67
ROBERT W. YARBROUGH

4. PAUL ON HELL   91
DOUGLAS J. MOO

5. THE REVELATION ON HELL   111
GREGORY K. BEALE

6. BIBLICAL THEOLOGY: THREE PICTURES OF HELL   135
CHRISTOPHER W. MORGAN

7. SYSTEMATIC THEOLOGY:
THREE VANTAGE POINTS OF HELL   153
ROBERT A. PETERSON

8. UNIVERSALISM: WILL EVERYONE ULTIMATELY
BE SAVED?   169
J. I. PACKER

9. ANNIHILATIONISM: WILL THE UNSAVED
BE PUNISHED FOREVER?   195
CHRISTOPHER W. MORGAN

10. PASTORAL THEOLOGY: THE PREACHER AND HELL   219
SINCLAIR B. FERGUSON

CONCLUSION   239
  CHRISTOPHER W. MORGAN AND ROBERT A. PETERSON

SELECTED BIBLIOGRAPHY   241

SCRIPTURE INDEX   245

AUTHOR INDEX   251

SUBJECT INDEX   253

CONTRIBUTORS

Gregory K. Beale (Ph.D., University of Cambridge), Chair of Biblical Studies and Professor of New Testament, Wheaton College Graduate School

Daniel I. Block (D.Phil., University of Liverpool), Associate Dean and Professor of Old Testament Interpretation, Southern Baptist Theological Seminary

Sinclair B. Ferguson (Ph.D., University of Aberdeen), Professor of Systematic Theology, Westminster Theological Seminary

R. Albert Mohler Jr. (Ph.D., Southern Baptist Theological Seminary), President and Professor of Christian Theology, Southern Baptist Theological Seminary

Douglas J. Moo (Ph.D., University of St. Andrews), Professor of New Testament, Wheaton College Graduate School

Christopher W. Morgan (Ph.D., Mid-America Baptist Theological Seminary), Associate Dean and Associate Professor of Theology, California Baptist University

J. I. Packer (D.Phil., Oxford University), Board of Governors and Professor of Theology, Regent College

Robert A. Peterson (Ph.D., Drew University), Professor of Systematic Theology, Covenant Theological Seminary

Robert W. Yarbrough (Ph.D., University of Aberdeen), Chair and Professor of New Testament, Trinity Evangelical Divinity School

ABBREVIATIONS

AB	Anchor Bible
ABD	*Anchor Bible Dictionary*
ACUTE	Evangelical Alliance Commission on Unity and Truth Among Evangelicals
AnBib	Analecta biblica
ANF	*Ante-Nicene Fathers*
BA	*Biblical Archaeologist*
BAR	*Biblical Archaeology Review*
BBR	*Bulletin for Biblical Research*
BibOr	Biblica et orientalia
BSac	*Bibliotheca sacra*
BST	The Bible Speaks Today
CBQ	*Catholic Biblical Quarterly*
ChrT	*Christianity Today*
COS	*The Context of Scripture*, ed. W. W. Hallo (3 vols.)
CTR	*Criswell Theological Review*
ESV	English Standard Version
EvQ	*Evangelical Quarterly*
ERT	*Evangelical Review of Theology*
HAR	*Hebrew Annual Review*
HNTC	Harper's New Testament Commentaries
HTR	*Harvard Theological Review*
ICC	International Critical Commentary
JANESCU	*Journal of the Ancient Near Eastern Society of Columbia University*
JAOS	*Journal of the American Oriental Society*
JBL	*Journal of Biblical Literature*
JETS	*Journal of the Evangelical Theological Society*
JSOTSup	Journal for the Study of the Old Testament Supplements Series

KTU	*Die keilalphabetischen Texte aus Ugarit*, ed. M. Dietrich, O. Loretz, and J. Sanmartín
LXX	Septuagint
NASB	New American Standard Bible
NCB	New Century Bible
NICNT	New International Commentary on the New Testament
NICOT	New International Commentary on the Old Testament
NIGTC	New International Greek Testament Commentary
NIV	New International Version
NIVAC	NIV Application Commentary
NLT	New Living Translation
NPNF	*Nicene and Post-Nicene Fathers*
NRSV	New Revised Standard Version
OTL	Old Testament Library
Presb	*Presbyterion*
RelS	*Religious Studies*
SJT	*Scottish Journal of Theology*
SNTSMS	Society for New Testament Studies Monograph Series
TDNT	*Theological Dictionary of the New Testament*, ed. Gerhard Kittel and G. Friedrich
TDOT	*Theological Dictionary of the Old Testament*, ed. G. J. Botterweck and H. Ringgren
TLOT	*Theological Lexicon of the Old Testament*, ed. E. Jenni and C. Westermann
TNIV	Today's New International Version
TNTC	Tyndale New Testament Commentaries
TOTC	Tyndale Old Testament Commentaries
TrinJ	*Trinity Journal*
UF	*Ugarit-Forschungen*
VE	*Vox evangelica*
VTSup	Vetus Testamentum Supplements
WBC	Word Biblical Commentary
ZNW	*Zeitschrift für die neutestamentliche Wissenschaft*

HeLL UNDeR fire

INTRODUCTION

CHRISTOPHER W. MORGAN AND ROBERT A. PETERSON

A business was opening a new store, and a friend of the owner sent flowers for the occasion. The flowers arrived at the new business site, and the owner read the card, inscribed "Rest in Peace."

The angry owner called the florist to complain. After he told the florist of the obvious mistake and how angry he was, the florist said, "Sir, I'm really sorry for the mistake, but rather than getting angry, you should imagine this: Somewhere there is a funeral taking place today, and they have flowers with a note that reads, "Congratulations on your new location."

If we believe the message sent by the contemporary media, the "new location" of everyone who dies is heaven. At first glance, popular polls seem to disagree with that conclusion, for they reveal that a large majority of Americans believe in the existence of hell. However, the same polls show that almost no one thinks that he or she is going there. Everyone hopes for heaven.

Hell is under fire. In one sense that is nothing new. It has been the case ever since the Enlightenment, but the past fifty years have seen a noteworthy turn of affairs. Attacks on the historic doctrine of hell that used to come from without the church are now coming from within. This is true especially with regard to two aberrations: universalism and annihilationism. Listen as two contemporary evangelicals, both scholars and churchmen, defend these views.

Universalism is the view that in the end all persons will experience the love of God and eternal life. All will be saved and none will be lost. Jan Bonda (who died in 1997), in *The One Purpose of God: An Answer to the Doctrine of Eternal Punishment*, makes a case for universalism, largely from Paul's letter to the Romans:

> In the letter to the Romans Paul presents the gospel as the message of salvation for all people. God brought about this salvation in the cross of Christ. Through his death, all humanity, from Adam onward—including all past generations—will receive "justification and life": "the many will be made righteous" (Rom. 5:18–19). That is God's one and only purpose. This was further confirmed when we discovered how that purpose is the bottom line of the one law that God gave humanity: that all of them, without exception, shall love him and their neighbors with all their heart. This eliminates the possibility that he might have another purpose for part of humanity. . . .

11

Christ called his apostles, and the church that resulted from their preaching, to serve him in his saving ministry. That ministry will not be completed until all humanity has been saved.[1]

Bonda is forthright in advocating universalism when he declares that Christ's ministry will not be complete until all humanity is saved.

Annihilationism—or as its contemporary proponents like to call it, conditionalism—is the view that the wicked will ultimately be exterminated and cease to exist. David Powys, in 'Hell': A Hard Look at a Hard Question: The Fate of the Unrighteous in New Testament Thought, includes the following among his conclusions:

> There is no certain support within the New Testament for an expectation of ongoing conscious suffering for the unrighteous. . . .
> The tentative finding of this study is that the unrighteous will have no life after death, save possibly to be raised temporarily to be condemned. The unrighteous, whoever they prove to be, will find that God respects them in death as in life—true to their own choice they will have no part in the restored Kingdom of God, indeed, severed from the source of life, they will be no more.[2]

Powys espouses annihilationism by teaching that the final end of the unrighteous is nonexistence.

Jan Bonda and David Powys are academics, churchmen, and evangelical Christians. They come from different theological traditions and do not agree on every point. While Bonda clearly favors universalism, he is willing to contemplate the possibility that all will not be saved, and in such a case, he regards annihilationism as a possibility.[3] Powys, however, rejects universalism.[4] We quote Bonda and Powys as proponents of universalism and conditionalism, respectively, to demonstrate that departure from received doctrine is now taking place from within the church and not only from without.

The contributors to this volume are united in affirming the historic Christian doctrine regarding the final destiny of the unsaved: They will suffer everlasting conscious punishment away from the joyous presence of God. The contributors defend the traditional teaching because they believe that it is the teaching of Scripture. Accordingly, Scripture occupies center stage in this book, not only because each essayist bases his theological conclusions on the Bible, but also because four chapters devoted entirely to biblical studies constitute the foundation of this volume.

---

[1]Jan Bonda, The One Purpose of God: An Answer to the Doctrine of Eternal Punishment (Grand Rapids: Eerdmans, 1998), 257.

[2]David Powys, 'Hell': A Hard Look at a Hard Question: The Fate of the Unrighteous in New Testament Thought (Paternoster Biblical and Theological Monographs; Carlisle, UK: Paternoster, 1998), 416.

[3]Bonda, The One Purpose of God, 259.

[4]Powys, 'Hell', 416, 417.

heLL UNDeR fire

First, Albert Mohler laments the departure of many people, including evangelicals, from historic Christian teaching concerning hell. Then follow four chapters penned by experts in biblical studies on the witness to hell of various sections of Scripture. Daniel Block treats the teaching of the Old Testament, Robert Yarbrough that of the Gospels, Douglas Moo that of Paul, and Gregory Beale that of the Revelation. Together, their work constitutes a powerful biblical witness for the truth of traditionalism.

Constructive theological chapters by the coeditors follow. Christopher Morgan, after surveying each New Testament author's teaching on hell, explores the implications of three predominate pictures: hell as punishment, destruction, and banishment. Robert Peterson examines three neglected systematic themes pertaining to hell: the Trinity, divine sovereignty and human freedom, and the "already" and the "not yet."

The next two chapters address the errors pertaining to the doctrine of hell described earlier in this introduction. J. I. Packer presents the arguments universalists use to defend their view but in the end is constrained by Scripture to regard universalism as a speculative distortion of clear biblical teaching that subverts the church's mission. Christopher Morgan answers the best arguments advanced by the proponents of annihilationism (conditionalism) and in the process presents a strong biblical case for eternal punishment.

In the final chapter Sinclair Ferguson contributes a powerful biblical and theological essay on the ways hell impacts the preaching ministry.

Without a doubt hell is under fire. We are thankful, therefore, that according to Scripture, without a doubt the sovereign and gracious God rules the world: "The LORD has established his throne in the heavens, and his kingdom rules over all" (Ps. 103:19 ESV). Our confidence that God's truth will ultimately prevail rests not in our abilities to persuade readers but in him who promised, "I will build my church, and the gates of Hades will not overcome it" (Matt. 16:18). This book is dedicated to his glory and goes forth with the prayer that it may be used of him to build up in the faith many who are confused by the discordant voices of the church's teachers today.

Chapter 1

modern theology:
the Disappearance
of Hell

R. Albert Mohler Jr.

At some point in the nineteen-sixties, Hell disappeared. No one could say for certain when this happened. First it was there, then it wasn't. Different people became aware of the disappearance of Hell at different times. Some realized that they had been living for years as though Hell did not exist, without having consciously registered its disappearance. Others realized that they had been behaving, out of habit, as though Hell were still there, though in fact they had ceased to believe in its existence long ago.... On the whole, the disappearance of Hell was a great relief, though it brought new problems.

David Lodge, Souls and Bodies[1]

A fixture of Christian theology for over sixteen centuries, hell went away in a hurry. The abandonment of the traditional doctrine of hell came swiftly, with centuries of Christian conviction quickly swept away in a rush of modern thought and doctrinal transformation. Historian Martin Marty reduced the situation down to this: "Hell disappeared. No one noticed."[2]

The traditional doctrine of hell now bears the mark of *odium theologium*—a doctrine retained only by the most stalwart defenders of conservative theology, Catholic and Protestant. Its defenders are seemingly few. The doctrine is routinely dismissed as an embarrassing artifact from an ancient age—a reminder of Christianity's rejected worldview.

The sudden disappearance of hell amounts to a theological mystery of sorts. How did a doctrine so centrally enshrined in the system of theology suffer such a wholesale abandonment? What can explain this radical reordering of Christian theology?

The answer to this mystery reveals much about the fate of Christianity in the modern world and warns of greater theological compromises on the horizon, for, as the church has continually been reminded, no doctrine stands alone. Each doctrine is embedded in a system of theological conviction and expression. Take out the doctrine of hell, and the entire shape of Christian theology is inevitably altered.

Background: Hell in Christian History

The traditional doctrine of hell was developed in the earliest centuries of Christian history. Based in the New Testament texts concerning hell, judgment, and the afterlife, the earliest Christian preachers and theologians understood hell

---

[1]David Lodge, *Souls and Bodies* (London: Penguin, 1980), 113.
[2]Martin E. Marty, "Hell Disappeared. No One Noticed. A Civic Argument," *HTR* 78 (1985): 381–98.

HeLL UNDeR fiRe

to be the just judgment of God on sinners without faith in Christ. Hell was understood to be spatial and eternal, characterized by the most awful biblical metaphors of fire and torment.

Following the example of Jesus, the early Christian evangelists and preachers called sinners to faith in Christ and warned of the sure reality of hell and the eternal punishment of the impenitent. Thomas Oden summarizes the patristic consensus on hell as this:

> Hell is the eternal bringing to nothing of corruption and ungodliness. Hell expresses the intent of a holy God to destroy sin completely and forever. Hell says not merely a temporal no but an eternal no to sin. The rejection of evil by the holy God is like a fire that burns on, a worm that dies not.[3]

As Oden notes, the terms "eternal fire" and "eternal punishment" are very common. These terms "have withstood numerous attempts at generous reinterpretation, but they remain obstinately in the received text."[4] A central example is Augustine, who encouraged his readers to take the biblical metaphors quite literally. Beyond this, Augustine was stalwart in his refutation of those who taught that the punishments of hell were not truly eternal:

> Moreover, is it not folly to assume that eternal punishment signifies a fire lasting a long time, while believing that eternal life is without end? For Christ, in the very same passage, included both punishment and life in one and the same sentence when he said, "So those people will go into eternal punishment, while the righteous will go into eternal life." [Matt. 25:46] If both are "eternal," it follows necessarily that either both are to be taken as long-lasting but finite, or both as endless and perpetual.[5]

The first major challenge to the traditional doctrine of hell came from Origen, whose doctrine of *apokatastasis* promised the total and ultimate restitution of all things and all persons.[6] Thus, Origen was the pioneer of a form of universalism. His logic was that God's victory would only be complete when the last things are identical to the first things. That is, the consummation would involve the return of all things to union with the Creator. Nothing (and no one) could be left unredeemed. Beyond this, in *Against Celsus*, Origen responded to one of the church's Greek critics by denying that hell would be punitive, at least in the end. Instead, hell would be purifying and thus temporal.[7]

---

[3]Thomas Oden, *Systematic Theology;* Vol. 3: *Life in the Spirit* (San Francisco: Harper & Row, 1992), 450.

[4]Ibid.

[5]St. Augustine, *Concerning the City of God Against the Pagans*, tr. Henry Bettenson (London: Penguin, 1972), 1001–2.

[6]For a review of patristic sources on hell and the reality of divine judgment, see David Powys, *"Hell": A Hard Look at a Hard Question* (Paternoster Biblical and Theological Monographs; London: Paternoster, 1997), and Graham Keith, "Patristic Views on Hell—Part 1," *EvQ* 71 (1999): 217–32.

[7]See Origen, *Contra Celsum*, tr. Henry Chadwick (Cambridge: Cambridge Univ. Press, 1965).

Origen's teaching was a clear rejection of the patristic consensus, and the church responded in 553 at the fifth ecumenical council (Constantinople II) with a series of anathemas against Origen and his teaching. The ninth anathema set the refutation in undeniable clarity: "If anyone says or thinks that the punishment of demons and of impious men is only temporary, and will one day have an end, and that a restoration [*apokatastasis*] will take place of demons and of impious men, let him be anathema."[8]

This general consensus held well through the medieval and Reformation eras of the church. Rejections of the traditional doctrine were limited to peripheral sects and heretics, and hell was such a fixture of the medieval mind that most persons understood all of life in terms of their ultimate destination by God's judgment. Men and women longed for heaven and feared hell. Yet by the end of the twentieth century, inhabitants of those lands once counted as Christendom lived with virtually no fear of hell as a place of eternal punishment, and no fear of divine judgment.

The contrast between the modern dismissal of hell and the premodern fascination with hell is evident when today's preaching is compared with the graphic warnings offered by preachers of the past. In the medieval era, an Italian preacher warned his congregation of the real danger of a very real hell:

Fire, fire! That is the recompense for your perversity, you hardened sinners. Fire, fire, the fires of hell! Fire in your eyes, fire in your mouth, fire in your guts, fire in your throat, fire in your nostrils, fire inside and fire outside, fire beneath and fire above, fire in every part. Ah, miserable folk! You will be like rags burning in the middle of this fire.[9]

Jonathan Edwards, the great theologian-preacher of the colonial era in America, offered a similar warning:

Consider that if once you get into hell, you'll never get out. If you should unexpectedly one of these days drop in there; [there] would be no remedy. They that go there return no more. Consider how dreadful it will be to suffer such an extremity forever. It is dreadful beyond expression to suffer it half an hour. O the misery, the tribulation and anguish that is endured![10]

Few congregations hear such warnings today. As a matter of fact, preachers who would dare to offer such graphic descriptions of hell and its terrors today would likely be considered eccentric, or worse. A major news magazine summarized hell's disappearance succinctly: "By most accounts, it has all but disappeared

[8]"The Anathemas Against Origen," in *The Seven Ecumenical Councils of the Undivided Church*, ed. Henry R. Percival (*NPNF*; Grand Rapids: Eerdmans, 1979 [1899]), 320.
[9]Quoted in Richard Marius, *Martin Luther: The Christian between God and Death* (Cambridge, Mass.: Harvard Univ. Press, 1999), 60.
[10]Jonathan Edwards, "The Torments of Hell Are Exceedingly Great," in *Sermons and Discourses, 1723–1729*, ed. Kenneth P. Minkema (The Works of Jonathan Edwards, vol. 14; New Haven, Conn.: Yale Univ. Press, 1997), 326.

HELL UNDER FIRE

from the pulpit rhetoric of mainline Protestantism. And it has fared only marginally better among evangelicals."[11]

Jesus warned his listeners to "be afraid of the One who can destroy both soul and body in hell" (Matt. 10:28b), and generations of Christians heard sermons filled with warnings to this effect. But the Rev. Robert Schuller, pastor of California's famous Crystal Cathedral, explains that he long ago revised his theology to focus on "generating trust and positive hope."[12] Thus revised, his theology would "emphasize that we're 'saved' not just to avoid 'hell' (whatever that means and wherever that is), but to become positive thinkers inspired to seek God's will for our lives and dream the divine dreams that God has planned for us."[13] Schuller's dismissal of the traditional doctrine of hell is evident in the quotation marks he put around the word, as if he must graphically depict his rejection. His parenthetical qualifications, "whatever that means and wherever that is," certainly pose no threat to his readers. Hell is on the landscape but understood to be harmless.

Hell as Question: The Seventeenth and Eighteenth Centuries

The seventeenth century witnessed the consolidation of Protestant theology as the children and grandchildren of the Reformers formalized and systematized their doctrines. Simultaneously, however, other currents were flowing into the river of European thought. Various atheisms emerged along with heretical groups such as the Socinians and the English Arians.

The century also gave birth to the first major stirrings against the traditional doctrine of hell. A belief in the annihilation of the wicked became apparent among the Socinians, which earned them the commendation of Pierre Bayle, the radical French polemicist, who considered hell "the greatest scandal of our theology for philosophical minds."[14] The Socinians argued that eternal torment was an unjust penalty for temporal sins and that the character of God would not allow such unjust punishments. Their logic was basically shared by the English Arians and Platonists, who also joined in their rejection of the doctrine of the Trinity.

As D. P. Walker argues, the basically heretical character of these groups marginalized their influence on the larger church. Their assaults on the traditional doctrine of hell had little impact on mainstream theology, but they did infect a certain elite. As described by Walker, this elite was forced to produce "a theory of double truth."[15] Their rejection of hell was confined to the knowledge of an intellectual elite, while the traditional doctrine was preached to the masses by intellectuals who no longer believed it.

The heretics were in a precarious social position, and the very real threat of prosecution or persecution caused them to hide their heresies concerning hell. At

---

[11]"Hell's Sober Comeback," *U.S. News and World Report* (March 25, 1991), 56.
[12]Robert H. Schuller, *My Journey* (San Francisco: HarperCollins, 2001), 127.
[13]Ibid., 127–28.
[14]Cited in D. P. Walker, *The Decline of Hell: Seventeenth Century Discussions of Eternal Torment* (London: Routledge & Kegan Paul, 1964), 77.
[15]Ibid., 5.

the same time, they seemed to accept the argument that hell—even if it did not exist as a place of eternal torment—was a doctrine necessary for social order and lawfulness. Walker summarizes their reticence:

> Thus people who had doubts about the eternity of hell, or who had come to disbelieve in it, refrained from publishing their doubts not only because of the personal risk involved, but also because of genuine moral scruples. In the 17th century disbelief in eternal torment seldom reached the level of a firm conviction, but at the most was a conjecture, which one might wish to be true; it was therefore understandable that one should hesitate to plunge the world into moral anarchy for the sake of only conjectural truth.[16]

If the seventeenth century marks the emergence of theological opposition to the traditional doctrine of hell, the eighteenth century marks the explosion of Enlightenment skepticism. As Gerald R. Cragg notes, the century "was secular in spirit and destructive in effect. It diffused a skepticism which gradually dissolved the intellectual and religious patterns which had governed European thought since St. Augustine. It proclaimed the autonomy of man's mind and his infinite capacity for progress and perfectibility."[17] Quite clearly, these proclamations were at odds with any notion of an eternal hell for the impenitent.

The question arose among philosophers, some of whom argued for a metaphorical understanding of hell. In his *Leviathan*, Thomas Hobbes argued that hell may be eternal, but the torments of the impenitent are not:

> The fire prepared for the wicked is an Everlasting Fire: that is to say, the estate wherein no man can be without torture, both of body and mind, after the Resurrection shall last for ever; and in that sense the Fire shall be unquenchable and the torments Everlasting: but it cannot thence be inferred, that he who shall be cast into that fire, or be tormented with those torments, shall endure, and resist them so, as to be eternally burnt, and tortured, and yet never be destroyed, nor die.[18]

Voltaire and the other Enlightenment *philosophes* rejected Christianity outright and as a whole. Their attacks were not directed at hell as an isolated doctrine but to the entire system of Christian theology and the very idea of divine revelation. The real doctrinal crisis for hell would come among those who considered themselves Christians in the next century. In Britain, the crisis befell the Victorians.

Hell as Scandal: The Victorian Crisis of Faith

The Victorian era is often sentimentalized as an era of great faith and Christian vitality. Queen Victoria was a steady if undemonstrative emblem of Christian

---

[16]Ibid.
[17]Gerald R. Cragg, *The Church and the Age of Reason, 1648–1789* (London: Penguin, 1960), 234.
[18]Thomas Hobbes, *Leviathan* (Cambridge: Cambridge Univ. Press, 1904), 335.

hell under fire

devotion and she took an active interest in church affairs. Christianity was a part of the fabric of the British Empire, and missionary zeal was mixed with colonial ambitions. Christianity was the solace for the masses of working poor in London. If they could aspire to no riches in this life, at least they had the hope of glories to come in heaven.

The Victorian age was an era of great churchgoing. Attendance at churches rural and urban was at an all-time high, and great churches such as Charles Spurgeon's Metropolitan Tabernacle numbered worshipers in the thousands. Nevertheless, Spurgeon's doctrinal conservatism was not shared by all Victorians.

To the contrary, when John Keble delivered his famous "Assize Sermon" at Oxford University in 1833, he lamented his age as "this funereal and discouraged epoch, where the faith is completely dead or dying."[19] Though many Britons of the nineteenth century gave evidence of robust Christianity and doctrinal conservatism, Jaroslav Pelikan reminds us that the age also produced "radical doubt" and "the negation of dogma."[20]

Among many Victorians, hell became something of an obsession. The rejection of the traditional doctrine extended throughout the elites of the society, including even William Gladstone, the evangelical *cum* high-churchman Prime Minister, who asserted that hell had been "relegated ... to the far-off corners of the Christian mind ... there to sleep in the deep shadow as a thing needless in our enlightened and progressive age."[21]

The Victorian "crisis of faith" has long fascinated historians, who have offered various accounts of the nineteenth-century dissipation of Christian conviction on both sides of the Atlantic. This collapse of Christian belief is well described by A. N. Wilson: "Perhaps only those who have known the peace of God which passes all understanding can have any conception of what was lost between a hundred and a hundred and fifty years ago when the human race in Western Europe began to discard Christianity."[22]

The devastating impact of Victorian doubt was visited upon the twentieth century as its lasting legacy. Leslie Stephen, the father of Virginia Woolf, was an ordained clergyman in the Church of England who lost his faith, renounced his ordination, and became a man of letters. His story was a paradigm for his age and the century to follow. Utilitarianism and various other philosophies had undermined the foundations of Christian conviction for Stephen, who saw through the Victorian experiment in hypocrisy:

---

[19]Cited by Jaroslav Pelikan, "Christian Doctrine and Modern Culture (Since 1700)," in *The Christian Tradition: A History of the Development of Doctrine*, vol. 5 (Chicago: Univ. of Chicago Press, 1989), 177.

[20]Ibid., 178.

[21]Cited in Geoffrey Rowell, *Hell and the Victorians: A Study of the Nineteenth-Century Theological Controversies Concerning Eternal Punishment and the Future Life* (Oxford: Clarendon, 1974), 212.

[22]A. N. Wilson, *God's Funeral: A Biography of Faith and Doubt in Western Civilization* (New York: Random House, 1999), 4. Wilson's analysis is especially poignant given his own abandonment of Christian belief.

The average Cambridge don of my day was (as I thought and think) a sensible and honest man who wished to be both rational and Christian. He was rational enough to see that the old orthodox position was untenable. He did not believe in hell, or in "verbal inspiration" or the "real presence." He thought that the controversies on such matters were silly and antiquated, and spoke of them with indifference, if not with contempt. But he also thought that religious belief of some kind was necessary or valuable, and considered himself to be a genuine believer.[23]

Stephen was not alone in his analysis or in his rejection of hell as an odious doctrine. Other literary figures shared his dismissal of hell and provided even more argument for their case.

In this regard the case of Lewis Carroll is especially instructive. Carroll, the famed author of *Alice in Wonderland* and other writings, was actually the pen name of Charles Lutwidge Dodgson, the son of an Anglican minister. Though in other respects a faithful Anglican, the younger Dodgson demonstrated what one biographer called an "instinctive repugnance" for the doctrine of everlasting punishment.[24]

Influenced by the new higher critical views of Scripture, largely imported from Germany, Dodgson declared that if the Bible really taught the doctrine of everlasting punishment, "I would give up the Bible."[25] Upon his death Dodgson left an unpublished manuscript entitled "Eternal Punishment," in which he presented what he thought was a tight logical case against hell.[26] He argued that the goodness of God is the first axiom and that biblical teachings on hell can be discounted because the doctrine of verbal inspiration "has been largely modified in these days."[27] Acceptance of any concept of eternal punishment would require, Dodgson argued, "the abandonment of the belief in a God, and the acceptance of Atheism."[28]

By the end of the Victorian age, poet Thomas Hardy would imagine himself observing God's funeral. The Victorian crisis of faith spread throughout the aristocracy and the educated classes, and some theologians and preachers added their voices to the calls for doctrinal reformulation. Hell was at the center of their attention.

Historian Geoffrey Rowell argues that for the Victorians the historic doctrine of hell, established in a straightforward acceptance of biblical texts, was simply too awful to contemplate, much less to accept and teach:

Of all the articles of accepted Christian orthodoxy that troubled the consciences of Victorian churchmen, none caused more anxiety than the everlasting punishment of the wicked. The flames of hell illuminated vividly the

---

[23]Ibid., 9.

[24]Donald Thomas, *Lewis Carroll: A Biography* (London: Heath, 1996), 320.

[25]See his June 28, 1889, letter to Mary Brown, published in *The Letters of Lewis Carroll*, ed. Morton N. Cohen (New York: Oxford Univ. Press, 1979), 747.

[26]Lewis Carroll, "Eternal Punishment," in *The Lewis Carroll Picture Book*, ed. Stuart Dodgson Collingwood (London: T. Fisher Unwon, 1899), 345–55.

[27]Ibid., 353.

[28]Ibid., 349.

HeLL under fire

tensions of an age in which men felt that old certainties were being eroded by new knowledge, and in which an optimistic faith in progress co-existed uneasily with forebodings of the consequences of increasingly rapid social change. A Bible whose Divine authority had been accepted rather than argued about was battered by the blasts of Germanic criticism and scientific theory, and the particular pattern of Christian orthodoxy which it had been assumed to uphold no longer carried full conviction.[29]

F. W. Robertson of Brighton, among the most popular Victorian preachers, acknowledged to his congregation that they had all "learned to smile" at the idea of an eternal hell, for "in bodily awful intolerable torture we believe no longer."[30] Robertson and his parishioners were not alone.

But if the Victorians seemed to develop an obsession with the scandal of hell, none appeared more scandalized than F. D. Maurice, an Anglican churchman and one of the organizers of the Christian Socialist Movement. Maurice repeatedly offended the faithful and attacked the cherished doctrines of orthodox Christianity. Hell was a special interest. Maurice argued that eternality was an attribute of God alone and could not be extended to something as ungodly as hell. Accordingly, Maurice advocated something like a concept of conditional immortality, arguing that eternal *death* is a more acceptable teaching than eternal *punishment*.[31]

F. W. Farrar, Canon of Westminster Abbey and for several years chaplain to Queen Victoria, went so far as to label the traditional doctrine of hell as "blasphemy against the merciful God."[32] He went on to pledge:

> But I here declare and call God to witness, that if the popular doctrine of Hell were true I should be ready to resign all hope, not only of a *shortened*, but of *any* immortality, if thereby I could save, not *millions*, but *one single human soul* from what fear, and superstition, and ignorance, and inveterate hate, and slavish letter-worship have dreamed and taught of Hell.[33]

This statement is incredibly revealing, for it demonstrates a momentous shift in theology and the culture. Whereas preachers in earlier eras were concerned to save persons from *punishment in hell*, Farrar and his like-minded colleagues were determined to save their congregations from the *fear of the idea of hell*. The Victorian concern for decency ruled hell out of bounds. It was simply not a doctrine that persons considered decent and respectable by Victorian standards would teach and hold.

---

[29]Geoffrey Rowell, *Hell and the Victorians: A Study of the Nineteenth-Century Theological Controversies Concerning Eternal Punishment and the Future Life* (Oxford: Clarendon, 1974), vii.

[30]Cited in Michael Wheeler, *Heaven, Hell, and the Victorians* (Cambridge: Cambridge Univ. Press, 1994), 187.

[31]Fredrick Denison Maurice, "Eternal Life and Eternal Death," in *Theological Essays* (London: Macmillan and Co., 1892), 377–407.

[32]Fredrick W. Farrar, *Eternal Hope: Five Sermons* (London: Macmillan & Co., 1904), 68–69.

[33]Ibid., 202.

Farrar was certain that the traditional doctrine was unacceptable, but he was agnostic concerning the reality of God's punishment, for "God has given us no clear and decisive revelation on the final condition of those who have died in sin."[34] Of course, once one is freed from what Farrar called "letter-worship"—meaning submission to the biblical text—there is no doctrine that cannot be denied or completely modified.

One other aspect of the Victorian mind deserves attention. The Victorian cult of the family featured a particular ideal of the father as a loving, respected, upright, reserved *pater familias*. Such a father would discipline his children, but never too severely. Eventually, the sentimental indulgence of the father would bring punishment to an end, leading to reconciliation. When this vision of fatherhood was extended to God, hell as eternal torment became unthinkable.

This point was clearly argued by the infamous J. W. Colenso, the Bishop of Cape Town in South Africa. Colenso had earned his infamy by denying the historical accuracy of the Pentateuch and the book of Joshua. In his commentary on Romans, Colenso acknowledged that God's punishment may last a very long time, depending upon the individual, but he rejected the doctrine of eternal punishment:

> But God's punishments are those of a Father. And, as a true, loving, earthly parent will never think of weighing out, by fixed laws, a certain definite measure of punishment, as the proper amount of penalty, in case his child commits such and such an offense, but will punish him with more or less severity, as he judges to be needful in each particular case, ever seeking, not merely to check the like fault in others of his children, but to amend or correct what is evil in the offender himself.[35]

As Gilbert and Sullivan put it to music in *The Mikado*, Victorians were insistent that "the punishment must fit the crime." Apparently, this argument was to become even more persuasive in the twentieth century.

The Victorians wanted to retain and reinforce a moral order in society, and the fear of hell was considered to be of prime importance as a curb on crime and what is now commonly called "anti-social behavior." For this reason, some elite Victorians considered the idea of hell to be socially important—even when they no longer believed hell to be real. This gives the appearance of double-mindedness to much Victorian hand-wringing over hell. As Rowell comments, "the need of hell as a moral sanction, and the underlying sense that, however crudely expressed and distorted the doctrine might be, it did attempt to state something of importance about ultimate ethical issues, meant that it could not be quietly discarded."[36]

The same currents of theological change were also evident in America, of course. Deists and Unitarians had rejected the idea of God as judge. In certain circles, higher criticism had undermined confidence in the Bible as divine reve-

---

[34]Ibid., 86.
[35]J. W. Colenso, *St. Paul's Epistle to the Romans* (New York: Appleton, 1863), 219.
[36]Rowell, *Hell and the Victorians*, vii.

HeLL under fire

lation, and churchmen increasingly treated hell as a metaphor. With the coming of Protestant liberalism, theological proposals virtually identical to those of Maurice and Farrar become common to the nation's divinity schools and liberal churches.

These precincts were increasingly shaped by what historian William R. Hutchinson has called "the modernist impulse," with its emphasis on divine immanence rather than transcendence.[37] American liberals of the Victorian era included influential preachers like Henry Ward Beecher, who rejected the old orthodoxy with its "spiritual barbarism" and "hideous doctrines."[38]

The Victorian revisions of theology were not limited, of course, to the doctrine of eternal punishment. As Western nations continued their push throughout the globe, the aspirations of empire confronted the discovery of other people with other gods, other practices, and other worldviews. This discovery of "the other" led Victorian liberals to emphasize the universal fatherhood of God, and they came up with numerous ways to modify the traditional claim of exclusivity for salvation through Christ. Various forms of universalism and inclusivism were introduced into British and American theological discussions. In Germany, the "history of religions" school treated Christianity as one form of human religion alongside others. Religion was understood to be a fundamentally human phenomenon.

As for the doctrine of God, the Victorians increasingly came to the conclusion that God was universally benevolent and would judge persons based on their response and access to truth. Christianity was the brightest light of revelation among lesser lights. Historian James Turner summarizes the picture well: "God had to be a humanitarian."[39] This concept of a humanitarian God would drive many of the theological reformulations of the twentieth century, with repercussions throughout the system of theology.

Hell as Myth: Twentieth-Century Theology and the Problem of Evil

"The cosmology of the New Testament is essentially mythical in character," declared Rudolf Bultmann. "The world is viewed as a three-storied structure, with the earth in the center, the heaven above, and the underworld beneath. Heaven is the abode of God and of celestial beings—the angels. The underworld is hell, the place of torment."[40]

Thus, according to Bultmann the Bible presents an essentially mythological picture of reality that is incompatible with the modern scientific worldview. This

---

[37]William R. Hutchinson, *The Modernist Impulse in American Protestantism* (New York: Oxford Univ. Press, 1976).

[38]Ibid., 79.

[39]James Turner, *Without God, Without Creed: The Origins of Unbelief in America* (Baltimore: Johns Hopkins Univ. Press, 1985), 71.

[40]Rudolf Bultmann (and five critics), *Kerygma and Myth*, ed. Hans Werner Bartsch (New York: Harper & Row, 1961), 1.

mythological worldview "is therefore unacceptable to modern man whose thinking has been shaped by science and is therefore no longer mythological."[41] The world-view of the modern age is simply a fact with which theology must come to terms, argued Bultmann, and those terms require the abandonment of any claim that hell is real as a place and as a threat.

Bultmann's project of *demythologization* was an attempt to rescue existential meaning from the Christian "myth." If, as he argued, modern men who turn on electric lights and use electric shavers cannot simultaneously believe in a literal hell (or heaven for that matter), then something must nevertheless be salvaged from the Christian *mythos*—something that would speak to modern humanity's anxiety about evil. Those anxieties had good reason to grow in the tragic soil of the twentieth century. Though born in nearly unbridled optimism, the century quickly turned into an age of unparalleled murder and carnage.

The seemingly interminable trench warfare of World War I established new benchmarks for carnage on the battlefield—and to no visible military result. The war brought the nineteenth-century's faith in human progress to a crushing col-lapse. Edward Grey, Great Britain's Foreign Secretary, lamented this fading dream as the world war began: "The lamps are going out all over Europe. We shall not see them lit again in our lifetime."[42]

Theologically, the century that began in comfortable Victorian eloquence quickly became fertile ground for nihilism and *angst*. What World War I did not destroy, World War II took by assault and atrocity. The battlefields of Verdun and Ypres gave way to the ovens of Dachau and Auschwitz as symbols of the century.

At the same time, the technological revolutions of the century extended the worldview of scientific naturalism throughout much of the culture of the West, especially among elites. The result was a complete revolution in the place of reli-gion in general, and Christianity in particular, in the public space. Ideological and symbolic secularization became the norm in Western societies with advanced technologies and ever-increasing levels of economic wealth. Both heaven and hell took on an essentially this-worldly character.

If the atrocities of the Holocaust and genocide represented hell on earth, what fear did secular moderns have of a hell to come? If the blessings of material abun-dance were so readily available to others, what solace was promised by the hope of heaven?

Neoorthodox theologians like Karl Barth and Dietrich Bonhoeffer acknowl-edged the fundamental threat of evil, and the Confessing Church had bravely opposed the Nazi regime. Nevertheless, Barth came to the theological conclu-sion that evil was fundamentally a negation, *Das Nichtige*, and held out hope that the victory of God in Christ would extend to a universal redemption and recon-ciliation. Hell would be no more. Theologians such as Reinhold Niebuhr saw hell in the impoverished ghettos of inner city America. The liberation theologians

---

[41]Rudolf Bultmann, *Jesus Christ and Mythology* (New York: Charles Scribner's Sons, 1958), 36.
[42]Cited in Eric Hobsbawm, *The Age of Extremes: A History of the World, 1914–1991* (New York: Pantheon, 1994), 22.

HeLL UNDeR fire

found hell in the situation of political and economic powerlessness and oppression experienced by millions around the world.

Jürgen Moltmann, who mixed Marxist and Christian concepts of eschatology into a "theology of hope," expressed the this-worldly focus of the new eschatology: "Salvation is not another world in the 'beyond.' It means that this world becomes finally different. In the liberations of the people, their redemption already becomes efficacious in germ."[43] Heaven is liberation, hell is oppression, and everything is essentially tied to the historical vision.

Roman Catholic theology had historically claimed continuity with Cyprian's famous dictum, *extra eccelesia nulla salus*—salvation is found only in the church, and the Roman Catholic Church *is* the church. The revolutions of Vatican II changed this picture dramatically. The "Dogmatic Constitution on the Church" (*Lumen Gentium*) declared, "Those who, through no fault of their own, do not know the Gospel of Christ or his Church, but who nevertheless seek God with a sincere heart, and, moved by grace, try in their actions to do his will as they know it through the dictates of their conscience—those too may achieve eternal salvation."[44]

Pope John Paul II redefined hell in a 1999 General Audience at the Vatican. The traditional doctrine of hell was redefined to remove virtually all threat of eternal torment and any sense of place. "Hell is not a punishment imposed externally by God, but the condition resulting from attitudes and actions which people adopt in this life," declared the Pope.[45] With this single sentence, the Pope denied that God imposes hell as a punishment and insisted that hell is now merely a "condition." He continued by explaining that "more than a physical place, hell is the state of those who freely and definitely separate themselves from God, the source of all life and joy. So eternal judgment is not God's work but is actually our own doing."[46]

Catholic theology had already been moving in this direction, which is actually the outworking of the dynamic and thought of Vatican II. Theologians such as Karl Rahner and Hans Urs von Balthasar had redefined salvation and eschatology so as to incorporate non-Christians into Christ's work of salvation and to leave little room for hell. Sincerity rather than explicit faith in Christ became the ground of salvation. Rahner's concept of "anonymous Christians" suggested that hell could have few inhabitants. Some conservative Catholics were unmoved. As an Australian priest opined, "Because Hell is not popular these days we cannot conclude that it is not populated. If Dante were to visit Hell in a new poetic reverie, would he find it closed up and boarded over?"[47]

---

[43]Jürgen Moltmann, *Experiences in Theology: Ways and Forms of Christian Theology* (Minneapolis: Fortress, 2000), 241–42.

[44]"Dogmatic Constitution of the Church," in *Vatican II: The Conciliar and Post-Conciliar Documents*, ed. Austin Flannery, O.P. (Collegeville, Minn.: Liturgical, 1975), 367.

[45]Pope John Paul II, "General Audience," Wednesday, July 28, 1999, released by the Vatican News Service.

[46]Ibid.

[47]David Watt, "Is Hell Closed Up & Boarded Over?" *New Oxford Review* 66 (February 1999): 28.

The liberal and self-described "mainstream" Christian theologians who taught in the university divinity schools and seminaries of mainline Protestantism were in basic agreement with the Roman Catholic position, and insofar as salvation was a real concern, the goal was more likely to be seen as political or psychological liberation. Any claim of exclusivity for the Christian faith was eagerly abandoned. These theologians had so accommodated themselves to the antisupernatural worldview of the age that belief in a literal hell as a place of eternal torment was simply incredible, unacceptable, and unspeakable. Hell was an epithet, a symbol, and an embarrassment.

Hell as Reality—But What Kind? Evangelicals Join the Debate

Though the Victorian elites no longer believed in hell, the evangelicals both believed and preached it. Charles Spurgeon's congregations heard him declare that hell was real and hot and eternal:

Suffice it for me to close up by saying, that the hell of hells will be to thee poor sinner, the thought, that it is to be *forever*. Thou wilt look up there on the throne of God, and it shall be written "For ever!" When the damned jingle the burning irons of their torments, they shall say, "for ever!" When they howl, echo cries "for ever!"[48]

Spurgeon and the other evangelicals were hardly unaware of the denials of hell common to their age. They had seen their theology parodied in the novels of George Eliot and Charles Kingsley. They knew full well that many Victorians had transformed hell into a mere metaphor, along with its horrors. Spurgeon would not have it:

Now, do not begin telling me that that is metaphorical fire: who cares for that? If a man were to threaten to give me a metaphorical blow on the head, I should care very little about it; he would be welcome to give me as many as he pleased. And what say the wicked? "We do not care about metaphorical fires." But they are *real*, sir—yes, as real as yourself. There is a real fire in hell, as truly as you now have a real body—a fire exactly like that which we have on earth in everything except this—that it will not consume, though it will torture you.[49]

The preaching of hell's threatening torments may have chagrined the Victorian elites, but evangelical preachers on both sides of the Atlantic made hell a major focus of their preaching. After all, did not Jesus offer such stern warnings? Did not the New Testament provide sufficient assurance of hell's fury in eternity?

A few figures on the periphery of evangelical thought offered revisions of the traditional doctrine of hell throughout the earlier decades of the twentieth century.

---

[48]Charles H. Spurgeon, "Paul's First Prayer," a sermon preached March 25, 1855, at Exeter Hall in London, *The New Park Street Pulpit* (London: Passmore and Alabaster, 1856), 124.
[49]Charles H. Spurgeon, "The Resurrection of the Dead," a sermon preached February 17, 1856, at New Park Street Chapel, Southwark (London: Passmore and Alabaster, 1857), 104.

HeLL UNDeR fiRe

Challenges to the doctrine moved from the periphery of evangelicalism to its center by the 1980s, and with the arrival of the new century, evangelicals were engaged in a full-scale debate over the existence and nature of hell and its punishments.

In 1974 a clear call for reconsideration of the doctrine of hell came from John Wenham, vice principal of Tyndale Hall, Bristol, and a well-known figure among British evangelicals. "The ultimate horror of God's universe is hell," Wenham acknowledged.[50]

> The other difficulties of the Bible and of Providence are real enough, but however appalling they may be, their seeming harshness and injustices are only temporary, cut short at death. The terrors of hell, on the other hand, belong to the world which lies beyond death. For a single being to endure pain hopelessly and unendingly, or even to pass out of existence and forfeit forever the joys of heaven, is more terrible than any temporal suffering.[51]

No evangelical would disagree with Wenham's assessment thus far. Indeed, many evangelicals would see this picture of hell as exceedingly accurate and to the point. Wenham stipulated that modern persons find the traditional doctrine of hell as everlasting torment to be unacceptable and unbelievable. Thus, theologians have initiated "intensive efforts to find alternatives to the teaching of traditional orthodoxy."[52]

These efforts have included proposals identified as universalism, which Wenham finds lacking in biblical support, and conditional immortality (or annihilationism), which Wenham seemed to affirm—at least partly. He warned that traditional orthodoxy is not to be given up lightly. "Beware of the immense natural appeal of any way out that evades the idea of everlasting sin and suffering. The temptation to twist what may be quite plain statements of Scripture is intense. It is the ideal situation for unconscious rationalizing."[53] He concluded this section of his book by calling for further study.

By 1991, however, Wenham emerged as a proponent of conditional immortality, which he defined as the belief "that God created Man only potentially immortal. Immortality is a state gained by grace through faith when the believer receives eternal life and becomes a partaker of the divine nature, immortality being inherent in God alone."[54] So those who are in Christ by faith receive immortality as God's gift. Those not in Christ simply are not given the gift and pass from existence after death and the judgment.

Wenham is certainly correct in his defense that his position is not universalism, which he still found to be lacking in biblical support. He claimed that no

---

[50]John Wenham, *The Goodness of God* (Downers Grove, Ill.: InterVarsity Press, 1974), 27.
[51]Ibid.
[52]Ibid., 33.
[53]Ibid., 37–38.
[54]John Wenham, *Facing Hell: An Autobiography* (London: Paternoster, 1998), 230. The 1991 date refers to a paper Wenham presented to an audience at Rutherford House, Edinburgh, in that year.

sufficient answer had come in light of his challenge to defenders of the traditional doctrine that they should argue him out of conditionalism. Of course, he set himself up as the judge of these arguments. "I regard with utmost horror the possibility of being wrong," Wenham stated.[55] Nevertheless, Wenham's indictment of the traditional doctrine of hell was scathing:

> Unending torment speaks to me of sadism, not justice. It is a doctrine which I do not know how to preach without negating the loveliness and glory of God. From the days of Tertullian it has been the emphasis of fanatics. It is a doctrine that makes the Inquisition look reasonable. It all seems a flight from reality and common sense.[56]

This impassioned, almost hysterical language indicates that the doctrine of hell, traditionally understood, had become for him a stumbling block to faith, a theological obstacle he could not overcome without rejecting it wholesale. Wenham's earlier call for "fresh study" had become a demand for doctrinal transformation among evangelicals.

John Wenham is not an insignificant figure among evangelicals, but his influence on this issue was quickly eclipsed by John Stott, one of the most important evangelical leaders of the twentieth century, respected throughout the world. Stott's reassessment of hell came in the context of his debate with David Edwards, a well-known figure among Anglican liberals. The debate was later published in book form and provides a fascinating view of Stott's mind at work. In one of his exchanges with Stott, Edwards called the traditional evangelical view of hell a "Hades doctrine" presenting God as "the Eternal Torturer" and accused Stott of a certain vagueness on the question of everlasting torment.

Stott responded to the challenge by affirming that the traditional doctrine has been held throughout the history of the church, right down to the Reformers and their heirs. "Do I hold it however? Well, emotionally, I find the concept intolerable and do not understand how people can live with it without either cauterizing their feelings or cracking under the strain."[57] Nevertheless, after giving vent to these emotions, Stott insisted that he must submit his theology to the test of Scripture, not the voice of his heart.

Stott then constructed an argument for annihilationism based on language, imagery, justice, and universalism. According to his argument, the church has misunderstood the meaning of the language of the biblical texts. In strategic texts such as Matthew 10:28, the Greek word *apollymi*, generally translated "to destroy," means utter destruction—annihilation of the individual, and not everlasting punishment.

Further, biblical imagery such as the "lake of fire" (Rev. 20:14–15), Stott argues, has been misunderstood. He acknowledges that the text says that the judged will "be tormented day and night for ever and ever," but insists that this

---

[55]Ibid., 256.
[56]Ibid., 254.
[57]David L. Edwards and John R. W. Stott, *Essentials: A Liberal-Evangelical Dialogue* (Downers Grove, Ill.: InterVarsity Press, 1988), 314.

heLL under fire

does not refer to impenitent humans. On the ground of God's justice, Stott argues that eternal punishment is incommensurate with finite sins. "Would there not, then, be a serious disproportion between sins consciously committed in time and torment consciously experienced throughout eternity?"[58]

Finally, Stott turns to the biblical texts speaking of the universal victory of God and argues that this does not speak of the salvation of every single human sinner, but to the total victory of God over sin and evil. "It would be easier to hold together the awful reality of hell and the universal reign of God if hell means destruction and the impenitent are no more," he explains.[59] Interestingly, Stott claims to affirm hell and "the eternal damnation of the impenitent" since those annihilated cease to exist eternally.[60] Yet, even if Stott affirms hell, it is certainly not a place populated by the damned for eternity.

Stott also claimed that New Testament scholar F. F. Bruce held that annihilationism "is certainly an acceptable interpretation of the relevant New Testament passages," though Bruce remained an agnostic on the question itself.[61] Later, Stott would defend himself against claims of changing his position by stating, "my position has been the same for about fifty years."[62]

By the mid–1980s, the number of evangelicals promoting annihilationism had reached the point that Anglican evangelical Peter Toon reflected, "In conservative circles there is a seeming reluctance to espouse publicly a doctrine of hell, and where it is held there is a seeming tendency toward a doctrine of hell as annihilation."[63]

In America the situation was much the same. In 1989 the National Association of Evangelicals and Trinity Evangelical Divinity School cosponsored a consultation known as "Evangelical Affirmations." The event had been conceived by Carl F. H. Henry and Kenneth S. Kantzer, two of American evangelicalism's most revered figures. A sense of theological crisis formed the background to the consultation, and the assembled theologians sought to define the essentials of evangelical conviction.

At the consultation, J. I. Packer, another of the most respected figures in evangelical thought, directly addressed the issue of hell and its meaning. Packer

---

[58]Ibid., 318.

[59]Ibid., 319.

[60]See John R. W. Stott, "The Logic of Hell: A Brief Rejoinder," *ERT* 18 (January 1994): 34.

[61]Ibid. Bishop Timothy Dudley-Smith, John Stott's generous biographer, includes a portion from a letter from F. F. Bruce to Stott dated October 26, 1989, in which Bruce states: "Eternal conscious torment is incompatible with the revealed character of God. I'd *like* to be a universalist, and Paul sometimes encourages me in this (cf. Rom. 11:32, 1 Cor. 15:22), but only (I fear) when he is read out of context. Our Lord's teaching seems plain enough: there are some who persist irretrievably in impenitence, and refuse to the end the only salvation that is available to them." See Timothy Dudley-Smith, *John Stott: A Global Ministry*, "The Later Years," (Downers Grove, Ill.: InterVarsity Press, 2001), 2:354–55.

[62]Ibid., 354. Dudley-Smith credits Basil Atkinson, teacher to both John Stott and Philip E. Hughes at Trinity College, Cambridge, with influencing his students toward this position (see p. 353). Atkinson was librarian of the college and a lay theologian who led a popular Bible study for students.

[63]Peter Toon, *Heaven and Hell* (Nashville: Thomas Nelson, 1986), 174.

allowed that evangelicals might *wish* universalism were true: "No evangelical, I think, need hesitate to admit that in his heart of hearts he would like universalism to be true. Who can take pleasure in the thought of people being eternally lost? If you want to see folks damned, there is something wrong with you."[64] Nevertheless, Packer warned that the Bible closes the door on any notion of universal salvation. The same is true, he asserted, in the case of conditional immortality. Here his comments were very pointed:

> What troubles me most here, I confess, is the assumption of superior sensitivity by the conditionalists. Their assumption appears in the adjectives (awful, dreadful, terrible, fearful, intolerable, etc.) that they apply to the concept of eternal punishment, as if to suggest that holders of the historic view have never thought about the meaning of what they are saying.[65]

As for the biblical arguments put forth by John Stott, they "are to my mind flimsy special pleading." Furthermore,

> the feelings that make people want conditionalism to be true seem to me to reflect, not superior spiritual sensitivity, but secular sentimentalism which assumes that in heaven our feelings about others will be present, and our joy in the manifesting of God's justice will be no greater than it is now. It is certainly agonizing now to live with the thought of people going to an eternal hell, but it is not right to reduce the agony by evading facts; and in heaven, we may be sure, the agony will be a thing of the past.[66]

Packer's presentation was followed with a response by John Ankerberg and John Weldon, who contended, "*The doctrine of eternal punishment is the watershed between evangelical and non-evangelical thought.*"[67] They described the interrelation of doctrines and cited this as a cause for evangelical alarm: "When friends such as John Stott, Philip Edgcombe Hughes, Clark Pinnock, John Wenham, Basil Atkinson and other well-known and reputedly evangelical leaders, reject the traditional view of eternal punishment, the Church suffers serious or even fatal erosion in its doctrinal foundation."[68]

Such erosion was evident in 1995 when the Church of England Doctrine Commission released *The Mystery of Salvation*, an official report commended by the House of Bishops. The report embraced a hope for universal salvation, arguing that it is "incompatible with the essential Christian affirmation that God is love to say that God brings millions into the world to damn them."[69] The report

---

[64]J. I. Packer, "Evangelicals and the Way of Salvation," in *Evangelical Affirmations*, ed. Kenneth S. Kantzer and Carl F. H. Henry (Grand Rapids: Zondervan, 1990), 117.

[65]Ibid., 125–26.

[66]Ibid., 126.

[67]John Ankerberg with John Weldon, "Response to J. I. Packer," in *Evangelical Affirmations*, 140. Italics in original.

[68]Ibid., 140–41.

[69]*The Mystery of Salvation, The Story of God's Gift: A Report by the Doctrine Commission of the General Synod of the Church of England* (London: Church House Publishing, 1995), 180.

HeLL UNDeR fiRe

included strains of both universalism and inclusivism, but thoroughly rejected exclusivism.

The report also considered eschatology, noting that a recent survey had found that only 69 percent of churchgoing Britons believed in a destiny after death—a figure that fell to 42 percent among the general public. "There can be no doubt," the report asserted, "that Christians need to articulate in a coherent way a doctrine of the 'Last Things.'"[70] Evidently, the Doctrine Commission did not consider the historic teaching of its own church to be coherent. In any event, the commissioners were ready to dispense with it:

> Over the last two centuries the decline in the churches of the western world of a belief in everlasting punishment has been one of the most notable transformations of Christian belief. There are many reasons for this change, but amongst them has been the moral protest from both within and without the Christian faith against a religion of fear, and a growing sense that the picture of a God who consigned millions to eternal torment was far removed from the revelation of God's love in Christ. Nevertheless it is our conviction that the reality of hell (and indeed of heaven) is the ultimate affirmation of the reality of human freedom. Hell is not eternal torment, but it is the final and irrevocable choosing of that which is opposed to God so completely and so absolutely that the only end is total non-being.[71]

Thus, hell is the ultimate exercise of the liberated human will—but not a place of everlasting punishment. "If God has created us with the freedom to choose, then those who make such a final choice choose against the only source of life, and they have their reward. Whether there be any who do so choose, only God knows."[72] Hell as annihilation is "a truer picture of damnation," the report asserts, but it then goes on to suggest that only God knows if anyone is finally annihilated.

Sadly, the picture was not much clearer among the evangelicals. *The Nature of Hell*, a report of the Evangelical Alliance Commission on Unity and Truth Among Evangelicals (ACUTE), affirmed hell as an evangelical belief but concluded that "specific details of hell's duration, quality, finality, and purpose which are at issue in the current evangelical debate are comparatively less essential."[73]

In America, no one has made the case for annihilationism more energetically than Clark Pinnock and Edward Fudge, but of the two Pinnock has the more

---

[70]Ibid., 188.

[71]Ibid., 199.

[72]Ibid. It is interesting to note that Jacques Ellul, a French figure popular among some evangelicals, argued for a radical concept of human libertarianism, but argued that the freedom to be damned is the one freedom God will not allow. See Jacques Ellul, *What I Believe* (Grand Rapids: Eerdmans, 1989), 192.

[73]*The Nature of Hell: A Report by the Evangelical Alliance Commission on Unity and Truth Among Evangelicals* (Carlisle, UK: ACUTE/Paternoster, 2000), 128. Interestingly, the report also reminds us that when the Evangelical Alliance was established in 1846, "a clause was added to the original draft of its doctrinal basis to align the new body with eternal punishment and against a then-emergent liberal universalism" (3).

expansive theological agenda.[74] As a matter of fact, Pinnock seeks a complete reordering of Christian theology, rejecting such doctrines as the substitutionary atonement, forensic justification, biblical inerrancy, and God's exhaustive foreknowledge and omniscience.

On salvation, Pinnock promotes a form of Christian inclusivism. "God's universal salvific will implies the equally universal accessibility of salvation for all people," he argues.[75] Significantly, Pinnock rejects absolute universalism, but argues that the traditional doctrine of hell has promoted universalism as an option:

> The idea that hell means everlasting conscious punishment contributes much to belief in universal salvation. If the choice is between hell as everlasting torture and universal salvation, who could resist the latter? Sensitive persons would be practically forced to accept it, since they cannot accept that God would subject anyone, even most corrupt sinners, to unending torture in both body and soul as Augustine and Jonathan Edwards taught. If that is what hell means, many will conclude that there should not be a doctrine of hell in Christian theology.[76]

In an article published in 1990, Pinnock rejected the traditional doctrine of hell as a monstrous concept:

> Let me say at the outset that I consider the concept of hell as endless torment in body and mind an outrageous doctrine, a theological and moral enormity, a bad doctrine of the tradition which needs to be changed. How can Christians possibly project a deity of such cruelty and vindictiveness whose ways include inflicting everlasting torture upon his creatures, however sinful they may have been? Surely a God who would do such a thing is more nearly like Satan than like God, at least by any moral standards, and by the gospel itself.[77]

What about those who never hear the gospel? Pinnock now espouses the concept of a postmortem opportunity for those who never heard the gospel to find faith in Christ.

> The logic behind a postmortem encounter with Christ is simple enough. It rests on the insight that God, since he loves humanity, would not send anyone to hell without first ascertaining what their response would have been to his grace. Since everyone eventually dies and comes face to face with the risen Lord, that would seem to be the obvious time to discover their answer to God's call.[78]

---

[74]For Fudge's argument see his *The Fire That Consumes* (Houston: Providential, 1982).

[75]Clark H. Pinnock, *A Wideness in God's Mercy: The Finality of Jesus Christ in a World of Religions* (Grand Rapids: Zondervan, 1992), 157.

[76]Ibid., 156–57. Here again we see a proponent of annihilationism arguing from a supposed position of moral superiority. "Sensitive persons" are driven to reject the traditional doctrine of hell. This means, by unavoidable implication, that all those faithful preachers and teachers throughout the history of the church who affirmed and believed the historic doctrine must be or have been insensitive and lacking in human compassion.

[77]Clark H. Pinnock, "The Destruction of the Finally Impenitent," *CTR* 4 (1990): 246–47.

[78]Pinnock, *Wideness*, 168–69.

HELL UNDER FIRE

Of course, this concept seems to run into direct conflict with specific biblical texts such as Romans 10:8–17 and the general shape of the New Testament's presentation of evangelistic urgency. As a matter of fact, the biblical support for a postmortem evangelistic opportunity is virtually nonexistent. Pinnock recognizes this and offers, "Although the scriptural evidence for postmortem encounter is not abundant, its scantiness is relativized by the strength of the theological argument for it. A postmortem encounter with Jesus actually makes very good sense."[79]

The scope of Pinnock's proposal for reordering evangelical theology became clear when he coauthored a book with Robert Brow announcing a "good news theology for the 21st century."[80] The book followed a manifesto by Brow published in *Christianity Today* magazine. Brow called for an "evangelical megashift" that would thoroughly redefine the essential theological identity of the evangelical movement. The "new-model" evangelicalism he described would redefine (and thus reject) "old-model" evangelical doctrines such as justification by faith, substitutionary atonement, sin, and the wrath of God. Brow would continue to use the words but infuse them with a different meaning—what he called a "different accent." He seemed to argue that the larger culture had already demanded these changes by reconceiving the language. Hell came under Brow's special scrutiny, and he denied that God *sends* persons to hell. The wrath of God "never means sending people to an eternal hell."[81]

Brow saw time on his side and argued that the tide of evangelical opinion had already turned his way. In fact, he claimed that most evangelical young people had already accepted the basic form of his proposals. The transformation of evangelical theology is inevitable, he stressed, for even though we "may use old-model language and assume that we believe as before ... our hearts are changing our minds."[82]

Pinnock and Brow joined forces in promoting what they called "creative love theism," the heart of their agenda for a reordered evangelical theology. Their system does include a doctrine of hell, but one that bears little resemblance to the traditional doctrine:

> Creative love theism does have a doctrine of hell, but hell cannot be an everlasting vindictive torment. God is not vindictive and does not practice sadism. The lurid portrayals of hellfire in the Christian tradition contradict God's identity, according to the gospel. God is not a pitiless, vengeful judge but One who loves his enemies and dies for them.[83]

By the last decade of the twentieth century, it was apparent that a battle for evangelical identity and evangelical conviction was well underway. Reformist theologians who claimed to be evangelicals felt perfectly free to deny or radically revise articles of faith that had been taught and defended by evangelicals of

[79]Ibid., 169.
[80]Clark H. Pinnock and Robert C. Brow, *Unbounded Love: A Good News Theology for the 21st Century* (Downers Grove, Ill.: InterVarsity Press, 1994).
[81]Robert Brow, "The Evangelical MegaShift," *ChrT* 34 (February 19, 1990), 13.
[82]Ibid., 14.
[83]Pinnock and Brow, *Unbounded Love*, 89–90.

previous generations—and even now by many, if not most evangelicals of the present day. Hell was but one significant doctrine under fire.[84]

Hell in the Balance: What Is at Stake?

Os Guinness notes that Western societies "have reached the state of pluralization where choice is not just a state of affairs, it is a state of mind. Choice has become a value in itself, even a priority. To be modern is to be addicted to choice and change. Change becomes the very essence of life."[85] Personal choice becomes the urgency, or what sociologist Peter Berger called the "heretical imperative."[86] In such a context, theology undergoes rapid and repeated transformation driven by cultural currents.

This process is often invisible to those experiencing it and denied by those promoting it. As David F. Wells comments, "The stream of historic orthodoxy that once watered the evangelical soul is now dammed by a worldliness that many fail to recognize as worldliness because of the cultural innocence with which it presents itself."[87] He continued:

> To be sure, this orthodoxy never was infallible, nor was it without its blemishes and foibles, but I am far from persuaded that the emancipation from its theological core that much of evangelicalism is effecting has resulted in greater biblical fidelity. In fact, the result is just the opposite. We now have less biblical fidelity, less interest in truth, less seriousness, less depth, and less capacity to speak the Word of God to our own generation in a way that offers an alternative to what it already thinks.[88]

The pressing question of our concern is this: What has happened so that we now find some who claim to be evangelicals promoting and teaching concepts such as universalism, inclusivism, postmortem evangelism, conditional immortality, and annihilationism—when those known as evangelicals in former times were known for opposing those very proposals?

The answer must be found in understanding the impact of cultural trends and the prevailing worldview on Christian theology. Ever since the Enlightenment, theologians have been forced to defend the very legitimacy of their discipline and proposals. A secular worldview that denies supernatural revelation must reject Christianity as a system and truth-claim. At the same time, it seeks to transform all religious truth-claims into matters of personal choice and opinion. Christianity, stripped of its offensive theology, is reduced to one "spirituality" among others.

---

[84]See R. Albert Mohler Jr., "Reformist Evangelicalism: A Circle without a Circumference," in *A Confessing Theology for Postmodern Times*, ed. Michael S. Horton (Wheaton, Ill.: Crossway, 2000), 131–52.

[85]Os Guinness, *The Gravedigger File* (Downers Grove, Ill.: InterVarsity Press, 1983), 92.

[86]Peter L. Berger, *The Heretical Imperative: Contemporary Possibilities of Religious Affirmation* (New York: Doubleday, 1980).

[87]David F. Wells, *No Place for Truth: Or Whatever Happened to Evangelical Theology?* (Grand Rapids: Eerdmans, 1993), 11.

[88]Ibid., 11–12.

HELL UNDER FIRE

All the same, there are particular doctrines that are especially odious and repulsive to the modern and postmodern mind. The traditional doctrine of hell as a place of everlasting punishment bears that scandal in a particular way. The doctrine is offensive to modern sensibilities and an embarrassment to many who consider themselves to be Christians. Those Friedrich Schleiermacher called the "cultured despisers of religion" especially despise the doctrine of hell.

Liberal Protestantism and Roman Catholicism have modified their theological systems to remove this offense. No one is in danger of hearing a threatening "fire and brimstone" sermon in those churches. The burden of defending and debating hell now falls to the evangelicals—the last people who think it matters. How is it that now so many evangelicals—including some of the most respected leaders in the movement—reject the traditional doctrine of hell in favor of annihilationism or some other option? The answer surely comes down to the challenge of theodicy.

Modern secularism demands that anyone who would speak for God must now defend him. The challenge of theodicy is primarily to defend God against the problem of evil. The societies that gave birth to the decades of megadeath, the Holocaust, the abortion explosion, and institutionalized terror now demand that God answer their questions and redefine himself according to their dictates.

In the background to all this is a series of interrelated cultural, theological, and philosophical changes that point to an answer for our question: What happened to evangelical convictions about hell?

The first issue is a changed view of God. The biblical vision of God has been rejected by the culture as too restrictive of human freedom and offensive to human sensibilities. God's love has been redefined so that it is no longer holy. God's sovereignty has been reconceived so that human autonomy is undisturbed. In recent years, even God's omniscience has been redefined to mean that God perfectly knows all that he can perfectly know, but he cannot possibly know a future based on free human decisions.

Evangelical revisionists promote an understanding of divine love that is never coercive and disallows any thought that God would send impenitent sinners to eternal punishment in the fires of hell. They are seeking to rescue God from the bad reputation he picked up by associating with theologians who for centuries taught the traditional doctrine. God is just not like that, they reassure. He would never sentence anyone—however guilty—to eternal torment and anguish.

Theologian Geerhardus Vos warned against abstracting the love of God from his other attributes, noting that while God's love is revealed to be his fundamental attribute, it is defined by his other attributes as well. It is quite possible to "overemphasize this one side of truth as to bring into neglect other exceedingly important principles and demands of Christianity," he stressed.[89] This would lead to a loss of theological "equilibrium" and balance. In the specific case of the love

---

[89]Geerhardus Vos, "The Scriptural Doctrine of the Love of God," in *Redemptive History and Biblical Interpreation: The Shorter Writings of Geerhardus Vos*, ed. Richard B. Gaffin (Grand Rapids: Baker, 1980 [1902]), 426.

of God, it often leads to an unscriptural sentimentalism whereby God's love becomes a form of indulgence incompatible with his hatred of sin.

In this regard, the language of the revisionists is particularly instructive. Any God who would act as the traditional doctrine holds would be "vindictive," "cruel," and "more like Satan than like God." Clark Pinnock has made the credibility of the doctrine of God to the modern mind a central focus of his theology: "I believe that unless the portrait of God is compelling, the credibility of belief in God is bound to decline."[90] Later he suggests, "today it is easier to invite people to find fulfillment in a dynamic, personal God than it would be to ask them to find it in a deity who is immutable and self-enclosed."[91]

Extending this argument further, it is surely easier to persuade secular persons to believe in a God who never judges anyone deserving of eternal punishment than it is to persuade them to believe in the God preached by Jonathan Edwards or Charles Spurgeon. But the urgent question is this: Is evangelical theology about marketing God to our contemporary culture, or is our task to stand in continuity with orthodox biblical conviction—whatever the cost? As was cited earlier, modern persons demand that God must be a humanitarian and must be held to human standards of righteousness and love. In the end, only God can defend himself against his critics.

A second issue is a changed view of justice. Retributive justice has been the hallmark of human law since premodern times. This concept assumes that punishment is a natural and necessary component of justice. Nevertheless, retributive justice has been under assault for many years in Western cultures, and this has led to modifications in the doctrine of hell.

The utilitarian philosophers such as John Stuart Mill and Jeremy Bentham argued that retribution is an unacceptable form of justice. Rejecting clear and absolute moral norms, they argued that justice demands restoration rather than retribution. Criminals were no longer seen as evil and deserving of punishment; rather, they are persons in need of correction. The goal—for all but the most egregious sinners—was restoration and rehabilitation. The shift from the prison to the penitentiary was supposed to be a shift from a place of punishment to a place of penance, but apparently no one told the prisoners. C. S. Lewis rejected this idea as an assault on the very concept of justice:

> We demand of a cure not whether it is just but whether it succeeds. Thus when we cease to consider what the criminal deserves and consider only what will cure him or deter others, we have tacitly removed him from the sphere of justice altogether; instead of a person, a subject of rights, we now have a mere object, a patient, a "case."[92]

---

[90]Clark H. Pinnock, "Systematic Theology," in *The Openness of God: A Biblical Challenge to the Traditional Understanding of God*, ed. Clark H. Pinnock et al. (Downers Grove, Ill.: InterVarsity Press, 1994), 101.

[91]Ibid., 107.

[92]C. S. Lewis, "The Humanitarian Theory of Punishment," in *God in the Dock: Essays on Theology and Ethics*, ed. Walter Hooper (Grand Rapids: Eerdmans, 1970), 288.

HELL UNDER FIRE

Penal reforms followed, public executions ceased, and the public accepted the changes in the name of humanitarianism. Dutch criminologist Pieter Spierenburg pointed to "increasing inter-human identification" as the undercurrent of this shift.[93] Individuals began to sympathize with the criminal, often thinking of themselves in the criminal's place. The impact of this shift in the culture is apparent in a letter from one nineteenth-century Anglican to another:

> The disbelief in the existence of retributive justice ... is now so widely spread through nearly all classes of people, especially in regard to social and political questions ... [that it] causes even men, whose theology teaches them to look upon God as a vindictive, lawless autocrat, to stigmatize as cruel and heathenish the belief that criminal law is bound to contemplate in punishment other ends beside the improvement of the offender himself and the deterring of others.[94]

The utilitarian concept of justice and deterrence has also given way to justice by popular opinion and cultural custom. The U. S. Constitution disallows "cruel and unusual punishment," and the courts have offered evolving and conflicting rulings on what kind of punishment is thus excluded. At various times the death penalty has been constitutionally permitted and forbidden, and in one recent U. S. Supreme Court decision, the justice writing the majority opinion actually cited data from opinion polls.

The transformations of legal practice and culture have redefined justice for many modern persons. Retribution is out, and rehabilitation is put in its place. Some theologians have simply incorporated this new theory of justice into their doctrines of hell. For the Roman Catholics, the doctrine of purgatory functions as the penitentiary. For some evangelicals, a period of time in hell—but not an eternity in hell—is the remedy.

Some theologians have questioned the moral integrity of eternal punishment by arguing that an infinite punishment is an unjust penalty for finite sins. Or, to put the argument in a slightly different form, eternal torment is no fitting punishment for temporal sins. The traditional doctrine of hell argues that an infinite penalty is just punishment for sin against the infinite holiness of God. This explains why all sinners equally deserve hell, except for salvation through faith in Christ.

A third shift in the larger culture concerns the advent of the psychological worldview. Human behavior has been redefined by the impact of humanistic psychologies that deny or reduce personal responsibility for wrongdoing. Various

---

[93]Pieter Spierenburg, *The Spectacle of Suffering: Executions and the Evolution of Repression* (Cambridge: Cambridge Univ. Press, 1984), cited in Kendall S. Harmon, "Finally Excluded From God? Some Twentieth-Century Theological Explorations of the Problem of Hell and Universalism with Reference to the Historical Development of These Doctrines" (D.Phil. Thesis, Oxford University, 1993), 110.
[94]Letter from Fenton J. A. Hort to F. D. Maurice, dated November 16, 1849, cited in ibid., 112.

theories place the blame on external influences, biological factors, behavioral determinism, genetic predispositions, and the influence of the subconscious—and these variant theories barely scratch the surface.

The autonomous self becomes the great personal project for individuals, and their various crimes and misdemeanors are excused as growth experiences or "personal issues." Shame and guilt are banned from public discussion and dismissed as repressive. In such a culture, the finality of God's sentencing of impenitent sinners to hell is just unthinkable.

A fourth shift concerns the concept of salvation. The majority of men and women throughout the centuries of Western civilization have awakened in the morning and gone to sleep at night with the fear of hell never far from consciousness—until now. Sin has been redefined as a lack of self-esteem rather than as an insult to the glory of God. Salvation has been reconceived as liberation from oppression, internal or external. The gospel becomes a means of release from bondage to bad habits rather than rescue from a sentence of eternity in hell.

The theodicy issue arises immediately when evangelicals limit salvation to those who come to conscious faith in Christ during their earthly lives and define salvation as anything akin to justification by faith. To the modern mind this seems unfair and scandalously discriminatory. Some evangelicals have thus modified the doctrine of salvation accordingly. This means that hell is either evacuated or minimized. Or, as one Catholic wit quipped, hell has been air-conditioned.

These shifts in the culture are but part of the picture. The most basic cause of controversy over the doctrine of hell is the challenge of theodicy. The traditional doctrine is just too out of step with the contemporary mind—too harsh and eternally fixed. In virtually every aspect, the modern mind is offended by the biblical concept of hell preserved in the historic doctrine. For some who call themselves evangelicals, this is simply too much to bear.

We should note that compromise on the doctrine of hell is not limited to those who reject the historic formulation. The reality is that few references to hell are likely to be heard even in conservative churches that would never deny the doctrine. Once again, the cultural environment is a major influence.

In his study of "seeker sensitive" churches, researcher Kimon Howland Sargeant notes that "today's cultural pluralism fosters an under-emphasis on the 'hard sell' of Hell while contributing to an overemphasis on the 'soft sell' of personal satisfaction through Jesus Christ."[95] The problem is thus more complex and pervasive than the theological rejection of hell—it also includes the avoidance of the issue in the face of cultural pressure.

The revision or rejection of the historic doctrine of hell comes at a great cost. The entire system of theology is modified by effect, even if some revisionists refuse to take their revisions to their logical conclusions. Essentially, our concepts of God and the gospel are at stake. What could be more important?

---

[95]Kimon Howland Sargeant, *Seeker Churches: Promoting Traditional Religion in a Nontraditional Way* (New Brunswick, N.J.: Rutgers Univ. Press, 2000), 198.

HeLL UNDeR fire

The temptation to revise the doctrine of hell—to remove the sting and scandal of everlasting conscious punishment—is understandable. But it is also a major test of evangelical conviction. This is no theological trifle. As one observer has asked, "Could it be that the only result of attempts, however well-meaning, to air-condition Hell, is to ensure that more and more people wind up there?"[96]

Hell demands our attention in the present, and now confronts evangelicals with a critical test of theological and biblical integrity. Hell may be denied, but it will not disappear.

---

[96]"Hell Air-Conditioned," *New Oxford Review* 58 (June 1998): 4.

Chapter 2

tHe
OLD testameNt
oN HeLL

Daniel I. Block

What does the Old Testament teach about hell? The simple answer to this question is, "Very little." Despite the Septuagint's consistent rendering of the Hebrew term $\check{s}^{e_{}}\bar{o}l$ as $had\bar{e}s$,[1] the Old Testament understanding of the place called Sheol bears little resemblance to the Gehenna/hell we read about in the New Testament. Nevertheless, in order to understand the few hints the Old Testament offers for postmortem punishment in a place we have come to know as hell, and in order to interpret the fuller revelation on this subject found in the New Testament, it is necessary to reconstruct a picture of ancient Israelite perspectives on this matter. This essay will therefore attempt to recapture the Old Testament views of the netherworld and afterlife by asking the following questions:

1. How does the Old Testament refer to the abode of the dead?
2. Who occupies the netherworld?
3. What conditions greet those who enter the netherworld?
4. What evidence does the Old Testament provide for the Christian doctrine of hell as a place of eternal torment?

The Old Testament Vocabulary for the Netherworld

The importance of and general interest in matters relating to death and the afterlife are reflected in the variety of expressions used to identify the place to which the deceased go when they die. Often their abode is described in phenomenological language derived from ancient burial practices. In each case one must decide whether the reference is to the grave or the abode of the dead.

The Grave (*qeber*)

Not surprisingly, the abode of the dead is often referred to simply as *haqqeber* ("the grave"). Genesis 23 describes in moving terms Abraham's desire to give his wife a proper burial and the actions he took to do so. His intention is expressed as acquiring "a burial site [*qeber*] here so I can bury my dead" (23:4). In this instance, it involved a cave at Machpelah. In ancient Israel, people with sufficient means would bury their dead in family tombs dug out of the limestone, which explains the euphemistic expression for death as (lit.) "being gathered to one's grave" (2 Kings 22:20 = 2 Chron. 34:28), "being gathered to one's fathers/ancestors" (Judg. 2:10), and "being gathered to one's people,"[2] and the burial place as (lit.) "the tomb of the fathers/ancestors."[3] The poor simply dug a hole in the ground and covered the corpse of the deceased with soil (2 Kings 23:6; Jer. 26:23).

---

[1] Only in Prov. 23:14 is the word rendered otherwise in the Septuagint, in this case with *thanatos* ("death").

[2] Gen. 25:8; 25:17; 35:29; 49:29, 33; Num. 27:13; 31:2; Deut. 32:50.

[3] 2 Sam. 2:32; 17:23; 19:38; 1 Kings 13:22; Neh. 2:3–5; 2 Chron. 35:24; cf. Judg. 8:32; 16:31; 2 Sam. 21:14.

HeLL UNDeR fire

The Pit (*bôr*)

Literally a *bôr* was a manmade hole dug in the ground or the limestone to trap and store rainwater.[4] However, the word is also often used of the abode of the dead,[5] especially when found in parallelism with *šᵉʾōl* (Ps. 30:3[4]; Prov. 1:12; Isa. 14:15; 38:18; Ezek. 31:16) or *šaḥat* ("trap"; Ps. 7:15[16]; Isa. 38:17–18).

The Trap (*šaḥat*)

The primary sense of *šaḥat* is reflected in Ezekiel 19:4, 8, where it denotes a pit dug for trapping game.[6] However, it is used most commonly of the place where the dead reside, especially in idioms like "to go down to the pit,"[7] "to approach the pit" (Job 33:22), "to die [in]to the pit" (Isa. 51:4), "to pass through the pit" (Job 33:28), "to see/experience the pit" (Pss. 16:10; 49:9[10]).

The Earth, Netherworld (*ʾereṣ*)

Although in the vast majority of cases *ʾereṣ* denotes "earth" in contrast to "the heavens" (see Gen. 1:1; Ezek. 8:3), in several contexts the term obviously refers to the "netherworld."[8] This sense is especially clear in contexts involving phrases like *ʾereṣ taḥtiyyôt* ("land of the depths"; Ezek. 32:18, 24; cf. 26:20), a distinctly Ezekielian variation of *ʾereṣ taḥtît* ("the lower world"; cf. 31:14, 16, 18; Deut. 32:33), and *taḥtiyyôt ʾereṣ* ("depths of the earth").[9] As such a designation for the abode of the dead, "land of the depths" represents a counterpart to *ʾereṣ haḥayyîm* ("land of the living").[10]

Sheol (*šᵉʾōl*)

Šᵉʾōl is a distinctly Hebrew expression of uncertain etymological derivation.[11] The most likely explanation relates the noun to the verb *šāʾal* ("to ask, inquire"), perhaps because of some association with the practice of necromancy.[12] Some

---

[4]Occasionally, dry cisterns would be used to store perishable goods or even criminals (Ex. 12:29; cf. Gen. 37:24; Jer. 37:16), or to seek cover from danger (Jer. 38:6). Compare the related expression *bᵉʾēr* ("well"; e.g., Gen. 21:19, 25).

[5]Pss. 28:1; 30:3[4]; 40:2[3]; 88:4[5]; 143:7; Prov. 1:12; Ezek. 26:2.

[6]Cf. N. J. Tromp, *Primitive Conceptions of Death and the Nether World in the Old Testament* (BibOr 21; Rome: Pontifical Biblical Institute, 1969), 69–71; M. H. Pope, "The Word *šaḥat* in Job 9:31," *JBL* 5 (1964): 269–78; idem, "A Little Soul-Searching," *Maarav* 1 (1978): 25–31. Cf. also M. Held, "Pits and Pitfalls in Akkadian and Biblical Hebrew," *JANES* 5 (1973): 173–90.

[7]Job 33:24; Pss. 30:10[9]; 55:24[23]; Ezek. 28:8.

[8]Isa. 26:19; Ps. 22:30; Jonah 2:6 [7]. Compare Ugaritic *ʾrṣ* and the Akkadian cognate *erṣetu*.

[9]Isa. 44:23; Pss. 63:9[10]; 139:15; cf. *bôr taḥtît*, Ps. 88:6[7]; Lam. 3:55.

[10]Pss. 27:13; 52:7; 116:9; 142:6; Job 28:13; Isa. 38:1; 53:18; Jer. 11:19; Ezek. 26:20; 32:23, 24, 25, 26, 27, 32. On these terms as designations for the netherworld, see L. J. Stadelmann, *The Hebrew Conception of the World: A Philological and Literary Study* (AnBib 39; Rome: Pontifical Biblical Institute, 1970), 167.

[11]The word occurs sixty-six times in the Old Testament (including Isa. 7:11). For references see A. Even-Shoshan, *A New Concordance of the Bible* (Jerusalem: Kiryat Sepher, 1981), 1098.

[12]Cf. Deut. 18:11; 1 Sam. 28:6; 1 Chron. 10:13. For discussion of the etymology and significance of the expression, see T. Lewis, "Dead, Abode of the," *ABD*, 2:101–5.

would always interpret the word as "grave," while others always interpret it as the place where the dead reside, that is, the netherworld. One enters Sheol by "the gates of Sheol" (Isa. 38:10) or "the gates of death" (Job 38:17; Pss. 9:14; 107:18).

Death, Place of Death (*māwet/môt*)

The term *māwet/môt* usually refers to the experience of death, though in some poetic texts with mythological backgrounds it appears to be used as a proper name identifying the chthonic power behind death, Mot of the Ugaritic texts.[13] In a few instances, *māwet/môt* refers to the place of the dead.[14]

Abaddon (*ᵃbaddôn*)

Usually translated "Perdition" or "Place of Destruction" (from *ᵓābad*, "to perish"), this is the most negative expression for the abode of the dead (Job 26:6; 28:22; 31:12; Ps. 88:12[11]; Prov. 15:11; 27:20). The personification of the word in Job 28:22 leads to the notion of Apollyon, "the destroying angel of the abyss" (from *apōleia*, "destruction," the LXX's rendering of the term) in Revelation 9:11.

The Occupants of the Netherworld

The Old Testament has several expressions to identify the deceased in the netherworld. Most naturally, they are called *hammētîm* ("the dead"),[15] but the Israelites also shared with the Canaanites a special expression for the deceased in Sheol, *rᵉpāᵓîm*, traditionally rendered "the shades." The most likely etymology derives this word from *rāpāᵓ* ("to heal"), but the precise relationship between the verb and the substantive *rᵉpāᵓîm* is uncertain. The latter term occurs twenty-seven times in the Old Testament. The majority of these are found in the historiographic writings, where the word is used as a proper noun to identify one of the groups of fearful and gigantic inhabitants of ancient Palestine.[16]

At Ugarit, the cognate noun *rpum* denoted in particular the deceased royalty that in some contexts appear divinized.[17] The royal sense of Hebrew *rᵉpāᵓîm* is

---

[13]Job 18:13–14; 28:22; Ps. 49:15; Song 8:6; Isa. 28:15,18; Hos. 13:14; Hab. 2:5; cf. also Isa. 5:14; Ps. 141:7; Prov. 1:12; 27:20; 30:15–16.

[14]Job 38:17; Pss. 6:5[6]; 9:14; 107:18; Prov. 7:27.

[15]Deut. 18:11; Pss. 88:5, 10[6, 11]; 106:28; 115:17; 143:3; Eccl. 4:2; 9:3, 5; Isa. 8:19; 26:14, 19; 59:10; Lam. 3:6; Ezek. 24:17. In Deut. 18:11 and Isa. 8:19 the reference is to consulting the dead on behalf of the living. Ps. 106:28 and Ezek. 24:17 involve rites for the dead.

[16]Gen. 14:5; 15:20; Deut. 2:11, 20a, 20b; 3:11, 13; Josh. 12:4; 13:12; 17:15; 1 Chron. 20:4 (cf. the singular *rāpāᵓ* in vv. 6, 8). To this list we should add the references to the Valley of Rephaim, southwest of Jerusalem and associated with the Valley of Hinnom, apparently named after this group: Josh. 15:8; 18:16; 2 Sam. 5:18, 22; 23:13 = 1 Chron. 11:15; 14:9; Isa. 17:5. The Rephaim were often linked with other terrifying peoples: Anakites, Emites, Zamzummites.

[17]As a designation for [divinized?] inhabitants of the netherworld, the term *rpum* is occasionally associated with *mlkm* ("kings") and even *ilnym* ("divine ones"). On the former, see B. Levine and J. M. Tarragon, "Dead Kings and Rephaim: The Patrons of the Ugaritic Dynasty," *JOAS* 104 (1984): 649–59; J. F. Healey, "*MLKM/RPᵓUM* and the Kispum," *UF* 10 (1978): 89–91. On the latter, see H. Rouillard, "Rephaim," in K. van der Toorn, B. Becking, and P. W. van der Horst, eds., *Dictionary of Deities and Demons in the Bible* (Leiden; New York: Brill, 1995),

HeLL UNDeR fiRe

evident in several Old Testament texts. Especially striking is Isaiah 14:9, which mentions among those who welcome the king of Babylon to Sheol "all the leaders [lit., goats] of the earth" (*kol-ʿattûdê ʾareṣ*) and "all the kings of the nations" (*kōl malkê gôyim*) in parallelism with *rᵉpāʾîm*:

> Sheol beneath is stirred up
>   to meet you when you come;
> it rouses the shades [*rᵉpāʾîm*] to greet you,
>   all who were leaders of the earth;
> it raises from their thrones
>   all who were kings of the nations.[18]

Here the community of *rᵉpāʾîm* embraces all the royal dead, whether they rest in graves or recline on beds of maggots. Though not quite as obvious, this is true also of Isaiah 26:13–14:

> O LORD our God,
> other lords besides you have ruled over us,[19]
>   but your name alone we bring to remembrance.
> They are dead, they will not live;
>   they are shades [*rᵉpāʾîm*], they will not arise;
> to that end you have visited them with destruction
>   and wiped out all remembrance of them.

In this "apocalyptic" oracle Isaiah distinguishes between the *rᵉpāʾîm* and "the dead" (*mētîm*), presumably the prophet's deceased fellow Israelites, who will participate in the national resurrection envisioned by Ezekiel in 37:1–14.

Elsewhere in the Old Testament, *rᵉpāʾîm* tends to refer to any deceased inhabitant of Sheol, without respect to class or status. This is most evident in Psalm 88, an individual lament in which the psalmist pleads for Yahweh to save him from imminent death, arguing that only the living can praise God for his acts of salvation and covenant faithfulness:

> [1]O LORD, God of my salvation;
>   I cry out day and night before you.
> [2]Let my prayer come before you;
>   incline your ear to my cry!

692–95. The traditional interpretation of *rᵉpāʾîm* as "the shades" finds some justification in the Ugaritic literature, inasmuch as in a funerary ritual text involving commemoration of a king's death the *rpum* are also called *ẓlm* ("shadows"). See *KTU* 1.161. For discussion, see M. Dietrich and O. Loretz, "Neue Studien zu den Ritualtexten aus Ugarit (II)—Nr. 6—Epigraphische und inhaltliche Probleme in *KTU* 1.161," *UF* 15 (1983): 17–24.

[18]Unless otherwise indicated, all biblical citations are based on the ESV.

[19]Although some would interpret the "other lords besides you" (*ʾᵃdōnîm zûlātekā*) who have lorded it over (*bāʿal*) the Israelites as the Baals worshiped by the people (Rouillard, "Rephaim," 696), it is preferable to see here a reference to foreign overlords. So also J. N. Oswalt, *The Book of Isaiah Chapters 1–39* (NICOT; Grand Rapids: Eerdmans, 1986), 481.

³For my soul is full of troubles,
and my life draws near to Sheol.
⁴I am counted among those who go down to the pit;
I am a man who has no strength,
⁵like one set loose among the dead [*mētîm*],
like the slain that lie in the grave,
like those whom you remember no more,
for they are cut off from your hand.
⁶You have put me in the depths of the pit,
in the regions dark and deep.
⁷Your wrath lies heavy upon me,
and you overwhelm me with all your waves.   *Selah*
⁸You have caused my companions to shun me;
you have made me a horror to them.
I am shut in so that I cannot escape;
⁹   my eye grows dim through sorrow.
Every day I call upon you, O LORD;
I spread out my hands to you.
¹⁰Do you work wonders for the dead [*mētîm*]?
Do the departed [*rᵉpāʾîm*] rise up to praise you?   *Selah*
¹¹Is your steadfast love declared in the grave,
or your faithfulness in Abaddon?
¹²Are your wonders known in the darkness,
or your righteousness in the land of forgetfulness? (Ps. 88:1–13[2–13])

Similarly, in three texts in Proverbs *rᵉpāʾîm* refers to the dead in general:

Her house sinks down to death,
and her paths to the departed [*rᵉpāʾîm*];
None who go to her come back,
nor do they regain the paths of life. (Prov. 2:18–19)

But he [the fool] does not know that the dead [*rᵉpāʾîm*] are there,
that her guests are in the depths of Sheol. (Prov. 9:18)

These verses describe the lethal effect of a visit to Dame Folly's house, creating the impression that immediately inside her doorway is a trap door that leads directly to the netherworld. Whereas these texts seek to warn the youthful fool to avoid Dame Folly, in Proverbs 21:16 the warning is more general:

One who wanders from the way of good sense
will rest in the assembly of the dead.

This statement is remarkable for its reference to the deceased resting in the "assembly of the dead" (*qᵉhal rᵉpāʾîm*).²⁰

---

²⁰In the context of this discussion of designations for the deceased, that is, the occupants of the netherworld, we note also the hapax expression in Isa. 19:3, *ʾiṭṭîm*, usually understood as

Besides these basic terms, the ancient Israelites had a series of additional specific terms to refer to the occupants of the netherworld. But no biblical author's vocabulary on this theme matched that of Ezekiel. Some are found elsewhere in the Old Testament; others are unique to him; *yôrᵉdê bôr* ("those who go down to the Pit") is the most general expression.[21]

The idiom *ḥalᵉlê-ḥereb* ("those slain by the sword") reflects the means whereby these were sent down to Sheol. Although in some contexts these may be simply passive victims of violence or soldiers who have died on the battlefield,[22] in Ezekiel the expression generally refers to executed murderers and evildoers, whose bodies may have been tossed in a heap in a separate burial place, or even left out in the open, instead of being given an honorable burial.[23]

Already Ezekiel 31:18 had mentioned the *ᶜᵃrēlîm* ("uncircumcised"), though only in passing. He applies this expression to inhabitants of Sheol no fewer than ten times in 32:17–32. Obviously, Ezekiel's usage of the term is metaphorical and culturally determined. In Israel, circumcision was the sign and seal of membership in the covenant community (Gen. 17), which in time became a symbol of cultural superiority. To call anyone "uncircumcised" was the ultimate insult. Those who did not bear this mark at the time of their deaths were excluded from the family grave. For Ezekiel this meant being sentenced to the most undesirable compartment of the netherworld along with other vile and unclean persons.[24]

Another designation Ezekiel uses for the residents of Sheol is *ḥittît bᵉ'ereṣ ḥayyîm* ("those who spread terror in the land of the living"; 32:23). The distinctly Ezekielian expression *ḥittît* occurs seven times in 32:17–32 (cf. 26:21). Deriving from a root meaning "to be filled with terror," it refers to the fear, confusion, and anguish created by a powerful foe. In this text, those nations who have created such Angst in others discover that their violent conduct while in the land of the living has determined their status in the realm of the dead.

In 26:20 Ezekiel announces that Tyre shall join the *ᶜam ᶜôlām* ("people of eternity"). The literary context suggests that this idiom should be associated with *mētê ᶜôlām* ("those long dead"), which in Psalm 143:3 and Lamentations 3:6 denotes the departed dead from long ago who dwell in dark places. By contrast, if we

---

"sorcerer," but rightly interpreted as "spirits of the dead" by the NRSV. Thus also L. Koehler, W. Baumgartner, and J. J. Stamm, *The Hebrew and Aramaic Lexicon of the Old Testament* (Leiden: Brill, 1994–1999), 37.

[21]Ezek. 26:20a, 20b; 31:14, 16, 32; 32:18, 24, 25, 29, 30. Cf. Pss. 28:1; 30:3[4]; 88:4[5]; 143:7; Prov. 1:12. Elsewhere Ezekiel speaks of people "going/bringing down to Sheol" (31:15, 16, 17; 32:27), or simply "going down" (vv. 32:18, 19, 21, 24, 30; cf. 26:20; 31:18). In 31:16, 18 the prophet identifies the occupants of Sheol as "all the trees of Eden."

[22]Isa. 22:2; Jer. 14:18; Lam. 4:9; Ezek. 35:8.

[23]Ezek. 31:17, 18; 32:30, 31, 32. On the ignominy of being denied a proper burial or exhumation, see Deut. 28:25–26; 1 Kings 13:77; 14:10–11; Jer. 16:4. For a discussion of the expression, see O. Eissfeldt, "Schwerterschlagene bei Hesekiel," in *Studies in Old Testament Prophecy* (Festschrift for T. H. Robinson; ed. H. H. Rowley; New York: Scribner's, 1950), 73–81.

[24]For a recent study on Israelite circumcision in its Near Eastern context, see R. C. Steiner, "Incomplete Circumcision in Egypt and Edom: Jeremiah (9:24–25) in the Light of Josephus and Jonckeere," *JBL* 118 (1999): 497–526.

understand *ʿôlām* substantively (i.e., "eternity") or more specifically the nether-world, then the *ʿam ʿôlām* may be the inhabitants of the *bêt ʿôlām* ("eternal house") referred to in Ecclesiastes 12:5, that is, "the people of the netherworld."[25]

In Ezekiel 39:11, 14 we find the curious phrase *gê hāʿōbᵉrîm*, which identifies the place of Gog's burial. Scholars have interpreted this expression in several ways, most notably as "Valley of the Travelers," a variant spelling of Abarim, or as a new name, "the Valley of Hamon-Gog," which plays on *gê hinnôm* ("the valley of Hinnom"). However, drawing on the support of the Ugaritic text KTU 1:22 I:12–17, some have recently argued that *hāʿōbᵉrîm* represents the inhabitants of the netherworld. This mortuary cultic document associates the *ʿbrm* with *mlkm*, departed kings who are identified elsewhere as *rpwm/rpym*. According to this interpretation, *hāʿōbᵉrîm* refers to these departed heroes, and the "valley of those who have passed on" is a cemetery where people disposed of their dead.

Ezekiel has several additional expressions for deceased heroes. In 32:21 he speaks of *ʾēlê gibbôrîm* (lit., "the rams of mighty men").[26] In 32:27 they are referred to as "the fallen heroes from ancient times" (*gibbôrîm nōpᵉlîm mēʿôlām*).[27] This phrase recalls Genesis 6:4, which labels the antediluvian progeny of the "sons of God" and human daughters Nephilim, identified more closely as "the heroes who were from ancient times, the men of renown" (*ʾanšê haššēm haggibbôrîm ʾᵃšer mēʿôlām*). According to Ezekiel 32:21, these heroic personages speak from the midst of Sheol, which may suggest that they are located in the heart of the nether-world, perhaps a more honorable assignment than "the remotest recesses of the pit" (*yarkᵉtê bôr*, Ezek. 32:23; cf. Isa. 14:15), where the uncircumcised and those who have fallen by the sword lie. The description in Ezekiel 32:27 indicates that these individuals have indeed been afforded noble burials. There they lie with their weapons of war, their swords laid under their heads, and their shields placed on their bones. Ancient burial customs in which personal items and symbols of status were buried with the corpses of the deceased provide the source of this image.[28]

The Nature and Conditions of the Netherworld

The vocabulary of the abode of the dead offers some hints concerning the Israelite perception of the netherworld, but the subject requires further explo-ration. The Israelites shared with their ancient Near Eastern neighbors the per-ception of a universe consisting of three tiers of existence that may be portrayed graphically as follows:[29]

---

[25]One finds semantic equivalents in Akkadian *šubat dārati/dārat* ("the dwelling place of eternity"), and *ēkal salāli kimah tap-šuḥti šubat dārati* ("a palace of sleeping, a resting tomb, a dwelling place of eternity") as well as *byt -ʿlm*, signifying "grave," in the Deir ʿAlla texts [II:6]. On these expressions see H. Tawil, "A Note on the Ahiram Inscription," *JANES* 3 (1970): 36.
[26]Ps. 88:4[5] employs the same root: *geber ʾên ʾᵉyāl* ("man without strength").
[27]Reading with LXX. MT reads *mēʿᵃrēlîm* ("from the uncircumcised").
[28]On the custom, see Bloch-Smith, *Judahite Burial Customs*, 72–93.
[29]This three-tiered structure is reflected in Ps. 115:16–18:

> The *heavens* are the LORD's heavens,
> but the *earth* he has given to the children of man.

| Heaven: The Realm of Deity |
| Earth: The Realm of the Living |
| Sheol: The Realm of the Dead |

In death a human being passes from the realm of the living to the realm of the dead. Israel's neighbors developed rather imaginative images of the state of the deceased in the netherworld, as witnessed, for example, by the following poetic account of the descent of Ishtar into the netherworld from Mesopotamia:

To the Kurnugu, land of [no return],
Ishtar daughter of Sin, was [determined] to go;
The daughter of Sin was determined to go
To the dark house, dwelling of Erkalla's god,
To the house which those who enter cannot leave,
On the road where travelling is one-way only,
To the house where those who enter are deprived of light,
Where dust is their food, clay their bread.
They see no light, they dwell in darkness,
They are clothed like birds, with feathers.
Over the door and the bolt, dust has settled.[30]

This text is reminiscent of Enkidu's description of the fate of the dead from the Epic of Gilgamesh:

I saw him, whom you saw [die] a sudden death:
He lies in bed and drinks pure water.
I saw him, whom you saw killed in battle:
His father and mother honour him and his wife weeps over him.
I saw him, whose corpse you saw abandoned in the open country:
His ghost does not sleep in the Earth.
I saw him whom you saw, whose ghost has nobody to supply it:
He feeds on dregs from dishes,
and bits of bread that lie abandoned in the streets.[31]

Obviously, ancient Mesopotamians perceived the netherworld as an inhospitable place, dark and dingy, and the afterlife as a miserable place to be in,

---

The dead do not praise the LORD,
  nor do any who go down into *silence*.
But we will bless the LORD
  from this time forth and forevermore.

For discussion of the relationships among the tiers, see B. Lang, "Life After Death in the Prophetic Promise," *Congress Volume: Jerusalem 1986*, ed. J. A. Emerton (VTSup 40; Leiden: Brill, 1988), 145–48.
[30]As translated by S. Dalley, *COS* 1:381; S. Dalley, *Myths from Mesopotamia: Creation, The Flood, Gilgamesh and Others* (Oxford: Oxford Univ. Press, 1989), 155.
[31]As translated by Dalley, *Myths from Mesopotamia*, 124.

especially for those who had been killed in battle and/or who had not been afforded a proper burial. In Canaanite mythology, the netherworld was viewed as the realm of Mot (cognate to Hebrew *mût*, "death"), the divine king of the netherworld. His residence is identified as ʾarṣ ("underworld/netherworld," cognate to Hebrew ʾereṣ), at the base of two mountains that either formed a barrier between the land of the living or provided a pass (gate) through which one entered his realm. This is how Baal describes Mot's abode to his messengers:

> Then you shall head out to Mount TRGZZ,
> To Mount THRMG,
> The two hills at Earth's edge.
> Lift the mountain on your hands,
> The hill on top of your palms.
> And descend to Hell, the House of "Freedom,"[32]
> Be counted among the descendants of Hell.
> Then you shall head out for [Divine Mot],
> At his town, the Pit [*hmry* = watery pit, ooze],
> Low, the throne where he sits,
> Filth, the land of his heritage.[33]

Mot himself is portrayed as a monster with a voracious appetite[34] and a huge mouth:

> But take care, divine servants:
> Do not get too close to Divine Mot,
> Do not let him take you like a lamb in his mouth,
> Like a kid crushed in the chasm of his throat. . . .
>
> But let me tear you to pieces,
> Let me eat flanks, innards, forearms.
> Surely you will descend into Divine Mot's throat,
> Into the gullet of El's Beloved, the Hero. . . .
>
> . . . .
>
> [One lip to He]ll, one lip to Heaven,
> [a to]ngue to the Stars.

---

[32]An antiphrastic expression for a prison-house.

[33]As translated by M. S. Smith in *Ugaritic Narrative Poetry*, ed. S. B. Parker (SBL Writings from the Ancient World Series; Atlanta: Scholars Press, 1997), 138–39.

[34]We hear allusions to Mot's disposition in two texts in Proverbs:

> Like Sheol let us swallow them alive,
>   and whole, like those who go down to the pit. (1:12)
> Three things are never satisfied;
>   four never say, "Enough":
> Sheol, the barren womb,
>   the land never satisfied with water,
>   and the fire that never says, "Enough." (30:15–16)

Baal will enter his innards,
Into his mouth he will descend like a dried olive,
Produce of the earth, and fruit of the trees.[35]

Old Testament writers occasionally hint at their awareness of pagan perspectives like these, generally with polemical intent, but as a rule their portrayals of the netherworld are much less imaginative. Her poets may indeed speak of death as passing through "the gates of Sheol" (Isa. 38:10) and "the gates of death" (Job 38:17; Pss. 9:14; 107:18) into Sheol. However, death itself was generally viewed more soberly as the retraction of the divine breath (*rûaḥ*) from the body (*bāśār/ʿāpār*).[36] The Old Testament offers only limited information on the status of the dead. Often their abode is described in phenomenological language, derived from ancient burial practices. One must decide in each case whether Sheol or the "Pit" refers to the grave or the abode of the dead.

Ezekiel offers the fullest description of the deceased in the netherworld in his oracles against the nations. The way he describes them in 32:22–23 creates the impression of a massive communal cemetery, in which the graves are arranged by nationality and organized in such a way that the principal grave is located in the center, surrounded by the graves of the attendants. The residents themselves are all reclining on their own beds (*miškāb*). The verb *šākab* ("to lie") occurs seven times in this text.[37] According to 26:20, which speaks of Tyre dwelling in the lower parts of the earth like *ḥʳrābôt mēʿôlām* ("waste places from eternity"), Sheol seems to appear as a massive wasteland filled with the refuse of collapsed civilizations.[38] Ezekiel's expression *yarkʳtê-bôr* ("the remotest parts of the Pit," 32:23) suggests a gradation of assignments in Sheol, with the most dishonorable occupants being sent to the farthest recesses. The fact that the uncircumcised and the victims of the sword are separated from the "mighty men of old," who receive an honorable burial with their weapons of war at their sides, reinforces this impression. It is unclear whether these compartments are arranged horizontally or vertically. The plural form *ʾereṣ taḥtiyyôt* ("land of depths") may point in the latter direction.

Ezekiel's picture of the netherworld is reminiscent of two well-known ancient mortuary customs. First, the arrangement of the grave complexes resembles that of a royal tomb, with the king's (in this instance the queen's) crypt (sarcophagus?) in the middle, and his (her) nobles all around. In fact, this oracle displays some

---

[35]Thus Smith, ibid., 139, 140, 141.

[36]See especially Job 10:9; 12:10; 27:3; 32:8; 33:4; 34:15; Ps. 104:29; Eccl. 12:7.

[37]Of course, Ezekiel's use of *šākab* ("to lie") as a euphemism for death is not unique to him. Compare the idiom "X lay/slept with his fathers and was buried [with his fathers] in Y," variations of which occur dozens of times in the Deuteronomistic and Chronistic historiographic works. See 1 Kings 11:21, 43; 14:20, 31; 15:8, 24; 16:6, 28; 22:40, 50; 2 Kings 8:24; 10:35; 13:9,13; 14:22, 29; 15:7, 22, 38; 16:20; 20:21; 21:18; 24:6; 2 Chron. 9:31; 12:16; 14:1; 16:13; 21:1; 26:2, 23; 27:9; 28:27; 32:33; 33:20.

[38]The image recalls a Mesopotamian view reflected in one of Nergal's titles, *šar ṣēri* ("King of the Wasteland"). On the netherworld as a wasteland, see further J. Pedersen, *Israel: Its Life and Culture* (London: Oxford Univ. Press, 1926), 464; C. Barth, *Die Errettung vom Tode in den indivuellen Klage- und Dankliedern des Alten Testaments* (Zurich: Zollikon, 1947), 86–87.

deliberate local coloring. The pyramid complexes, in which the pharaoh's tomb (the pyramid itself) was surrounded by the tombs of his princes, courtiers, and other high officials, provide the closest analogue to Ezekiel's portrayal of Sheol.[39] Second, the image of the beds recalls the pattern of ancient tombs in which the place where the corpse was laid was designed as a bed, often complete with headrest.[40]

Given this image of Sheol as a place where the dead lie on beds, it is not surprising that death was also perceived as sleep. In Psalm 13:3[4] the psalmist had appealed to God:

> Consider and answer me, O LORD my God;
> light up my eyes, lest I *sleep the death*.[41]

Even more telling is Jeremiah's twofold invective against Babylon: "May they sleep a perpetual sleep and not awake" (*weyāšenû šenat-ʿôlām welōʾ yāqîṣû*, 51:39, 57). And Job expresses a similar disposition in Job 14:12:

> So a man lies down and rises not again;
> till the heavens are no more he will not awake
> or be roused out of his sleep.

If death is viewed as sleep, we need to interpret this not as "soul sleep" in Sheol, as understood by Seventh-day Adventists,[42] but "that the state of dying is a falling asleep to awake in another world."[43] Neither Jeremiah's nor Job's statement should be interpreted as dogmatic assertions about the state of the deceased. In the case of the former, it represents Yahweh's firm determination that the Babylonians will never arise to oppress Yahweh's people again; in the case of the latter, ironically, Job sees death as deliverance from the horrible nightmare he has been experiencing in real life.

What then was the state of those who had entered this other world? Here the Old Testament texts (more precisely the characters in the Old Testament) are not monolithic. On the one hand, in Ezekiel's oracles against Tyre, the prophet presents death as the termination of existence. Three times in roughly equiva-

---

[39]On Egyptian burial patterns, see P. Montet, *Eternal Egypt* (New York: New American Library, 1964), 199–234; esp. 212–23; C. Aldred, "Grablage, Auszeidmung durch," *Lexikon der Aegyptologie*, ed. W. Helck and E. Otto (Wiesbaden: Otto Harrassowitz, 1977), 2:859–62.

[40]On Judahite bench tombs, see E. Bloch-Smith, *Judahite Burial Practices and Beliefs about the Dead* (JSOTSup 123; Sheffield: Sheffield Academic Press, 1992), 25–62. Cf. the superbly illustrated presentation of a complex Israelite family tomb by G. Barkay and A. Kloner, "Jerusalem Tombs from the Days of the First Temple," *BAR* 12/2 (1986): 22–39.

[41]See also Pss. 76:5–6[6–7] (*nûm šēnâ*, "to sink into sleep"; *nirdām*, "to sleep deeply"); 90:5 (substantive *šēnâ*, "sleep").

[42]Listed among Adventist "Fundamental Beliefs" is the notion "that the condition of man in death is one of unconsciousness [and that] all men, good and evil alike, remain in the grave from death to the resurrection." Thus *Seventh-day Adventists Answer Questions on Doctrine* (Washington: Review and Herald, 1957), 13. For discussion, see Millard J. Erickson, *Christian Theology* (Grand Rapids: Baker, 1985), 1176–78.

[43]Thus C. A. Briggs, *A Critical and Exegetical Commentary on the Book of Psalms* (ICC; Edinburgh: T. & T. Clark, 1906), 101.

HeLL UNDeR fire

lent terms he announces, "I shall bring terrors upon you and you will be no more" (Ezek. 26:21; 27:36; 28:19). In fact, according to 26:21, any efforts by search parties to find the lost city will prove futile. However, the broader context of this verse shows that we should not interpret these statements literally. The language is rhetorical and phenomenological; no one ever returns from the realm of the dead.

Job presents a slightly different image of the afterlife in his protests over his undeserved disasters. Twice he expresses his intense longing for death, for then his suffering would be over. In 3:11–19 he exclaims:

> Why did I not die at birth,
> come out from the womb and expire?
> Why did the knees receive me?
> Or why the breasts, that I should nurse?
> For then I would have lain down and been quiet;
> I would have slept; then I would have been at rest,
> with kings and counselors of the earth
> who rebuilt ruins for themselves,
> or with princes who had gold,
> who filled their houses with silver.
> Or why was I not as a hidden stillborn child,
> as infants who never see the light?
> There the wicked cease from troubling,
> and there the weary are at rest.
> There the prisoners are at ease together;
> they hear not the voice of the taskmaster.
> The small and the great are there,
> and the slave is free from his master.

Later, in 10:18–22, he directs his bitterness at God himself:

> Why did you bring me out from the womb?
> Would that I had died before any eye had seen me
> and were as though I had not been,
> carried from the womb to the grave.
> Are not my days few?
> Then cease, and leave me alone,
> that I may find a little cheer
> before I go—and I shall not return—
> to the land of darkness and deep shadow,
> the land of gloom like thick darkness,
> like deep shadow without any order,
> where light is as thick darkness.

In his first outburst, death is viewed as the great equalizer, for in the grave all, rich and poor, free and slave, sleep with no one to torment them. In the second, the abode of the dead is perceived as a place of deepest darkness.[44] It is doubtful whether either of Job's statements should be taken as authoritative and accurate declarations of netherworldly reality, on two counts. First, these are the passionate outbursts of a man in deep emotional and physical strain trying to make sense of his predicament. Second, the language is phenomenological, the first being derived from the image of a corpse in calm repose in his burial chamber, the second derived from the deep darkness of those burial chambers.[45] Job finds both prospects more attractive than what he is currently experiencing.

From other texts it is evident that, although the deceased lie in their beds, they are fully conscious of their surroundings and their relative positions in the netherworld. This is suggested by Isaiah's taunting oracle against the king of Babylon in Isaiah 14:4–21:

How the oppressor has ceased,
    the insolent fury ceased!
The LORD has broken the staff of the wicked,
    the scepter of rulers,
that struck the peoples in wrath with unceasing blows,
    that ruled the nations in anger with unrelenting persecution.
The whole earth is at rest and quiet;
    they break forth into singing.
The cypresses rejoice at you,
    the cedars of Lebanon, saying,
"Since you were laid low,
    no woodcutter comes up against us."
Sheol beneath is stirred up
    to meet you when you come;
it rouses the shades to greet you,
    all who were leaders of the earth;
it raises from their thrones
    all who were kings of the nations.

---

[44]This point is highlighted by the repetitious references to darkness in vv. 21–22: ʾereṣ ḥōšek wᵉṣalmāwet, "a land of darkness and deep darkness"; ʾereṣ ʿêpātâ kᵉmô ʾōpel, "a land of gloom like thick darkness" (ʿêp- occurs elsewhere only in Amos 4:13, where it is paired with šāḥar, "blackness"); ṣalmāwet wᵉlōʾ sᵉdārîm, "like deep darkness without order"; wattōpaʿ kᵉmô-ʾōpel, "where light is as thick as darkness."

[45]Several additional texts present the abode of the dead as a dark place:

The enemy has pursued my soul;
    he has crushed my life to the ground;
    he has made me sit in darkness like those long dead. (Ps. 143:3)

He has made me dwell in darkness
    like the dead of long ago. (Lam. 3:6)

Cf. Ps. 88:11–12[12–13], which speaks of Sheol as "a land of forgetfulness."

HeLL UNDeR fiRe

All of them will answer
    and say to you:
"You too have become as weak as we!
    You have become like us!"
Your pomp is brought down to Sheol,
    the sound of your harps;
maggots are laid as a bed beneath you,
    and worms are your covers.

How you are fallen from heaven,
    O Day Star, son of Dawn!
How you are cut down to the ground,
    you who laid the nations low!
You said in your heart,
    "I will ascend to heaven;
above the stars of God
    I will set my throne on high;
I will sit on the mount of assembly
    in the far reaches of the north;
I will ascend above the heights of the clouds;
    I will make myself like the Most High."
But you are brought down to Sheol,
    to the far reaches of the pit.
Those who see you will stare at you
    and ponder over you:
"Is this the man who made the earth tremble,
    who shook kingdoms,
who made the world like a desert
    and overthrew its cities,
    who did not let his prisoners go home?"
All the kings of the nations lie in glory,
    each in his own tomb;
but you are cast out, away from your grave,
    like a loathed branch,
clothed with the slain, those pierced by the sword,
    who go down to the stones of the pit,
    like a dead body trampled underfoot.
You will not be joined with them in burial,
    because you have destroyed your land,
    you have slain your people.
"May the offspring of evildoers
    nevermore be named!
Prepare slaughter for his sons
    because of the guilt of their fathers,
lest they rise and possess the earth,
    and fill the face of the world with cities."

The imagery is striking. The prophet envisions Yahweh cutting off the king of Babylon and sending him to Sheol, where those who preceded him greet him. On the one hand, the latter recognize the advantage the death of the king of Babylon poses for the inhabitants of the land of the living. On the other hand, although the deceased rulers of the nations rise from their thrones to greet the king of Babylon, they also announce to him that maggots and worms are waiting for him in his bed. And in the end (Isa. 14:19), they recognize the particular ignominy of the Babylonian king's demise.

Ezekiel's portrayal of the state of the deceased in Ezekiel 32:17–32 is similar. On the one hand, he envisions the demise of a specific person who had ruled brutally on earth—in this instance the king of Assyria. But when he gets to Sheol, he is surrounded by a host of folks who had predeceased him. On the other hand, he offers several interesting clues concerning the condition of the deceased in the afterlife. First, that which survives of the deceased is not simply the spiritual component of the human being, but a shadowy image of the whole person, complete with head and skeleton. Second, as we have already noted, the deceased lie on beds in their respective wards, arranged according to nationality (Ezek. 32:21, 27, 28, 29, 30, 32). Third, the inhabitants of Sheol are not asleep, but fully conscious.[46] They are not only aware of one another and their relative positions; they also know that their conduct during their tenure "in the land of the living" has determined their respective positions in Sheol. Those who were high and mighty on earth express grief over their loss of status and power (Ezek. 32:31) and consciously bear the disgrace associated with dishonorable burial (32:24, 25, 30). This description agrees with Israelite burial practices, which suggest that the tomb was not considered the permanent resting place of the deceased. While the physical flesh decomposed, the person was thought to descend to the vast subterranean mausoleum in which the dead continued to live in a remarkably real sense as "living corpses."[47]

The Old Testament Background for the Christian Doctrine of Hell

The Old Testament does not sound a clear bell with respect to distinctions between the wicked and the righteous in death. From the foregoing, with the exception of a few emotional outbursts in which a person expresses the notion that death ends everything, the general tenor of the Old Testament seems to reflect a conviction that people continue to live even after they die. Logic would suggest that any belief in the resurrection would be based on this supposition. It is beyond the scope of this essay to discuss this notion in detail.

However, the doctrine of personal eschatological resurrection represents a natural corollary to Israelite anthropological views. As noted earlier, the Hebrews

---

[46]Compare Job's desire as expressed in 3:13, 18; 7:9, and the phenomenological language of Dan. 12:2; Matt. 9:24; John 11:11; 1 Cor. 11:30; 15:51; 1 Thess. 4:14; 5:10.

[47]Cf. R. E. Cooley, "Gathered to His People: A Study of a Dothan Family Tomb," in *The Living and Active Word of God: Studies in Honor of Samuel J. Schultz*, ed. M. Inch, et al. (Winona Lake, Ind.: Eisenbrauns, 1983), 47–58.

looked on a human being as a unity, a *nepeš ḥayyâ* ("a living being"), so constituted by the infusion of divine life-breath into the physical matter (Gen. 2:7; 3:19). At death, which was viewed as the divine sentence for sin, the physical matter and life-giving breath divorce and the *nepeš ḥayyâ* dissolves (Job 34:14–15; Ps. 104:29; Eccl. 3:18–21; 12:7). It follows that any hope of victory over death and a beatific afterlife would require a reunion of the divorced components, which is exactly what Ezekiel envisions in 37:1–14. Admittedly, this is a visionary text, and the resurrection envisioned is that of the nation of Israel, but the rhetorical force of the prophecy depends on its correspondence to and/or basis in a general aware-ness (if not acceptance) of the idea.

Precursors and hints of the doctrine of personal eschatological resurrec-tion that would develop later may be seen also in the life-giving miraculous work of Elijah and Elisha (1 Kings 17:17–24; 2 Kings 4:18–37; 13:20–21). To be sure, these cases could be interpreted simply as postmortem healings, inas-much as the raised persons had recently died and their flesh was certainly still on the bones. But the fact remains that through the involvement of a prophet, the dead come to life. Furthermore, the psalmists regarded having one's life threatened as being in the grip of Sheol, and to be delivered from this dan-gerous situation as being brought back to life (e.g., Pss. 16:11–12; 49:15–16). Admittedly, the concern is for an early, if not immediate, rescue rather than an eschatological deliverance from Sheol, but the language of resurrection can scarcely be denied. Finally, earlier prophets anticipate Ezekiel's vision of a national resurrection. Hosea 6:1–3 may be toying with the notion, but in Isaiah 26:19 we find a clear anticipation.[48]

It is difficult to imagine a doctrine of resurrection without an understand-ing of the continued existence of the person in some (spiritual) form after death. Would one really cease to exist at death and then be recreated at the time of the resurrection? Even if these texts assume that the deceased live on in Sheol as *rᵉpāʾîm*, there is no hint in any of the texts cited so far of the netherworld as a "hellish" place where the wicked suffer eternal punishment. In fact, the Old Testament is not clear with respect to distinctions between the wicked and the righteous in death. Ezekiel paints imaginative word pictures of the gradations of existence in Sheol, but he never contemplates the fate of the righteous—only those condemned to an ignominious fate. We find hints of the netherworld and the afterlife as a place/time of eternal torment (in contrast to a beatific afterlife for the righteous) as we know it from the New Testament in only two Old Testament texts: Isaiah 66:24 and Daniel 12:2. We shall comment on each of these briefly.

Isaiah 66:24

The book of Isaiah closes on a remarkable note:

---

[48]For further discussion of the nature and roots of the Old Testament understanding of resurrection see Daniel I. Block, "Beyond the Grave: Ezekiel's Vision of Death and Afterlife," *BBR* 2 (1992): 13–41. Further bibliography is provided there.

wᵉyāṣᵉᵓû	And they shall go out
wᵉrāᵓû bᵉpigrê hāᵓᵃnāšîm	and look on the dead bodies of the men
happōšᵉᶜîm bî	who have rebelled against me.
kî tôlaᶜtām lōᵓ tāmût	For their worm shall not die,
wᵉᵓššām lōᵓ tikbeh	their fire shall not be quenched,
wᵉhāyû dērāᵓôn lᵉkol-bāśar	and they shall be an abhorrence to all flesh.

In order to understand this text we must place it in its context.[49] In Isaiah 66 the prophet casts his gaze far beyond his own historical present to the eschatological renewal of heaven and earth, when people from every tribe and nation will come to Zion to worship Yahweh on his holy mountain. But Isaiah's vision of the final day is anything but soteriologically universalist. On the contrary, from the outset he draws a stark contrast between the righteous and the wicked. On the one side are the humble and contrite of spirit and those who tremble at the word of Yahweh (Isa. 66:2); on the other are those who go through the motions of liturgical worship but reject his word and persist in evil (66:3–6, esp. v. 4). The former receive the favorable look of Yahweh (v. 2); the latter receive the due reward of their rebellion (vv. 4, 6). The former flourish and rejoice in Zion (vv. 7–14c); the latter experience the full and direct force of his fury (vv. 14c–17).

The chapter climaxes with the glorious picture of Yahweh displaying his glory and setting a sign (the cross!) among the nations, which rallies worshipers to find whatever means they can to bring their gifts and offerings to Zion. But when the worshipers leave the city, they pass by the city dump, where they observe the endless fire consuming the refuse and the maggots (*tôlaᶜt*) ceaselessly eating away at the decaying corpses of those who have been unceremoniously dumped there— undoubtedly those whom Yahweh has slain in his fury (Isa. 66:16). The gaze of the worshipers has less to do with gloating over the deaths of their enemies than with recalling the fate that would have been theirs—but for the grace of God.

It is tempting to interpret this verse as an Isaianic vision of hell, equivalent to the Gehenna (*eis tēn geennan*) spoken of by Jesus in Luke 12:5, the fiery Gehenna (*eis tēn geennan tou pyros*) of Matthew 5:22, and the Gehenna of unquenchable fire of Mark 9:43 (*eis tēn geennan, eis to pyr to asbeston*).[50] However, we should not do so too hastily, primarily because the sight that greets the worshipers coming out of Jerusalem is not a netherworldly scene. On the contrary, the image is realistic and earthly.

During much of Judah's history the valley was associated with idolatrous worship, particularly of the sacrificing ("passing through the fire") of children to

---

[49]For helpful interpretations of this chapter, see J. N. Oswalt, *The Book of Isaiah, Chapters 40–66* (NICOT; Grand Rapids: Eerdmans, 1998), 680–93; J. A. Motyer, *Isaiah: An Introduction and Commentary* (TOTC; Downers Grove, Ill.: InterVarsity Press, 1999), 400–408; B. S. Childs, *Isaiah* (OTL; Louisville: Westminster John Knox, 2001), 532–47.

[50]The name "Gehenna," derives from the transliterated version of Hebrew *gê-hinnōm*, "Valley of Hinnom." See D. F. Watson, "Gehenna," *ABD*, 2:926–28; idem, "Hinnom," *ABD*, 3:202–3.

HeLL UNDeR fire

Molech.[51] The valley seems also to have been used as a garbage dump, which meant that smoke would constantly have been rising from the refuse burning there, and maggots would have feasted endlessly on the carcasses of dead animals thrown into the valley. The sight and smell of the place must have been familiar to Isaiah, who lived in Jerusalem. At the same time, we must realize that this is a battle scene. The image is also that of a pile of corpses, victims in battle, ignominiously dumped in a heap and torched.

Even if Isaiah was not hereby speaking of the netherworld, let alone Sheol, as a "hellish" place where the wicked suffer eternal punishment, it is not difficult to see why this text came to be associated with hell in the intertestamental period and in the New Testament.

First, since the valley was associated with the worship of Molech, in syncretistic and pagan circles considered a chthonic deity who ruled the netherworld,[52] it was not that great a stretch to see in Isaiah's description a reflection, if not a picture, of the netherworld. Second, the reality envisioned by Isaiah is clearly cast in an eschatological context, loosening the immediate link with current phenomena. Third, the context clearly involves a contrast between the ultimate destiny of the righteous (those who are humble and contrite and tremble at the word of Yahweh, Isa. 66:2) and the wicked (who are subjected to the fire of divine wrath). Fourth, although Sheol is never linked with eschatological judgment elsewhere, the motif of fire as an instrument of divine judgment is a common motif in the Old Testament (cf. 66:16). While Isaiah himself may not have had in mind hell as we later learn about it, it was a small and natural step for Jesus and later New Testament writers to utilize Isaiah's image for their own purposes.

Daniel 12:1-3

ûbāʿēt hahîʾ yaʿᵃmōd mîkāʾēl	At that time shall arise Michael,
haśśar haggādôl hāʿōmēd ʿal-bᵉnê	the great prince who has charge of
ʿammekā	your people.
wᵉhāyᵉtā ʿēt ṣārâ	And there shall be a time of trouble,
ʾᵃšer lôʾ- nihyᵉtâ	such as never has been
mihyôt gôy ʿad bāʿēt hahîʾ	since there was a nation till that time.
ûbāʿēt hahîʾ yimmālēṭ ʿammᵉkā	But at that time your people shall be delivered,
kol-hannimṣāʾ kātûb bassēper	everyone whose name shall be found written in the book.
wᵉrabbîm miyyᵉšēnê	And many of those who sleep
ʾadmat-ʿāpār yāqîṣû	in the dust of the earth shall awake,
ʾēlleh lᵉḥayyê ʿôlām	some to everlasting life,
wᵉʾēlleh laḥᵃrāpôt lᵉdirʾôn ʿôlām	and some to shame and everlasting contempt.

---

[51]See 2 Kings 16:3; 21:6; 23:10; 2 Chron. 28:33; 33:6; Jer. 7:31; 19:4–5; 32:35.

[52]Though some suggest that the application of the name gê-hinnōm/gehenna to the netherworld was a natural development, given the fact that the latter was the realm of Molech, who was worshiped in Gehenna. See L. R. Bailey, "Gehenna: The Topography of Hell," *BA* 49 (1986): 189–91.

wᵉhammaškilîm yazhirû	And those who are wise shall shine
kᵉzôhar hārāqîaᶜ	like the brightness of the sky above;
ûmaṣdîqê hārabbîm	and those who turn many to righteousness,
kakkôkābîm lᵉᶜôlām wāᶜed	like the stars forever and ever.

In Daniel 12:1–3, the exilic statesman takes Isaiah's pregnant notions and declares explicitly what is at best implicit in Isaiah's last utterance.[53] Like Isaiah 66:24, Daniel 12:2 must be interpreted primarily within its present context rather than lifting it out and exploiting it as a proof text for a later, more developed, eschatology. The chapter division after 11:45 is unfortunate, obscuring the fact that Daniel 12:1–2 represents the climax of a lengthy and complex prophecy concerning the distant future of Daniel's people. Daniel envisions an extremely stressful time, but Michael, the angelic patron of Israel, will stand guard over them, apparently guaranteeing that all whose names are written in the book of life will be rescued (12:1).

The context of the events described is established by the opening phrase, "at that time," which raises the question, "At what time?" The answer is provided by a series of expressions in Daniel 11: "the end time" (Dan. 11:35), "the appointed time" (11:35), "at the end of time" (11:40). These assertions cast doubt on the interpretation of some that Daniel is still speaking about Antiochus IV Epiphanes in 11:36–40. To be sure, the text contains no formal signals pointing to a referential transition from the violent historical Seleucid king to the Antichrist of the eschaton. Nevertheless, these chronological markers and other features in 11:36–40 that seem to point to events and personalities larger than life suggest that the perspective of this paragraph goes far beyond the Maccabean historical situation.

As Jesus' own use of this and other passages in Daniel will confirm (Matt. 24:5–31; Mark 13:5–27; Luke 21:8–28), we now find ourselves face to face with the Antichrist.[54] Accordingly, based on the testimony of Daniel 12:1–3 itself, Daniel envisions unprecedented convulsions at the end of history as we know it, in the context of which God's people will experience incredible stress, even to the point of martyrdom.

Within this context, Daniel 12:2 is a most remarkable text, which, as W. S. Towner rightly observes, contains "the first and only unambiguous reference to the double resurrection of the dead in the entire Old Testament."[55] By double resurrection he means the resurrection of both the righteous and the wicked. The contrasting fates of these two groups may be highlighted in a tabular manner as follows:

---

[53] Our conviction of a link between these texts is secured by the term *dērāʾôn* ("contempt, abhorrence"), which occurs only in these two contexts.

[54] For helpful introductory discussions of the issues involved, see J. Baldwin, *Daniel: An Introduction and Commentary* (TOTC; Downers Grove, Ill.: InterVarsity Press, 1978), 198–201; T. Longman III, *Daniel* (NIVAC; Grand Rapids: Zondervan, 1999), 280–83.

[55] W. S. Towner, *Daniel* (Interpretation; Atlanta: John Knox, 1984), 166. J. E. Goldingay (*Daniel* [WBC 30; Dallas: Word, 1989], 308), is more cautious, seeing in "the many" a reference only to a few—those who lost their lives in the conflict—while the masses of faithful Israel remain in Sheol.

Feature	The Righteous	The Wicked
The Principals	"Many" (*rabbîm*)	"Many" (*rabbîm*)
Their State	"Asleep in the dust"	"Asleep in the dust"
Their Experience	"They will awake"	"They will awake"
Their Destiny	"Everlasting life"	"Disgrace and everlasting contempt"

Although nothing in this text precludes the final resurrection of all the dead, strictly speaking Daniel's attention is focused on the "many," which here refers on the one hand to the righteous who have been martyred at the hands of the Antichrist and his forces, and on the other hand to their enemies who have perished in these conflicts at the hands of God.[56]

Daniel characterizes the state of the dead, both righteous and wicked, as "asleep in the ground of the dust" (*miyy^{e}šēnê ʾadmat-ʿāpār*). The latter expression is uniquely redundant, highlighting the "earthy" destiny of all humanity in view of their sin.[57] But as we noted above, Daniel is not the first to speak of death (i.e., the departure from the "land of the living") as "sleep." However, whereas under normal circumstances those who "fall asleep" expect to awaken in the "land of the deceased" (i.e., Sheol), in Daniel's utterance the "awaking" involves leaving the dust (i.e., Sheol). Undoubtedly he envisions a picture such as that presented by Ezekiel in 37:12–14, according to which Yahweh will open up the graves, infuse his people with his animating Spirit (*rûaḥ*), causing them to come back to life. According to this text, both righteous and wicked will rise from the dust.

So far the experiences of the righteous and the wicked follow parallel lines. However, the contrast in the *destinies* of the righteous and wicked could scarcely be painted more starkly. We might have expected Daniel to say that whereas the righteous awaken to eternal life, the wicked awaken to eternal death. Instead, the latter awaken to disgrace and eternal contempt.

Life in this context means the recovery of that for which humankind was created in the beginning—free and open fellowship with God and a restoration of all the privileges and responsibilities involved with being the image of God, namely, once more governing the world as God's representative and deputy. The fate of the wicked is the opposite. They are sentenced to perpetual disgrace (*ḥⁿrāpôt*) and shame (*dērāʾôn*). The former expression refers to the taunts and reviling

---

[56]Daniel's use of "many" (*rabbîm*) may be inspired by Isa. 66:16: "And the ones slain by Yahweh will be many" (*w^{e}rabbû haḷlê yhwh*). The preposition *min* after Daniel's "many" is best interpreted as a partitive *min*, that is, "separated from those who sleep." So also E. J. Young, *The Prophecy of Daniel: A Commentary* (Grand Rapids: Eerdmans, 1949), 256; Baldwin, *Daniel*, 204.

[57]One may recognize in the expression an intentional echo of Gen. 3:19: "For dust you are and to dust you shall return" (*kî-ʿāpār ʾattâ w^{o}el-ʿāpār tāšûb*).

of all who pass by, the latter to the revulsion and loathing that passers-by feel toward the sight. This interpretation of this rare word is confirmed by Isaiah 66:24, the only other occurrence of *dērā'ôn*. It describes the disposition one has toward the putrid and malodorous carcass of a dead animal infested with maggots and in an advanced stage of decay. Daniel does not specify to whom the resurrected wicked will be so loathsome, but we may imagine that he has in mind those who are raised to life as well as the members of the heavenly court, of whom Michael was but one representative, and God himself.

Under normal circumstances, when a person dies the body decomposes fairly rapidly. While the sight and the smell of decomposition are loathsome for a while, eventually the body returns to dust and the repugnancy ends. Not so in this case. Daniel notes that just as the righteous awake to *eternal* life, so the wicked awake to *eternal* disgrace and contempt. Both expressions—"eternal life" and "eternal disgrace and contempt"—occur only here in the Old Testament. The word *'ôlām* refers not to the end of time (i.e., the eschaton), but to time without end.[58] Just as God is *eternal* (Ps. 90:2), so those who are created as his images are eternal. With this statement Daniel answers Qoheleth's pessimistic view of the grave as a *bêt 'ôlāmô* ("his eternal house") in Ecclesiastes 12:5,[59] hereby asserting that the grave is not the end for anyone—righteous or wicked.

Conclusion

Modern readers often wish that Old Testament prophets and authors had been more forthright and explicit in their comments concerning the afterlife in general, and the netherworld in particular. The fact remains that biblical writers and ancient Israelite characters tended to be preoccupied with the here and now. Their goal was to enjoy a long full life, secure in the knowledge of God's presence and rich in the blessings that attend a life of covenant faithfulness. Furthermore, inasmuch as children were viewed to be extensions of the lives of their parents, eternal life was often viewed in terms of living on in one's children. Accordingly, a man "with a full quiver" (Ps. 127:3–5) was considered most blessed; a person who was childless was deemed under the curse. At the risk of being simplistic, we reduce Israelite perceptions regarding death to several basic propositions.

(1) Ancient Israelites perceived the universe as a three-tiered structure: heaven, the residence of God and his heavenly court; earth, the residence of humankind and all creatures; Sheol, the residence of the deceased.

(2) Through death people passed from the land of the living to Sheol, the realm of the dead. The transition could be described as falling asleep in the "land of the living" and awakening in the netherworld.

---

[58]For a superb discussion of the word, see E. Jenni, "עוֹלָם *'ôlām,*" *TLOT*, 2:852–62.

[59]Qoheleth's pessimism concerning old age and death is reflected in his characterization of his future as "days of evil" (*y'mê hārā'â*) and years of which he says, "I have no pleasure in them" (*'ên-lî bāhem ḥēpeṣ*), in contrast to the delights of youth (11:7–12:1). The expression *bêt 'ôlām* apparently originates in Egypt, but it occurs on Palmyrene and Punic inscriptions. See J. L. Crenshaw, "Youth and Old Age in Qoheleth," *HAR* 10 (1986): 9 n. 33.

(3) Although it is obvious that the physical body decomposed after death, the deceased continued to exist as "living corpses" in Sheol. Although rhetorically persons could refer to death as the end of existence, any tendency toward contemporary theories of annihilationism, either for the wicked or the righteous, would have been rejected.

(4) Although they existed as shadowy figures ($r^ep\bar{a}\,^{\circ}\hat{\imath}m$), the residents of Sheol were fully conscious, aware that their conduct on earth had determined their status in Sheol and aware of gradations of status in Sheol. As a corollary, orthodox Yahwists will have recognized the absolute justice of God in his consignment of the dead to Sheol.

(5) Although earlier poets and prophets had toyed with the idea of the resurrection of God's people, in Daniel 12:2 we find the first notice of general resurrection for both the righteous and the wicked.

(6) Prior to Daniel 12:2 we find no clear evidence of belief in hell, if by hell we mean a place of eternal torment and judgment for the wicked. It would be left to later revelation in the New Testament to develop this image. When the doctrine of hell develops in the New Testament, it borrows much of its imagery from the Old Testament, particularly the images of perpetual suffering through maggots and unquenchable fire in Isaiah 66:24.

Chapter 3

Jesus on Hell

Robert W. Yarbrough

Throughout church history Christians have generally understood Jesus' preaching and teaching to have carried not only a joyful message but also a severe warning. Christ affirmed that those who oppose God by failing to seek him so as to secure redemption, or who openly spurn the gospel of salvation in his name, will be consigned to hell at some point following earthly death, there to face a misery that will never end. As John G. Stackhouse Jr. remarks, "Christian tradition weighs in heavily on this side" when it comes to the question of whether hell is everlasting,[1] and as we will see below, Jesus' teaching bears much of the burden for this belief.

A recent official statement of the Evangelical Alliance Commission on Unity and Truth Among Evangelicals (ACUTE) in Great Britain states that "the interpretation of hell as eternal conscious punishment is the one most widely attested by the Church.... We also recognize that it represents the classic, mainstream evangelical position."[2] Because of its dominance and persistence, this may be termed the "historic" view. We will refer to it by this label below.

Since by common consent Jesus Christ (with the other members of the Godhead) is a central authority for Christians, his teachings on hell are a primary point of reference in assessing the propriety of what the church has most commonly affirmed. Does the historic view find support in his teaching? Or, as many are now insisting, did Christ rather say that the wicked will at some point after death simply cease to exist rather than undergo eternal conscious suffering?

Does Anyone Really Know What Jesus Taught?

Since the flowering of the Enlightenment in the late eighteenth century, skepticism about the reliability of the four Gospels has slowly increased, first in literary and academic circles and then gradually extending to the general public.[3] Typifying the low respect accorded to the Gospels' truth-telling value in recent times, in North America the 1990s saw ongoing media coverage of the Jesus Seminar, a maverick collection of scholars who pressed the sensationalist claim that only a small percentage of Jesus' words can be credibly traced to the historical figure of Jesus of Nazareth.[4] The work of this group has been exposed as ten-

---

[1]John G. Stackhouse Jr., ed., *No Other Gods before Me?* (Grand Rapids: Eerdmans, 2001), 199.

[2]*The Nature of Hell: A Report by the Evangelical Alliance Commission on Unity and Truth Among Evangelicals* (Carlisle: Acute/Paternoster, 2000), 134.

[3]For key essays marking this movement see Gregory W. Dawes, ed., *The Historical Jesus Quest* (Louisville: Westminster John Knox, 2000).

[4]See esp., as representative of a sizable literature, Robert W. Funk, Roy W. Hoover, and the Jesus Seminar, *The Five Gospels* (New York: Macmillan, 1993); Robert W. Funk, *Honest to Jesus* (San Francisco: HarperSanFrancisco, 1996); Robert W. Funk and the Jesus Seminar, *The Acts of Jesus* (San Francisco: HarperSanFrancisco, 1998).

dentious and unconvincing overall.[5] But the corrosive effects of over two centuries of assault on the Gospels' credibility is not easily undone.[6]
The argument, by no means new, that even evangelical scholars and theological training institutions are witnessing a dwindling commitment to the full
authority of Scripture continues to be pressed,[7] probably with increasing justification. A recent valuable book on the gospel message passes over explicit extended
treatment of the Bible's inspiration, infallibility, and full authority,[8] no doubt for
strategic reasons. Nor can it be said to lay much stress on eternal punishment.
Irving Hexham rightly excoriates the loss of will among evangelicals to be clear
about their beliefs in the face of postmodern and world religions forces that mil-
itate against robust articulation of Christian doctrine.[9] He could have added the
pressure of popular evangelicalism that in North America likes to dwell on feelings and blessings but not on unpleasant doctrines like eternal hell.[10]
Or take the study by David Powys, *"Hell": A Hard Look at a Hard Question*.[11]
His book is marketed by a broadly evangelical publishing house and is endorsed
by a well-known British New Testament scholar who is by no means radical as
Gospels specialists go. Yet Powys challenges the following "widely held" conviction: "the view that the New Testament writings yield access to Jesus, his life, and
ministry, and to the proclamation which he stimulated, rather than access only to

---

[5]See, e.g., Markus Bockmühl, *This Jesus: Martyr, Lord, Messiah* (Edinburgh: T. & T. Clark,
1994); Michael J. Wilkins and J. P. Moreland, eds., *Jesus under Fire: Modern Scholarship Reinvents
the Historical Jesus* (Grand Rapids: Zondervan, 1995); Luke Timothy Johnson, *The Real Jesus*
(San Francisco: HarperSanFrancisco, 1996); Raymond E. Brown, *An Introduction to the New
Testament* (New York: Doubleday, 1997), 817–30.

[6]Helpfully surveyed by Robert B. Strimple, *The Modern Search for the Real Jesus*
(Phillipsburg, N.J.: Presbyterian and Reformed, 1995).

[7]Among early analyses was James Davison Hunter, *Evangelicalism: The Coming Generation*
(Chicago: Univ. of Chicago Press, 1987); see 34–40 on erosion in traditional views of eternal
life and damnation. More recently see Iain H. Murray, *Evangelicalism Divided*
(Edinburgh/Carlisle: Banner of Truth Trust, 2000), 173–214; cf. the chapters by D. G. Hart and
R. Albert Mohler Jr. in Michael S. Horton, ed., *A Confessing Theology for Postmodern Times*
(Wheaton, Ill.: Crossway, 2000). Continuing the conversation is Corwin Smidt and James M.
Penning, *Evangelicalism: The Next Generation* (Grand Rapids: Baker, 2002).

[8]John N. Akers, John H. Armstrong, and John D. Woodbridge, eds., *This We Believe*
(Grand Rapids: Zondervan, 2000). The strong faith in Scripture of contributors to this volume
is not in question. But the contrast between this book's approach to pressing home the gospel's
claims and the approach of, for example, *The Fundamentals: A Testimony for the Truth* (the mem-
ory of which *This We Believe* invokes on 16–17), is striking. *This We Believe* simply assumes
rather than documents or argues for the truth of the Bible. The book's summary statement does
in one place refer to "the infallible Scriptures" (241). But there is no affirmation regarding
Scripture in the key "Affirmations and Denials" section (244–48). This omission may be in def-
erence to postmodern readers' aversion to external authority, but it deserves notice as a possible harbinger of future trends.

[9]Irving Hexham, "Evangelical Illusions," in Stackhouse, ed., *No Other Gods before Me?* 137–60.

[10]Cf. Tony Lane, "The Wrath of God as an Aspect of the Love of God," *Nothing Greater,
Nothing Better: Theological Essays on the Love of God*, ed. Kevin Vanhoozer (Grand Rapids:
Eerdmans, 2001), 153–54.

[11]David Powys, *"Hell": A Hard Look at a Hard Question* (Paternoster Biblical and
Theological Monographs; Carlisle: Paternoster, 1998).

the early church and their struggles."[12] The logical implication of this statement in context is twofold: (1) The New Testament writings do not furnish reliable knowledge of Jesus' life and teachings; (2) instead, the New Testament writings furnish knowledge "only" of the early church and its disputes.

In Powys's thinking, apparently, Jesus' numerous and consistent statements about hell in the Gospels are not necessarily direct evidence of our Lord's convictions on the subject at all. This impression is supported by reading his chapter "The Fate of the Unrighteous in the Synoptic Gospels," in which there is little direct statement of what Jesus thought—in keeping with Powys's views that the Gospels do not yield such information.[13]

Furthermore, Powys makes the remarkable claim that "the fate of the unrighteous is never directly addressed within the Synoptic Gospels."[14] What about the numerous texts (see below) in which Gospel writers repeatedly place talk of eternal punishment on Jesus' lips? Powys claims that, in addition to not necessarily coming direct from Jesus, these texts are "used motivationally rather than informatively."[15] Lacking is an explanation of why they could not have been both. To this first forced dichotomy he adds a second: "Reference to fire connoted destruction rather than retribution."[16] No wonder his conclusion is, "No positive doctrine of the fate of the unrighteous can be proclaimed with confidence."[17] The reader should not overlook the irony of this confident claim, which has the effect of setting aside the historic understanding of hell by giving at least measured confidence to those who have decided to jettison it.

In such a climate it is increasingly tempting to take the Gospels' teaching on hell as at best only partially reflective of Jesus' actual outlook. Perhaps the words of "Jesus" about hell are actually later church teaching projected back into well-meaning but largely allegorical accounts of his life. Perhaps they are ultimately relative in meaning and therefore open to thoroughgoing reinterpretation, since they refer to things that lie beyond the space-time world as we know it.[18] Or

---

[12]As I understand him, Powys contests this in "*Hell*," 419, along with a dozen other "major convictions" that his book challenges. The somewhat pessimistic assessment of the link between the Gospels' claims and Jesus actual work and words stands in tension with a more optimistic statement found on p. 274 and in quotations from other writers affirmed on p. 295. See also p. 295, n. 4, in which Powys states that he "will treat the sayings of Jesus as reported in the Synoptic Gospels as being dominical, though without precluding redactional influences." Various hermeneutical moves appear to prevent such hopeful-sounding methodological affirmations from having the effect one might have expected.

[13]Actually this is not quite true: Powys seems to think the Gospels do contain recoverable Jesus material when Jesus can be interpreted as saying things with which Powys agrees—see, e.g., ibid., 274, 277, 279.

[14]Ibid., 293.

[15]Ibid.; cf. the statement by Walle, cited approvingly on p. 295 n. 2.

[16]Ibid.

[17]Ibid., 417.

[18]The view proposed in "Hell," *New Dictionary of Biblical Theology*, ed. T. D. Alexander and Brian S. Rosner (Downers Grove, Ill.: InterVarsity Press, 2000), 544. Cf. ACUTE, *The Nature of Hell*, 125.

HeLL UNDeR fire

maybe Christianity, contrary to age-old convention, is now quite simply free to rethink what used to be nonnegotiable teachings. What harm can there be in jettisoning a presumably lower-order, difficult doctrine like an eternal hell if doing so helps gain a more positive regard for the central core of the Christian message? Why not view this issue as a question of adiaphora—matters on which there is not clear biblical teaching, with the result that each Christian must make his or her own personal decision about the matter (cf. Rom. 14).[19]

The problem is that if Jesus spoke as frequently and directly about hell as Gospel writers claim, then it may not be the Christian message that we end up proclaiming if we modify his doctrine of posthumous existence. At some point divergence from the edges of his teaching (assuming for now that the doctrine of eternal punishment is at the edge) must necessarily affect perception and representation of the central core.

This is not the place to embark on a full investigation of the Bible's reliability and authority or to explore how much Christian teaching we can bracket without beginning to misrepresent the faith we claim to uphold. But we do well not to overlook possible connections between a waning appetite for Jesus' teaching on hell on the one hand, and a flagging conviction that if we call ourselves Christians we are bound to accept the whole Gospel witness to Jesus' teachings on the other. As E. J. Schnabel has observed:

> The Deists' view of God and the resulting focus on the primacy of human reason gave rise to biblical criticism in the 18th century. The Romantic view of religion in the 19th century was more concerned with human religious experience than with divinely revealed truths. It is more than probable that the pluralistic and panentheistic parameters of contemporary (e.g. New Age) thinking will increasingly influence the way Christians will view and use Scripture; all sincere religious utterances and experiences will be treated as of equal worth, and the voice (or voices) of the Bible as just one (or some) of many. In this context it is as important as ever to maintain the traditional Christian view that Scripture is the word of God.[20]

In sum, we should be wary of the temptation of our era to dilute the Bible's message about hell because it is currently acceptable, not only in society but increasingly even in the church, to pick and chose what one wishes to believe. We should be skeptical of arguments that overturn age-old understandings of Scripture on ultimately speculative grounds. And we should not be surprised to encounter suggestions that we are free to reinterpret Jesus' words so they no longer support Christians' historic view of hell, even from writers who insist they seek to do full justice to what the Bible says. As Scot McKnight notes, "What Christians have believed about hell has been constructed almost entirely out of" what Jesus teaches in the Gospels.[21] If the historic doctrine of hell is to be set

---

[19]This is the tack suggested by ACUTE, *The Nature of Hell*, 123–26.
[20]"Scripture," *New Dictionary of Biblical Theology*, 42.
[21]Scot McKnight, *A New Vision for Israel* (Grand Rapids: Eerdmans, 1999), 139.

aside, it is most of all Jesus' teachings that must be neutralized. We could be seeing that take place in current discussion on the subject. That is why there is need to look again at Jesus' teaching on eternal punishment.

What Jesus Said

Let us examine all the Gospel passages in which Christ speaks of hell. We will note the main thrust of all he says from nine different vantage points, and we will be particularly alert to allusions he makes regarding hell's duration. Is it ongoing and conscious with no end? Or does Jesus indicate that while heaven is eternal, hell is not, at least not in anything like the same sense?

1. The Sermon on the Mount

The almost offhand, assumed central place accorded to hell in Christ's teaching is already obvious from perhaps his best-known recorded sermon (Matt. 5–7). Christ warns against hateful anger, because "anyone who says, 'You fool!' will be in danger of the fire of *hell*" (5:22; emphasis added throughout this section). He warns against adulterous looks and actions, lecherous sins of the eye and hand. Gouge out the eye, cut off the hand, Christ states, because "it is better for you to lose one part of your body than for your whole body to be thrown into *hell*" (5:29–30). It is widely agreed that he overstates here for rhetorical effect, but even as a figure of speech the impact is graphic. Later in his ministry Jesus repeats these statements in a different connection (18:9), and he makes it clear that hell involves a fire that never ends: "It is better for you to enter life maimed or crippled than to have two hands or two feet and be thrown into *eternal fire*" (18:8).

Such passages suggest that Jesus apparently viewed hell as real, awful, and "eternal" (we will discuss the meaning of this word more fully below). The statement that nothing in Jesus' teaching on hell (or Gehenna) "specifically mentions the duration" of it appears ill-founded.[22] Jesus also presented hell as motivational, inciting people to take painful measures now, if necessary, to avoid a fate worse than mere physical death later, as fearful as that can be.

2. Jesus' Teaching When Commissioning His Disciples

When Jesus sent out the Twelve, he realized they would be harassed, hated, and persecuted. The temptation to cowardice or compromise would be strong. Christ's own example of courage under fire is one incentive for them to take heart: "A student is not above his teacher, nor a servant above his master.... If the head of the house has been called Beelzebub, how much more the members of his household!" (Matt. 10:24–25). But there is another incentive: the fear of God, whose disapproval is more terrible than any harm inflicted by people. In this connection Christ states: "Do not be afraid of those who kill the body but cannot kill the soul. Rather, be afraid of the One who can destroy both soul and body in *hell*" (10:28).

---

[22]ACUTE, *The Nature of Hell*, 43.

Once again we see Christ appeal to hell, this time as a positive motivation to grasp the nettle of Christian service boldly even when it involves the likelihood of loss, pain, and earthly destruction. Temporary discomfort here and now is preferable to permanent calamity in the age to come.

3. Jesus' Teaching about the Destiny of His Opponents

All of the above passages are addressed to disciples. Those whose faithfulness to their master flags and fails can expect not the promise of heaven but the certainty of hell.[23] But Christ extends this grim prospect to those who oppose his message too. Among these were the religious leaders of Jerusalem and Judea, whose authority in matters both civic and religious brought them into conflict with Jesus repeatedly. He called these leaders "hypocrites," in part because by opposing Christ they "shut the kingdom of heaven in men's faces" (Matt. 23:13). Jesus accused them of turning people away from his kingdom message, producing a convert who is then "twice as much a son of *hell*" as the misguided religious leaders were (23:15).

In biblical usage "son of" normally means physical descendent. But it also has a metaphorical use. It can mean "to share the characteristics" of someone or something. "Sons of thunder" are boisterous and impulsive young men (Mark 3:17; cf. Luke 9:54). "Sons of the light and sons of the day" (1 Thess. 5:5) are people whose lives reflect God's moral brilliance, his holy radiance (cf. 1 John 1:5). "Sons of the kingdom" and "the sons of the evil one" (Matt. 13:38) are expressions depicting people who hark to Christ's kingdom message or who are content with allegiance to "the prince of demons" (9:34; 12:24) or "the prince of this world" (John 12:31, 14:30, 16:11).

Therefore, "a son of *hell*" in Matthew 23:15 is someone whose life shows the same qualities as the religious leaders who discouraged people from acknowledging Jesus as the promised Messiah. Here Jesus' teaching implies that hell exerts an influence on people that can make them stand pat in their native religious and moral condition rather than respond with a whole heart to Jesus' call to repentance, personal trust, and kingdom service. Hell is a sphere of influence in the present as well as an eschatological destination.

4. The Gospels of Mark and Luke

All the references treated so far are found in Matthew. But other Gospels sound identical notes in their references to hell. Jesus' words of Matthew 10:28, for example, are paralleled in Luke 12:5: "But I will show you whom you should fear: Fear him who, after the killing of the body, has power to throw you into *hell*. Yes, I tell you, fear him." Jesus also speaks of hell in Luke's Gospel in the story of the rich man and Lazarus: "In *hell*, where he was in torment, he looked up and saw

---

[23]In our view such disciples were never truly committed to Christ in the first place. They are like the first three classes of people in Jesus' parable of the sower (Mark 4:13–19). For a fresh study of this issue see Thomas R. Schreiner and Ardel B. Candeday, *The Race Set Before Us* (Downers Grove, Ill.: InterVarsity Press, 2001).

Abraham far away, with Lazarus by his side" (Luke 16:23). It is widely accepted that this story is parabolic and not intended to furnish a detailed geography of hell. Yet the picture of an impious sinner tortured by unquenchable thirst, with painful but unmitigated anxiety about his brothers who may end up in the same place, is far from irreconcilable with other allusions and images used by Christ in Matthew's Gospel. There is no justification for supposing that the Lucan parable presents Jesus' teaching on hell in some different light than the Matthew passage does. Significantly, this is yet another passage that points to a conscious and unending torment endured by hell's inhabitants.

As for the Gospel of Mark, when John asks Christ what to do about people who cast out demons in Jesus' name but are not part of the Twelve, Jesus repeats his Sermon on the Mount teaching with a dramatic threefold flourish. (1) Disciples must be willing to go to any lengths necessary to be at peace with each other (cf. Mark 9:50) rather than please themselves and as a result "go into *hell*, where the fire never goes out" (9:43). It requires a studied effort not to see eternal conscious punishment implied in the words "where the fire never goes out." (2) It is preferable, Jesus goes on to say, "to enter life crippled than to have two feet and be thrown into *hell*" (9:45). (3) Finally, "it is better for you to enter the kingdom of God with one eye than to have two eyes and be thrown into *hell*, where 'their worm does not die, and the fire is not quenched'" (9:47–48).

In this Marcan setting Jesus is at conspicuous pains to underscore the unending nature of hell's affliction. He does this, first, by speaking of the "fire that never goes out." Then he does it by quoting Isaiah 66:24. This is one of at least two Old Testament passages that clearly teach "the notion of eternal punishment" (cf. Dan. 12:2).[24] In Mark 9, then, Jesus teaches that hell's agonies are ongoing and neverending. This is a view at least as old as Isaiah, an eighth-century B.C. prophet; the oft-heard assertion that "in ancient Israel there was no belief in life after death"[25] is an overstatement. There was at the very least belief in some quarters in a conscious "life" consisting of the experience of eternal punishment. If we hold to the doctrine of biblical inspiration, the ultimate source of this belief is God himself, who spoke to and through prophets like Isaiah and Daniel. Jesus endorsed this view and this doctrine when he appropriated their teachings as part of his own.[26]

5. The Gospel of John

The Fourth Gospel does not contain the word "hell." But the reality of unending affliction as a result of God's wrath is present: "Whoever believes in the Son has eternal life, but whoever rejects the Son will not see life, for God's wrath remains on him" (John 3:36). As we will see below, virtually everyone agrees that "eternal life" refers to unending blessedness in God's presence. But some wish to

---

[24]Paul Achtemeier, ed., *The HarperCollins Bible Dictionary* (San Francisco: HarperCollins, 1996), 901.

[25]Ibid., 310.

[26]A point elaborated at length in John Wenham, *Christ and the Bible*, 3d ed. (Grand Rapids: Baker, 1994).

limit the duration of "God's wrath" to a limited time or experience. In this view, wrath "remains" but is not experienced consciously, despite other Johannine passages in which the same Greek word likely connotes everlasting duration (see, e.g., 6:27, 56; 8:35; 12:34). Those who die without Christ, it is argued, are eventually simply destroyed or annihilated and then cease all existence.

The evidence of John's Gospel makes this unlikely. Particularly in Jesus' discourses, it juxtaposes "eternal life" and a cluster of negative expressions: "perish" (John 3:16; 10:28), "condemned" (3:18; 5:24, 28), "judgment" (5:22, 30), "death" (5:24), and "die" (6:50). The blessed state of eternal life is logically opposite to the condemned state of eternal destruction. If salvation and conscious bliss are everlasting, so are perdition and conscious torment.

It is possible, but by no means necessary, to interpret terms like "perish," "condemned," "judgment," and "death" as excluding eternal conscious punishment. Jesus did not indulge in melodramatic description of coming horrors but was frequently content to let the normal language of mortal death suffice to refer to the eternal torment that he explicitly warned of in various Synoptic passages. We must see his clear teaching on eternal conscious punishment as interpreting less explicit references to perishing, dying, and destruction; the latter should not be used as grounds to question and ultimately set aside his explicit references.

John's view, it appears, amounts to the same plain teaching found in Matthew, Mark, and Luke. There is certainly no reason to suppose that John understood Jesus in a fundamentally different manner.

6. The Meaning of "Eternal" in Jesus' Teaching

A minority view holds that "eternal" means "unending in conscious experience" when referring to heaven, but "unending only in effect" when referring to hell—that is, the unbelieving are destroyed and then cease existence. This view has a pedigree extending back several centuries.[27] In response to this position, for now we may simply cite the results of one of North America's earliest Bible scholars, Moses Stuart, who already in 1830 carefully examined the biblical data in the ancient languages and arrived at this conclusion:

The result seems to be plain, and philologically and exegetically certain. It is this; either the declarations of the Scriptures do not establish the facts, that God and his glory and praise and happiness are *endless*; nor that the happiness of the righteous in a future world, is *endless*; or else they establish the fact, that the punishment of the wicked is *endless*. The whole stand or fall together. There can, in the very nature of antithesis, be no room for rational doubt

---

[27]See, e.g., D. P. Walker, *The Decline of Hell: Seventeenth-Century Discussions of Eternal Torment* (Chicago: Univ. of Chicago Press, 1964); Powys, "*Hell*," 17–60; D. A. Carson, *The Gagging of God: Christianity Confronts Pluralism* (Grand Rapids: Zondervan, 1996), esp. 515–36; David George Moore, *The Battle for Hell: A Survey and Evaluation of Evangelicals' Growing Attraction to the Doctrine of Annihilationism* (Lanham, Md.: Univ. Press of America, 1995); Larry Dixon, *The Other Side of the Good News* (Wheaton, Ill.: Crossway, 1992); Jon Braun, *Whatever Happened to Hell?* (Nashville: Thomas Nelson, 1979).

here, in what manner we should interpret the declarations of the sacred writers. WE MUST EITHER ADMIT THE ENDLESS MISERY OF HELL, OR GIVE UP THE ENDLESS HAPPINESS OF HEAVEN.[28]

The continuing validity of this finding is suggested by the identical conclusions of recent scholars like D. A. Carson, Murray Harris, and, in an earlier generation, H. Sasse.[29] In the debate over whether the punishment of hell will be everlasting, "this argument is often seen as conclusive."[30]

7. So What Did Jesus Teach About Hell?

It is seemingly straightforward. There will be a bodily resurrection of all persons, the good and the wicked (John 5:28–29). The good (those who have savingly received Christ's kingdom message) will enter heaven. This is a place of blessing and of unending joy in the presence of the Lord. The wicked (those who have not savingly received Christ's message) will enter hell: "Then they will go away to *eternal* punishment, but the righteous to *eternal* life" (Matt. 25:46). The symmetry is starkly simple. As McKnight concludes, Jesus clearly teaches "punishment in an individual, eternal, sense."[31] Or again: "We must admit that Jesus taught the possibility and reality of an eternal, conscious punishment for Israelites."[32]

A recent massive study of pre-Christian Judaism comports with Jesus' teaching in Matthew that individual Jews who did not receive his teaching leading to eternal conscious life would receive condemnation resulting in eternal conscious death.[33] Within the first decades of the early church, apostles and others were spreading this sobering message across the length and the breadth of the Roman world.

We have seen that Jesus depicted hell as real, awful, everlasting, motivational (people should strive to avoid it), and influential (people can reflect its reality in this life). In view of modern doubts about whether the torments of hell are really unending (see below), Jesus' apparent stress on hell's everlasting duration should be underscored.

8. Echoes of Jesus' Teaching Elsewhere in the New Testament

Jesus' teaching about hell is found primarily in the Gospels. But in a sense the whole of New Testament teaching can be viewed as coming from Jesus, since writers like Paul (see next chapter) claim to be passing along or applying Jesus'

---

[28]Moses Stuart, *Exegetical Essays on Several Words Relating to Future Punishment* (Philadelphia: Presbyterian Publication Committee, 1867 [reprint of 1830 edition]), 62; Stuart's emphasis throughout.
[29]Cf. D. A. Carson, *The Gagging of God*, 523 (Carson cites passages from Harris and Sasse in n. 23).
[30]"Hell," *New Dictionary of Biblical Theology*, 54
[31]McKnight, *A New Vision for Israel*, 38.
[32]Ibid.
[33]Mark A. Elliott, *The Survivors of Israel* (Grand Rapids: Eerdmans, 2000).

HeLL UNDeR fire

doctrine, either directly (e.g., 1 Cor. 11:23) or indirectly by the Spirit of Jesus (e.g., Rom. 15:19, 30; 1 Cor. 2:10–14, 7:40; Eph 3:5; 1 Thess. 1:5; 1 Tim. 4:1). Even if someone should minimize the importance of an individual Gospel passage in establishing Jesus' teaching about hell, the evidence of other passages by other writers—all followers of Jesus claiming to pass along his divine teaching and not their own—would remain. Jesus' early followers teach nothing essentially different on this subject from their Master. Some New Testament books, such as Hebrews and Revelation, actually extend and amplify aspects of Jesus' teaching as epitomized above.

9. Foundation of Jesus' Teaching

Furthermore, what Jesus teaches concerning the afterlife claims continuity with the Old Testament. There is a direct connection between Christ's understanding of eternal life and death on the one hand, and the hope extended to the patriarchs generally (Matt. 22:31), to Abraham in particular (John 8:56), to Moses (5:46), and to Isaiah (12:41), on the other hand. This is the message of eternal reward, and its corollary eternal misery, to which the entire Old Testament testifies (5:39). While Christ certainly extends, solidifies, and applies Old Testament teaching, so that it can be said that he fulfills it and in that sense transcends it, he does not contradict it.

Christ's teaching on hell, therefore, draws persuasive force from its basis in the Old Testament witness and not only from the scattered references to the actual word "hell" discussed above. The one who came down from heaven to reveal God (John 4:13) corrected views about the age to come (e.g., in the case of the Sadducees) when they were out of sync with a proper understanding of the Old Testament. But Christ did not set aside or change—he merely purified, clarified, extended, and intensified—Old Testament views of redemption and judgment that existed in various forms among the Jewish sects of his time and stretched back for many centuries.

Just as we can be sure that the Messiah of Old Testament promise who offers eternal life has prepared an eternal abode for his people in heaven (cf. John 14:2–3), we can be confident that he spoke knowledgeably and authoritatively about the everlasting woes of hell he urged all to avoid.

Jesus' Teaching: A Different Understanding

Edward W. Fudge has become well known as a leading advocate of the view that when the wicked die, their punishment is "eternal" in the sense that its consequences last forever, not in the sense that the wicked experience unending torment. This view is called conditional immortality, conditionalism, or annihilationism.[34] "Hell is real. It is fearful beyond human imagination, and those who go there will never come out again."[35] But they will not experience torment

---

[34]Cf. ACUTE, *The Nature of Hell*, 4–5.
[35]Fudge in Edward W. Fudge and Robert A. Peterson, *Two Views of Hell* (Downers Grove, Ill.: InterVarsity Press, 2000), 19.

forever; they will simply cease to exist. Against the view outlined in the previous section—that Jesus warned of a hell that is as everlasting as heaven is—Fudge writes:

> The fact is that the Bible does not teach the traditional view of final punishment. Scripture nowhere suggests that God is an eternal torturer. It never says the damned will writhe in ceaseless torment or that the glories of heaven will forever be blighted by the screams from hell. The idea of conscious everlasting torment was a grievous mistake, a horrible error, a gross slander against the heavenly Father, whose character we truly see in the life of Jesus of Nazareth.[36]

Some of Fudge's language can be set aside as overwrought rhetoric. The historic view does not view God as "an eternal torturer"; hell is not unjust torture but is rather, according to Scripture, a just recompense for people who are without excuse for not seeking God so as to be saved.[37] "Will not the Judge of all the earth do right?" (Gen. 18:25). Is God "unjust in bringing his wrath on us? . . . Certainly not! If that were so, how could God judge the world?" (Rom. 3:5–6). Scripture clearly faces the implications of God's inflicting eternal wrath, but biblical writers have more fear of God than to call him a "torturer" with the implication of injustice and cruelty.

Similarly, "the glories of heaven" will not "forever be blighted by the screams from hell." Scripture implies that the smoke from the judgment of God's enemies will not mar heavenly praise but if anything enhance it (Rev. 14:11; 19:3). Furthermore, in heaven "there will be no more death or mourning or crying or pain, for the old order of things has passed away" (21:4). So hell's woes will ultimately be transcended by those blessed in the heavenly presence. This may appear callous at first glance, but it is what Scripture says, and as Fudge agrees,[38] this is the main issue in the debate.

Finally, to call Jesus' apparent belief in conscious everlasting punishment "a grievous mistake, a horrible error, a gross slander against the heavenly Father" is a risky charge in light of the Scriptures we have cited in the previous section. For Jesus appears to assert precisely the "traditional" view that Fudge associates with torture, error, and slander of God.

Fudge's claims do call for response. We may first appeal to Jesus' language in the previous section. It is difficult to avoid the impression that Jesus believed that

---

[36]Ibid., 20; see also 82.
[37]This has been widely recognized for many years: "The word 'retribution' is to be preferred to 'punishment' because the Bible teaches us that the fate of the wicked is not an arbitrary (much less a vindictive) infliction, but the necessary consequence of their own sins" (W. C. Procter, "What Christ Teaches Concerning Future Retribution," *The Fundamentals* [Chicago: Testimony Publishing Company, n.d.], 9:85–86).
[38]Cf., e.g., *Two Views of Hell*, 21, where Fudge comments: "The growing evangelical rejection of the traditional doctrine of unending conscious torment is not propelled by emotionalism, sentimentality or compromise with culture but by absolute commitment to the authority of Scripture. . . ."

HeLL UNDeR fire

persons born into this world receive an existence that thereafter never terminates. It appears to be part of the theological convictions he embraced as a result of his complex personal circumstances molded by his unique identity as God's Chosen One, his religious upbringing in a Jewish home and synagogue, and his careful attention to the Old Testament Scriptures[39] prior to and during his earthly ministry. We will expand on these thoughts by looking at key Gospel passages in detail.

The Prima Facie Meaning of Jesus' Statements on Hell

In a previous section we pointed out a number of passages where Jesus appears to teach that hell's woes are unending. Fudge has a different understanding of each passage.[40] We cannot discuss all of these texts in detail, but below we deal with enough of them, we believe, to call in question Fudge's understanding. Taking five key passages, we will cite the text, summarize Fudge's interpretation, and suggest a more plausible way of understanding Jesus' teaching.

1. *Matthew 5:22: "But anyone who says, 'You fool!' will be in danger of the fire of hell [Gehenna]."* Fudge points to the referent of the Hebrew word underlying the Greek word *geenna*.[41] It is often claimed to have been a site near Jerusalem where refuse was burned.[42] So Fudge relates it directly to fire at that location, having the effect that fire has on combustibles. In the physical realm fire consumes, burns up, and destroys; in its wake nothing much is left. This is the argument of Fudge's best-known book[43] and the sheet anchor of his argument that hell is a place of annihilation, not of eternal torment. In a word, Jesus warns in Matthew 5:22 that deadly anger and hatred will result in fiery pain and then loss of consciousness.

Fudge appears to underinterpret Gehenna. He does this in part by committing the exegetical fallacy of confusing referent (the Valley of Hinnom outside of Jerusalem and the mundane burning that allegedly occurred there) and sense (a place of extraordinary punishment prepared by God for his enemies).[44] By focusing so wholly on the former, Fudge gives short shrift to the latter. But it is the latter that Jesus warns against; the connotative meaning (sense) of Matthew 5:22 is primarily God's hell, not a Judean waste disposal site.

A more plausible interpretation is that Jesus uses a despicable, disgusting, and harrowing geographical reference familiar to him and his listeners to warn of an eschatological destiny that his listeners should seek to avoid at all costs. Gehenna

---

[39]Rightly stressed in McKnight, *A New Vision for Israel*, 3.

[40]Note Fudge's chapter "The Teachings of Jesus" in Fudge and Peterson, *Two Views of Hell*, 36–52.

[41]Ibid., 42–43.

[42]But Peter Head writes: "There is no convincing evidence in the primary sources for the existence of a fiery dump in this location" ("Duration of Divine Judgment," in *Eschatology in Bible and Theology*, ed. Kent E. Brower and Mark W. Elliott [Downers Grove, Ill.: InterVarsity Press, 1997], 223).

[43]Edward W. Fudge, *The Fire That Consumes*, rev. ed. (Carlisle: Paternoster, 1994). See also Fudge and Peterson, *Two Views of Hell*, 37–39.

[44]Cf. D. A. Carson, *Exegetical Fallacies*, 2d ed. (Grand Rapids: Baker, 1996), 63–64. See also G. B. Caird, *The Language and Imagery of the Bible* (Grand Rapids: Eerdmans, 1997), 8–12.

is a pale image for a much more vivid coming reality, just as a golden street (cf. Rev. 21:21; 22:2) is a weak description of glories mortal flesh cannot grasp (cf. 1 Cor. 2:9). Loss of consciousness is what normal people welcome every night; Christ's threat must be drawing on something more fearful than that. Subsequent Gospel references indicate that he is, indeed, pointing to endless discomfort of a conscious nature.

Yet I agree with Fudge[45] that Matthew 5:22 needs to be explained with reference to subsequent sayings of Jesus, and so we turn to the next passage.

2. *Matthew 5:29–30: "If your right eye causes you to sin, gouge it out and throw it away. It is better for you to lose one part of your body than for your whole body to be thrown into hell. And if your right hand causes you to sin, cut it off and throw it away. It is better for you to lose one part of your body than for your whole body to go into hell."*

For Fudge, Jesus threatens "the loss of the total self."[46] Fudge characterizes this as "rejection, banishment, and expulsion" and likens it to "loss inflicted by fire." But this is too weak to do justice to the words. "Thrown into hell" is not just "rejection, banishment, and expulsion" but active punishment. The image is not of a judge turning his back, exiling someone to a lonely place, or sending someone out of the courtroom. "To go into hell" is not just a passive loss or lamentable setback; it is an active image of someone entering a location of extreme misery and discomfort. "The loss of the total self" is a feeble psychologization of an execrable state in comparison to which bodily mutilation and amputation are much to be preferred, according to Jesus. Again it must be asked whether ultimate loss of consciousness can be taken seriously as the awful outcome the Lord warns against.

We again agree with Fudge, however, that this "loss inflicted by fire" begs for interpretation in conjunction with other sayings of Jesus, so we turn to the next text.

3. *Matthew 10:28: "Do not be afraid of those who kill the body but cannot kill the soul. Rather, be afraid of the One who can destroy both soul and body in hell."* Fudge stresses that "kill" and "destroy" are parallel. By "destroy" he understands annihilate. So Jesus' warning is to fear God because he can make both soul and body cease to exist any longer.[47]

Doubtless God could have chosen to do this; the question is whether Scripture means here that he does or will so choose. It makes better sense to view Jesus' warning a different way. Matthew 10 is about Jesus' sending out the Twelve. They will face danger, treachery, and things like flogging (10:17). It will be tempting to be cowardly rather than face pain or even death. But there is a second death more fearful than any earthly end. God is able to inflict an unending misery on the whole person, "soul and body." We say "unending" for two reasons.

First, Jesus elsewhere calls this affliction "eternal" (see discussion in this essay both above and below), and there is no compelling reason to interpret a death Jesus calls "eternal" elsewhere as "temporary" here.

---

[45]Fudge and Peterson, *Two Views of Hell*, 43.
[46]Ibid.
[47]Ibid., 43–44.

HeLL UNDeR fire

Second, in Jesus' usage "destroy" can also mean to inflict enduring torment. That is, unclean spirits who ask whether Jesus will "destroy" them (*apollymi*; Mark 1:24; Luke 4:34) understand that destruction in terms of unending torment (*basanizō*; Matt. 8:29; Mark 5:7; Luke 8:28). In other words, the verb *apollymi* ("to destroy") in Matthew 10:28 is parallel not only with *apokteinō* ("to kill") in the same verse, where the reference is plainly to earthly death; *apollymi* can also be parallel with *basanizō* ("to torment, torture"), where the reference is to the sphere of existence beyond this earthly one. The spirits were not afraid of being "destroyed" or "tormented" by Jesus on this earth, as if he might take time now and then to inflict pain on them when it suited him and at worst even terminate their conscious existence. They rather feared the pain of the "forever and ever" torment that the Spirit of Jesus later revealed to John as the destiny of the devil and all those loyal to him (Rev. 14:11)—such as the unclean spirits.

While Matthew 10:28 taken alone is inconclusive, Fudge's interpretation of it is unconvincing. The evidence is beginning to mount that to view Jesus as an annihilationist does a disservice to the Gospel texts. Two additional passages bear this out.

4. Matthew 18:8–9: "It is better for you to enter life maimed or crippled than to have two hands or two feet and be thrown into eternal fire.... It is better for you to enter life with one eye than to have two eyes and be thrown into the fire of hell [Gehenna]." Fudge understands this as threatening "total destruction that will be forever."[48] He suggests that Gehenna is called "eternal" because "it is not part of the present age but of the age to come.... It does not belong to time but to eternity." This implies a timeless view of eternity, a Platonic understanding[49] (which is surprising in view of how avidly Fudge condemns the Platonic view of the immortality of the soul).[50] If echoes of Platonic belief are, as Fudge contends, fatal to one's views on everlasting punishment, then with this he has painted himself into a corner.

But Fudge appears here also to run afoul of a logical difficulty. If Gehenna is really about an eternal destination and not about either the Valley of Hinnom and what happened there,[51] or about Sodom, which was destroyed with "eternal fire" and "was never seen again,"[52] then Fudge's appeals to those earthly locations as descriptive of hell's fire lose persuasive force. By his own admission they are fleeting earthly prefigurements of enduring eschatological realities. I agree with Fudge here. As interpreters we should therefore be prepared to find in the future Gehenna dimensions that transcend earthly bounds. Fudge cannot have it both ways. He errs in equivocating when he likens Gehenna so strictly to the Valley of Hinnom when it suits his purpose to unpack one saying of Jesus (Matt. 5:22; see

---

[48]Ibid., 44.
[49]Cf. Oscar Cullmann, *Christ and Time*, rev. ed., trans. by Floyd Filson (Philadelphia: Westminster, 1964), 61–68.
[50]Cf. Fudge and Peterson, *Two Views of Hell*, 22, 43, 62, 187.
[51]Cf. ibid., 42.
[52]Ibid., 44 and Jude 7.

above), then defines it differently when he finds it necessary to make sense of Jesus' teaching here. We should rather simply understand the "eternal fire" of 18:8 as parallel with "the fire of hell" in 18:9.

We must note carefully that in both verses, Jesus *speaks of people being cast into hell as closely parallel with "entering life."* Clearly Jesus has in mind the picture of someone who causes others to stumble, dies, and stands before the eternal Judge. Persons appearing before that Judge enter eternal "life," their final destination (cf. Matt. 25:31–46). That destination could be heaven, and if so, the duration of the experience will be conscious and unending. Fudge does not dispute that. There is no justification, then, to deny that by the same token, Jesus teaches here that *the "life" of those who enter Gehenna will be conscious and unending.* Fudge forces an unnatural interpretation on these verses that cannot do justice to the details of Jesus' utterance.

5. Mark 9:47–48: "It is better for you to enter the kingdom of God with one eye than to have two eyes and be thrown into hell, where 'their worm does not die, and the fire is not quenched.'" The Marcan parallel to Matthew 18:8–9 is Mark 9:47–48, a verse that sheds additional light on Jesus' teaching.

In dealing with this verse[53] Fudge sticks to his guns: "The devouring worm is aided by unquenchable fire that cannot be put out and that therefore continues to destroy until nothing remains. And when that destruction is completed, it will last for all eternity." He appeals to a reading of Isaiah 66:24 that insists on seeing nothing in the imagery but corpses that decompose or are burned into oblivion: "Their worm will not die, nor will their fire be quenched."[54]

But this is an unlikely rendering of Isaiah's meaning. For one thing, the logic is strained. A fire that "continues to destroy until nothing remains" is not unquenchable; it is rather quenched—if "nothing remains," as Fudge claims, the fire must go out. Fudge makes exactly the opposite point of Jesus and Isaiah. Their fire never goes out; Fudge's goes completely out. Isaiah and Jesus may be right, or Fudge may be right, but their statements stand in flat contradiction to each other. We must make a choice.

Furthermore, destruction cannot be both "completed" and therefore over with and at the same time "last for all eternity." Of course, Fudge is free to venture the speculation that Jesus (or Isaiah) was referring to the *consequences* of the destruction, but that is not what either text says. Rather, both refer to the destroying and ongoing ravages of maggot and flame. The grotesqueness of the image and the sternness of the warning are dependent precisely on the macabre spectacle of such horrors being ongoing. As Peter Head shows, this is the understanding of Isaiah that prevailed in Second Temple Judaism, as seen in texts from Judith, *1 Enoch*, and the *Sibylline Oracles*.[55] It is the most natural and straightforward reading of what Jesus says in Mark.

[53]Ibid., 44.
[54]Ibid., 32–33.
[55]Peter Head, "Duration of Divine Judgment," in *Eschatology in Bible and Theology*, ed. Brower and Elliott, 223–34.

HELL UNDER FIRE

Thus, J. Alec Motyer is likely correct in seeing in the worm image used by Isaiah "ceaseless corruption" and in the fire "unending holy wrath."[56] Robert Gundry thinks Jesus in Mark 9:48 understood Isaiah this way; as against annihilation, "these expressions seem more likely to mean that the worm and the fire feed forever on the body of the damned."[57] There is strong support here from the Old Testament apocryphal book of Judith 7:17, written prior to New Testament times; it speaks of God's giving "fire and worms" to the flesh of the nations, who "shall weep in pain forever." Fudge, calling on the usual whipping boy (see next section), attributes Judith's reading of Isaiah to "the pagan Greek notion that souls are immortal and cannot die,"[58] but this is speculative and less likely, overall, than that Judith is drawing on the same conviction that Isaiah voiced. In any case, Jesus understood Isaiah to be implying eternal punishment. And it is impossible, of course, that Isaiah 66:24 (and Dan. 12:2; see previous discussion) derives from Greek thought.

In light of Old Testament teaching and the five texts just examined, in which Christ underscores the unending nature of the punishment that awaits the ungodly, it strains credulity to maintain that he did not mean what most interpreters both ancient and modern have reluctantly but steadfastly understood: ceaseless conscious torment. Fudge fails to overturn the prima facie meaning of Jesus' teaching on hell as recorded in the Gospels.[59]

Jesus' Teaching: Did It Come from Plato?

We have shown Fudge's claim to be unconvincing that Jesus never intended to give the impression that hell's miseries are conscious and everlasting. This was rather Christ's clear teaching. Yet Fudge has a second line of argument. He maintains that it was the Greek (Platonic) doctrine of immortality of the soul that caused ancient thinkers like Augustine to suppose that those cast into hell could never die; their torment would have to be unending. "The traditionalist notion of everlasting torment in hell springs directly from that nonbiblical teaching."[60] In other words, because Plato and other Greeks taught that the human soul, once created, can never pass out of existence, church history came to be dominated by theologians and preachers who understood Scripture as teaching that the fate of the damned is eternal conscious punishment. We ought therefore to ask whether the earliest known postcanonical interpreters of the Gospels considered the pain of hell to be unending. And if they did affirm this, was it because of the Greek doctrine of the immortality of the soul, as Fudge claims?

---

[56]J. Alec Motyer, *The Prophecy of Isaiah* (Downers Grove, Ill.: InterVarsity Press, 1993), 544.
[57]Robert Gundry, *Mark* (Grand Rapids: Eerdmans, 1993), 526.
[58]Fudge and Peterson, *Two Views of Hell*, 35.
[59]We do not have space to examine all parallel or relevant Gospel texts, but we have found nothing in them that conflicts with the findings presented above. Particularly, we believe that in-depth exploration of Jesus' urgent call to repentance and faith, his teaching on God's kingdom, his doctrine of Satan and demons and his exorcisms, as well as his willingness to endure the hell of dereliction on the cross and in the tomb, would yield additional warrants for declaring the historic view of hell the best interpretation of his reported teachings.
[60]Fudge and Peterson, *Two Views of Hell*, 185.

There is no escaping the conclusion that early Christian writers typically held to the view that hell's punishments would be unending. But Augustine is not the problem, for people were saying the same thing three hundred years earlier. And biblical considerations, not philosophical ones, seem to have furnished primary impetus. The *Epistle of Barnabas*, dating to around A.D. 70–100, states: "The way of darkness is . . . the way of eternal death with punishment."[61] The same writer holds to the doctrine of the bodily resurrection (*Barnabas* 5:6), a doctrine at which Hellenistic thinkers typically scoffed (cf. Acts 17:32). It is more likely that *Barnabas*, with its teachings of resurrection and ongoing punishment, is more dependent on the Gospels, which it cites some half-dozen times, than on Plato or other Hellenistic writers, with which it shows little affinity. Moreover, the corpus that *Barnabas* cites by far most frequently is the Old Testament, not a marker of Platonic thinking by any measure.

Papias of Hierapolis, a hearer of the apostle John before the end of the first century, affirmed the millenarian view of Revelation and its related view of eternal rewards.[62] There is no reason to suppose that he denied the view of hell as eternal torment affirmed in Revelation and for that matter in the Gospel, which his mentor John the apostle penned. The fragments of Papias's writings that survive suggest disaffection with Hellenistic thought (the dominant religious milieu of his native Phrygia) in favor of Jesus' teachings, not some capitulation to Platonism. It is widely recognized that Eusebius invented an "elder John" to whom Revelation could be traced, thus freeing the apostolic John from millenarian taint and making apostolic Christianity more amenable to Eusebius's neo-Platonic outlook.[63] In other words, Papias was too far removed from Plato to suit Eusebius. Clearly Papias's eschatology is in no sense Platonic. If, like Revelation, he affirms eternal conscious punishment, the reason is far more likely to lie in the teachings of Jesus and the apostolic circle than in Platonic philosophy.

Other writers from the second century A.D. likewise speak of hell's unending torment. The *Martyrdom of Polycarp* (ca. A.D. 135) states: "They despised all the torments of this world, redeeming themselves from eternal punishment by the suffering of a single hour. . . . For they kept before their view escape from that fire which is eternal and will never be quenched."[64] Justin Martyr (ca. A.D. 160) writes, "We know from Isaiah that the members of those who have transgressed will be consumed by the worm and unquenchable fire."[65] Tatian (ca. A.D. 160) summaries the gospel promise in these words: "We who are now easily susceptible to death,

---

[61]*ANF* 1.149, cited in David W. Bercot, ed., *A Dictionary of Early Christian Beliefs* (Peabody, Mass.: Hendrickson, 1998), 242.

[62]Irenaeus, *Against Heresies* 5.33.3, 4; Eusebius, *Church History* 3.39; Jerome, *De vir. illust.* 18. See J. B. Lightfoot, *The Apostolic Fathers* (London: Macmillan, 1891), 527–34.

[63]Cf. Robert Yarbrough, "The Date of Papias: A Reassessment," *JETS* 26 (1983): 181–91. See also Glenn F. Chesnut, *The First Christian Histories* (Macon, Ga.: Mercer Univ. Press, 1986), 164–66.

[64]*ANF* 1.39, cited in Bercot, ed., *A Dictionary of Early Christian Beliefs*, 242.

[65]*ANF* 1. 264, 265, cited in ibid., 242.

HeLL UNDeR fire

will afterwards receive immortality with either enjoyment or with pain."[66] Similar views can be found in Athenagoras (ca. A.D. 175), Theophilus (ca. A.D. 180), Irenaeus (ca. A.D. 180), and Tertullian (ca. A.D. 197).[67] The line from these views back to Jesus (or in Justin's case to Isaiah) is short and direct. There is no reason to adduce Platonic or Hellenistic theology as the major factor.

In fact, even a source friendly to conditionalism admits that it is not until Arnobius (died ca. A.D. 330) that we find "the first explicit defence of the annihilation of ungodly souls in hell." Moreover, "Arnobius is among the least biblically-grounded of the early church fathers." It is therefore not surprising that this view "was deemed heretical by the Second Council of Constantinople in 553 and again by the Lateran Council in 1513."[68] In other words, earlier writers with demonstrated ties to Scripture repeat what Jesus says in the Gospels about eternal punishment. A later writer like Arnobius, with less clear biblical orientation, explicitly diverges. Why should the earlier writers be charged with following Plato, whom they do not claim as their Lord, but the lone voice of a discredited Arnobius be given praise for discerning what Christ actually intended to communicate?

It is a little baffling that some wish to set aside the evidence of early patristic writers. It is suggested that we disqualify from consideration passages such as those in the *Martyrdom of Polycarp* and *2 Clement* that use biblical phrases like "everlasting punishment," "everlasting fire," and "fire that is never quenched." Because "it is precisely the meaning of these phrases that is the question at issue," they should not be introduced as evidence in the debate.[69] This move would be satisfactory if it could be shown that these writers were so prone to syncretism on the matter of life after death that they could not distinguish in their teachings between Christ and classical philosophers like Plato.

But while it is inevitable that Greek thought suffuses their writings—many wrote in Greek, and some were converted out of Hellenistic paganism—their appeal to Scripture and Bible-based doctrinal warrants should be taken seriously. They were definitely not brainwashed by Plato, as is evidenced by common patristic convictions backed by Scripture but hardly sanctioned by Platonism:

- the uniqueness of Jesus Christ as the divine and human Son of God
- the necessity of personal faith in his death and resurrection for salvation
- the resurrection of the body, both of Christ and of all persons following death
- the doctrine of creation, to say nothing of creation *ex nihilo*
- Christian millenarianism
- the revelatory authority of the Old and New Testaments over human reason

[66]*ANF* 1.71, cited in ibid., 242.
[67]Cf. ibid., 242–45.
[68]ACUTE, *The Nature of Hell*, 62.
[69]E. Earle Ellis, "New Testament Teaching on Hell," in *Eschatology in Bible and Theology*, ed. Brower and Elliott, 201 n. 8.

- the intrinsic tie between religion and morality (the grounding of ethics in theology)
- humans as the unique *imago dei*
- the mediation of redemption for all via the saving history of the chosen Hebrew people
- the doctrine of the Fall and original sin

None of these doctrines would be readily embraced by a Platonic thinker. Yet they were generally affirmed by patristic writers. Tony Gray points out that Justin and Irenaeus agreed with the Stoic teaching, not Platonism, on the corruptibility of the soul.[70] They fervently opposed the Platonically-inclined Gnostics.[71] The first anti-Christian Greek philosopher whose writings we possess in any length, Celsus (ca. A.D. 180), shows with his allegiance to Plato[72] and hostility toward Christian doctrine the wide gulf that generally separated mainstream second-century church teaching from Platonism on a number of key points.[73]

Therefore, for a cluster of reasons we need something more than the vague charge of "a conception rooted in Platonic philosophy"[74] to convict the writers cited above of culpable subservience to Plato in their teaching on hell. If they were following Plato's doctrine of the immortality of the soul so close to the letter, they would not have believed in the resurrection of bodies to damnation in the first place. Plato and derivative teachings played godfather to the pagan mystery religions[75] and perhaps Gnosticism[76] far more than to early patristic Christianity.

This is not to deny that by the second-century Christian thinkers (and indeed writers from the first century) were being influenced by Hellenistic ideas. How could they not be, writing in Greek in the Greco-Roman world? Yet even thinkers like Origen, whose thinking unquestionably was grounded in a Hellenistic worldview, wrestled with Scripture texts, affirmed the bodily resurrection, and concluded (against Greek Stoic thought) that hell's miseries could not be terminated by suicide.[77] Justin

---

[70]Tony Gray, "The Nature of Hell," in *Eschatology in Bible and Theology*, ed. Brower and Elliott, 237.

[71]J. N. D. Kelly, *Early Christian Doctrines*, rev. ed. (New York: Harper & Row, 1978), 35–41.

[72]On Celsus' Platonism, cf. ibid., 20.

[73]*Celsus on the True Doctrine*, R. Joseph Hoffmann trans. (New York/London: Oxford Univ. Press, 1987). For Celsus, who bitterly opposes the Christian doctrine of resurrection on the basis of Plato's teaching, Plato is quite simply "the Philosopher" (ibid., 81). For other references to Plato and important examples of how a Platonist viewed patristic Christianity, see, e.g., pp. 77, 88–89, with notes 85–88, 92–95, 103–4, 109–11, 113–14. Clearly Celsus did not detect any hint of concession to Plato's doctrine of the immortality of the soul in the Christian doctrine of eternal punishment (ibid., 121), which Celsus viewed as common to all religions of his time—except that civilized religions, in his view, did not believe that departed souls are reunited with a body prior to eternal perdition.

[74]Ellis, "New Testament Teaching on Hell," 212.

[75]Cf. Jack Finegan, *Myth and Mystery: An Introduction to the Pagan Religions of the Biblical World* (Grand Rapids: Baker, 1989), 169–85.

[76]Kelly, *Early Christian Doctrines*, 22–28.

[77]*ANF* 4.294, 295, cited in Bercot, ed., *A Dictionary of Early Christian Beliefs*, 246. Origen's doctrine of universal redemption did, however, imply that hell must be of limited duration; see Kelly, *Early Christian Doctrines*, 473–74.

　　　　　　　　　　　　　　　　　HeLL UNDeR fire

used "language strongly colored by the Platonizing Stoicism of his day" but did not go along with Plato's dualism.[78] And even someone like Augustine, frequently accused of being the main conduit of (nonbiblical) interpretations of hell as eternal conscious punishment, "was a theologian of the [biblical] text, even though, as with all theology, he was subject to other influences."[79]

It is therefore by no means clear that Plato was anything like the authority for early church leaders that, say, Aristotle was for Thomas Aquinas.[80] To demonstrate Plato's influence it would be helpful to see at least a fair number of patristic authorities explicitly adducing Plato to help ground their interpretations of Jesus' teaching on hell. To my knowledge no one has produced such a study.

The question we are seeking to answer in this section is whether the doctrine of eternal conscious punishment in hell is primarily the result of early church acquiescence to Plato's teaching on the immortality of the soul. Actually we could argue the opposite: It is precisely an inveterate Platonizer like Origen[81] who arrives at a doctrine that hell, though serious, is not eternal conscious punishment. We have shown that the source of patristic teaching is far more likely to be the teaching of Jesus in the Gospels and in passages such as Isaiah 66. If our aim is to be faithful to Scripture, we must face what Jesus' teachings have been understood to assert by most biblical interpreters over many centuries, cutting across a wide assortment of confessional and denominational settings. This is not to say that conditionalist or annihilationist teaching can make no appeal to Scripture. It is only to say that the frequent first move of discrediting the historical view by accusing it of early and direct Platonic origin lacks credible basis. This move deserves to be abandoned until compelling evidence for the claim is forthcoming.

The Lord Jesus through the Scriptures, not Plato through surreptitious historical influences, bequeathed the discomfiting doctrine of hell to the church. Early patristic theologians "generally, in spite of a good deal of confusion, are on their guard against the current Platonic theory of immortality."[82] The church has not been perfect and often errs in many ways. It has undoubtedly erred at times in the spirit with which it has upheld the historic doctrine of hell. But it has not been unfaithful to Christ in confessing that this is what the Scriptures teach.

---

[78]Kelly, *Early Christian Doctrines*, 84–85. Cf. p. 170: "However ready [Justin] might be on occasion to avail himself of the idiom of Hellenistic speculation, he remained all the time a churchman, with his feet firmly planted in the Church's living liturgical and Scriptural traditions."

[79]Gray, "The Nature of Hell," 238.

[80]In the same way that Plato is "the Philosopher" for Celsus (see note 73 above), Aristotle is "the Philosopher" for Aquinas. See Vernon J. Bourke, ed., *The Pocket Aquinas* (New York: Washington Square, 1960), 43, 94, 191, 300, etc. In the index of this book, under "Philosopher, the," one is referred to Aristotle (ibid., 370). To my knowledge early patristic writers do not defer to Plato in this way with respect to the doctrine of the immortality of the soul. It is more likely they inferred it from a combination of Old Testament teaching and views expressed by Jesus (e.g., his teaching on eternal punishment) and various New Testament writers.

[81]Kelly, *Early Christian Doctrines*, 74, 128, 131, 213, 230f., 470, etc.

[82]Ibid., 466.

Conditionalist Scruples, Post 9/11 Belief, and Jesus' Teaching

Disenchantment with the historic view of Jesus' teaching on hell has been on the increase for several centuries, but among evangelicals John Stott in 1988 lent fresh legitimacy to the conditionalist view. While he felt he could produce biblical warrants for his position, he spoke for many with "emotive force"[83] when he stated: "I find the concept [of eternal conscious torment] intolerable and do not understand how people can live with it without cauterizing their feelings or cracking under the strain."[84]

This kind of reasoning has long been a staple of nonevangelical thinkers.[85] But Stott's admission has had incalculable influence *among the international evangelical community*, which looks to leaders like him for guidance in an age of rapid change and increasing doctrinal controversy. While people generally, and Christians perhaps much more, can empathize with such compassionate angst, our study above justifies several observations in response.

First, if the New Testament exegesis and patristic readings above are headed in the right direction, Jesus did not find the concept of eternal conscious punishment intolerable. On the contrary, it was much on his mind and on his lips. Yet his feelings were not cauterized, and while the pressures he faced (e.g., in Gethsemane and at Golgotha) were enormous, he does not seem to have cracked under the strain.

If Jesus bore and passed this teaching on without it driving him to distraction, we should probably assume that he felt his followers would receive the grace to bear it with a comparable solemnity, robust trust in a God who both loves and judges, and resultant zeal for the salvation of sinners like themselves. They were to go into the world teaching all the things that Jesus commanded (Matt. 28:20). There is no reason to suppose that he granted them a bye when it came to this doctrine. Nor does it seem likely that Jesus' teaching allows for times to come when Christians more humane than Christ might be permitted to improve on his too-stern beliefs.

Second, while Stott's warning about emotional hardening is salutary, there is another sort of cauterization and cracking to which we are equally subject. If one kind of hell is found in the Bible's story of a loving but zealous God who consigns the wicked, whom he deems deserving, to permanent woe, a plausible analogy might be the vacuous moral vertigo in which much contemporary human consciousness languishes. Along with the postmodern loss of a sense of transcendence has come, notoriously, the demise of any tangible sense of right and wrong. There is little ethical firm ground here and now, and there will be no final reckoning, no

---

[83]The words are Tony Gray's in his essay "The Nature of Hell," 234.

[84]Cited in ibid., 233–34; cf. David L. Edwards and John R. W. Stott, *Evangelical Essentials: A Liberal-Evangelical Dialogue* (Downers Grove, Ill.: InterVarsity Press, 1988), 314.

[85]Note, e.g., the grim light in which Harry Emerson Fosdick casts his boyhood belief in the historic doctrine of hell (*The Living of These Days* [New York: Harper & Row, 1956], 33–36). See also from more recent Continental quarters: "The traditional idea of a final judgment at the end of time is hardly viable" (Heinrich Ott, ed., *Die Antwort des Glaubens: Systematische Theologie in 50 Artikeln* [Stuttgart/Berlin: Kreuz Verlag, 1972], 466). "Hell" is at most to be conceived of as "an ultimate remoteness from God" (ibid., 471).

HeLL UNDeR fire

great Day of Judgment, in times to come. The only unpardonable sin left, it seems, is intolerance.

Meanwhile, barbarity of all descriptions rages in on many fronts and may even be growing worse, from child abuse to Internet porn to AIDS-inducing sexual behavior and its genocidal consequences to abortion to idolatrous consumerism to murderous racial or ethnic struggles—most of them religiously based—on virtually every continent. These things are not eternal hell, but they are permanent symptoms of the human condition, and they are certainly hellish. Jesus spoke of a time when "because of the increase of wickedness, the love of most will grow cold" (Matt. 24:12). We suppose we have voted out of office a God who would inflict eternal conscious punishment. Have we replaced him with a weak moral policeman lacking power to pronounce a sentence that the condemned will never cease to feel? In many quarters the answer is, "Yes, and with good riddance."

With the destruction of the World Trade Center towers on September 11, 2001, at least some old certainties were swept aside. Many have acknowledged anew the stark reality of evil. It may well be a time when the infinite heinousness of humans—and our corporate predicament of being able to restrain senseless killing chiefly by additional killing—renders the infinite duration of hell a slightly more thinkable notion. In any case, having just emerged from a century in which the harvest of fresh corpses from war and war-related causes has been put at 187 million,[86] we are in no position to flatter ourselves that the moral sense in which we might ground kinder views of hell is part of a larger movement away from the barbarism of days of yore. We possess limited ground to affirm the moral inferiority of those of former ages who more readily affirmed Jesus' teaching on eternal punishment, and we have to face the possibility that the zeal to reform his doctrine now could be a sign of misguided sentimentality or some other malaise rather than discovery of new meaning in Scripture by eyes having purer moral light.

When it comes to cauterized feelings and cracking under the strain of an eternal conscious hell, it can be replied that a look at any major newspaper reveals horrors that we are equally powerless to rationalize: two dozen blown to death and hundreds injured in a single weekend of suicide bombings in Israel; George Harrison's death from a brain tumor; fifteen people removed from a public bus in Colombia and shot through their heads by far-right paramilitary; forty-nine women slain by an alleged serial killer in the Pacific Northwest of the United States.

Or how about Taliban justice in the Kabul Sports Stadium before a packed crowd in July 1998?[87] Ghulam Farooq, an apprentice ironworker, had been accused of theft.

> More than three years later, Farooq, 26, bowed his head to hold back tears as he described the final minutes before the silent doctor jabbed a hypodermic needle into his hand and put him to sleep.

---

[86]British Marxist historian Eric Hobsbawm as quoted in *Time International* 49 (December 5, 1994): 93.
[87]See sec. 1 of the December 2, 2001 *Chicago Tribune*.

The mullahs already had finished their speeches about justice and the Koran and the will of God. The only sound Farooq remembers hearing as he drifted off were a few shouts from the stands.

"They were crying out to the Talibs not to do it, but they didn't care," he recalled last week.

When Farooq awoke about two hours later, he was in Kabul's Wazir Akbar Khan Hospital, minus his right hand and left foot. He was screaming in pain. The Taliban hung his severed hand and foot on lampposts as a warning to others.[88]

With Stott I affirm that the doctrine of eternal conscious punishment strains our sense of justice. It weighs heavily on our emotions when we ponder the implications. But so does the daily news. Can anyone take it in? Could anyone make sense of things to the world's Ghulam Farooq's? To the bereaved of the suicide bombers in Israel? To the hapless victims of a decadent Western serial killer? To any of their moms and dads?

I conclude that there is a difference primarily in degree rather than in kind between the woes of this world and those of the age to come as portrayed by Jesus Christ. I cannot make sense of any of it, really, and I confess suspicion of anyone who says he or she can. Any, that is, but Christ.

No one seeking theological understanding from Scripture is a stranger to the experience of arriving at more and more unanswerable questions, the nearer one comes to plumbing the depths of divine love and justice. One response to the pain, fears, and frustration of our questions is to allow the sensibilities we absorb from our age to dictate what Scripture can mean. A second response is to defer to the God who has created the world and promises that he is even now redeeming it, and to the Redeemer he has sent to establish the righteousness that all the world longs for. If our best hope is that Redeemer, then our best counsel may be to receive his teachings, undiluted, in the same grave earnest that our sources say he set them forth.

---

[88]Paul Watson, "Taliban Justice: Public Executions and Amputations," in ibid., 9. Other portions of Watson's report are even more harrowing.

Chapter 4

Paul on Hell

Douglas J. Moo

On the basis of a concordance, one might expect an article on Paul's teaching about hell to be very short. In most English versions, the word "hell" never appears in the letters of Paul.[1] And for good reason: Paul never uses the Greek words usually translated "hell" (*geenna* and *hadēs*). But this book is not about the word "hell" but about the doctrine of hell. If that doctrine is defined as teaching about the ultimate destiny of the wicked, then Paul says much about it.

In this chapter, we first will survey what Paul says about hell. Our conclusion is that Paul teaches that God will visit eternal punishment on people who do not respond to God's grace revealed in the gospel of Jesus Christ. Then we will tackle a major contemporary challenge to this conclusion—that Paul teaches that all people will eventually be saved and that hell eventually will have no human occupants (universalism). After dismissing this challenge, we will investigate further the nature of hell in Paul's teaching, dealing especially with the question of annihilationism or conditional immortality. Put simply, we will probe Paul to discover his teaching about the reality of hell, the eternality of hell, and the nature of hell.

The Reality of Hell

Since Paul never uses the Greek words normally translated "hell," we will have to depend on the various ways in which Paul depicts the fate of the wicked to determine what he teaches on this matter. The words he uses to speak of hell make a useful starting point. They are (from most common to least common):

1. "Death," "die" (usually *apothnēskō, thanatos*; Rom. 1:32; 5:12, 14, 15, 17, 21; 6:16, 21, 23; 7:5, 9, 10, 11, 13, 24; 8:2, 6, 13; 1 Cor. 15:21, 22; 2 Cor. 2:16; 3:6, 7; 7:10; Eph. 2:1). Typical is the well-known Romans 6:23: "For the wages of sin is death, but the gift of God is eternal life in Christ Jesus our Lord."[2]
2. "Perish," "destroy," "destruction" (usually *apollymi, apōleia*, three times *olethros*, once *phthora*; Rom. 2:12; 9:22; 14:15[?], 20[?]; 1 Cor. 1:18; 15:18; 2 Cor. 2:15; 4:3; Gal. 6:8; Phil. 1:28; 3:19; 1 Thess. 5:3; 2 Thess. 1:9; 2:10; 1 Tim. 6:9). Typical is Galatians 6:8: "Those who sow to please their sinful nature, from that nature will reap destruction; those who sow to please the Spirit, from the Spirit will reap eternal life."
3. "Wrath" (usually *orgē*, once *thymos*; Rom. 1:18; 2:5, 8; 3:5; 5:9; 9:22; Eph. 2:3; 5:6; Col. 3:6; 1 Thess. 1:10; 2:16; 5:9). Typical is Ephesians 5:6: "Let

---

[1]The NLT is an exception, paraphrasing the "powers" (*dynameis*) of Rom. 8:38 as "the powers of Hell."

[2]Unless otherwise noted, all New Testament quotations are from the TNIV.

HeLL UNDeR fire

no one deceive you with empty words, for because of such things God's wrath comes on those who are disobedient."

4. "Condemn," "condemnation," "judge," "judgment" (all words built on the Gk. root *krin-*; Rom. 2:1, 2, 3, 5, 12; 3:7, 8; 5:16, 18; 8:1; 1 Cor. 11:32; 2 Cor. 3:9; 2 Thess. 2:12; 1 Tim. 5:24). Typical is Romans 5:18: "Consequently, just as one trespass resulted in condemnation for all people, so also one righteous act resulted in justification and life for all."

5. "Curse," "cursed," "eternally condemned" (*anathema, katara*; Rom. 9:3; Gal. 1:8, 9; 3:10, 13; cf. 1 Cor. 12:3; 16:22).[3] Typical is Galatians 3:10: "All who rely on observing the law are under a curse, for it is written: 'Cursed is everyone who does not continue to do everything written in the Book of the Law.'"

6. "Punish" (*ekdikos, ekdikēsis, dikē*; 1 Thess. 4:6; 2 Thess. 1:8, 9). Typical is 2 Thessalonians 1:8: "He [God] will punish those who do not know God and do not obey the gospel of our Lord Jesus."

7. "Trouble and distress" (*thlipsis kai stenochōria*). See Romans 2:9: "There will be trouble and distress for every human being who does evil: first for the Jew, then for the Gentile."

Several comments on this list are in order. First, some may object that many of the instances we have cited do not clearly refer to the fate of human beings after death (e.g., Rom. 5:18 and 6:23, quoted, respectively, under 1 and 4). And the same is true for the concepts of God's wrath (Rom. 1:18; 9:22; Eph. 2:3), the experience of the curse, and the language of "perishing," which Paul sometimes describes as a present condition (e.g., 1 Cor. 1:18; 2 Cor. 2:15). Nevertheless, we have included them as evidence for Paul's view of hell because Paul implies, either in the context or by his use of the same words elsewhere, that the state they describe will continue after death if it is not reversed through faith in Christ. "Death," "condemnation," "wrath," and the "curse" all descended on human beings as a result of Adam's sin. Human beings are, therefore, already in a state of "perishing." This condition is fixed forever for those who do not respond to God's grace in Christ and the work of his Spirit. But it is also clear that the condition that follows final judgment is an intensified form of what unbelievers now experience.

Therefore, as we find in Paul an inaugurated eschatology of life—believers enjoy life now as the first stage of life eternal—so we find an inaugurated eschatology of death—human beings suffer condemnation and wrath now as the first stage of eternal death. This is almost certainly the way we are to explain the sequence in Romans 1:18–2:11. Paul begins by proclaiming that the "wrath of God is being revealed from heaven against all the godlessness and wickedness of

---

[3]Edward Fudge, a prominent annihilationist, argues that "anathema," because it reflects the Hebrew/Old Testament concept "devoted to destruction," implies the extinction of the wicked (*The Fire That Consumes: A Biblical and Historical Survey of Final Punishment* [Houston, Tex.: Providential, 1982], 251–53). But Fudge errs in thinking that the original connotations of the imagery must be present in Paul.

human beings who suppress the truth by their wickedness" (1:18). But he concludes by threatening people who are stubborn and unrepentant with "wrath" on "the day of God's wrath, when his righteous judgment will be revealed" (2:5; cf. vv. 8–9). The latter is typical of Paul, who usually associates God's wrath with the Day of Judgment. Some scholars argue that 1:18 might have a similar focus; they take the present tense "is being revealed" as futuristic.[4] But the parallelism between verses 17 and 18 makes clear that the present tense must be taken seriously: the revelation of God's righteousness in the gospel is needed precisely because God's wrath is also being revealed from heaven.[5]

This "inaugurated eschatology" of judgment is an important consideration in appreciating Paul's teaching about hell. The judgment of hell is not, for Paul, the imposition of a new state of affairs but the continuation and intensification of a situation that already exists. People do not come to the Day of Judgment in a neutral state. They come as people already condemned to death because of their relationship to Adam (Rom. 5:12–21). The verdict of "guilty" and the fearsome reality of punishment for that verdict is the backdrop against which Paul proclaims the good news of Jesus Christ. Only those who have identified themselves with Jesus Christ will be saved from the wrath of final judgment (Rom. 5:9, 10).

Second, the various word groups that Paul uses to depict the fate of unbelievers are interrelated. In the same context, for instance, Paul can shift from "perish" to "condemn" (2 Thess. 2:9–10); from "condemnation" to "death" (Rom. 5:12, 18; 2 Cor. 3:6, 7, 9); from "condemnation" to "wrath" (Rom. 2:1–5); from "punish" to "wrath" to "destroy" (2 Thess. 1:8–10); and from "perish" to "judge" (Rom. 2:12). Clearly Paul uses these different word groups to describe the same reality.

Third, turning to individual words and concepts, we cannot always pin down the exact meaning of the "death" that Paul highlights especially often in Romans 5–8. The background for his use of the language in these chapters is the Genesis 3 account of the Fall (Rom. 5:12–21). In this account, as in Paul's appropriation of it, physical death and "spiritual" death are intertwined in ways that make it difficult neatly to separate.

In Romans 5:14, for instance, the "death" that reigns over human beings between the time of Adam and Moses includes at least physical death. But the parallel between "death" and "condemnation" (cf. Rom. 5:12, 18) reveals clearly enough that "death" also has a spiritual side. Some scholars therefore speak of

---

[4]See esp. H. J. Eckstein, "'Den Gottes Zorn wird von Himmel her offenbar werden.' Exegetische Erwägungen zu Röm 1:18," *ZNW* 78 (1987): 74–89; William Sanday and Arthur C. Headlam, *A Critical and Exegetical Commentary on the Epistle to the Romans*, 5th ed. (ICC; Edinburgh: T. & T. Clark, 1902), 41.

[5]The exercise of this wrath is not simply "permissive," as if God simply allows human beings to take the course they have chosen (contra David Powys, '*Hell*': *A Hard Look at a Hard Question: The Fate of the Unrighteous in New Testament Thought* [Carlisle: Paternoster, 1997], 309–11). The thrice-repeated "God gave them over" (Rom. 1:24, 26, 28) makes clear that God's wrath even at the present time is an active judgment. Powys is to be faulted for constantly seeking to minimize the judicial and punitive aspects of God's wrath and judgment.

Paul's concept here in terms of a "physical-spiritual entity—total death."[6] Since believers undergo physical death and yet enjoy eternal life, it is clear that death does not signify extinction but the "unnatural separation of the person from bodily life."[7] Paul, with other New Testament authors, teaches that all people, including believers, must still experience physical death (e.g., 8:10), the "last enemy" (1 Cor. 15:26). But believers have been rescued from spiritual death through their union with Christ (note the past tense in Eph. 2:1: "You were dead in your transgressions and sins"); and, while having to pass through death, they are assured that they will escape the "eternal death" that unbelievers will suffer.

Fourth, the Greek *krin-* root occupies a broad spectrum of usage in Paul, and it is not always easy to determine which occurrences are applicable to our study. Paul often uses the root, for instance, to refer to the "judgment" that all human beings must face, a judgment whose outcome may be either positive or negative (e.g., Rom. 2:16; 2 Cor. 5:10). We have included above only those occurrences that seem clearly to denote the negative verdict of judgment or the state resulting from that negative verdict.

Despite initial impressions, therefore, Paul's teaching about hell is widespread and clear. People who do not respond to the gospel of Jesus Christ will experience the unambiguously distressing fate that we have outlined above. Nevertheless, rarely, if ever, does Paul devote himself to explicit teaching about hell as a central purpose within his letters. How are we to evaluate this circumstance? Some might cite Paul's failure to provide extended treatment about hell as evidence that the doctrine was of minimal importance to him. Some might go so far as to view the references we have cited above as holdovers from the tradition Paul inherited, concluding that Paul himself was not fully persuaded of the doctrine. But another conclusion is equally tenable: Paul and his readers assumed the doctrine of hell as so basic that he did not need to provide extensive evidence for it. There are good reasons to think that this is the more likely conclusion to be drawn.

While Paul was in some respects a theological innovator, in many other respects he simply built on the theological tradition he inherited. A fairly extensive theological tradition about the fate of the wicked had developed by Paul's day. While the Old Testament does not have a lot to say about the afterlife—and what it does say is disputed—many passages emphasize the reality of God's judgment for sin. At least two (Isa. 66:24 and Dan. 12:2) present that judgment in terms of eternal punishment.[8] Considerable development in the notion of life after death took place in the intertestamental period. To be sure, some Jews focused exclusively on this life as the context for both God's reward and punishment. But more

---

[6]J. C. Beker, *Paul: The Triumph of God in Life and Thought* (Philadelphia: Fortress, 1980), 224; cf. also T. Barrosse, "Death and Sin in Saint Paul's Epistle to the Romans," *CBQ* 15 (1953): 449–55.

[7]John W. Cooper, *Body, Soul, and Life Everlasting: Biblical Anthropology and the Monism-Dualism Debate* (Grand Rapids: Eerdmans, 1989), 214. This point is important in countering annihilationists (see below), who sometimes argue that "death" implies extinction.

[8]See, e.g., Robert A. Peterson, *Hell on Trial: The Case for Eternal Punishment* (Phillipsburg, N.J.: Presbyterian & Reformed, 1995), 21–37; see also ch. 2 in the present book.

typical was an increasing emphasis on resurrection as the point of entry into a far more extensive system of reward and punishment.

Even Jewish theologians who taught a resurrection of the body differed on who would experience that resurrection. Most taught that only the righteous would be raised; some extended the privilege to all Israel, and some to both the particularly righteous and the most notorious sinners. But several Jewish works attest the idea of a general resurrection as a prelude to reward and punishment (e.g., *T. Ben.* 10:8; 4 Ezra 7:32, 37; *2 Bar.* 30:2–5; 42:8; 49:1–51:10).[9] The Pharisees held this last view.[10] Paul, of course, was a Pharisee (e.g., Acts 23:6; 26:5; Phil. 3:5), who expresses his agreement with the notion of a resurrection of both the righteous and the unrighteous (Acts 24:15). We would expect, then, unless we find evidence to the contrary, that this is the position Paul assumed on eschatology, with its teaching about resurrection as the portal to eternal reward and eternal punishment. Moreover, as the previous chapter has made clear, the notion of punishment after death was a staple in the teaching of Jesus; and from him, it made its way into early Christianity. It is this tradition that Paul assumes as common knowledge.

But evidence equally important in appreciating the reality of hell in Paul comes from what he assumes in his repeated emphasis on the need for the preaching of the gospel. Paul makes clear that "salvation" and "life" come only through response to the good news of Jesus Christ (e.g., Rom. 1:16; 10:9–10). He goes to great lengths to proclaim this message (e.g., 2 Cor. 11:22–29) and bemoans the fate of those who do not respond to his message (e.g., Rom. 9:3; 10:1). One cannot adequately explain this passion for preaching the gospel without assuming that Paul believed human beings who did not respond to the gospel face a bleak and extremely distressing fate.

The Eternality of Hell

Few interpreters deny that Paul in some passages teaches the reality of a punishment for the wicked in the afterlife. But a significant number of contemporary scholars minimize this evidence, arguing either that the punishment will be only temporary, followed by restoration to fellowship with God, or that warnings about final punishment serve a rhetorical purpose and do not represent the true heart of Paul's theology.[11] In one way or another, then, these interpreters deny the reality of hell in the sense of irreversible judgment. Put positively, they argue for universalism: the doctrine that all human beings will in the end be saved.

---

[9]See the survey in Murray J. Harris, *From Grave to Glory: Resurrection in the New Testament* (Grand Rapids: Zondervan, 1990), 69–79.

[10]See esp. Josephus, *War* 2.164. Josephus certainly accommodates the Jewish views of his day to standard Greek conceptions; but his reliability on this point is confirmed by other sources. See also the conclusion of E. P. Sanders: Most Jews in Paul's day probably believed in an afterlife of reward and punishment (*Judaism: Practice and Belief, 63 BCE–66 CE* [Philadelphia: Trinity Press International, 1992], 303).

[11]For instance, M. E. Boring notes two strands of passages in Paul—one affirming the reality of eternal judgment, the other universalism—and concludes that they cannot be reconciled ("The Language of Universal Salvation in Paul," *JBL* 105 [1986]: 269–92).

HeLL UNDeR fiRe

Universalism is on the rise in our day. The global village has brought people of different religious persuasions together to an unprecedented degree. Other religions are no longer strange teachings held by people far away in another country; they are the beliefs of people right next door. And as people get to know one another at this level, the claim that Christianity is the only way to salvation begins to sound arrogant. Added to the cultural mix is the postmodern tendency to question absolute truth. Multiculturalism combines with postmodernism to elevate tolerance to the chief of virtues—and hell is the ultimately intolerant doctrine.

If universalism were simply a modern cultural phenomenon with no basis in the biblical text, it would be easy to dismiss. But, in fact, several key texts in Scripture appear to provide initial support for the idea, and most of the texts are in Paul's letters. We must deal with these texts to defend the doctrine of hell that we presented in the first part of this essay. For if Paul's theological position is universalistic, hell has no ultimate place in his eschatological landscape. Universalism finds ostensible support in five key Pauline texts.

1 Corinthians 15:20–28

In his spirited defense of the doctrine of the resurrection of the dead, Paul appeals first of all to the reality and fundamental importance of the resurrection of Christ (1 Cor. 15:12–19): "And if Christ has not been raised, your faith is futile; you are still in your sins" (v. 17). In verses 20–28, Paul goes on to argue positively that the resurrection of Christ is the "firstfruits," the inaugural stage in the program of eschatological resurrection. In other words, God's raising Christ from the dead guarantees the resurrection of all who belong to him and is the first stage in the ultimate conquering of death, "the last enemy." Paul, therefore, affirms that "in Christ all will be made alive" (v. 22) and that everything will ultimately be subjected to God, so that he might be "all in all" (v. 28).

Here, according to some interpreters, Paul expresses his characteristic optimism about the ultimate fate of the world. Borrowing from Jewish apocalyptic, Paul teaches a future universal extent of God's life-giving power. For God to reclaim his sovereignty over creation, he must bestow on all human beings a new resurrection life, a life that conquers death itself.[12] But this conclusion is not warranted by the text. Paul's claim in 1 Corinthians 15:22 that "in Christ all will be made alive" is occasionally taken to refer to the general resurrection of the dead.[13] But even if this is Paul's reference, universalism does not follow, for a universal resurrection does not entail universal salvation. The New Testament clearly affirms that all people will be raised, but some will be raised not to eternal life but to eternal condemnation (see John 5:29).

More importantly, however, it is unlikely that verse 22 refers to a universal resurrection. "In Christ all will be made alive" is interpreted in verse 23: "But in

---

[12]See, e.g., Arland J. Hultgren, *Paul's Gospel and Mission: The Outlook from His Letter to the Romans* (Philadelphia: Fortress, 1985), 104.

[13]E.g., Robert D. Culver, "A Neglected Millennial Passage from St. Paul," *BSac* 113 (1956): 141–52.

this order: Christ, the firstfruits; then, when he comes, those who belong to him." Paul is thinking in this verse of the resurrection of Christians. Just as all those who belong to Adam die, so all those who belong to Christ will be raised from the dead.[14] Nor is it necessary, for God to be "all in all," for every creature to enter finally into a saving relationship with him. Paul affirms that God's nature and purposes demand that all creatures be finally subject to his authority, but the nature of that submission is not spelled out.

Romans 5:18

Somewhat similar to 1 Corinthians 15:22 is Romans 5:18: "Consequently, just as one trespass resulted in condemnation for all people, so also one righteous act resulted in justification and life for all." Paul again portrays Adam and Christ as the two key figures in salvation history, through whom, respectively, came condemnation (or death; see 5:12) and life. Again, Paul paints on a broad canvas, affirming the universal reach of both Adam's trespass and of Christ's "righteous act." But one key difference between these texts is that "life" in Romans 5:18 does not refer to resurrection but to spiritual or eternal life (cf. 5:17, 21). Even more clearly than 1 Corinthians 15:22, then, Romans 5:18 seems to affirm universalism: The extent of eternal life will match the extent of death and condemnation.[15]

In response, we must reiterate at the outset that such a view requires that Paul contradict himself on a rather fundamental point within the same letter, for he affirms unequivocally that the reign of sin and death can be escaped only through the gospel of Jesus Christ. Universalists do not always deny this, but they suggest that some people may be embraced by the power of the gospel only after death. But Paul makes equally clear that the gospel has the power to save only those who believe (e.g., Rom. 1:16–17; 3:21–22) and that judgment will be based on the decisions made in this life (e.g., 2 Cor. 5:10). Indeed, Paul suggests just such a limitation on the scope of the "all" in Romans 5:18b in verse 17: "Death reigns" through the "trespass of the one man" (Adam), but it is only those who *"receive"* God's gift of grace who will reign in life. Human response is required to experience the benefits of God's work in Christ.[16]

---

[14]See esp. William V. Crockett, "The Ultimate Restoration of All Mankind: 1 Corinthians 15:22," in *Studia Biblica 1978: Papers on Paul and Other New Testament Authors* (ed. E. A. Livingstone; Sheffield: Sheffield Academic Press, 1980), 83–87; and also, e.g., Gordon D. Fee, *The First Epistle to the Corinthians* (NICNT; Grand Rapids: Eerdmans, 1987), 749–51; Anthony C. Thiselton, *The First Epistle to the Corinthians: A Commentary on the Greek Text* (NIGTC; Grand Rapids: Eerdmans, 2000), 1224–29. Hultgren objects to this interpretation by arguing that the phrase "in Christ" must be adverbial, modifying "will be made alive" rather than adjectival, modifying "all" (*Paul's Gospel and Mission*, 104). But our interpretation does not require that "in Christ" be adjectival; it simply insists that the word "all" be defined—as it always must be—by the context.

[15]See, again, Hultgren, *Paul's Gospel*, 82–124; and also C. K. Barrett, *The Epistle to the Romans* (HNTC; New York: Harper & Row, 1958), 116–17.

[16]To be sure, there is debate about whether the "receive" in 5:17 is active (humans must act) or passive (humans simply accept what comes to them). But the very introduction of the language, in contrast to the Adam-side of the situation, implies an active response.

Hell under fire

What then does Paul mean by claiming that through Christ there is justification and "life for all"? One possibility is that he is affirming that Christ's work on the cross is of potential benefit to all people. Christ has won for all people "the sentence of justification" and this justification is offered freely to all.[17] But Paul usually uses "justification" language to refer to the actual transfer from the realm of sin and death to the realm of righteousness and life. Probably, therefore, as in 1 Corinthians 15:22, the "all" in the second half of verse 18 refers to "all who are in Christ."[18] This interpretation meshes perfectly with Paul's overall purpose in Romans 5:12–21. He seeks to assure believers of their ultimate salvation (see 5:9–10) by reminding them that Christ has more than cancelled the damaging effects of Adam's sin. All who belong to Adam are condemned. But all who belong to Christ can be absolutely certain of eternal life. Paul is not claiming that all people will be saved but, rather, that all believers will be saved.

Romans 11:26, 32

Paul's defense of God's faithfulness to his promises to Israel in chapters 9–11 climaxes with two sweeping promises: "All Israel will be saved" (11:26a), and "For God has bound everyone over to disobedience so that he may have mercy on them all" (11:32). The latter verse obviously constitutes a problem for the view of hell that we outlined above: If all people will receive mercy in the end, no one will be left in hell. The former verse does not technically suggest universalism, since the promise in it appears to be confined to Israel. But we need at least to glance at it as well, because it is often taken as an indicator that Paul's theology is ultimately universalistic: If all Jews will be saved, will not all people as well?

Careful attention to context and background is indispensable if we are to arrive at an accurate interpretation of these verses. Beginning in 11:12, Paul seeks to stifle the arrogance of certain Gentile Christians (see 11:18, 25) by showing how God is using the unbelief of so many Jews and the salvation of Gentiles to bring salvation again to Israel. As Jews reject the message of salvation in Christ, that message goes out to Gentiles. But their acceptance of the message and inclusion within the people of God are designed to stimulate the Jews to jealousy (11:11, 14, referring to Deut. 32:21, quoted in Rom. 10:19). Some interpreters think that the promise of verse 26, "All Israel will be saved," summarizes this entire process. "All Israel," then, would be a way of referring to all the people of God, Jew or Gentile.[19]

But most interpreters, rightly in my estimation, insist that the context requires that "Israel" have a national rather than a spiritual meaning here. Paul may then be referring to a cumulative effect (it is as Jews come to Christ throughout the church age that "all Israel" is saved) or to a climactic act (in the last days "all Israel"

---

[17]E.g., F. Godet, *Commentary on Romans* (repr.; Grand Rapids: Kregel, 1977), 224–25.
[18]See, e.g., Herman Ridderbos, *Paul: An Outline of His Theology* (Grand Rapids: Eerdmans, 1974), 340–41.
[19]E.g., John Calvin, *Commentaries on the Epistle of Paul the Apostle to the Romans* (repr.; Grand Rapids: Eerdmans, 1947), 437–38; N. T. Wright, *The Climax of the Covenant* (Minneapolis: Fortress, 1993), 249–50.

will be saved). The latter is the more likely view, since 11:26b probably refers to the Parousia.[20] Whatever the exact scenario, what is especially important for our purposes is the background of the phrase "all Israel." As a survey of the Old Testament and Jewish literature quickly reveals, this phrase does not usually refer to all Jews, or even to all Jews alive at a given time. It has a representative significance, as in, for instance, Joshua 7:25, where "all Israel" is said to have stoned Achan. Romans 11:26 gives no support for even a qualified universalism.

Context is also critical to the correct interpretation of Romans 11:32. Paul's focus throughout this section, as we have seen, is on the relationship of Jews and Gentiles. The "all" consigned to disobedience on the one hand (for which, see 1:18–32), and the "all" who receive mercy on the other, are "all nations."[21] The universalism of this verse—as much of the universalism of Romans—is a universalism of people groups, not of individuals.

Colossians 1:20

In Colossians, Paul counters a heretical teaching that diminished the place of Jesus Christ in redemption by emphasizing the importance of other angelic mediators. Colossians 1:15–20, probably reproducing or at least based on an early Christian hymn, responds to such a limitation on Christ's significance by asserting his supremacy in the spheres of both creation (1:15–17) and redemption (1:18–20). At the climax of this passage, Paul asserts that through Christ God has purposed to "reconcile to himself all things, whether things on earth or things in heaven." We find here another verse that is often cited as evidence that all people will eventually be saved and that hell will not therefore exist forever.

Particularly significant in Colossians 1:20 is the language of "reconciliation," which Paul elsewhere applies theologically only to people who are saved (see Col. 1:22; see also Rom. 5:10, 11; 11:15; 2 Cor. 5:18–20; Eph. 2:16). Despite this normal Pauline use of the language, however, it is doubtful that Paul here refers to salvific reconciliation. The objects of the reconciliation in this verse are "all things" (*ta panta*, a neuter construction). This phrase could refer to human beings (see, perhaps, Gal. 3:22), but, with the elaboration "whether things on earth or things in heaven," this is unlikely. Human beings must certainly be included, but Paul uses language that embraces the entire created world (see the somewhat parallel Eph. 1:10).

If this is the case, then the reconciliation of which Paul here speaks is not only the salvific reconciliation enjoyed by those in Christ but includes also the universal "pacification" of the entire universe in Christ.[22] At the minimum, the "all

[20]So most modern commentators. See Douglas J. Moo, *The Epistle to the Romans* (NICNT; Grand Rapids: Eerdmans, 1996), 720–22.
[21]See esp. Stephen Pegler, "The Nature of Paul's Universal Salvation Language in Romans" (Ph.D. dissertation, Trinity Evangelical Divinity School, 2002).
[22]See esp. F. F. Bruce, *The Epistles to the Colossians, to Philemon, and to the Ephesians* (NICNT; Grand Rapids: Eerdmans, 1984), 74–76; Eduard Lohse, *Colossians and Philemon* (Hermeneia; Philadelphia: Fortress, 1971), 59–61; Peter T. O'Brien, *Colossians, Philemon* (WBC 44; Waco, Tex.: Word, 1982), 53–57.

HELL UNDER FIRE

things" must include the "thrones or powers or rulers or authorities" of Colossians 1:16, since the phrase "whether things on earth or things in heaven" clearly echoes "things in heaven and on earth" in verse 16. On the basis of this interpretation, Origen in the early church and others since him have advanced the idea of *apokatastasis*, the ultimate reconciliation of all people and spiritual beings to God (the word itself is taken from Acts 3:21). Yet, as Peter O'Brien points out, this interpretation does not match the teaching of Paul elsewhere about hostile spiritual powers: "These forces are shown as submitting against their will to a power they cannot resist. They are reconciled through subjugation."[23] The final submission of all things to God in Christ awaits the last day (Phil. 2:10–11). Yet the last phrase of the verse suggests that Paul here refers to the "pacification in principle" that took place through the death of Jesus on the cross. God through the cross of his Son provided the basis for the subjugation of all things to himself.

1 Timothy 2:4

The final text sometimes used to support universalism in Paul is 1 Timothy 2:4, with its famous claim that God "wants all people to be saved and to come to a knowledge of the truth." Universalists argue that an omnipotent God will surely accomplish what he "wishes." If God wants all people to be saved, then all people will be saved—whether through faith in this life, through an encounter with Christ after death, or by some other means.[24] The problem with this interpretation is that Paul teaches quite explicitly in this very letter—indeed, in the next verse—that faith, which Paul confines to this life and limits only to some people, is necessary for salvation (see also 1:16; 3:16; 4:10).

Moreover, it is not at all clear on logical or theological grounds that whatever God "desires" he accomplishes. Theologians since the early days of the church have recognized the need to distinguish between God's "general" will—his "desires," as it were—and his effective will. One must analyze carefully biblical expressions about God's "will" before deciding in which category to place them.

What, then, does Paul mean in this verse? Two interpretations deserve mention. (1) Since Paul seems to be combating in the Pastoral letters a heresy that confined salvation to a select few, the point of verse 4 might be that God extends a gracious offer of salvation to all human beings. Only some, however, will accept.[25] (2) Or Paul might be emphasizing that God's will for salvation extends to "all kinds of people." We have seen that Paul uses universal language in this sense elsewhere (Rom. 11:32), and 1 Timothy 2:1, with its call for prayers to be offered for "everyone" (same Greek words as in 2:4), supports this nuance.[26] A

[23]O'Brien, *Colossians, Philemon*, 56.
[24]See, e.g., John Hick, *Evil and the God of Love* (London: Macmillan, 1966), 378–80.
[25]See, for a recent defense of this view, I. Howard Marshall (in collaboration with Philip H. Towner), *A Critical and Exegetical Commentary on the Pastoral Epistles* (ICC; Edinburgh: T. & T. Clark, 1999), 426–27.
[26]E.g., George W. Knight III, *The Pastoral Epistles: A Commentary on the Greek Text* (NIGTC; Grand Rapids: Eerdmans, 1992), 307.

decision between these two interpretations is difficult and, fortunately, not necessary for our purposes. Either interpretation does justice to the language in its context and avoids an untenable salvific universalism.

We conclude that none of the verses usually cited as evidence that Paul taught universalism must be interpreted in that way. Could they be so interpreted? Of course—but only by isolating them from the entire fabric of Paul's teaching. But Paul is clear elsewhere about the reality of judgment and wrath for all human beings and that escape from that judgment comes only via a vital connection, by faith, with Christ.

To be sure, John Hick and others argue that the passages in which Paul threatens eternal judgment are just that: threats that will not necessarily come to pass.[27] But Hick ignores Paul's teaching about the desperate condition of humankind because of sin. Only a positive act can rescue people from that condition. So universalism would be consistent with this teaching only if it could be shown that all people will in fact believe. But not only does Paul never suggest universal belief; he also teaches that faith is tied to God's election, an election that clearly does not extend to all human beings (see esp. Rom. 9:22–24).

We must also remember the context in which Paul is writing. The Old Testament emphasizes the contrasting fates of those who align themselves with the God of Israel and those who do not (e.g., Deut. 30:15–20). The distinction between those who will be saved and those who will be punished eternally for their sin is fundamental in Judaism as well. As A. Oepke notes, the idea of a final restoration of all sinners is simply foreign to Paul's Jewish heritage.[28] The claim that Paul breaks away from that heritage to a new insight about universalism at certain key moments in his letters (e.g., Rom. 5:18; 11:32; 1 Cor. 15:20–28) does not explain how Paul in those same letters can continue explicitly to assert the usual Jewish viewpoint. If Paul had truly diverged from that viewpoint, he would have had to make his break much more explicit and argue for it far more consistently. Hell, Paul teaches, is real, and some people will end up there.

The Nature of Hell

Hell exists—people who do not respond to the gospel will go there after death. And hell will always exist—since escape from the consequences of sin is possible only in this life, people who die in their sin will never leave hell. What, then, is the nature of hell? Or, to put the matter another way, what exactly is the fate awaiting those who die apart from Christ?

The historic view of the Christian church is that hell involves unending conscious punishment and exclusion from the presence of God. Challenges to this interpretation have arisen periodically in the history of the church. The dominant challenge in our day is "annihilationism." According to this view, people who die apart from Christ do not experience conscious torment in hell forever. Rather,

[27]John Hick, *Death and Eternal Life* (New York: Harper & Row, 1976), 247–50.
[28]A. Oepke, "ἀποκαθίστημι, ἀποκατάστασις," *TDNT*, 1:392.

hell under fire

after perhaps a period of conscious suffering, they simply cease to exist. This teaching about the destiny of the wicked is closely tied to another view, "conditional immortality." Human beings are not naturally immortal but are given immortality only as a gift from God through Jesus Christ. We would therefore naturally expect that, contrary to believers, who receive the gift of immortality and so live forever, unbelievers would not exist forever.

Proponents of this general interpretation claim that it has strong historical precedent and that it better explains the biblical data about hell. The decisive data for and against this teaching do not occur in Paul. But it is important to establish that, contrary to the claims some have made, Paul's teaching does not at all clearly lend support to the view. In fact, we will find some evidence in Paul that creates difficulties for annihilationism.[29] When this evidence is compared with the clearer evidence of other New Testament passages, we are justified in concluding that it is most unlikely that Paul taught annihilationism.

We will focus on three key issues: the language of "destruction" that Paul uses to describe the final state, the significance of the word "eternal" as it is applied to God's judgment, and the nature of immortality in Paul. Our study of the first two of these issues will be anchored in what may be the most important Pauline text on the doctrine of hell, 2 Thessalonians 1:8–9. In verses 5–10, Paul comforts the Thessalonian Christians, who are suffering persecution, by reminding them that a great role reversal is coming. When "the Lord Jesus is revealed from heaven in blazing fire with his powerful angels" (v. 7), God will reveal his justice. Christians will be granted "relief" while those who are "troubling" the Thessalonians will in turn be "troubled" (v. 6): "He will punish those who do not know God and do not obey the gospel of our Lord Jesus. They will be punished with everlasting destruction and shut out from the presence of the Lord and from the glory of his might" (vv. 8–9). Two questions especially relevant for our discussion need to be answered: (1) Who receives the punishment? and (2) What is that punishment?

(1) The TNIV translation, "who do not know God and do not obey the gospel of our Lord Jesus," implies that Paul has in view one group of people described in two different ways. But other English versions suggest that Paul may have two separate groups in mind; see, for example, the ESV: "vengeance on those who do not know God and on those who do not obey the gospel of our Lord Jesus." This construction does echo the Greek, which repeats the article before "those who do not obey" (*tois mē hypakouousin*). If this is what Paul intends, the two groups might be, respectively, Gentiles and Jews. Paul elsewhere describes Gentiles as those who "do not know God" (see esp. 1 Thess. 4:15), while he frequently accuses the Jews of disobedience (e.g., Rom. 10:16, 21; 11:30–31).[30] But this distinction

---

[29]For convenience sake, I will use this term to embrace any view that posits a cessation of existence for unbelievers. I recognize that some who hold this view are not happy with the label. For instance, in the recent study on *The Nature of Hell* (London: Evangelical Alliance, 2000), put out by The Evangelical Alliance Commission on Unity and Truth Among Evangelicals, the term "conditionalism" is preferred (72).

[30]For this view, see, e.g., I. Howard Marshall, *1 and 2 Thessalonians* (NCB; Grand Rapids: Eerdmans, 1983), 177–78.

is not always maintained in Paul (cf. Rom. 11:32), and the context provides no reason to think Paul would introduce a Jew/Gentile distinction here. The strong Old Testament influence on this whole passage suggests instead that "those who do not know God" and "those who do not obey the gospel" stand in synonymous parallelism. Almost certainly, then, Paul intends to describe one group of people from two perspectives.[31] Who are they? Best claims that the context limits the focus to the persecutors of Christians.[32] But this is most unlikely, for two reasons. First, Paul has moved from pronouncing judgment on the Thessalonians' persecutors (1:6) to a general description of the judgment of God, borrowing extensively from Old Testament theophanic passages. As Chrysostom pointed out long ago, the people are condemned not because they persecuted the Thessalonians but because they refused to acknowledge God.[33] Second, as Wanamaker notes for this passage and Crockett for Paul's teaching generally, a strong dualism pervades Paul's teaching about the respective fate of believers and unbelievers. "The language of verse 8 is that of social exclusion by virtue of contrast with the implied condition of the readers, who are those knowing God and obeying the gospel of the Lord Jesus. Not to be part of the community that knows God and obeys the Lord is to be excluded from salvation itself and condemned to divine retribution."[34] The description is not therefore limited only to the actual persecutors of the Thessalonians, nor is it limited to people who have explicitly rejected the proclamation of the gospel. As Paul elsewhere makes clear, all people have been confronted with knowledge of God and have turned from that knowledge to fashion idols of their own making (Rom. 1:19–23). People in their natural state are those who do not know God and who do not obey the gospel. What Paul says about judgment here, therefore, applies to all those who have not responded to God's grace in the gospel of his Son.[35]

(2) But what is the nature of the judgment that they suffer? Annihilationists, naturally enough, point to the language of "destruction" used here and in many other passages about the destiny of the wicked (see the survey above). Two Greek words or word groups are involved: *olethros* (used here and in 1 Cor. 5:5; 1 Thess. 5:3; 1 Tim. 6:9—these are the only occurrences in the New Testament), and *apollymi/apōleia* (see Rom. 2:12; 9:22; 14:15, 20; 1 Cor. 1:18; 15:18; 2 Cor. 2:15; 4:3; Phil. 1:28; 3:19; 2 Thess. 2:3, 10; 1 Tim. 6:9; cf. also *phthora* in Gal. 6:8). Definitive

---

[31]So most commentators. See, e.g., E. Best, *A Commentary on the First and Second Epistles to the Thessalonians* (London: Adam & Charles Black, 1977), 260; Charles A. Wanamaker, *The Epistles to the Thessalonians* (NIGTC; Grand Rapids: Eerdmans, 1990), 227; Abraham J. Malherbe, *The Letters to the Thessalonians: A New Translation with Introduction and Commentary* (AB; New York: Doubleday, 2000), 400–401.

[32]Best, *First and Second Thessalonians*, 261–63.

[33]Chrysostom, *PG* 62.470, quoted in Malherbe, *The Letters to the Thessalonians*, 400.

[34]Wanamaker, *The Epistles to the Thessalonians*, 228. On the use of this same strategy more broadly in Paul, see William V. Crockett, "Will God Save Everyone in the End?" in *Through No Fault of their Own: The Fate of Those Who Have Never Heard*, ed. William V. Crockett and James S. Sigountos (Grand Rapids: Baker, 1991), 159–66.

[35]Malherbe, *The Letters to the Thessalonians*, 401.

conclusions about the meaning of these words in each case are not easy to attain. But this much can be said: The words need not mean "destruction" in the sense of "extinction." In fact, leaving aside for the moment judgment texts, none of the key terms usually has this meaning in the Old and New Testaments.[36] Rather, they usually refer to the situation of a person or object that has lost the essence of its nature or function.

This is the case even when the words are applied to physical death (as in, e.g., 1 Cor. 10:9, 10 [*apollymi*]; Judith 11:15 [*olethros*]). What is "destroyed" is "life as we know it in this world"; whether this implies extinction is not at all clear and can be decided only after the broader teaching about life after death has been decided. But note that most evangelical annihilationists posit that unbelievers exist for some time after death—so clearly they cannot argue that the language of destruction when applied to physical death must mean extinction. The key words for "destroy" and "destruction" can also refer to land that has lost its fruitfulness (*olethros* in Ezek. 6:14; 14:16); to ointment that is poured out wastefully and to no apparent purpose (*apōleia* in Matt. 26:8; Mark 14:4); to wineskins that can no longer function because they have holes in them (*apollymi* in Matt. 9:17; Mark 2:22; Luke 5:37); to a coin that is useless because it is "lost" (*apollymi* in Luke 15:9); or to the entire world that "perishes," as an inhabited world, in the Flood (2 Pet. 3:6). In none of these cases do the objects cease to exist; they cease to be useful or to exist in their original, intended state. In other words, these key terms appear to be used in general much like we use the word "destroy" in the sentence, "The tornado destroyed the house." The component parts of that house did not cease to exist, but the entity "house," a structure that provides shelter for human beings, ceased to exist.

What particular connotation would this language therefore have in the many passages in both Old and New Testaments where it is applied to God's judgment of the wicked? We have shown that annihilation is not the required meaning; but, of course, it is a possibility. Dan Reid, for instance, notes the many Old Testament passages that present God as the "divine warrior," visiting vengeance and destruction on his enemies (e.g., Isa. 66:15–16).[37] In these texts God is uniformly presented as annihilating his enemies. To Reid, Paul, who undoubtedly borrows from this tradition, probably intends the same thing.

But this does not follow. The language of judgment in the New Testament is drawn from a variety of sources and employs a variety of metaphors. The metaphor of "destruction" may, indeed, be drawn from the divine warrior tradition. But the meaning of that language need not be confined by the parameters of that tradition. The language of "destruction" as a way of depicting the end of

---

[36]Indeed, Best claims that *oletheros* never has the meaning "annihilation" in the LXX (*The First and Second Epistles to the Thessalonians*, 261–62, though he admits Wisd. Sol. 1:14 might be an exception).

[37]Daniel G. Reid, "2 Thessalonians 1:9: 'Separation from' or 'Destruction from' the Presence of the Lord?" A paper read at the November, 2001, meeting of the Pauline Studies Group at the Evangelical Theological Society National Meeting in Colorado Springs, Colorado.

the wicked must be set alongside the other words and metaphors Paul uses to depict this end (see the survey above). Moreover, we must also question Reid's claim that the Old Testament texts teach that Yahweh annihilates his enemies. The divine warrior concept is itself, of course, drawn from the arena of human warfare—where the victorious warrior kills his enemy. But we should not therefore assume that the victory of Yahweh over his enemies must likewise take the form of physical destruction.

We would suggest, therefore, that the "destruction" of which Paul here speaks may just as likely refer to "ruin." In this sense *olethros* would mean not that the wicked simply cease to exist but that they suffer ruin: "an eternal plunge into Hades and a hopeless destiny of death."[38] "Ruin" must be placed alongside other Pauline depictions of the state of the wicked: suffering wrath, spiritual death, tribulation, and condemnation.

Two contextual factors suggest that "ruin" in this sense is the meaning of *olethros* in 2 Thessalonians 1:9. First, the "destruction" is called "eternal." In the nature of the case, a punctiliar action, such as "annihilate," cannot be "eternal." By so qualifying *olethros*, therefore, Paul indicates that it must describe a state ("ruin") rather than an action. Defenders of annihilationism will sometimes respond by arguing that the word "eternal" (*aiōnios* in the Greek) has a qualitative rather than temporal sense; it refers to destruction that lasts "for an age" (*aiōn*, "age," is the root of the word). But even if this were the case, the "age" in question is the age to come—an age that had no end.[39] Nevertheless, most scholars today agree that the word has a mainly temporal significance in our literature.[40]

A more promising way of squaring *aiōnios* with annihilationism, therefore, is to argue that the word refers not to the action itself but to the results of the action.[41] The "destruction" has "eternal" consequences. There is some point to this claim: In other New Testament passages where "eternal" describes a noun of action, it is sometimes the results of the action that are indicated. The "eternal sin" of Mark 3:29, for instance, means "a sin whose consequences last forever" (see also Heb. 5:9; 6:2; 9:12; Jude 7). Nevertheless, even if this is the sense of the word here, one must still ask how a destruction whose consequences last forever can be squared with annihilationism. For eternal consequences appear to demand an eternal existence in some form.

A second reason for thinking that "destruction" refers to the end of any prospect of a meaningful relationship with God is that Paul expands the concept of "destruction" with just this idea: People are "shut out from the presence of the Lord and from the glory of his might" (2 Thess. 1:9b). This TNIV translation, it must be pointed out, reflects a key decision about the meaning of the Greek preposition *apo* that occurs at the beginning of the phrase. The TNIV translators,

---

[38]Oepke, "ἀποκαθίστημι, ἀποκατάστασις," 1:396.
[39]See, e.g., Leon Morris, *The First and Second Epistles to the Thessalonians*, rev. ed. (NICNT; Grand Rapids: Eerdmans, 1991), 205.
[40]See, e.g., H. Saase, "αἰών, αἰώνιος," *TDNT*, 1:197–209; Harris, *Raised Immortal*, 182–83.
[41]E.g., Fudge, *The Fire That Consumes*, 37–50.

HELL UNDER FIRE

following most commentators,[42] take the preposition to denote separation and thus translate as "shut out from." To be sure, other options are possible; it could denote source ("destruction that comes from the presence of the Lord"), cause ("destruction because of, or through, the presence of the Lord"),[43] or even time ("destruction when the Lord comes"). But *apo* is most often used in the New Testament in the sense of separation. Confirming this meaning is the almost certain dependence of Paul on Isaiah 2:10–21:

> Go into the rocks,
>   hide in the ground
> from dread of the LORD
>   and the splendor of his majesty!
> The eyes of the arrogant man will be humbled
>   and the pride of men brought low;
> the LORD alone will be exalted in that day.

> The LORD Almighty has a day in store
>   for all the proud and lofty,
>   for all that is exalted
>   (and they will be humbled),
> for all the cedars of Lebanon, tall and lofty,
>   and all the oaks of Bashan,
> for all the towering mountains
>   and all the high hills,
> for every lofty tower
>   and every fortified wall,
> for every trading ship
>   and every stately vessel.
> The arrogance of man will be brought low
>   and the pride of men humbled;
> the LORD alone will be exalted in that day,
>   and the idols will totally disappear.

> Men will flee to caves in the rocks
>   and to holes in the ground
> from dread of the LORD
>   and the splendor of his majesty,
>   when he rises to shake the earth.
> In that day men will throw away
>   to the rodents and bats
> their idols of silver and idols of gold,
>   which they made to worship.

---

[42]E.g., Best, *The First and Second Letters to the Thessalonians*, 263; Malherbe, *The Thessalonian Letters*, 402–3.

[43]See, e.g., Reid, "2 Thessalonians 1:9," 10–11.

They will flee to caverns in the rocks
and to the overhanging crags
from dread of the LORD
and the splendor of his majesty,
when he rises to shake the earth. (NIV)

Three times in this passage, the wicked are said to hide "from the dread of the LORD and the splendor of his majesty." The wording of the LXX is almost identical in each case to 2 Thessalonians 1:9 (the only difference is that Paul drops *phobos*, translated "dread" in the NIV). The point, then, is this: Paul elaborates the meaning of "eternal destruction" with the idea of being separated from the presence of God.[44] Not only does this suggest that our interpretation of "destruction" is on the right track; it also implies that the people who are the objects of destruction continue to exist in some form. It makes little sense to describe people who have been annihilated as being separate from the presence of God.[45]

In our interpretation of 2 Thessalonians 1:8–9, we have tackled two of the main issues that are raised by the annihilationist viewpoint: the meaning of "destruction" and "eternal." There remains the final issue of "conditional immortality." Many who hold the view we have labeled generally "annihilationism" prefer this way of approaching the matter. They argue that the concept of inherent human immortality is unbiblical, a notion introduced into the church from Platonic philosophy. The Bible emphasizes resurrection, not immortality; and the "eternal life" secured by resurrection is a gift only for the righteous. Unbelievers may, therefore, experience a resurrection (see John 5:29), but that resurrection does not confer on them immortality. Lacking that gift from God, they at some point cease to exist. In this sense, God need not "annihilate" them; his withholding from them the gift of immortality ensures their eventual extinction.[46]

This is not the place to critique "conditional immortality" as a general theological perspective or in terms of the history of the doctrine.[47] We will confine ourselves to some remarks on Paul. At first sight, "conditional immortality" seems to find solid support in the letters of Paul. He affirms that God only is immortal (Rom. 1:23; 1 Tim. 6:15–17) and attributes immortality only to believers as a result of resurrection transformation. In 1 Corinthians 15:52, for instance, Paul proclaims that "the dead will be raised imperishable" (*aphthartoi*, "immortal")— referring clearly to believers only. Murray Harris has shown that Paul uses

---

[44]We are not suggesting that exclusion from God's presence exhausts the meaning of "ruin"; the language of this text (e.g., "punish") and others indicates that the fate of the wicked is not simply deprivation (as serious as that is) but involves a positive infliction of pain as well.

[45]See Peterson, *Hell on Trial*, 80–81.

[46]For this view, see, e.g., Fudge, *The Fire That Consumes*, 263–64; Basil Atkinson, *Life and Immortality* (n.p., n.d.); LeRoy Edwin Froom, *The Conditionalist Faith of our Fathers*, 2 vols. (Washington: Review and Herald, 1966); John W. Wenham, "The Case for Conditional Immortality," in *Universalism and the Doctrine of Hell*, ed. Nigel M. de S. Cameron (Grand Rapids: Baker, 1992), 161–91; Philip E. Hughes, *The True Image: The Origin and Destiny of Man in Christ* (Grand Rapids: Eerdmans, 1989), 398–407.

[47]See Christopher Morgan's chapter on annihilationism in this book.

HeLL UNDeR fire

"immortality" to mean "the immunity from death and decay that results from having or sharing the eternal divine life."[48]

Does this mean, then, that Paul teaches "conditional immortality"? Yes and no. If we define "immortality" as Paul uses the terminology, then the answer is yes. But Paul's way of using the word is not the same as the way the word is usually used in theology. In this broader sphere the word usually has the sense of unending existence. Because Paul's focus is restricted, nothing in his letters denies the immortality of human beings in this broader sense. To be sure, one looks in vain for any clear Pauline affirmations of the idea. But the idea does find biblical support elsewhere, and Paul's claim that both the righteous and the wicked experience eternal rewards and punishments would seem to presuppose the idea.[49]

We conclude that annihilationism finds no clear support in the teaching of Paul and that, indeed, the language of 2 Thessalonians 1:8–9 (not to mention other passages) tends to undercut the notion. The wicked, Paul suggests, do not simply cease to exist; they undergo "eternal ruin," punishment, and exclusion from God's presence as long as the new age shall last.

Conclusion

As we noted at the outset of this essay, Paul never uses the Greek words that are normally translated "hell," nor does he teach as explicitly about the concept of hell as do some other New Testament writers. To some extent, then, our purpose has been a negative one: to show that Paul teaches nothing to contradict the picture of hell that emerges more clearly from other portions of the New Testament. But the evidence we do have from Paul suggests that he agrees with that larger New Testament witness in portraying hell as an unending state of punishment and exclusion from the presence of the Lord. Such a fate is entirely "just," Paul repeatedly stresses (e.g., Rom. 1:18–2:11; 2 Thess. 1:8–9), because human beings have spurned God and merited his wrath and condemnation.

Paul, therefore, presents the judgment that comes on the wicked as the necessary response of a holy and entirely just God. For Paul, the doctrine of hell is a necessary corollary of the divine nature. Negatively, Paul never in his letters explicitly uses hell as a means of stimulating unbelievers to repent. But he does— a sobering consideration!—use it as a warning to believers to stimulate us to respond to the grace of God manifested in our lives (e.g., Rom. 8:12–13).

---

[48]Harris, *Raised Immortal*, 189.
[49]See, e.g., Peterson, *Hell on Trial*, 176–78. On the larger question of immortality in the Bible, see Cooper, *Body, Soul, and Everlasting Life*, esp. 215–17.

Chapter 5

tHe

ReveLatioN

oN HeLL

Gregory K. Beale

The debate over whether the suffering of "hell" in John's Apocalypse endures eternally or for a limited time is complicated by the figurative language of the book. Nevertheless, pictorial language can be interpreted. Metaphorical speech contains a "literal meaning" or, should we say, an author's intended meaning. There are, of course, several thorny questions in this book. For example, does the visionary portion of 4:1–22:5 refer to the future, the past, the present, or a mix of all of these?

Despite such difficult issues, I believe that the answer to the question about John's conception of final judgment is more comprehensible. Revelation 14:10–11; 20:10; and 20:14 are the three most debated passages in Revelation concerning the nature of the final punishment. These passages will be the focus of this exegetical essay, though other relevant passages in the book may be considered tangentially, and in passing I will evaluate the annihilationist view.[1] The goal of this discussion is not only to determine John's concept of "final punishment," but also how it fits into the flow of ideas in the wider context of each passage.

Revelation 14:9–12

And another angel, a third one, followed them, saying with a loud voice, "If anyone worships the beast and his image, and receives a mark on his forehead or upon his hand,

he also will drink of the wine of the wrath of God, which is mixed in full strength in the cup of His anger; and he will be tormented with fire and brimstone in the presence of the holy angels and in the presence of the Lamb.

And the smoke of their torment goes up forever and ever; and they have no rest day and night, those who worship the beast and his image, and whoever receives the mark of his name."

Here is the perseverance of the saints who keep the commandments of God and their faith in Jesus.[2]

In Revelation 14:9 a third angel appears in a vision after the first two (14:6–8). Like them, he also announces judgment, declaring that if people give ultimate allegiance to the beast, they will suffer a much worse death than that which believers were decreed to suffer by the false prophet (13:15).[3] The present tense in "wor-

---

[1]See my commentary, *The Book of Revelation* (Grand Rapids: Eerdmans, 1999), in loc., for more in-depth comment on the various passages in Revelation than this essay allows.

[2]Unless otherwise indicated, this essay uses the NASB translation of the Bible.

[3]Robert H. Mounce, *The Book of Revelation* (NICOT: Grand Rapids: Eerdmans, 1977), 274.

ships" and "receives" connotes that continued worship of the beast and allegiance to him, despite the warning of judgment in 14:6–8, warrants the penalty stated in verses 10–11.[4] Like verse 8, the declaration further elaborates on the nature of the judgment mentioned in verse 7 ("the hour of His [God's] judgment has come").

Revelation 14:10 introduces the consequences of beast worship. Those will be punished who express greater devotion to the beast than to Christ in order to maintain economic security. The punishment fits their crime. Verse 8 has explained that the nations have allowed themselves to drink from Babylon's wine, which has made them desire to cooperate with her economic-religious system. Therefore, since the nations have willingly drunk "from the wine of the passion" for Babylon (14:8), God will make them "drink of the wine of [his] wrath" in demonstration of the "eye for an eye" principle.

The picture of pouring out wine resulting in intoxication indicates the unleashing of God's wrath under which people are completely subjugated through judgment, resulting in extreme suffering (Pss. 60:3; 75:8; Isa. 51:17, 21–23; 63:6; Jer. 25:15–18; 51:7; cf. Job 21:20; Obad. 16). Sometimes the drunken stupor ends in physical death and destruction (Jer. 25:27–33; Obad. 16; Rev. 18:6–9). This imagery is inspired especially by the wording of Psalm 75:8 and Jeremiah 25:15; 51:7. These three texts are grouped together and applied by Jewish exegetical tradition to the wicked who will "drink in the time to come" (*Midr. Rab. Gen.* 88.5; *Midr. Ps.* 11.5; 75.4; cf. *Midr. Rab. Gen.* 16.4).

While the intoxicating effect of Babylon's wine seemed strong, it is nothing in comparison to God's wine. Babylon's wine made the nations submissive to her will only for a temporary time. The effect of her wine will wear off at the end of time. Then the ungodly will become drunk with God's wine. The effect of this wine, however, will not be temporary. God's wine will make the nations submissive to his judicial will forever (see comments on 14:11). The thorough and enduring effect of the judgment is expressed through the portrayal of the divine draught being "mixed unmixed" (*kekerasmenou akratou*).[5] To be "mix unmixed" sounds contradictory, but "mix" refers generally to the preparation of the wine for drinking. It is prepared in full strength. This implies a metaphor of Babylon's wine being mixed with water and diluted in verse 8 (as in Isa. 1:22); that is, her influence is not permanently effective. This anticipates the eternal punishment about to be described in contrast to mere earthly temporary punishments.

The following clause, "in the cup of His anger," reiterates the preceding "he ... will drink of the wine of the wrath of God" in order to emphasize the definitiveness and severity of the last judgment to which all unbelievers are forced to submit.[6] At the last day they will be "tormented with fire and brimstone." As throughout the book, the image of fire is figurative for judgment (1:14; 2:18; 3:18;

---

[4]Ibid., 275.

[5]See Beale, *Revelation*, 760, for amplification of the meaning of this unusual expression.

[6]In 16:19 the repetition of synonyms in the phrase "the cup of the wine of his *fierce anger* [*tou thymou tēs orgēs*]" has the same force; note the same force of the repetitive synonyms in 19:15.

4:5; 8:5, 7–8; 15:2; 19:12).[7] Uppermost in thought is the suffering that results from judgment (see 9:17–18; 11:5; 16:8–9; 20:10).[8] The idea of suffering is emphasized when "brimstone" is added to the image of "fire" (so *pyr* + *theion* in 9:17–18; 19:20; 20:10; 21:8). The combination of the noun "torment" (*basanismos*) and verbal (*basanizō*), both of which appear in 14:10–11, occurs also with the same meaning in 9:5–6 (see also 11:10).

The "torment" is primarily spiritual and psychological suffering, which is the meaning of the word elsewhere in the book with reference to the nature of trials that either precede the Final Judgment or are part of it (9:5–6; 11:10; 18:7, 10, 15; 20:10). The psychological notion of suffering is enforced by the uses in chapter 18, which are synonymous with the emotional pain of "weeping" and "mourning." In mind is thus a "tormenting" of unbelievers' minds by assuring them of their hopeless spiritual plight, which will result in extreme depression.

That the torment takes place not only "in the presence of the Lamb" but also of the "holy angels" suggests that they are not merely present when the judgment occurs, but take part in its execution, though their presence may only be intended to call attention to the Lamb. The point is that those who have denied the Lamb will be forced to acknowledge him as they are being punished "before" him (cf. 6:16). A similar purpose is achieved when Judaism depicts the wicked beholding the reward of the righteous.[9]

The Old Testament Background of the "Smoke of Their Torment Goes Up Forever and Ever"

Together with the conclusion of Revelation 14:10, the portrait of verse 11a is drawn from Isaiah 34:9–10, which describes God's judgment of Edom (LXX): "Her valleys shall be turned into *pitch*, and her land into *brimstone*; and her land shall be as *pitch burning night and day*; and it shall *never* [*ou . . . eis ton aiōna chronon*] be quenched, and *her smoke shall go up*; it shall be made desolate *throughout* her *generations . . .* for a long time [*eis chronon polyn*] . . . desolation will be cast over it"

---

[7]In addition to the above references elsewhere in Revelation, for the picture of fire as figurative for judgment, especially the suffering which results from judgment, note that 17:16 and 18:8 refer to annihilation on the earthly level, as in the Old Testament the metaphors of "fire and brimstone," sometimes together with "smoke," indicate a fatal judgment (Gen. 19:24, 28; Deut. 29:23; 2 Sam. 22:9 ["coals" instead of "brimstone"]; Ps. 11:6; Isa. 30:27–33; 34:9–10; Ezek. 38:22; 3 Macc. 2:5; cf. Job 18:15–17); observe also the addition of "the wrath of the LORD" in Isa. 30:33. For fire as the last judgment that endures forever, see *1 En.* 91:9, 1 QS 2.6–18 and 4.12–14.

[8]Also falling into this category are 19:20; 20:9–10, 14–15; and 21:8, though see discussion below.

[9]Compulsory acknowledgment of God through the process of punishment is expressed in Judaism when the wicked are depicted as beholding the reward of the righteous: *1 En.* 108:14–15; Wisd. Sol. 5:1–5; 2 Bar. 51:5–6; *4 Ezra* 7:85; *Midr. Ps.* 23.7; *Midr. Rab. Lev.* 32.1; *Midr. Rab. Eccl.* 7.14. The apocalyptic belief was that the wicked would be punished, often by fire, in the presence of the righteous (*1 En.* 48:9; 62:12; 108:14–15; Wisd. Sol. 5:1–14; *4 Ezra* 7:93; *Targ. Isa.* 33:17) forever (Isa. 66:22–24; *1 En.* 27:2–3; cf. with *1 En.* 21). Even this belief did not underscore gleeful revenge but drew attention to the truth formerly denied by the unrighteous.

(italics added). Isaiah pictures the historical annihilation of Edom because of her sin. Once destroyed by God's judgment, Edom would never rise again. Likewise, the judgment of unbelievers at the end of time would be absolute and complete.

Like Isaiah 34, the depiction in Revelation 14 may be that of the historical destruction of the last generation of beast worshipers living on earth. If so, the description of Isaiah has been universalized from Edom to all unbelieving nations (cf. Rev. 14:6, 8). Similarly, Judaism applies the description of Isaiah 34:9–10 to Rome's judgment (*Targ. Isa.* 34:9, followed by *Midr. Rab. Exod.* 9.13, and *Midr. Ps.* 18.11).

But it is just as possible, if not probable, that this passage concerns the final judgment of all unbelievers throughout history who have given allegiance to the ungodly world system, which the beast, in his various forms, heads up during the era of the church. In this case, the universalization of Isaiah will be even more radical. As the case with the wording "he drinks" (*pietai*) in verse 10, so the present tense portrayal in verse 11 of the last assize (*ho kapnos tou basanismou autōn ... anabainei, kai ouk echousin anapausin*) is to be taken with future sense: "The smoke of their torment ... *will go up* and *they will have* no rest." Verse 11 in relation to verse 9 could be paraphrased, "[if] they worship the beast ... and if they receive the mark, they will suffer torment and they will have no rest."[10]

There is theological debate, however, about the nature of the Final Judgment. Does the portrayal mean the annihilation of unbelievers so that their existence is abolished forever? Or does it refer to a destruction involving not absolute annihilation but the suffering of unbelievers for eternity? The Old Testament context of Isaiah 34 could support the former view, since there the historical annihilation of Edom is portrayed. Since God's judgment of Edom meant that she ceased to exist, the same meaning appears appropriate to Revelation 14:10–11. Accordingly, the image of continually ascending smoke in Isaiah 34 would serve as a memorial of God's annihilating punishment for sin, the message of which never goes out of date (see Wisd. Sol. 10:6–7; cf. Sodom in Gen. 19:28). Likewise, to an escalated degree, in Jude 7 Sodom is "exhibited as an example in [others] undergoing the punishment of eternal fire."

A Memorial of a Past Judgment or a Sign of an Ongoing Punishment?

The lack of rest "night and day" also has its background in Isaiah 34:9, where, like the smoke, it refers to the enduring effects of the extinction of Edom. In particular, "day and night" (*hēmeras kai nyktos*) in Revelation 14:11 can be taken as a qualitative genitival construction, indicating not duration of time (as does purportedly the accusative construction of the same phrase) but kind of time—the time of ceaseless activity.[11] The lack of rest will *continue uninterrupted* as long as

---

[10]Cf. Steven Thompson, *The Apocalypse and Semitic Syntax* (SNTSMS 52; Cambridge: Cambridge Univ. Press, 1985), 95–96.

[11]E.g., Mark 5:5; Luke 18:7; Acts 9:24; 1 Thess. 2:9; 3:10; 2 Thess. 3:8; 1 Tim. 5:5; 2 Tim. 1:3 (so also the LXX of the following texts: Pss. 21[22]:2; 31[32]:4; 41[42]:3; 54[55]:10; Isa. 34:9; 60:11; Jer. 9:1; 14:17; Lam. 2:18; following the standard Greek grammars of Robertson, 495, and Dana and Mantey, 77, 93; cf. Blass-Debrunner, § 161.2).

the period of suffering lasts, though there will be an end to the period. Therefore, the imagery of Revelation 14:10–11 could indicate a great judgment that will be remembered forever, not one in which people suffer forever.[12]

Nevertheless, two considerations support the view that 14:10–11 evokes eternal, ongoing punishment. First, the parallel of 20:10 refers to the devil, the beast, and the false prophet undergoing the judgment in "the lake of fire and brimstone" where "they will be tormented day and night forever and ever." This does not say that their existence will be abolished forever but that they will suffer torment forever (see comments on 20:10 below). The ungodly suffer the same fate as their three satanic leaders, who represent them.

This identification of the fate of the wicked and their satanic representatives is also supported by the concept of corporate representation in the Old and New Testaments.[13] There is no justification for Edward Fudge's attempt not to identify the fate of those in 14:10–11 with that of their satanic representatives in 19:20 and 20:10.[14] The fact that the ungodly are thrown into the same "lake of fire" as their satanic leaders further confirms this (so 20:15; on the "second death" see discussion below on 20:14). Furthermore, 22:14–15 implies that the existence of the wicked is coterminus with the eternal blessedness of the righteous.

Second, the word "torment" (*basanismos*) in 14:10–11 is used nowhere in Revelation or biblical literature in the sense of annihilation of one's existence (against Fudge, who defines it as "lifeless desolation"[15]). Without exception, in Revelation it refers to conscious suffering on the part of people (9:5; 11:10; 12:2; 18:7, 10, 15; 20:10). In chapter 18 the word alludes to the conscious torment that Babylon underwent *as* she was undergoing earthly destruction at the very end of history. Her earthly torment there perhaps ended when she was finally destroyed as a historical institution (though note our possible qualification of this below).

The various forms of the word "torment" (the *basanismos* word group) elsewhere in the New Testament and LXX, when applied to people, also refer to conscious suffering, not annihilation (see Matt. 4:24; 8:6, 29; 18:34; Mark 5:7; 6:48; Luke 8:28; 16:23, 28; 2 Peter 2:8). The word group occurs approximately a hundred times in the LXX, always referring to conscious suffering (see, e.g., the concordance of Hatch-Redpath, 1:191–92). One exception to this could be Ezekiel 32:24, 30, which may refer only to death, yet there the dead are portrayed as existing after death in their tormented condition (cf. 32:20, 31). Only once in biblical literature is the word applied to something other than people (Matt. 14:24), but even this may be a parallel with the use in Mark 6:48.

Therefore, the genitival phrase "the smoke of torment" (*ho kapnos tou basanis-*

[12]For these arguments see Edward W. Fudge, *The Fire That Consumes* (Houston: Providential, 1982), 295–96.

[13]On which see Beale, *Revelation*, 217–19.

[14]Fudge, *Fire That Consumes*, 304–7. One of the Achilles' heels of Ralph G. Bowles's article discussed below ("Does Revelation 14:11 Teach Eternal Torment? Examining a Proof-Text on Hell," *EvQ* 73 [2001]: 21–36) is the inattention to the parallels between 14:11 and 20:10 and precisely how the latter passage is developing the earlier—which it is.

[15]Fudge, *Fire That Consumes*, 307.

mou) is a mixed metaphor, where "smoke" is figurative of an enduring memorial of God's punishment involving a real, ongoing, eternal, conscious torment. The genitive in the above phrase of 14:11a does not express the source of the smoke ("the smoke arising from [their] torment") but is a genitive of association or reference: "the memorial to [their] torment." The metaphorical meaning of smoke as a memorial is confirmed not only by the Isaiah 34 background but also by Revelation 8:4, where "the smoke of the incense, with the prayers of the saints, went up before God." The smoke there is a picture of the saints' prayers and the continual ascent of the smoke is figurative of continually reminding God of the activity and content of those prayers.

Early Judaism and early Christian literature also expressed the same notion of eternal torment by fire. *Jubilees* 36:9–11 directly links God's burning of Sodom to the burning of the land of sinners and to their "condemnation," which is always "renewed ... in wrath and in torment ... and in plagues and in disease for ever" (though in *Jub.* 30:4 "torments" refer to suffering immediately before earthly death). *Fourth Maccabees* 9:9 pronounces that the evil Antiochus will suffer "eternal torture by fire" (*aiōnion basanon dia pyros*) because of his killing of Jewish saints. *Fourth Maccabees* 10:11 likewise decrees with respect to the tyrant, "for your impiety and murdering you will endure *indissoluble [or indestructible, endless] torments* (*akatalytous ... basanous*)." *Fourth Maccabees* 12:12 asserts that "the divine vengeance is reserving you [Antiochus] for *eternal fire and torments* (*aiōniō pyri kai basanois*), which will cling to you *unto all time* (*eis holon ton aiōna*)." *Fourth Maccabees* 12:19 affirms to the king, "but you, both while living and while dying, he [God] will punish." "Eternal torment" (*en aiōniō basanō*) is reserved for the lawless (*4 Macc.* 13:15).[16]

These are relevant parallels for Revelation 14, since those being punished in 14:9–11 have also persecuted and killed the saints under the lead of a tyrannical beastly king. Furthermore, not only is the idea the same, even the Greek expressions are virtually identical, employing three of the same Greek words: "fire" (*pyr*), "eternal" (*aiōnios*), and "torment" (*basanismos*). Since *4 Maccabees* predates Revelation, it is possible that John partially alludes to it, but if not, the two appear to stand in the same tradition on the Last Judgment. Fudge barely considers *4 Maccabees* in his three chapters on intertestamental literature, merely summarizing it in two brief paragraphs and making no evaluation of it one way or the other.[17] This is a strange omission, since it stands closer to Revelation 14 than any other extrabiblical text.

The Picture of Those Who "Have No Rest Day and Night"

The adverbial classification of the phrase "day and night" (*hēmeras kai nyktos*) in the second part of Revelation 14:11 clarifies the ceaseless nature of the restlessness

---

[16]For an ongoing, eternal and conscious suffering in fire see *Apoc. Peter* 6—13: e.g., ch. 7 (Ethiopic) reads, "the fire of their punishment ... we did not know that we would come into everlasting torture ... they are tormented without rest, as they feel their pains ... [we] did not believe that we would come to this place of eternal judgment" (cf. also *Apoc. Peter* 32 [Akmim]).

[17]Fudge, *Fire That Consumes*, 153.

(i.e., a qualitative genitive; sometimes the phrase is in parallelism with such words as "unceasingly," "continually," etc. [Isa. 60:11; Jer. 14:17; Lam. 2:18; 2 Tim. 1:3]). There will be no rest as long as the duration of the suffering continues. Fudge argues that this time of suffering does not last forever.[18] While it is true that the idea of ceaseless activity more than time is intended, the idea of time is nevertheless not lost sight of. In Isaiah 34:9–10 "night and day" (*nyktos kai hēmeras*) is a parallel expression with "unto the age of time" (*eis ton aiōna chronon*), "unto generations" (*eis geneas*), and "unto a long time" (*eis chronon polyn*), which may mean that "night and day" there also alludes to a long duration of time. And, at the least, in context the phrase refers to an *uninterrupted* memorial of Edom's judgment that *lasts for a long time*. Hence, the notion is of a ceaseless activity that endures a very long time.

The only other occurrences of the phrase *hēmera kai nyx* are in Isaiah 60:11 (genitive) and 62:6 (accusative), both of which refer to the eternal blessing of the new Jerusalem. In Isaiah 60:11 it is parallel conceptually with "eternal gladness, a joy of many generations," which appears a few verses later in 60:15 (62:6 has "I have set watchmen day and night, who *never* cease making mention of the Lord"). Likewise, in Revelation 14:11 "day and night" (*hēmeras kai nyktos*) is parallel with the preceding "unto ages of ages" (*eis aiōnas aiōnōn*), so that the idea expresses a long period of uninterrupted restlessness.

This is further evident in Revelation 20:10, where the phrase "day and night" (*hēmeras kai nyktos*) is directly followed by "unto the ages of the ages" (*eis tous aiōnas tōn aiōnōn*) in explaining the intensity and duration of the torment of the devil, the beast, and the false prophet. The phrase "unto the ages of the ages" (*eis tous aiōnas tōn aiōnōn*) occurs twelve other times in Revelation[19] and always refers to eternity (i.e., God's or Christ's eternal being, God or the saints' eternal reign; 19:3 is a parallel to 14:11). In particular, the expression describing the eternal duration of the punishment in 20:10 appears to be balanced antithetically by the identical phrase describing the eternal duration of the saints' reign in 22:5.

This analysis is supported not only by observing that the temporal expression "day and night" (*hēmeras kai nyktos*) clearly refers to ceaseless activity that endures for eternity in 20:10, but the identical sense is strongly implied in 7:15 and 4:8. In 7:15 the clause alludes to the worship of the whole congregation of saints in God's temple in the new creation at the end of the age. The expression is part of a larger portrayal of the heavenly relief saints have from their former hardships while on earth (in parallelism with 14:13). Such worship and relief will continue forever. The recollection that 7:15 is an allusion to Ezekiel 37:26–28 confirms the eternal perspective: "I [God] will make ... an *everlasting* covenant with them ... and will set My sanctuary in their midst *forever*. And My dwelling place also will be with them ... when My dwelling place is in their midst *forever*" (italics added).

The phrase "the smoke of their torment goes up forever and ever" (Rev. 14:11) is not a mere reminder of past judgment, but ongoing judgment as well. It

---

[18]Ibid., 299–300.
[19]See 1:6, 18; 4:9, 10; 5:13; 7:12; 10:6; 11:15; 15:7; 19:3; 20:10; 22:5.

HeLL UNDeR fire

is not the smoke of a completed destruction that goes up, but "the smoke of their torment." The nature of the torment is explained in the second part of verse 11 not to be annihilation but lack of rest. Indeed, annihilation would be a kind of rest or relief from the excruciating torment of the brief, final judgment (those who support euthanasia do so usually because they believe it is merciful to relieve people of pain by annihilating their physical life). Therefore, the smoke is metaphorical of a continued reminder of the ongoing torment of restlessness, which endures for eternity.

That the restlessness endures for an unlimited time is evident from two other uses of "rest" (*anapausis*) and "to rest" (*anapauō*) elsewhere in Revelation. Only two verses later in 14:13 believers find eternal "rest" when they die, which appears as the opposite corollary of the restlessness of unbelievers (though 6:11 mentions that deceased saints "should rest a little while longer," it refers primarily to ceasing from their anxious cries for vindication). Further, the phrase "they have no rest day and night" (*kai ouk echousin anapausin hēmeras kai nyktos*) of 14:11, describing "those who worship" the beast, is a verbatim repetition of the same phrase in 4:8, describing the ceaseless and eternal worship of the cherubim in heaven, which they had been doing at least since the time of Ezekiel 1 (the eternal worship of these heavenly beings is explicitly stated in *1 En.* 39:12–40:5; cf. 61:10–12). As long as God lives, and he lives forever (see Rev. 4:9–10!), the cherubim worship him.

The judgment portrayed in Revelation 14:10–11 is not self-imposed or self-perpetuated by the ungodly,[20] but is inflicted by God and the Lamb, as is clear from 14:14–20 (as well as 6:12–17; 11:18; 16:17–21; 18; 19:2, 11–21). Even if the phrase "unto the ages of the ages" is viewed as not referring to eternity but to "a long, indefinite time," it does not leave room for a classic "annihilationist view," which typically holds that the "torment" and "restlessness" of the last judgment is of short duration and then concluded by absolute destruction because God's justice and mercy could not allow any longer period of suffering.[21]

A punishment of unending restlessness is supported by a series of early Jewish texts: *1 Enoch* 63:1–6 has ungodly, deceased kings begging for "a little respite from his angels of punishment"; they ask, "Would that we had rest," and they plead "for a little rest but find it not . . . [in] darkness . . . for ever and ever." Note also:

- "You sinners will be cursed forever, and you will have no peace." (*1 En.* 102:3)

- "And what will they [sinners] receive and what will they see for ever? Behold, they too have died, and henceforth for ever will they see no light." (*1 En.* 102:8)

---

[20]Against R. H. Preston and A. T. Hanson, *The Revelation of St. John the Divine: The Book of Glory* (London: SCM, 1968), 102–4.

[21]The notion of eternal punishment in 14:10–11 should not be diluted by affirming that the imagery of the verses has only a rhetorical function of warning without conveying any doctrinal idea of a future state of punishment.

- "And the spirits of you who have died in righteousness will live and rejoice, and their [the wicked] spirits will not perish, nor their memorial from before the face of the Great One unto all the generations of the world: wherefore no longer fear their humiliation." (*1 En.* 103:4)[22]
- "And into darkness and chains and a burning flame where there is grievous judgment will your spirits enter; and the great judgment will be for all the generations of the world. Woe to you, for you will have no peace." (*1 En.* 103:8)
- "Burning in much fire . . . they will call death fair, and it will evade them. No longer will death or night give these rest." (*Sib. Or.* 2: 305–8)
- "The deeds of iniquity shall not sleep. And then shall the pit of torment appear . . . the furnace of Gehenna shall be made manifest . . . [the ungodly will experience] there fire and torments . . . for thus shall the Day of Judgment be . . . all shall be destined to see what has been determined (for them). And its *duration shall be as it were a week of years.*" (*4 Ezra* 7:35–44; the latter phrase being figurative, if not for eternity, for a very long period of time)[23]

The Relationship of Revelation 14:11 to 19:3

Ralph Bowles perceptively argues that the parallel of *destroyed* Babylon's "smoke rising up forever and ever" in Revelation 19:3 (cf. also 18:18) establishes that the same picture in 14:11 must refer to a "final, decisive destruction, not ongoing torment."[24] But we must ask, as Bowles rightly addresses in his article, which verse is the ultimate interpreter of the other. Does 14:11 show that the description of 19:3 involves eternal conscious suffering, or does the annihilating judgment of Babylon in chapter 18 demonstrate that chapter 14 refers precisely to the same thing? Ultimately, only the immediate and broad context of both passages can determine this. It is possible that there is an ultimate antinomy between the two texts or that they merely refer to two unrelated realities (though neither Bowles nor I take these routes). Of course, how the context bears on 14:11 is debated.

The analysis of this essay so far, especially the investigation of the immediate syntactical context, points to the probability that Revelation 14:11 involves eternal conscious suffering. The image of "the smoke of their torment" has revealed that this is not a picture of a mere memorial of past annihilation but evidence of an ongoing penal suffering. Thus, the description of the precise nature of the "smoke" is more in depth than in 19:3. Our examination of those who have "no

---

[22]But note that the translation of Isaac, "1 Enoch," in J. H. Charlesworth, *The Old Testament Pseudepigrapha* (Garden City: Doubleday, 1983), 1:83–84, suggests that the whole line concerns the righteous.

[23]So similarly Isa. 66:24; Matt. 25:41, 46; Mark 9:47–48; *1 En.* 10:6–22; 22:10–13; *2 Bar.* 44:12–15; 51:2, 6; *Sib. Or.* 2:284–310. Cf. *1 En.* 91:9, 1 QS II, 6–18 and IV, 12–14, which could fit into either a view of "annihilationism" or of "eternal punishment." See *4 Ezra* 7:75–87, 93–94 for conscious torture during the intermediate state for the unbeliever.

[24]Bowles, "Revelation 14:11," 29.

HeLL UNDeR fire

rest day and night" has further confirmed that the "torment" is ceaseless activity that has no end. Thus, the more detailed and clearer text of 14:11 most likely interprets the shorter and less clear one.[25] In addition to the picture of ascending smoke, what brings 19:3 more in line with 14:11 is the phrase "forever and ever" and the observation that it too is an allusion to Isaiah 34:9–10.

Furthermore, the next closest parallel to 19:3 in 18:18 does not refer exactly to smoke from a completed destruction but from an ongoing destruction: "They saw the smoke of her *burning*" (italics added). Therefore, the combined portrayal of 18:18 and 19:3 is that "her smoke rises up forever and ever," which is almost identical to Revelation 14:11, that "the smoke of their torment goes up forever and ever." The precise point is that the smoke indicates an ongoing punishment in both scenes and not a mere memorial of a past-completed punishment! Bowles would want to say that the "burning" of 18:18 (and destruction of all humans in Babylon) has ceased by the time of the statement of 19:3, but that is not what the text says. True, the word "burning" is left out of 19:3. Nevertheless, the parallel to 14:11 and our interpretation of the parallel indicates that the "burning" begins with Babylon's earthly demise, but the suffering it entails also likely continues eternally according to 19:3. We will also see below that probably the destruction of Babylon did not entail the actual physical death of all of its inhabitants.

This would mean that the Old Testament passages describing the destruction of Babylon or Edom become typological or analogical of eternal punishment. One response to this is that it "totally reverses" and contradicts the meaning of the Old Testament; the meaning of annihilation of existence is transformed into existence, albeit an existence of torment.[26] This is not necessarily, however, a contradiction. If one views eternal death essentially to be existence in separation from God (which I do but annihilationists do not), then a finite physical death that separates a human from others would be a good type of an escalated, infinite spiritual death.

Further, one could argue that it is grotesque and even contradictory that an emblem of a snake or that the death of a heinous criminal could foreshadow the death of Jesus Christ. But that is just what the New Testament portrays (see John 3:14; Gal. 3:13–14)! There are even several passages in the New Testament, including the Apocalypse, that could be categorized as "ironic" or "antithetical typology."[27] In addition to the ones just mentioned, the first sinful Adam, as a "type" of the last sinless Adam, is certainly a potential candidate to be included in this category of "*apparently* contradictory types."

---

[25]Though I suspect that Bowles would say that 19:3 is the more detailed passage (together with ch. 18), indicating clearly the notion of "destruction"; the clear organic parallels between 14:11 and 20:10 add to our analysis of 14:11's syntactical context (on which see discussion above and below). This would indicate either that 14:11 interprets 19:3 or that they deal with different kinds of judgments (on which see below).

[26]Bowles, "Revelation 14:11," 32.

[27]See my chapter, "[The Use of the Old Testament in] Revelation," in *It Is Written: Scripture Citing Scripture*, D. A. Carson and Hugh G. M. Williamson, eds. (Cambridge: Cambridge Univ. Press, 1988), 330–32.

But let us consider an alternative reading of Revelation 19:3 that does not include a notion of eternal suffering. This reading would be more in line with Bowles, yet differing from his judicial annihilationist perspective. It is possible that 19:3 describes *only* the earthly destruction of the Babylonian world system. According to Bowles, this verse represents the decisive annihilating judgment apparently of all humanity, or at least all who would be considered as the authorities and citizens of the Babylonian system. Whether or not the depiction means that everyone was actually "killed," however, is not so clear. It appears that the essential underbelly of the idolatrous economic system is decimated. This would presumably include the death of many, but certainly not necessarily of all in that system.

The Old Testament model of the fall of Babylon, and even possibly of Edom, did not entail the literal death of every inhabitant, but the geopolitical demise of the Babylonian government and the erasing of its culture and way of life. Many Babylonians continued to "live" physically, but their identification as Babylonian citizens and authorities was destroyed and many were deported into exile as slaves. The scene of Revelation 18 appears to follow this Old Testament model (recall also that Israel's destruction in the sixth century B.C. and later in A.D. 70 was like that of Babylon with respect to the fact that many were not killed but the nation's political and economic infrastructure were laid waste and its inhabitants exiled).

Indeed, Revelation 18:6–24 does not once mention the death or destruction of even one individual in Babylon. The destruction that is in focus is the annihilation of the economic system (18:11–14, 17). It is Babylon's "wealth" that "has been laid waste" (18:17). When its inhabitants are described, they are not depicted as slain[28] but as no longer engaged in economic dealings or living according to their former comfortable lifestyle (18:22–23). The destruction of old localized Babylon (and Edom) is typological of an eschatological worldwide system of like nature.[29] Therefore, according to this alternative reading, Bowles's claim that Revelation 18–19 contains "no suggestion that Babylon is defeated while her inhabitants are . . . suffering"[30] appears not to be correct after all.

Consequently, Bowles would have to produce a lot more exegetical analysis to demonstrate that Revelation 19:3 represents the *death* of everyone identified as a part of "Babylon." Even if it did, the portrayal certainly does not speak of the death of all the earth's unbelieving inhabitants, which is evident from those classes of people who mourn over Babylon's fall (18:9, 11, 15). And since it is a judgment of the final wicked living on earth at Christ's coming, it could not include the judgment of people who were identified with Babylon but who had already died in earlier generations or even near to the end. In addition, Babylon's defeat does

---

[28]Though 17:16 says that her opponents "will eat her flesh," it is unlikely that is to be taken literally as cannibalism or even that all in Babylon would die physically.
[29]Note that Mal. 1:2–4 depicts Edom's demise in terms of not annihilating the population so that no more Edomites are left, but of desolating the habitable dwellings and the political and economic structures, which the Edomites will attempt to rebuild again ("we will return and build up the ruins")!
[30]Bowles, "Revelation 14:11," 29.

HeLL UNDeR fire

not include the "beast" and the "false prophet," who are likely not merely two individuals but representative of many (cf. 19:19–21).

This leaves Bowles with the problem that 19:3 is not the "final decisive destruction," even of a part of ungodly humanity, which he claims it is. This leaves a picture of some kind of a punishment, but not one in which there is destruction of the body and soul of every individual in the world *or even of those who compose only Babylon*. The same conclusion may be reached of 14:14–20, which Bowles understands as a like destructive judgment. While the picture of a massive outpouring of "blood" at that judgment likely portrays the death of many, it must be remembered that it is a figurative picture. We need not conclude that it depicts the death of all without exception on analogy with the same kind of picture in Babylon's fall (even Christ's defeat of the nations with a "sword" in Rev. 19 may not necessarily be referring to actual physical death, but an indictment resulting in an imminent declaration of the "second death" in 20:11–15 [see comments below]).[31] Bowles undergirds his annihilationist perspective by consistently attempting a literal "physical" reading of what are clearly figurative judgment scenes. There is always a "literal" reality to these scenes, but to assume that the judgment they all portray entails the physical death of all judged is assuming too much.

Nevertheless, this reading of Revelation 19:3 is still a viable alternative for the view we have put forward so far about 14:11. How so? Babylon's destruction is but the final earthly judgment of that system. The final, ultimate punishment of those in Babylon, both the ones who physically died and those who survived in the midst of the system's demise, will come later. As most commentators acknowledge, Revelation expands on its scenes and themes in each succeeding chapter. Most of the Last Judgment scenes throughout the book describe the last judgment of the generation living on the earth when Christ returns (e.g., 6:12–17; 11:18; 14:14–20; 16:17–21; 18:4–24; 19:17–21).[32]

There are occasional anticipated snapshots of the final, eternal judgment (such as 14:10–11), but the full scenario of that punishment is given in 20:10–15. There we find that all people will be resurrected. Some will be punished eternally while others will receive eternal life. This is the final punishment that 14:11 is describing, especially because of the parallels with 20:10 that introduce the Final Judgment scene. Annihilationist theologians understand this final scene apparently to be of the same destructive nature as the final earthly judgment scenes (though I have questioned whether these earthly scenes are even fully destructive of body and soul). It is more probable, however, that in 20:10–15 not only the effect of the punishment ("death") will be eternal, but so will be the activity of the punishment itself (so that a concept of an eternal "living death" is in mind).[33] This conclusion is based on our study so far of 14:11 and below of 20:10.

---

[31]On which see Beale, *Revelation*, 961–62, 970–71; note the clearly figurative use of "sword" itself that "proceeds out of the mouth" of Christ in 19:15, as well as in 1:16; 2:12, 16.

[32]A commentary on Rev. needs to be written from a consistent "annihilationist" view, since it is sometimes hard to speculate how this perspective would take certain passages in the book.

[33]On which see Beale, *Revelation*, in loc.

It is at this very point that the study of Bowles is imprecise. He wants to say that 19:3 is a definitive destruction (as well as 14:11 by implication), which argues for his overall "annihilationist" position. Not only is he unclear about whether this includes all unbelieving humanity,[34] but then he also must posit another "final, decisive destruction" in 20:11–15 (if this is a resurrection of all throughout history who have died, which is the consensus view). The first earthly destruction was not sufficiently decisive, since 20:13–15 portrays resurrected unbelievers undergoing such a definitive punishment. This punishment is in "the lake of fire," which does not happen until the very end of the age (so 19:20; 20:10; cf. 21:8), after the earthly defeat of the impious at Messiah's last advent.

Therefore, it appears that annihilationists (at least in Bowles's version) must view the final earthly judgments noted above as destroying all living on the earth when Christ returns. Accordingly, 20:11–15 is the same kind of destructive judgment on all the resurrected ungodly who died before the Second Coming who had not yet been destroyed at Christ's coming. The problem with this view is that 20:11–15 is likely a final *judgment of all* who have lived, both unbelieving and believing. Virtually all commentators acknowledge that the scene includes all believers who ever lived. The only way to avoid this conclusion is to say that 20:11–15 refers only to the resurrection of unbelievers who died before the final earthly punishment of the wicked at Christ's return, which is unlikely.

The telltale indication that the scene of Revelation 20:11–15 also refers to all unbelievers is that this is the only judgment whereby people are indicted on the basis of "opened books" and "judged from the things which were written in the books, according to their deeds" (20:12). This courtroom scene is lacking from the earthly judgment scenes, and it is unlikely that it is to be read into them (John 5:28–29 seems to confirm this). There must be a final legal accounting of sins before God that precedes the Final Judgment of all sinners.

If this analysis is correct, then the annihilationist will have to acknowledge two distinct annihilating judgments: a judgment of some unbelievers on earth at Christ's advent and a judgment subsequent to that. This does not result in a coherent view. An additional similar problem with this perspective is that it would seem not to include in "the lake of fire" those defeated on earth at the eschaton. Again, such an image would have to be "read in" to the final earthly judgment scenes, which is possible but is an argument from silence.

The Question of a Possible Chiasm in Revelation 14:11 and Its Bearing on the Issue of Eternal Punishment

It is possible but unlikely that Revelation 14:9–11 forms a type of parallelism known as a "chiasm," as has been recently proposed:[35]

---

[34]He apparently does think so because of the equation that he draws between 19:3 and 14:11, though his position on 14:11 is not necessarily dependent on such an apparent inference.

[35]Bowles, "Revelation 14," 26–28.

HeLL UNDeR fiRe

A If anyone worships the beast and its image, and receives a mark on his forehead or on his hand, (v. 9)

B he also shall drink the wine of God's wrath, poured unmixed into the cup of his anger, (v. 10a)

C he shall be tormented with fire and sulphur in the presence of the holy angels and in the presence of the Lamb. (v. 10b)

C' And the smoke of their torment goes up forever and ever, (v. 11a)

B' and they have no rest day or night, (v. 11b)

A' these worshipers of the beast and its image, and whoever receives the mark of its name. (RSV)

If these lines were in a strict chiastic arrangement, they *might* argue for an annihilationist perspective.[36] There is, however, no verbal parallelism between the proposed inner lines (except for "torment" in C and C') as there is for the outside lines, nor is there a precise thematic parallelism between the inside lines. In particular, such a chiasm would demand that verse 10a ("he also shall drink the wine of God's wrath, poured unmixed into the cup of his anger") is the mutually interpreting parallel to verse 11b ("and they have no rest day or night").

The reason this chiasm has been proposed is to argue that verse 11b does not refer to eternal suffering but a brief point in time at an annihilating final judgment, which the parallel of verse 10a apparently clearly represents (though this itself is questionable).[37] While it is true that both these expressions pertain generally to judgment, that they are precisely about the same aspects of judgment is far from clear. But if they were parallel, it may then be that the clearer eternal perspective of verse 11b is the key to interpreting likewise the more vague temporal expression of verse 10a. Nevertheless, verse 10a appears not to be a temporal statement like verse 11b, so that it is not highlighting the "quenchless" and "unremitting" nature of judgment, as is verse 11b. Furthermore, this means that verses 10b and 11a are not the central elements of any chiasm and are not, therefore, synonymous; "he shall be tormented with fire and sulphur in the presence of the holy angels and in the presence of the Lamb" is not precisely the same thing as "the smoke of their torment goes up forever and ever."

Nevertheless, it is apparent that verses 9 and 11c do form an inclusio, which is a literary arrangement whereby the beginning and ending of a segment are

---

[36]As Bowles, ibid., 26–28, contends.

[37]Even if v. 11b did refer to a definitive judgment at a point in time, possibly it could refer to that ungodly generation living at the very end when Christ returns and who is judged by him on earth at that time. Whether or not this judgment necessarily involves actually killing them on a kind of battlefield or some other kind of judgment is not completely clear. But even if so, the question remains: What happens to the other unbelievers throughout history who have died before this last battle? Quite plausibly, if Rev. 14:11b refers to such a destruction of a last wicked generation, then this would be the prelude to a subsequent judgment of all unbelievers throughout history, which our comments so far and below contend will be an eternal conscious judgment. I think, however, that all of vv. 9–11 refer to the eternal judgment.

almost identical. Such a device helps to delineate literary segments and to indicate the main subject matter of the pericope. As can be seen, the verbal similarity between the outer boundaries of the pericope in verses 9 and 11c are clearly parallel.[38] Any further internal parallels within these boundaries must remain speculative.

In fact, the closest parallels are verses 11a and 11b, which appear to refer to the same "eternal" perspective, though they are in different, parallel positions in the purported chiastic framework. Discerning chiasms is a tricky business, especially when verbal parallelisms are lacking. In such cases the interpretative identification of supposedly corresponding expressions can be a subjective enterprise, not the least when matters of theology are at stake.[39] But even if the chiasm were more apparent, it would not be determinative for the issue at hand, since the parallels could still be interpreted according to either an "annihilationist" or an "eternal suffering" perspective.

Concluding Comments on Revelation 14:11

Verse 12 gives an exhortation to true saints to persevere through temporary suffering because of loyalty to Christ in order to avoid the eternal consequences of loyalty to the beast and receive instead an eternal reward (v. 13). The warning of verses 6–11 intends to motivate believers to persevere. Verses 9–13 follow the pattern of 13:11–18. In the latter passage, mention of the worshipers of the beast and his image who bear the mark on their forehead and hand is followed by reference to the persevering faith of believers, which enables them not to be deceived by the beast. In the same manner, 14:12–13 follows 14:9–11.[40]

The fact of coming judgment against their persecutors also motivates Christians to persevere. This is not a motivation arising from revenge but from a desire that judgment will show their cause to be true and will vindicate the righteous name of God that has been blasphemed by the beast and his allies (cf. 6:10). That judgment as the motivation for perseverance is also in mind is evident by the close links between 14:13, 18 with the saints' prayers for vindication in 6:9–11.

If Christians remain loyal to the Lamb, they will suffer in the present, but afterward they will gain a reward of eternal rest. The desire to persevere is to be motivated not only by the warning of judgment (14:6–11) but also by the promise of reward. Their reward will stand in contrast to the lack of eternal rest that the beast worshipers will experience (14:11). Just as 14:8 and 9–11 were interpretative elaborations of judgment noted in 14:6–7, so 14:13 likewise expands on the statement of persevering faith in 14:12.

---

[38]See N. W. Lund, *Studies in the Book of Revelation* (Chicago: Covenant Press, 1955), 156, who structurally identifies Rev. 14:9–11 as an inclusio. Lund identifies a number of chiasms and other kinds of parallelisms in Revelation but does not identify 14:9–11 as a chiasm. Likewise in his *Chiasmus in the New Testament* (Peabody, Mass.: Hendrickson, 1992), he does not even include discussion of Rev. 14:9–11 in his survey of the Apocalypse.

[39]See Lund, *Chiasmus*, for various examples of chiasms that are suggestive but questionable.
[40]For more, see Beale, *Revelation*, in loc.

HeLL UNDeR fiRe

Revelation 20:10

And the devil who deceived them was thrown into the lake of fire and brimstone, where the beast and the false prophet are also; and they will be tormented day and night forever and ever.

As in Revelation 20:7–8, the devil is highlighted in 20:10 as the one who deceived the nations to attack the saints. The reason for reiterating his deceiving activities is to show that he will undergo judgment because of such deception. The devil will be "cast into the lake of fire and brimstone, where the beast and false prophet are also [or "are also cast"]" (see comments on 14:10 for the Old Testament background of "fire and brimstone"). He is cast into the fire together with, or immediately after, the casting of his two fiendish allies. The probability that 20:7–10 is a recapitulation of 19:17–21 makes unlikely the supposition that he is cast into the fire many ages after his satanic cohorts at the end of chapter 19. Some think that if 20:10 recapitulates the same events associated with the demise of the beast and false prophet, then one would expect more explicit language, such as: "After the battle of Gog and Magog, Satan was thrown into the lake of fire *along with* the beast and false prophet."[41] However, this is not a necessary expectation, since the style of recapitulations in Old Testament prophetic literature is not characterized by such explicitness, nor are the recapitulations elsewhere in Revelation so characterized.

The satanic trinity "will be tormented day and night for ever and ever" (cf. *T. Judah* 25:3, "Beliar . . . shall be cast into the fire forever"). This wording is best taken to mean that they will not be annihilated but will suffer torment, which they will endure endlessly for eternity (for argument that the language of 20:10b cannot connote annihilation but endless suffering see the discussion on 14:10–11). Some, like Fudge, contend that the beast's and false prophet's judgment does not refer to eternal torment but only the absolute end to persecuting institutions. This is based on the idea that they are not personal beings but personifications of oppressive institutions.[42] Even Fudge, however, acknowledges the difficulty of understanding 20:10 as annihilation instead of the eternal torment of *Satan*.[43]

The difficulty with this analysis of the beast's and false prophet's destiny is that it involves a logical fallacy. Institutions are composed of people, so that if the institution is said to suffer something, so will the people composing the institution.[44] We saw above with respect to Babylon that her suffering was not purely

---

[41]So William J. Webb, "Revelation 20: Exegetical Considerations," *The Baptist Review of Theology/La revue baptiste de théologie* 4 (1994): 15–16.

[42]Fudge, *Fire That Consumes*, 303, 307. Likewise, following Fudge, see also David Powys, '*Hell': A Hard Look at a Hard Question* (Paternoster Biblical and Theological Monographs; Carlisle: Paternoster, 1998), 371, 391. I have not found Fudge's subsequent works to add anything substantial to his earlier interpretation of Rev. 20 or Rev. 14 (e.g., see Edward W. Fudge and Robert A. Peterson, *Two Views of Hell* [Downers Grove, Ill.: InterVarsity Press, 2000]).

[43]Fudge, *Fire That Consumes*, 304, 307.

[44]See Beale, *Revelation*, in loc. For the individual-corporate definition of beast and false prophet, see Beale, *Revelation*, ch. 13.

figurative but involved the demise of an economic and social system that caused suffering of people (though not necessarily the death of all).

In support of Fudge, however, it could be argued that institutions can arise from and generate a blindness or false consciousness, which can be personified. "Eternal torment" of such a personification would be a metaphor for its permanent removal, implying torment of those identified with it, in contrast with the blessedness of those set free from it. In this light, the main point would be only a general notion of an annihilating judgment for individuals identified with the ungodly institutions of the beast and false prophet. Accordingly, Fudge believes that to understand the judgment as involving eternal torment is to take the figurative language too literally.

Nevertheless, that individuals are more directly in mind and not merely implied is evident from the following considerations. If the people of God can be referred to as a "city," which will be secure forever (21:2–4), so can oppressing unbelievers be called, or at least included in the image of, the "beast and false prophet," who will suffer forever. There is little basis for Fudge's conclusion that the language of endless torment applied to the devil, beast, and false prophet could mean just that for the devil because he is an individual being, but mean annihilation for the latter two, since they are personifications of oppressive institutions and not representative of individuals (note "*they* will be tormented" in 20:10b!). This is such an inconsistency that it "breaks the back" of Fudge's argument.

Indeed, 14:10–11 and 20:15 demonstrate that unbelieving individuals also suffer the eternal torment of fire. That 14:10–11 also has the phrase "fire and brimstone" as part of the description of humans suffering further identifies 20:10 with an eternal, ongoing punishment of personal beings. Matthew 25:41 corroborates this: "Depart from Me, *accursed ones*, into the eternal fire which has been prepared for the devil and his *angels*" (the latter of which are also personal beings; italics added). The "lake of fire" of Revelation 20:10 is not literal since Satan (and his angels) is a spiritual being.

Therefore, the "fire" describes a punishment that is not physical but spiritual in nature.[45] Neither are "the beast and the false prophet" merely two literal individuals but figurative for unbelieving institutions composed of people. Even the phrase "day and night" is not literal but figurative for the idea of the *unceasing* nature of the torment (see comments on 14:11). Strictly speaking, even the expression "they will be tormented *forever and ever*" is figurative, since the phrase *eis tous aiōnas tōn aiōnōn* literally can be rendered "unto the ages of the ages." At the least, the figurative point of the phrase connotes a very long time. The context of the passage and of the book must determine whether this is a long but limited time or an unending period. Both immediate and broad contexts of the book indicate that the expression refers to an unending period. The "torment" refers to conscious suffering, especially spiritual and psychological suffering (for this meaning of "torment" see comments on 14:10–11).

---

[45]George E. Ladd, *Commentary on the Revelation of John* (Grand Rapids: Eerdmans, 1972), 270.

HeLL UNDeR fiRe

The reality of an unending suffering of Satan, the beast, and the false prophet in 20:10 is borne out by observing that the phrase "unto the ages of the ages" (*eis tous aiōnas tōn aiōnōn*) elsewhere in the book refers to the eternal reign of God (11:15), the eternal power and glory of God (1:6; 5:13; 7:12), the eternal life of God (4:9–10; 10:6; 15:7) or of Christ (1:18), and the eternal reign of the saints (22:5). In particular, the use of the same expression to connote explicitly an unending reign for the saints in 22:5 must mean that the very same temporal phrase in 20:10, only about one chapter earlier, refers to an unending period. That this is a real, ongoing suffering for those represented by the images of "beast and false prophet" is apparent, since the same expression of eternal punishment applies to the *individual* devil in this verse, and since virtually the same expression is applied to the *individual* followers of the beast in 14:10–11.

The phrase "the lake of fire" occurs in 20:10 as well as in 20:14–15 and 21:8. In the latter two texts, the "lake of fire" is called "the second death," that is, the final, eternal punishment, which begins at the time of the consummate destruction and re-creation of the cosmos (so 20:10–15; 21:1–8). Though "lake of fire" does not appear in 14:10–11, there is virtual unanimous agreement (excepting, of course, "annihilationist" commentators) that the portrayal there also refers to the same consummate punishment because of its similar wording, especially with 20:10: "tormented [with fire and brimstone] day and night forever and ever." The first death (= physical death) occurs until the present cosmos is destroyed. All unbelievers suffering the first death are held in the sphere of "death and Hades," which is a temporary, preconsummate holding tank, finally replaced by the permanent, consummate "lake of fire," which is "the second death." The "second death" cannot begin until all have died the first physical death. On any millennial view, the first death will cease at the destruction and renovation of the creation.

Therefore, most likely the punishment of the beast and false prophet in "the lake of fire" (19:20) is the eternal, consummate judgment and occurs at the same time as the eternal, consummate punishment of the devil (20:10) and of unbelievers (14:10–11), the latter of which happens after the close of the Millennium. They all begin to suffer "the second death" together.

Revelation 20:14

Then death and Hades were thrown into the lake of fire. This is the second death, the lake of fire.

What does it mean "death and Hades were thrown into the lake of fire"? Some contend that it refers to deceased unbelieving people who had died and whose spirits had gone to reside in "Hades," the sphere of the dead. At the very end of the age, this sphere will be destroyed, so that those spirits will be annihilated, along with Hades that had housed them. This conclusion, however, is not the most preferable. There are several possible interpretations of this phrase.

(1) Some interpret it to mean that death itself will be annihilated forever, and 21:4 may bear this out: "There will no longer be *any* death" (1 Cor. 15:54–55 and Isa. 25:8 are cited in this respect).

(2) The expression could be a figurative way of saying that in the eternal, consummated state (the first) physical death will no longer be a reality, but only "the second death," which involves endless spiritual and, perhaps, physical torment. Just as Satan, the beast, and the false prophet have lost all of their power as a result of being cast into the fiery lake, so death and Hades have completely lost their power.[46] That "death and Hades" do not represent personal beings who will suffer forever is suggested by the omission of any reference to their "torment" in the "lake of fire."

(3) Alternatively, "death and Hades" may be a metonymy in which the container is substituted for the contained; that is, it is another way of reiterating that unbelievers formerly held in the *temporary* bonds of "death and Hades" will be handed over to the *permanent* bonds of the lake of fire.[47] Verse 15 may support this, where the same precise phrase "were thrown into the lake of fire" is repeated but clearly refers to unbelievers consigned to judgment.

(4) Or, possibly, 20:14 affirms that "death and Hades," as the place of those having suffered the first physical death in the preconsummation age, has come to its end and is now being incorporated with or superseded by the "lake of fire" as the place of those suffering the "second [spiritual] death" in the postconsummation age.[48] Therefore, final, endless perdition now enters in place of the provisional.[49] *Fourth Ezra* also conveys the same idea: "Death is hidden, Hades fled away, corruption forgotten" (*4 Ezra* 8:53) at the time of the latter-day resurrection of the wicked and righteous (7:37; 8:54), which is followed by eternal "paradise" for the righteous (7:36; 8:52), but for the wicked only "the pit of torment," "the furnace of Gehenna," and "fire and torments" (7:36–38).

(5) Just as plausibly "death and Hades" may not be mere abstract regions that retain the bodies of the deceased but actual satanic forces that govern these regions. The combined names appear in Revelation 6:8 to identify the fourth rider (and his associate), who appears to be a personal, satanic agent. The names in 1:18 may also refer to satanic forces defeated by Jesus. That personal beings beginning to suffer torment are represented by "death and Hades" being thrown into the fire is suggested by the reference to the torment of personal beings in everlasting fire mentioned in 14:10–11 and 20:10. If this is correct, it would refer to the eternal punishment of Satan's demonic forces. It is difficult, if not impossible, to conceive of abstract institutions or realms suffering torment (see comments on 20:10).

Any of the above five options are possible, though the third or fourth may be preferable.

The "lake of fire" has already been defined as unending, conscious punishment for all consigned to it (see comments on 20:10; cf. 14:10–11). Now it is also

---

[46]Leon Morris, *The Revelation of St. John*, rev. ed. (TNTC; Grand Rapids: Eerdmans, 1987), 242.

[47]So also J. Webb Mealy, *After the Thousand Years* (JSNTSup 70; Sheffield: Sheffield Academic Press, 1992), 181; for Hades as the region of the dead see J. Jeremias, "ᾅδης," *TDNT*, 1:146–49.

[48]Cf. Moses Stuart, *Commentary on the Apocalypse* (New York: Newman, 1845), 372.

[49]Ernst W. Hengstenberg, *The Revelation of St. John* (New York: Carter, 1853), 2:380.

termed "the second death." This is not a second physical death. The unbelievers undergoing judgment have already died physically and been resurrected (20:5, 12–13). Revelation 20:10 shows that suffering the torment of the "lake of fire" does not involve physical death but suffering that is primarily spiritual in nature, since Satan and his angels are only spiritual beings. Corporeal suffering may be included for unbelieving humans, but only because they suffer spiritually while possessing resurrected bodies that never die physically.

This ongoing suffering must be considered a figurative "second death." A figurative understanding of the "second death" is supported not only by the obviously nonliteral "lake of fire," but also by 20:4–6, which refers to a physical and spiritual resurrection as well as a physical and spiritual death.[50] The qualitatively different first and second deaths are supported also by 21:4 and 21:8. There, physical death is part of the "first things" that "have passed away," which is contrasted with "the lake that burns with fire and brimstone, which is the second death." The reference to "fire and brimstone" in 21:8 identifies the "second death" with the eternal, conscious torment by "fire and brimstone" in 14:10–11 and 20:10.

A facet of suffering the "second death" is also being separated forever from the presence of God who dwells in the "city" of God. The same categories of wicked people who will suffer this death are also said to dwell outside the heavenly city, while the righteous enjoy the blessings of participation in it (cf. 21:8 with 22:15; so also 21:27; 22:14–15, 19). Elsewhere the New Testament can speak of a spiritual death that separates people from God (e.g., Luke 15:24, 32; Eph. 2:1, 12; Col. 2:13).

In Judaism the concept of the "second death" and the phrase itself could refer to the punishment of eternal suffering or, more predominantly, exclusion from the resurrection.[51] This latter meaning could be understood as unbelievers remaining in the grave forever, which would be contradictory to its other usage. Exclusion from resurrection, however, could mean being excluded from the blessings of the resurrection of the righteous. This could allow for a resurrection of the unrighteous in which they pass into punishment instead of endless bliss.[52]

Martin McNamara is correct to see that the phrase in Revelation 20:14 is not referring to a general Jewish concept of the "second death" but derives from Isaiah 65:14–18 and 66:22–24 and its associated Targumic tradition.[53] He supports this from the observation that only two verses after mention of "the second death" in

---

[50]See Beale, *Revelation*, in loc. on 20:4–6, which involves the thorny problem of the timing and nature of the thousand years (the Millennium).

[51]For references supporting the second meaning in the Targums see Deut. 33:6; Isa. 22:14; Jer. 51:39, 57; cf. *Pirke Rab. Eliezer* 34; *Midr. Ps.* 15.6; see Martin McNamara, *The New Testament and the Palestinian Targum to the Pentateuch* (AnBib 27; Rome: Pontifical Biblical Institute, 1966), 119ff.

[52]As in Dan. 12:1–2; indeed, *b. Sanh.* 92a cites Deut. 33:6 and explains it by citing Dan. 12:2, and the conclusion of *Pirke Rab. Eliezer* 34 states that the wicked "*shall arise* for the day of judgment, but they shall not live"; that is, they will not live the kind of resurrection life that God's saints live.

[53]McNamara, *New Testament and Palestinian Targum*, 123–24.

Revelation 20:14, explicit allusion is made to the prophecy of new creation from Isaiah 65:17 and 66:22 (so 21:1). The same allusion is repeated in Revelation 21:4. It is unlikely coincidental that in the *Targum of Isaiah* mention of "the second death" also directly precedes the new creation prophecy (so *Targ. Isa.* 65:6, 15). In addition, "the second death" there is associated with a "fire [which] burns all the day" (*Targ. Isa.* 65:5). The *Targum of Isaiah* 66:24 develops 65:5–6 by concluding that "their spirits [or breaths] shall not die, and their fire shall not be quenched."[54] This is strikingly similar to Revelation 20:10, 14–15, where the wicked are punished forever in "the lake of fire," which is defined as "the second death." The Isaiah background supports further a concept of the second death as a punishment of endless suffering.[55]

Conclusion

Possibly the judgment narrated in Revelation 14:9–11 is only for a future generation living at the end of history, but an analysis of Revelation 13 reveals that worship of the beast occurs throughout history, so that all worshiping the beast during the course of history will also be judged at the end of history. Some affirm, however, that this passage refers not to the unrighteous in general but only to the judgment of "apostates" who compromise with the beast.[56] While it is true that this passage focuses on apostates, the judgment they suffer appears to be the same as that of all the unrighteous as well as of Christ's superhuman opponents and notorious human foes (e.g., the Antichrist).

All of these categories of the ungodly experience "the lake of fire": beast and false prophet (19:20); beast, false prophet, and satanic dragon (20:10); "death and Hades" (20:14); and the unrighteous in general (20:15; 21:8). Some contend, nevertheless, that human unbelievers will not suffer eternally but will be annihilated, since "the second death" is applied only to them (20:14; 21:8; by implication 2:11 and 20:6) and not to God's superhuman enemies, with regard to whom only is attributed endless suffering in the lake of fire (20:10).[57]

This conclusion is improbable for three reasons. First, as we have seen, the precise phrases "torment forever and ever" and "have no rest day and night" are

---

[54]Though *Targum Isa.* 66:24b could be seen as putting a time limit on the suffering: "and the wicked shall be judged in Gehenna *until* the righteous will say concerning them, 'We have seen *enough*'" (following the translation of B. D. Chilton, *The Isaiah Targum* [The Aramaic Bible 11; Wilmington, Del.: Michael Glazier, 1987], 128). The Aramaic here, however, could just as easily read, "and the wicked shall be judged in Gehenna *while* [a possible rendering of ʿad] the righteous will say concerning them, 'We have seen *plenty*.'" But even if the temporally limited reading be favored, one does not need to assume that John would have endorsed every interpretative addition introduced by the Targum, including this last phrase of Isa. 66:24b.

[55]David E. Aune, "The Apocalypse of John and Greco-Roman Revelatory Magic," *NTS* 33 (1987), 495–96, observes that the motifs of the lake of fire together with the second death occur in early Egyptian texts (e.g., *The Book of the Dead*), though he concludes that neither the parallels there nor any possible parallels in the Old Testament, Judaism, or Greco-Roman literature provide the background for Rev. 20:6, 10.

[56]Powys, 'Hell', 366–68.

[57]Ibid., 368–72.

HeLL UNDeR fiRe

applied both to human unbelievers and the beast, false prophet, and dragon (cf. 14:11 and 20:10). Furthermore, the precise phrase "fire and brimstone" occurs both in 14:10 and 20:10, which most likely identifies both the sphere and means (note the preposition *en* [= "in"] in 14:10) of the judgment in chapter 14 to be "the lake of fire and brimstone" of 20:10. Hence, John describes both human and supernatural foes with the same language of "eternal torment" in the same "lake of fire."

Second, it is a logical and contextual fallacy to conclude that since the "second death" is applied only to human foes and not supernatural ones that this means human unbelievers will be annihilated and not supernatural foes like the devil and his angels.[58] This wrongly assumes that "second death" is purely a description of a punishment that is applied to ungodly people but not the devil. While it is likely that "second death" does allude to *punishment*, it is also a further identification of a *place*, "the lake of fire." In both 20:15 and 21:8 "the second death" is directly appended to "the lake that burns with fire and brimstone" in order to identify the latter place in more detail. It is more likely that this further identifies the place where both human and supernatural enemies go for their eternal destiny than that it differentiates the kind of punishments of the two.

It is a typical stylistic pattern of the Apocalypse to mention a phrase early and then add descriptively to it later (e.g., see 4:5; 8:5; 11:19; 16:18, all referring to the Final Judgment). In so doing, John does not alter the meaning in these cases but amplifies it. Therefore, 20:15 and 21:8 merely further define the earlier mention of "the lake of fire" in order to enlarge its original meaning in 19:20 and 20:10 and not to differentiate the nature of the judgments. If the latter were the case, then more would need to have been said by John to make this clear. As the text stands, however, whatever John means by "the lake of fire" and "the second death," it is a place where all the ungodly go to be "tormented forever and ever."

Third, as we have seen with Fudge's argument above, the idea that human unbelievers suffer a less severe fate than that of the beast, the false prophet, and the devil rests on the notion that these latter three figures are not human. Accordingly, it must be argued that in 20:10 the beast and false prophet are personifications of unbelieving institutions that are definitively abolished and that the "dragon" is the only being that undergoes eternal, conscious punishment.[59] As we have argued above, however, it is inconsistent, or at least unusual, to use the identical language of "thrown into the lake of fire and brimstone" and "they will be tormented day and night forever and ever" to describe the end of institutions and, at the same time, the eternal suffering of a personal being. Furthermore, the devil is "thrown into the lake of fire and brimstone, where the beast and false prophet are also"; this appears to indicate that the Devil is joining other personal beings in the fiery lake.

In addition, "the beast and false prophet" do not appear to be personifications of ungodly institutions but metaphors for historical institutions *composed of*

---

[58]Powys attempts to argue this in '*Hell,*' 368–72.
[59]Powys (like Fudge) attempts to argue this in '*Hell,*' 368–72.

actual people. For example, the beast represents ungodly governmental systems that coerce people into idolatry and persecute those not compromising their faith. This is clear from the use of the same metaphor for similar unbelieving nations in Daniel 7, from which John draws his beast metaphor.[60] Likely in mind is the leader of such nations and the loyal subjects represented by the leader (this is known as "corporate solidarity" or "corporate representation"; this is indicated by comparing Dan. 7:17, which compares the "beasts" to "kings," with 7:23, where they are referred to as "kingdoms").

For example, 1 John 2 refers to false prophets as "antichrists" as well as "antichrist" in order to show that they function in solidarity with the "spirit" of the individual Antichrist, who will make his incarnate appearance at the end of history (cf. 1 John 2:18 with 2:22–23; 4:1–3; so almost identically cf. 2 Thess. 2:3–4 with 2:7). The "beast" in Revelation is an image that is much the same as the "one and many" Antichrist figure of 1 John and 2 Thessalonians. The "false prophet" is the same kind of historical figure.[61] Consequently, it is unlikely that the beast and false prophet in Revelation 20:10 do not refer to real personal human beings, both the ultimate leaders and those represented by the leaders, who were a part of history. Thus, the singular beast and false prophet are probably used in such a corporate manner. They together with the devil and his angels will all suffer the same eternal fate.

It is hard not to resist the conclusion that only someone with a prior theological agenda to defend a particular view of divine love and justice could deny that the judgment of all unbelieving humans in Revelation will be different from that of the devil and his angels. Would, for example, an atheistic biblical commentator "without a theological axe to grind" over this issue but with historical sensitivities about ancient authors and texts really see such a difference, especially between the punishments portrayed in chapters 14 and 20?

This essay has attempted to interpret in detail some of John's references to final punishment in their respective contexts in order better to understand the temporal extent of that punishment. It still remains true that Revelation 14:11 and 20:10–15 are the Achilles' heel of the annihilationist perspective. Though some argue that the suffering of unbelievers is temporary, the likelihood is that John believed in an endless judgment of the ungodly.

---

[60]See Beale, *Revelation*, 680–730, for substantiation of the allusion to Dan. 7.
[61]See ibid., 831.

HeLL UNDeR fiRe

Chapter 6

Biblical theology: three Pictures of Hell

Christopher W. Morgan

This chapter endeavors to provide a basic overview of the New Testament teaching on hell with the goal of uncovering its primary depictions. The essay will do so in a rudimentary biblical theology format—by simply citing and summarizing each biblical author's teaching related to hell. There is no need to supply a thorough exegesis of the major New Testament passages on this topic because Robert Yarbrough, Douglas Moo, and Gregory Beale have already provided that in their chapters. In addition, no attempt will be made to interact significantly with the Old Testament teaching on hell since that has already been successfully accomplished in Daniel Block's chapter. Rather the focus here is threefold—to summarize the teaching on hell as portrayed by each New Testament author (which is supplied as a foundation for the average reader but may be skimmed by the scholar), to show how three predominant pictures of hell (punishment, destruction, and banishment) emerge from this survey, and to offer some proposals for interpreting these three pictures.

Hell in the New Testament: A Basic Overview

Each New Testament author addresses the concept of future judgment/hell. Following a modified biblical theology order, this section will highlight the teachings of hell in Mark, Matthew, Luke, Paul, Hebrews, James, Peter/Jude, and John's writings. Along this journey, we will pay special attention to three themes—punishment, destruction, and banishment. Punishment is frequently portrayed as retribution, judgment, suffering, and torment by fire. Destruction is often described as perishing, death, or the second death. Banishment is commonly pictured as separation from the kingdom of God, exclusion from the presence of God, or being cut off from something living.

Hell in Mark

The doctrine of hell does not play a prominent role in the Gospel of Mark. It is central in only one passage—Mark 9:42–48.[1] There Mark records Jesus' teachings about future punishment. First, Jesus stresses that hell is worse than death (it is better to drown in the sea than cause someone to sin and be thrown into hell; 9:42) and earthly suffering (it is better to be on earth maimed than in hell whole; 9:43). Jesus also teaches that hell is a punishment for sin. The overall thrust of the passage communicates, "Stop sinning or else you will suffer the consequences."

---

[1]See also Robert W. Yarbrough, "Jesus on Hell," 74, 82–83.

Mark 9 also instructs us that people in hell are excluded from the kingdom of God and are "thrown into hell" by God (9:45, 47). Notice that although persons are responsible for their sin and the resultant destiny of hell, God is the one who casts them into hell. In addition, hell is a place where the fire never goes out (9:43) and where suffering never ends. The agents of suffering (the worm and the fire) are never extinguished (9:48; cf. Isa. 66:24). The implication is strong: The agents of suffering never end because those in hell experience conscious suffering forever.[2]

Hell in Matthew

The doctrine of hell is a prevalent theme in Matthew. John the Baptist warns people about it. Most importantly, Jesus teaches about it throughout his ministry: in the Sermon on the Mount and the narratives that follow, in his commissioning the twelve disciples, in his parables of the kingdom and the narratives that follow, in the denunciation of the scribes and Pharisees, and in the Mount of Olives Discourse.

Matthew 3 recounts how John the Baptist prepares the way for Jesus. In 3:7–12, he proclaims several truths about final punishment. He warns that hell is a real danger for all who fail to repent—even for Jewish religious elites like the Pharisees and Sadducees (3:7). This future punishment is pictured as the "coming wrath" (3:7) and impending ("the ax is already at the root of the trees" in 3:10). John also cautions that those devoid of good fruit will be "cut down and thrown into the fire" (3:10). Finally, John points to a final separation of the wheat from the chaff, when the chaff will be burned "with unquenchable fire" (3:11–12).

Matthew 5–7 records Jesus' famous Sermon on the Mount. Known mostly for its emphasis on love and the kingdom of God, the Sermon on the Mount also includes some stern teaching about the reality and nature of hell (5:20–30; 7:13–27). In 5:20–30, Jesus contrasts hell with the kingdom of heaven, which cannot be attained unless one's righteousness exceeds that of the scribes and Pharisees (5:20). Hell is a real danger to unrepentant sinners (5:22; cf. 3:7). The "fire of hell" (5:22), the justice of hell (5:20–30; the passage is essentially saying, "Stop sinning or else you will suffer the consequences"), and the extreme suffering in hell (5:29–30) are particularly stressed. As in Mark 9:42–48, the unrepentant are "thrown into hell" by God (5:29) and warned to use extreme measures to avoid being cast into it (5:30).

In Matthew 7:13–27, Jesus brings the Sermon on the Mount to a climax by stressing the importance of entering the kingdom. In doing so, he contrasts the kingdom of heaven with the horrors of hell. Jesus cautions that hell is a place of destruction, depicted as the end of a broad road (7:13). He also contrasts hell with life, shown as the end of a narrow road (7:14). Jesus points out that those devoid of good fruit (the context implies especially false prophets) will be "cut down and thrown into the fire" (7:19) and warns that hell awaits everyone who does not enter the kingdom of heaven (7:21–23). Because of this, hell is a danger for some

---

[2]Robert A. Peterson, *Hell on Trial: The Case for Eternal Punishment* (Phillipsburg, N.J.: Presbyterian and Reformed, 1995), 61–64.

who profess to know Christ but who continue in sin (7:21–23). Here Jesus also depicts himself as Judge and King who personally excludes the wicked from his presence and the kingdom of heaven: "Then I will tell them plainly, 'I never knew you. Away from me, you evildoers!'" (7:23).

Jesus then concludes the Sermon by painting a graphic scene of future punishment. Those who fail to respond obediently to Jesus' message are likened to a house that is built on the sand and ultimately comes crashing down (7:24–27).

In the narrative section that follows the Sermon on the Mount, Jesus again speaks of hell. In 8:10–12 (as well as in 22:1–14, which contains essentially the same teaching on the subject), Jesus warns that the people of Israel who are devoid of faith are in danger of hell ("the subjects of the kingdom will be thrown outside" in 8:12; cf. 22:13). Jesus also portrays hell as "darkness" (8:12; cf. 22:13) and a place of intense suffering, "where there will be weeping and gnashing of teeth" (8:12; cf. 22:13).

Jesus reasserts the theme of future punishment when he commissions his twelve disciples: "Do not be afraid of those who kill the body but cannot kill the soul. Rather, be afraid of the One who can destroy both soul and body in hell" (10:28). In Jesus' parable of the weeds (13:36–43) and the parable of the net (13:47–50), the doctrine of hell again surfaces. Both parables teach the same truths: Hell is exclusion/separation from the kingdom of God (13:40–41, 49–50); it is described as "the fire" (13:40; cf. 3:10–12), "the fiery furnace" (13:42, 50), and a place of suffering, and again depicted as a place "where there will be weeping and gnashing of teeth" (13:42, 50; cf. 8:12).

In Matthew's next narrative section, Jesus offers yet another firm warning about hell. In 18:6–9, he reiterates several truths about hell that are parallel to the passage in Mark 9:42–48. The primary difference for us is that he describes hell as a place of "eternal fire" (Matt. 18:8; cf. the similar thought in Mark 9:43, "where the fire never goes out"). In his denunciation of the scribes and Pharisees, Jesus rhetorically asks them, "How will you escape being condemned to hell?" and shows that hell offers inescapable punishment for the impenitent (Matt. 23:33).

In the Mount of Olives Discourse, Jesus speaks of future punishment in three parables: the parable of the slaves (24:45–51), the parable of the bridesmaids (25:1–13), and the parable of the talents (25:14–30). He then teaches about hell and the final judgment in the section concerning the separation of the sheep from the goats (25:31–46). Jesus teaches several truths about hell in these passages. First, hell is punishment for disobedience to the master (all three parables). It is also graphically expressed as being "cut into pieces," a place where people are placed "with the hypocrites" (24:51), and as a place of suffering, again "where there will be weeping and gnashing of teeth" (24:51, 25:30; cf. 8:12; 13:42, 50; 22:13). Jesus also likens hell to being outside or a place of exclusion/separation (25:10–12, 30; cf. 8:12), a place "outside ... darkness" (25:30; cf. 8:12), a place of personal banishment from his presence and the kingdom ("depart from me" in 25:41; cf. 7:21–23), and a place of just condemnation/punishment (25:41, 46). Hell is then described as a place of "eternal fire prepared for the devil and his angels" (25:41; cf. 18:8 "eternal fire") and of "eternal punishment" (25:46).

Hell in Luke

Like the Gospel of Mark but unlike the Gospel of Matthew, Luke includes some important material on future punishment but does not employ it as a central theme. Some of Luke's teaching concerning hell has already been summarized in parallel Gospel accounts. For example, Luke 3:7–12 parallels Matthew 3:7–12, and Luke 12:5 relates the same account of Jesus' teaching as Matthew 10:28. Luke does not appear to refer frequently to this doctrine in Acts, but he does relate a few fresh insights concerning the future punishment in his Gospel— particularly in Luke 13:1–5 and 16:19–31. In Luke 13:1–5, hell is described as a place for the unrepentant, and those in hell are portrayed as perishing. In Luke 16:19–31, Jesus depicts hell as a place where justice prevails, consisting of suffering, torment, and agony (16:23–25, 27), and as a place of fire (16:24). Jesus graphically illustrates that this future punishment is final and inescapable separation and exclusion from heaven (16:25–26).

Hell in Paul

The word "hell" does not occur in the writings of Paul. But make no mistake, Paul clearly teaches about hell when he addresses the future punishment of unbelievers. Because it would be too cumbersome to highlight all that Paul relates about hell, Romans and 2 Thessalonians will serve as representative—Romans because it illustrates Paul's diverse handling of future punishment, and 2 Thessalonians because it contains Paul's most explicit and thorough teaching on hell.

Romans. In his letter to the church at Rome, Paul from the beginning stresses the necessity of proclaiming the gospel because it is God's appointed means of bringing people to personal faith in Christ. Preaching the gospel is crucial because of the current sinful state of all humanity. Jews and Gentiles alike are all under sin, under God's wrath, and will be judged accordingly. Only those who have faith in Christ will escape God's just judgment. In this portrayal of the predicament of sinners, Paul relates some important truths about the future punishment of the wicked.[3]

(1) In Paul's theology, future punishment is connected to God's wrath. The wicked are presently under his wrath (1:18–32), are objects of his wrath (9:22), continually store up wrath for the day of wrath (2:5–8; 3:5), and can only be saved from this coming wrath by being justified by faith in Christ (5:9–21).

(2) Paul connects future punishment with God's judgment. The wicked are presently and deservedly condemned under the judgment of God, which is impartial, true, righteous, and certain (2:1–12; 3:7–8). This condemnation is the result of sin, is connected to Adam's headship (5:12–21), and is just punishment for sin (6:23).

(3) Paul stresses that future punishment will consist of "trouble and distress." This suffering shows no favoritism between Jews and Gentiles (2:8–11).

(4) Future punishment is often portrayed as "death" and "destruction." Sinners deserve death (1:32), in Adam all die (5:12–21), the wages of sin is death (6:16–23; cf. "perish" in 2:12), as sinners we bear fruit for death (7:5), and those

---

[3]See also Douglas J. Moo, "Paul on Hell," 91–110.

CHRISTOPHER W. MORGAN

who live according to the flesh should expect death (8:13). Paul also asserts that the reprobate are vessels of wrath "prepared for destruction" (9:22; cf. Phil. 1:28, 3:19; 1 Thess. 5:3; 1 Tim. 6:9).

(5) Paul seems to suggest that the present state of sin and the corresponding future punishment is separation from Christ ("cursed and cut off from Christ" in 9:3). Here Paul expresses his desire to be separated from God if that would mean the salvation of his kindred people.

2 Thessalonians. It is in 2 Thessalonians that Paul teaches most directly concerning hell. In the midst of encouraging these believers suffering persecution, Paul stresses that God's justice will prevail (1:5–10). In just these few verses, Paul emphasizes several important truths about hell, and in the rest of the letter, he brings in additional pictures of final punishment. (1) He portrays hell as the result of God's retributive justice on sinners ("God is just. He will pay back trouble to those who trouble you," 1:6). (2) He teaches that hell is punishment/condemnation for those who do not know God and for those who do not obey the gospel (1:8; 2:12). (3) Hell is displayed as eternal destruction (1:9; cf. 2:3, 8, 10). (4) Hell is depicted as exclusion/separation from Jesus' presence and majesty ("shut out from" in 1:9).

Hell in Hebrews

The doctrine of future punishment emerges in two passages in Hebrews (6:1–3 and 10:27–30). Hebrews 6:1–3 refers to the future punishment of the wicked as "eternal judgment" (6:2). Interestingly, eternal judgment is considered a foundational "elementary teaching" (6:1–3). Hebrews 10:27–30 depicts this judgment as fearful and dreadful (10:27, 31), and as a "raging fire that will consume the enemies of God" (10:27; cf. 10:31). Hebrews also clearly teaches that hell comes from God as punishment, judgment, and retribution (10:27–30).

Hell in James

The letter of James does not put much stress on the doctrine of hell, though it does offer some general thoughts concerning the future punishment of the wicked. (1) Unbelievers are said to wither away/be destroyed (1:11). (2) James also asserts that sin produces the offspring of death (1:15). (3) He shows that God is the Lawgiver and Judge, who is able to save and destroy sinners (4:12; cf. Matt. 10:28). (4) James warns that the wicked deserve to be punished severely and that this suffering is indeed coming upon the wicked (James 5:1–5). To portray this graphically, James uses the prophetic judgment imagery of coming "misery," "eating flesh with fire," and the day of slaughter. James even concludes his letter by emphasizing that sinners need to be turned from impending "death" (5:20).

Hell in Peter and Jude

There is no clear teaching about hell in 1 Peter. Debates continue to rage over the interpretation of 3:19. But for our purposes, little can be gained, much time could be wasted, and few truths can be gleaned about hell by devoting significant space there.

140   HeLL UNDeR fiRe

Peter's second letter, however, is filled with references to the future punishment of the wicked in hell. Since Jude closely parallels 2 Peter 2, we will also tie in Jude here. Peter and Jude both depict hell as "destruction" (2:1, 3, 12; 3:7, 9; Jude 5, 10, 11). They both liken hell to condemnation hanging over the wicked (2 Peter 2:3; Jude 4; the contextual reference is to false teachers). Hell is a place like a gloomy dungeon where rebellious angels are held for judgment (2 Peter 2:4; Jude 6 is similar—God has kept rebellious angels in darkness, bound with everlasting chains for judgment on the great day). Peter illustrates the future punishment by referring to the account of Sodom and Gomorrah burning to ashes (2 Peter 2:6) and warns that God holds the unrighteous for the Day of Judgment while continuing their punishment (2:9). It is also noteworthy that Peter unmistakably instructs us that hell is a place of retribution ("paid back" in 2:13) and "blackest darkness" reserved for the wicked forever (2:17; Jude 13). Jude adds to Peter's portrait that hell is the punishment of eternal fire (Jude 7, 15, 23).

Hell in John

The doctrine of hell emerges infrequently in John's Gospel. John's enigmatic style sometimes leaves the reader wondering the full implications of his message. For example, do the contrasting themes of light versus darkness or life versus death at times imply the continuation of the sinful state after death or do they imply future punishment? In any event, three passages clearly teach about the future punishment of unbelievers: 3:16–36; 5:24–29; and 15:1–8. John describes future punishment as "condemnation" (3:17–21; 5:24, 29) and the continuation/culmination of God's wrath on those without faith in Christ (3:36). John also pictures hell as destruction and exclusion—unbelievers cannot enter the kingdom of God (3:3–5), will "perish" (3:16; 10:28), and will be "cut off" from Christ (15:1). Hell is also likened to being thrown away into the fire and burned (15:6–7).

No clear references to hell emerge in the three letters of John. Revelation, however, contains some of the most noteworthy passages on hell in all of Scripture. Revelation 14:9–11, 20:10–15; 21:8; and 22:15 disclose some important truths about hell.[4] In 14:9–11, John asserts that hell is a place where God's fury and wrath are felt at full force (14:10). Hell is also a place of intense suffering—even torment (14:10). John also likens hell to a place with "fire and sulfur" (14:10; cf. a lake of "fire and sulfur" in 20:10, a "lake of fire" in 20:14–15, and a "lake that burns with fire and sulfur" in 21:8) and a place where "the smoke of their torment rises forever and ever" (14:11). This torment is continual: "There will be no rest day or night" (14:11) and "they will be tormented day and night forever and ever" (20:10).

In Revelation 20:10–15, John emphasizes that hell is just punishment for the wicked. He also shows that God casts the devil, the beast, and the false prophet into hell. Notice that they are "thrown" there. They do not rule or have any power there (20:10). Hell will contain everyone whose name is not found in the book of

---

[4]See also Gregory K. Beale, "The Revelation on Hell," 111–34.

life (20:15). John also emphasizes separation as he juxtaposes heaven and hell. This is particularly clear in Revelation 20–22 and especially in 21:6–8. Revelation 21:8 calls hell the "second death." And in 22:15, hell is likened to being outside/banished from heaven.

Three Predominant Pictures of Hell

This brief overview clearly demonstrates that the future punishment of the wicked in hell is a significant theme in the New Testament. It is woven into the whole fabric of New Testament teaching. In fact, future punishment is addressed in some way by *every* New Testament author. Matthew, Mark, Luke, John, Paul, James, Peter, Jude, and the unknown author of Hebrews *all* mention it in their writings. That could not be said of many important biblical truths.

Another observation to be drawn from this overview is that the New Testament teaching concerning hell is somewhat diverse. At times, the pictures of hell even seem irreconcilable. How can burning fire coexist with the blackest darkness, for example? How can someone experience intense torment and yet perish? These presentations of hell should not be viewed as contradictory, however. Instead, they are better understood as complementary. Similar to the way in which different artists highlight varied characteristics of their particular subject, different depictions of hell bring out various shades that a monochromatic rendering could not.

Yet it should be noted that these different depictions of hell did not emerge as one might expect. It would seem plausible to expect that Matthew might focus on one aspect of hell, Mark another, Luke another, and even John another. In some ways, this is correct. Paul incorporates wrath into his doctrine of hell more than the others. James and Peter seem to place more stress on the destruction or death of the wicked. And Matthew places hell in contrast with the kingdom.

But an interesting thing to notice is that overall each New Testament writer's descriptions closely resemble those of the others. In fact, the diverse portraits of hell often come from the *same* biblical writer. Of course, it would be unwise to suppose that we could discover a detailed theology of hell in the brief excerpts on the subject by Mark, Luke, James, Peter, Jude, or the author of Hebrews. That is *not* the point of this chapter. But it is fascinating that similar pictures of hell emerge throughout the New Testament.

The following descriptions of hell recur throughout nearly all New Testament writers. Every author pictures hell as just punishment or judgment. Most also depict it in terms of destruction or death. Most also portray it as exclusion, banishment, or separation. Suffering and fire are often included in the pictures of hell as well, but they are often subsumed under a more prominent idea like punishment or destruction. So the three predominant pictures of hell that emerge from this study are hell as punishment, destruction, and banishment.[5] Each description offers a valuable way of looking at the nature of hell.

---

[5]Some could argue that other prominent depictions like fire could be included. I did not include fire because it is usually subsumed under other pictures—especially punishment and destruction. Though with notable difference in emphasis and some distinctions in terminology,

HeLL UNDeR fiRe

Punishment

The chief description of hell in the New Testament is punishment. That hell is punishment is communicated by every New Testament author. For clear examples, see Mark 9:42–48; Matthew 5:20–30; 24–25; Luke 16:19–31; 2 Thessalonians 1:5–10; Hebrews 10:27–31; James 4:12, 5:1–5; 2 Peter 2:4–17; Jude 13–23; and Revelation 20:10–15.

Three passages are most striking in stressing hell as punishment. In Matthew 25:31–46, Jesus claims the prerogative as the judge who determines the destinies of the world. He consigns the wicked to "eternal punishment" and grants the righteous "eternal life."[6]

In 2 Thessalonians 1:5–10, the apostle Paul encourages believers who are suffering at the hands of persecutors. He comforts them by proclaiming: "God's judgment is right. . . . God is just: He will pay back trouble for those that trouble you. . . . He will punish those who do not know God and do not obey the gospel of our Lord Jesus. They will be punished." In this passage Paul pictures God as the just judge. Hell is dispensed as appropriate retributive punishment on unbelievers.[7]

The apostle John also stresses that hell is just punishment in his familiar account of the final judgment in Revelation 20:10–15. In the end, justice prevails. The wicked are cast into hell, and the righteous experience the unhindered and glorious presence of God on the new earth.[8]

The punishment of hell is depicted as just, consists of suffering (often connected with fire), is conscious, and is eternal.

(1) The punishment is deserved and therefore *just*. The justice of the future punishment of the wicked is axiomatic. Yet for clarity and emphasis, the biblical writers stress the justice of the retributive punishment (i.e., "pay back" in 2 Thess. 1:6; 2 Peter 2:17, etc.) in many passages (see Matt. 5:20–30; 23:33; 24:45–25:46; Mark 9:42–48; Luke 16:19–31; Rom. 1:18–3:20; 2 Thess. 1:5–10; Heb. 10:27–31; James 4:12, 5:1–5; 2 Peter 2:4–17; Jude 6–23; Rev. 20:10–15).

Kendall Harmon follows C. S. Lewis and also proposes these three pictures of hell. See Kendall S. Harmon, "The Case Against Conditionalism: A Response to Edward William Fudge," in *Universalism and the Doctrine of Hell: Papers Presented at the Fourth Edinburgh Conference on Christian Dogmatics, 1991*, ed. Nigel M. de S. Cameron (Grand Rapids: Baker, 1992), 193–224. David Powys also suggests rejection, destruction, and retribution. Unfortunately, he continually strives to minimize the biblical teaching concerning hell as punishment, especially retributive punishment. See David Powys, *'Hell': A Hard Look at a Hard Question* (Paternoster Biblical and Theological Monographs; Carlisle: Paternoster, 1998). When John Benton describes Jesus' teaching on hell, he uses the categories of deprivation, punishment, and disintegration. See John Benton, *How Can a God of Love Send People to Hell?* (Durham, England: Evangelical Press, 1995), 44–53.

[6]For a more thorough analysis of this passage, see Robert W. Yarbrough's chapter, "Jesus on Hell," 76, 82.

[7]For a more thorough analysis of this passage, see Douglas J. Moo's chapter, "Paul on Hell," 103–9.

[8]For a more thorough analysis of this passage, see Gregory K. Beale's chapter, "The Revelation on Hell," 127–32.

(2) The punishment also consists of *suffering*. Those in hell suffer intense and excruciating pain. This pain is likely both emotional/spiritual and physical (John 5:28–29). Hell is a fate worse than being drowned in the sea (Mark 9:42). It is worse than any earthly suffering—even being maimed (Matt. 5:29–30; Mark 9:43). The suffering never ends (Matt. 25:41; Mark 9:48). The wicked will be "burned with unquenchable fire" (Matt. 3:12). Those in hell will be thrown into the fiery furnace and will experience unimaginable sorrow, regret, remorse, and pain. The fire produces the pain described as "weeping and gnashing of teeth" (Matt. 8:12; 13:42, 50; 22:13; 24:51; 25:30). The intensity of the suffering seems to be according to the wickedness of the person's behavior (Rom. 2:5–8). Hell is utterly fearful and dreadful (Heb. 10:27–31). This punishment is depicted as "coming misery," "eating flesh with fire," and "the day of slaughter" (James 5:1–5).

Those in hell will feel the full force of God's fury and wrath (Rev. 14:10). They will be "tormented" with fire (14:10–11). This suffering is best understood as endless since the "smoke of their torment rises forever and ever" (14:11).[9] This suffering is constant because it is said that those in hell "will have no rest day or night" (14:11) and "will be tormented day and night forever and ever" (20:10).

(3) All these depictions make it best to conclude that the punishment is *conscious*. If hell did not consist of conscious suffering, it is hard to see how it could in any meaningful sense be worse than death, be worse than earthly suffering, be filled with weeping and gnashing of teeth, or be a place of misery. These images demonstrate that people in hell will be perfectly aware of their suffering and just punishment.

(4) This punishment is *eternal*. The fire is eternal, the smoke of the torment rises forever and ever, and the instruments of suffering are eternal. More than that, hell is called "eternal punishment" (Matt. 25:46). This eternal punishment is placed alongside "eternal life" in the passage in such a way that the natural interpretation should keep them parallel. The continual nature of the punishment is shown in Revelation 14:11, where it is said that the wicked "will have no rest day or night." Jude 7 speaks of the "punishment of eternal fire." The endlessness of this punishment is also confirmed by the forceful pronouncement in Revelation 20:10, "They will be tormented day and night forever and ever." It is hard to imagine a stronger affirmation of endless punishment than that.[10]

Destruction

Punishment is not the only picture of hell, however. Hell as destruction or death also plays a central role in Scripture. The theme of destruction occurs in the writings of most New Testament authors. The only exception seems to be Mark.

---

[9]For a carefully articulated defense, see Gregory K. Beale's chapter, "The Revelation on Hell," 112–26.

[10]For a more thorough and critical evaluation of conditionalism, the belief that hell is not endless, see my chapter, "Annihilationism: Will the Unsaved Be Punished Forever?" 195–218.

HELL UNDER FIRE

Mark addresses hell in just one passage, however, so it is not at all surprising that he does not allude to hell as destruction (and if Mark 1:24, which speaks of Jesus' destruction of the demons, refers to hell—which is possible but uncertain—then even Mark portrays hell as destruction). Destruction is clearly used as a depiction of hell in Matthew 7:13–14, 24–27; 24:51; Luke 13:3–5; John 3:16; Romans 9:22; Galatians 6:8; Philippians 1:28; 3:19; 1 Thessalonians 5:13; 2 Thessalonians 1:5–10; 1 Timothy 6:9; Hebrews 10:27; James 1:11, 15; 4:12; 5:3–5, 20; 2 Peter 2:6; and Revelation 21:8.

Conditionalists have been quick to point out that the historic view of hell lays most of its stress on hell as punishment and not as destruction. This charge is not without merit. This imbalance may result from the marked emphasis on sin as guilt, salvation as justification, and God as Judge in Protestant theology. With those themes as primary, it seems natural to stress hell as punishment. This imbalance may also have arisen because the more familiar extended passages on hell emphasize punishment more than destruction (i.e., Matt. 25:31–46; Rev. 20:10–15). Hell as punishment is clearly a predominant theme in the New Testament teaching concerning hell and is likely even the major picture of hell (cf. the previous section).[11] But it should not lead us to ignore the other pictures of hell—destruction and banishment.

The more familiar passages portraying hell as destruction are generally smaller in scope and do not develop their teachings. A notable exception is 2 Thessalonians 1:5–10, where Paul stresses hell as punishment but also brings in the picture of destruction, even calling it "eternal destruction" (1:9). It is indeed interesting that the theme of destruction has been downplayed in church history because it is found in many well-known verses. The most-quoted passage in the world says, "For God so loved the world that he gave his one and only Son, that whoever believes in him shall not *perish* but have eternal life" (John 3:16). Romans 6:23 asserts, "For the wages of sin is *death*, but the gift of God is eternal life in Christ Jesus our Lord." Jesus declared in Matthew 7:13–14, "Enter through the narrow gate. For wide is the gate and broad is the road that leads to *destruction*, and many enter through it. But small is the gate and narrow the road that leads to life, and only a few find it." Revelation 20:14 and 21:8 speak of the "*second death*."

The growing emphasis on the theme of destruction has been a factor in the rising popularity of conditionalism. In his case for conditionalism, John Stott highlights Scripture's "vocabulary of destruction" and suggests: "It would seem strange, therefore, if people who are said to suffer destruction are in fact not destroyed; and as you put it, it is difficult to imagine a perpetually inconclusive

---

[11]Harmon, "The Case Against Conditionalism," 193–224. Harmon correctly asserts, "A fully biblical theology of hell must do justice to all three images of hell to which C. S. Lewis draws our attention—punishment, destruction, and exclusion. And here is where the traditional view may be faulted, because it focuses too much on punishment and leaves little room for the other two pictures. At this point the conditionalists' critique of traditionalism should be heard when they insist that some New Testament texts do not speak of eternal torment but instead use different language" (216).

process of perishing."[12] Conditionalist John Wenham argues that when the Bible speaks of the unrighteous' perishing, destruction, and death, it indicates total extinction, utter loss, or complete ruin.[13] Conditionalist David Powys even claims, "Destruction is the most common way of depicting the fate of the unrighteous within the Synoptic Gospels."[14]

These conditionalists correctly remind us that destruction is a central motif in depicting hell in the New Testament. But in their interpretation of the destruction passages, they tend to assume a connotation of extinction or annihilation rather than the more probable sense of loss, ruin, or corruption. D. A. Carson shows this in his critique of Stott's previously-quoted objection: "Stott's conclusion ... is memorable, but useless as an argument, because it is merely tautologous: *of course* those who suffer *destruction* are *destroyed*. But it does not follow that those who suffer destruction cease to exist. Stott has assumed his definition of 'destruction' in his epigraph" (emphasis his).[15]

So then what does hell as destruction signify? Douglas Moo addresses the meaning of destruction in his chapter of this book. He asserts that definitive conclusions are "not easy to attain," but they do not necessarily connote "extinction." Laying aside the judgment texts, Moo points out that none of the key terms usually has this meaning in the LXX or New Testament. Instead, the words usually "refer to the situation of a person or object that has lost the essence of its nature or function." Moo notes that "destroy" and "destruction" can refer to barren land (*olethros* in Ezek. 6:14; 14:16), to ointment that is poured out wastefully (*apōleia* in Mark 14:4; Matt. 26:8), to wineskins with holes that no longer function (*apollymi* in Mark 2:22; Matt. 9:17; Luke 5:37), to a lost coin (*apollymi* in Luke 15:9), or even to the entire world that "perishes," as the inhabited world in the Flood (2 Peter 3:6). Moo concludes, "In none of these cases do the objects cease to exist; they cease to be useful or to exist in their original, intended state."[16]

So hell as destruction is best understood to show that hell is final and utter loss, ruin, or waste. Destruction is a graphic picture that those in hell have failed to embrace the meaning of life and have wasted it. Trying to find life in themselves and sin, they have forfeited true life. Only ruin and garbage remains.[17]

---

[12]David L. Edwards and John R. W. Stott, *Evangelical Essentials: A Liberal-Evangelical Dialogue* (Downers Grove, Ill.: InterVarsity Press, 1988), 316.

[13]John Wenham, "The Case for Conditional Immortality," in *Universalism and the Doctrine of Hell: Papers Presented at the Fourth Edinburgh Conference on Christian Dogmatics, 1991*, ed. Nigel M. de S. Cameron (Grand Rapids: Baker, 1992), 170–78.

[14]Powys, '*Hell*,' 284.

[15]D. A. Carson, *The Gagging of God: Christianity Confronts Pluralism* (Grand Rapids: Zondervan, 1996), 522.

[16]See Douglas J. Moo's chapter, "Paul on Hell," 104–9.

[17]Studies on Gehenna have often suggested the centrality of suffering and fire. Is the "garbage" motif actually present in it? That has been the subject of some debate. If so, then it would be an interesting study to see if historically Gehenna could be connected to this theme of hell as destruction. For some steps in this direction, see Hans Scharen, "Gehenna in the Synoptics," *BSac* 149 (1992): 324–37, 454–70. See also David Powys, '*Hell*,' 172–293. See also Edward William Fudge, *The Fire That Consumes: The Biblical Case for Conditional Immortality*, rev. ed. Peter Cousins (Carlisle: Paternoster, 1994), 93–145.

HeLL UNDeR fire

Banishment

The third central picture of hell in the New Testament is banishment. The idea of hell as banishment, separation, exclusion, or being left outside is found in the writings of most New Testament authors, with the exception of James or Hebrews. Hell as banishment is especially prominent in the teachings of Jesus, particularly in Matthew. This is to be expected because of the kingdom themes developed in Jesus' teaching in this Gospel. The contrast is vivid: Believers are welcomed into the kingdom while the wicked are banished outside of it.

Mark 9:42–48 reveals that those who do not enter the kingdom of God will be thrown into hell by God. John the Baptist stresses the final separation of the righteous from the wicked, noting that the wicked will be thrown into hell and "burned with unquenchable fire" (Matt. 3:1–12). In his Sermon on the Mount, Jesus proclaims that he will judge the world and declare to unbelievers, "Away from me!" (7:21–23). In doing so, he personally banishes them from his kingdom. Jesus regularly portrays hell as being outside the kingdom (and in outer darkness) and the wicked as excluded from God's kingdom (8:12; 13:42, 50; 25:10–12, 30). In the Olivet Discourse, Jesus again shows that he will personally banish the wicked from the kingdom: "Depart from me into the eternal fire prepared for the devil and his angels" (25:41). Luke recounts Jesus' story of the rich man and Lazarus, in which Jesus depicts the rich man in Hades as separated by a great chasm from Lazarus in heaven (Luke 16:19–31). John's Gospel also incorporates Jesus' warning about being "cut off" from him (John 15:1–7).

In 2 Thessalonians 1:5–10, the apostle Paul asserts that those in hell will be "shut out from" Jesus' presence and majesty. This is a strong picture of banishment.

The literary context in Revelation 20–22 makes it clear that hell should be understood in part through its contrast with heaven. In heaven, believers experience the glorious presence of God. The wicked, by contrast, are left outside, unable to enter the heavenly city and forever excluded from wondrous fellowship with God (22:14–15).

Whereas punishment stresses the active side of hell, banishment shows the horror of hell by highlighting what a person misses. When average evangelical church members are asked what hell is like, their likely response will be that hell is "separation from God." While the idea of separation is certainly correct and included in this New Testament concept of banishment, separation alone does not do justice to the force of this picture of hell. Banishment is much stronger than separation. It suggests God's active judgment while separation could simply imply divine passivity. Banishment also stresses the dreadfulness and finality of the predicament. The Scriptures demonstrate that Christ eternally excludes the unrighteous from the kingdom. The wicked never experience unhindered fellowship with God. They are forever banished from his majestic presence and completely miss out on the reason for their existence—to glorify and know their Creator.

Kendall Harmon suggests three aspects of hell associated with banishment. (1) Hell is being cut off from Christ and the kingdom of God. This is what scholastic theologians called the *poena damni*, the spiritual agony of exclusion from God's presence. (2) Hell is God's judgment in completely giving over the sinner to himself (Rom. 1:24, 26, 28). (3) Hell is not being known by God (Luke 13:22–30).[18] Addressing the banishment of the wicked from God and the glory of heaven, Augustine observed:

> To be lost out of the kingdom of God, to be an exile from the city of God, to be alienated from the life of God, to have no share in that great goodness which God has laid up for them that fear him, has wrought out for them that trust in him would be a punishment so great that, supposing it to be eternal, no torments that we know of, continued through as many ages as man's imagination can conceive, could be compared with it.[19]

Interpreting the Three Pictures of Hell

Important Considerations

It is important to note that the three pictures of hell are each characterized as *eternal*. Matthew 25:46 speaks of hell as "eternal punishment"; 2 Thessalonians 1:9 teaches that hell is "eternal destruction" and suggests eternal separation.

The three pictures of hell should also be viewed independently before synthetically. Harmon astutely observes that Edward Fudge mistakenly supposes that God's final sentence begins with banishment, continues with a period of punishment, and ends with destruction.[20] The Scripture offers no such order. Just as each Gospel account deserves to be read and interpreted as a whole before being harmonized or systematized, each portrait of hell should be allowed to stand on its own. Much can be learned about hell by considering it as punishment. Other insights can be gleaned by viewing it as destruction. Even further light can be shed on hell by seeing it as banishment. Three pictures are more helpful and produce more clarity and understanding than only one. Harmon suggests:

> The crucial point is that the different images each refer to a single reality and that combining different images is not like putting together the pieces of a jigsaw puzzle, but rather like letting the sunlight reflect through a diamond and seeing each ray's colors as pointing towards a single eschatological truth.[21]

Next, the three pictures of hell should be held in balance. Those of us holding the historic view of hell should be careful not to allow the motif of punishment to dominate our thoughts about hell. Conditionalists should make sure they are not stretching the destruction theme beyond what Scripture actually teaches. And most evangelicals need to guard against the tendency to view hell only in passive terms, like separation.

---

[18]Harmon, "The Case Against Conditionalism," 220–24.
[19]Augustine, *Enchiridion* 112, in *The Works of Aurelius Augustine* (Edinburgh: T. & T. Clark, 1873), 9:254. Quoted in Harmon, "The Case Against Conditionalism," 220.
[20]Harmon, "The Case Against Conditionalism," 213.
[21]Ibid., 224, n. 70.

Finally, one must not assume that these three pictures of hell cannot stand together. Indeed, they can and do converge in the same passages. The three pictures of hell are sometimes used by the same author in the same passage. Thus, Jesus uses all of them in Matthew 24:45–25:46.[22] The wicked servant is "cut into pieces"—destruction (24:51). He is assigned to a place with the hypocrites—banishment (24:51). And he suffers extreme pain in the punishment. In the next parable, the bridesmaids are shut outside—banishment (25:10–12). Jesus then moves to a different parable in which the worthless servant is thrown outside into the darkness—banishment (25:30). The servant also suffers intensely—punishment (25:30). In his next analogy, Jesus proclaims to the wicked, "Depart from me," and banishes them to hell as a place of "eternal fire prepared for the devil and his angels" (25:41). Yet he concludes the section by declaring that the wicked will "go away to eternal punishment" (25:46). This passage is not unique in interweaving these pictures of hell. The apostle Paul also uses the portraits of punishment, destruction, and banishment in 2 Thessalonians 1:5–10—and even in one verse (1:9)! Paul declares that God will punish unbelievers (1:6, 8, 9). But he also stresses that they will receive "eternal destruction" and will be "shut out" from Christ's presence. Revelation 20:10–22:15 likewise brings these three pictures together when John depicts punishment (20:10–15), destruction in the sense of "second death" (20:14; 21:8), and banishment by declaring that those in hell will remain outside heaven and will never enter it. So punishment, destruction, and banishment can stand together—they do so in three of the central passages on hell.

Systematic Implications

The three pictures of hell are not easily integrated into a simplified whole, however. Jesus says in Matthew 25:41 and 46, "Then he will say to those on his left, 'Depart from me, you who are cursed, into the eternal fire. . . .' Then they will go away to eternal punishment, but the righteous to eternal life." From this passage, someone might propose that the banishment leads to punishment. But that is reading too much into Jesus' intentions because Paul asserts in 2 Thessalonians 1:9, "They will be punished with eternal destruction and shut out from the presence of the Lord and from the majesty of his power." Here someone could conclude the opposite—the punishment is the destruction and exclusion. And in Revelation 20:10–22:15, the ideas of punishment, death, and exclusion are never integrated. So great caution should be taken when trying to systematize these three pictures of hell.

But this does not mean that these three pictures do not have important systematic implications. Quite the contrary, understanding them will further biblical and systematic theology. These pictures of hell correspond to the biblical teaching concerning God, sin, the atonement, salvation, and heaven.

The three pictures of hell interweave with biblical portraits of God. Hell as punishment vividly depicts God as Judge, who justly sentences the wicked (cf. Rev.

[22]I owe this insight into Matt. 24–25 to Harmon.

20:10–15). Hell as destruction seems to portray God as Warrior or Victor who defeats his enemies (cf. 2 Thess. 1:6–9).[23] Hell as banishment views God as King who allows only his citizens into his kingdom (cf. Matt. 7:21–23).

The three pictures of hell flow naturally from biblical portraits of sin. Each picture of hell seems to be the logical result of the particular portrait of sin. Hell as punishment recognizes sin as guilt, crime, trespass, or transgression. Hell as destruction/death sees sin as opposition or spiritual death (e.g., Rom. 5:12–21; Eph. 2). Hell as banishment/separation views sin as alienation from God.

Various pictures of hell even seem to show an "inaugurated eschatology" of sin/death.[24] God's wrath is on sinners, and hell is the culmination and release of that wrath (Rom. 1:8–2:8; 5:6–11). Sinners are condemned already, but they await the ultimate condemnation in hell (John 3:16–36; 5:24–28). Sinners are now dead spiritually but await the second death. Unbelievers are alienated from God now but will be finally excluded from his presence. Sinners' hearts are dark now but will eternally be in the "outer darkness" and "blackest darkness" of hell. The evidence is compelling: In some sense the descriptions of hell can be viewed as culminations, extensions, intensifications, and/or logical continuations of the unbeliever's current state of sin.

It is also important to note how the pictures of punishment, destruction/death, and banishment have Old Testament roots. These three pictures can be found as early as the Fall recorded in Genesis 3. The curses of the Fall are depicted as punishment for Adam's sin (cf. Rom. 5:12–21). God also warned Adam of sin's consequence of death, and he banished Adam and Eve from the Garden of Eden (cf. Cain's banishment in Gen. 4:16).

The three pictures of hell also appear to illustrate the biblical doctrine of the atonement. On the cross, Jesus died as a substitute for our sins and drank the cup of wrath—punishment (Matt. 26:42; Rom. 3:21–31; 1 Peter 3:18). On the cross, Jesus offers himself as a sacrifice for our sins—death (cf. Heb. 9–10). On the cross, Jesus experiences separation from the Father's fellowship as he cries, "My God, my God, why have you forsaken me?" (Matt. 27:46).[25]

The three pictures of hell stand in contrast with biblical portraits of salvation. Hell as punishment remains for those who were not justified by faith. Hell as destruction awaits those who never received the new birth/new life in Christ. Hell as banishment/separation is in store for all who have never been reconciled to God in Christ.

Finally, the three pictures of hell stand in contrast with biblical portraits of the kingdom of heaven. Hell as punishment stands opposite of heaven as inheritance/reward

---

[23]For intriguing arguments that the divine warrior motif is a key for interpreting 2 Thess. 1:9, see Daniel G. Reid, "2 Thessalonians 1:9: 'Separation from' or 'Destruction from' the Presence of the Lord?" A paper read at the November 2001 meeting of the Pauline Studies Group at the Evangelical Theological Society Annual Meeting in Colorado Springs, Colorado.

[24]For more on Paul's inaugurated eschatology of death, see Douglas J. Moo, "Paul on Hell," 92–96.

[25]For a development of this theme, see Sinclair B. Ferguson's chapter, "Pastoral Theology: The Preacher and Hell," 228–34.

　　　　　HeLL UNDeR fIRe

(Matt. 25:31–46). Hell as destruction or death is the other extreme to heaven as eternal life. Hell as banishment stands in contrast with heaven as entrance into the kingdom and marvelous presence of God. Instead of inheriting the kingdom in Christ, unbelievers are punished eternally. Though God extends the invitation for new life in Christ, non-Christians opt for eternal destruction. Rather than experiencing unhindered fellowship with God through the calling of Christ ("come" in Matt. 25:34), the wicked are banished forever from God's glorious presence. Christ graciously offers heaven, but sadly many people still refuse him and are cast into hell—the dreadful place of punishment, destruction, and banishment.

Chapter 7

Systematic theology: three Vantage Points of Hell

Robert A. Peterson

Consider three different vantage points with reference to the 2003 National League championship baseball series between the Chicago Cubs and the Florida Marlins. First, some Chicago fans, devoted to their Cubbies, wept openly as the last out of the seventh game secured the series for the Marlins. Marlins fans, however, celebrated jubilantly as their heroes posted a second improbable victory (the first was over the San Francisco Giants) and headed for a World Series confrontation with the New York Yankees. A third vantage point is that of "neutral" baseball watchers like me, who are devoted to neither the Cubs nor the Marlins, but who enjoyed an exciting series without the strong pull of emotions that partisan fans experienced.

The biblical doctrine of hell has been explored from many vantage points as well. This essay will consider three neglected ones, namely:

• the Trinity
• divine sovereignty and human freedom
• the "already" and the "not yet"

Hell from the Vantage Point of the Trinity

It is surprising that many who reject the old liberal caricature of the angry God of the Old Testament—wrathful Jehovah—and the loving God of the New—meek and mild Jesus—fall into a similar trap in viewing the work of judgment as largely, if not entirely, the work of the Father. The Son, it is assumed, is the Savior, not the Judge. And the Holy Spirit is usually not brought into the picture at all. This picture is a distorted one. I will attempt to show that, while the Son is indeed primarily Savior of the world, according to more than a dozen passages of Scripture he is also the Judge of the world. In addition, I will argue that, although Scripture never explicitly says so, the unity of the Godhead demands that we must ascribe to the Holy Spirit a place in the divine work of judgment. Only by viewing the Last Judgment from a Trinitarian perspective will we gain a proper holistic vision.

Numerous passages teach that God the Father is the Judge before whom sinners will stand on the last day. Citing just a few biblical references is sufficient. It is the "Father who judges each man's work impartially" (1 Peter 1:17). The Father, portrayed as sitting on "a great white throne" of judgment, is the One from whose awesome presence "earth and sky fled" (Rev. 20:11). And the Father is depicted as the divine host from whom the wicked "will drink of the wine of God's fury, which has been poured full strength into the cup of his wrath" (14:10).

A doctrine of judgment that merely affirms the Father's role is incomplete, however, for the Son too is Judge. This truth appears in every major section of the

New Testament. The Synoptic Gospels ascribe judgment to "the Son of Man," who "is going to come in his Father's glory with his angels, and then will reward each person according to what he has done" (Matt. 16:27). Notice that although the Son plays the role of Judge, he will "come in his Father's glory." That is, there is an implied harmony between the Father and Son in the work of judgment. Notice too that, contrary to some contemporary conceptions of judgment, the Last Judgment will be to display God's glory. The Father will be glorified as the Son performs the work of judgment.

Matthew 25 powerfully presents the Son of God as Judge. The returning King Jesus will sit on his throne with all humankind gathered before him. He will separate the people of the world and consign them to one of two destinies: "eternal punishment" or "eternal life" (25:31, 32, 46). What he says to the two groups leaves no doubt that *he* is the Judge. He has warm words of welcome for those he ushers into eternal blessing: "Come, you who are blessed by my Father; take your inheritance, the kingdom prepared for you since the creation of the world" (25:34). But he has terrible words of woe for those headed to hell: "Depart from me, you who are cursed, into the eternal fire prepared for the devil and his angels" (25:41).

The Synoptic Gospels present the Son as Judge of unclean spirits and unsaved human beings. The former cried out to him during his earthly ministry, "What do you want with us, Jesus of Nazareth? Have you come to destroy us? I know who you are—the Holy One of God!" (Mark 1:24). Another time a demon shouted from within a possessed man, "What do you want with me, Jesus, Son of the Most High God? Swear to God that you won't torture me!" (5:7). With various pictures the Synoptics portray Christ as Judge of human beings. At the consummation of the present age he will command the angels to gather the wicked and cast them "into the fiery furnace, where there will be weeping and gnashing of teeth" (Matt. 13:41–42). He will spurn those who performed miracles in his name but who didn't obey the Father: "I will tell them plainly, 'I never knew you. Away from me, you evildoers!'" (Matt. 7:23).

The Gospel of John also ascribes the work of judgment to the Son. After healing a man who had been an invalid for thirty-eight years, Jesus preaches a sermon in which he claims to bestow eternal life. Then he announces, "Moreover, the Father judges no one, but has entrusted all judgment to the Son, that all may honor the Son just as they honor the Father" (John 5:22–23). Note that the Son's performing the divine work of judgment qualifies him for the honor that is due the Father. That is, when the Son executes divine justice, he reveals that he too is God.

John 5 reminds us also that the Son did not come to condemn sinners but to save them. Whoever hears his word and believes in the Father "has eternal life and will not be condemned" (John 5:24). But those who reject the Son as Savior will face him as Judge, for the Father has given the Son "authority to judge because he is the Son of Man" (5:27). In his role as Son of Man he will judge even those who have died. John writes, "Do not be amazed at this, for a time is coming when all who are in their graves will hear his voice and come out—those who have done good will rise to live, and those who have done evil will rise to be condemned"

(5:28–29). Jesus explains that when he performs the work of judgment, he accomplishes the Father's will: "By myself I can do nothing; I judge only as I hear, and my judgment is just, for I seek not to please myself but him who sent me" (5:30).

In addition to the Gospels' presentation of Jesus as Judge, the book of Acts bears witness to the fact that the Son of God is the world's Savior and Judge. At Cornelius's house, Peter preaches the death and resurrection of Christ, but he does not stop there. He says of Christ that God "commanded us to preach to the people and to testify that he is the one whom God appointed as judge of the living and the dead" (Acts 10:42). Paul, in his sermon at Athens, agrees that God "has set a day when he will judge the world with justice by the man he has appointed. He has given proof of this to all men by raising him from the dead" (17:31). That person whom the Father has designated to judge the world is Jesus Christ. Again notice the harmony in the work of judgment of the Father and the Son.

The classic Pauline text for the Last Judgment is 2 Thessalonians 1:6–10. On that day God's justice will be vindicated as he delivers his persecuted people and punishes the wicked (2 Thess. 1:6–7a). Paul follows this up with verses 7b–10a:

This will happen when the Lord Jesus is revealed from heaven in blazing fire with his powerful angels. He will punish those who do not know God and do not obey the gospel of our Lord Jesus. They will be punished with everlasting destruction and shut out from the presence of the Lord, and from the majesty of his power on the day he comes to be glorified in his holy people and to be marveled at among all those who have believed.

Paul is emphatic concerning the Christological focus of the judgment. It is the returning "Lord Jesus" who "will punish" the wicked (2 Thess. 1:7–8). The reasons for condemnation include ignorance of God and disobeying "the gospel of our Lord Jesus" (v. 8). Spurning the good news of the Savior is bad news, because even as Jesus is a wonderful Savior, he is a terrifying Judge. But Paul also makes another connection between Christ and hell: Hell is separation "from the presence of the Lord and from the majesty of his power." There is no mistaking whom Paul means by "the Lord" here. It is the same one who returns "to be glorified in his holy people and to be marveled at among all those who have believed" (v. 10). Hell, therefore, is being deprived of the majestic and blessed presence of Christ.

The book of Revelation completes our survey of the New Testament witness to the fact that the Son is the Judge. This book puts matters in proper balance when it extols the virtues of the Lamb who is worthy of eternal praise for his work of redemption (Rev. 5:6, 8, 12–14; 7:10; 15:3). The very symbol "Lamb" points to the fact that Christ "was slain and with [his] blood purchased" sinners (5:9). "Lamb" is a symbol for Christ as Savior. But that is not the whole story. Because of the ugliness of sin and the reality of rebellion against God, the Lamb plays some surprising roles in the Revelation. The enemies of God "make war against the Lamb, but the Lamb will overcome them because he is Lord of lords and King of kings" (17:14).

Since he is the triumphant Savior, the Lamb alone is qualified to open the sealed book of the awful judgments of God (Rev. 5:5; 6:1). By the time Christ opens the sixth seal of judgment, all the wicked of the earth try to hide from God and beg the mountains and rocks, "Fall on us and hide us from the face of him who sits on the throne and from the wrath of the Lamb! For the great day of their wrath has come, and who can stand?" (Rev. 6:16–17). We are taken aback by the strangeness of the expression "the wrath of the Lamb," but that is what John intends. Jesus is not first of all Judge, but the Savior of all who believe in him. Yet those who refuse to bow before him willingly in this life will be compelled to do so in the next! Again we see the theme of harmony between the Father and Son in the work of judgment. The wicked fear the Father and the Son and "the great day of *their* wrath" (6:16–17; italics added).

The most startling passage in Revelation concerning Christ and judgment occurs in 14:10. There we learn that the unsaved will "drink of the wine of God's fury, which has been poured full strength into the cup of his wrath"; that is, they will personally experience the holy anger of Almighty God. The lost will undergo unceasing torment "in the presence of the holy angels and of the Lamb" (14:10–11). The word "Lamb" appears twenty-seven times in the Revelation and in every appearance except one (where it is used in a simile in 13:11) it refers to Christ. Christ is not only the Judge who sentences sinners to hell; he is here depicted as the One before whom they must bow. Greg Beale captures the main idea: "The point is that those who have denied the Lamb will be forced to acknowledge him as they are being punished 'before' him (as in 6:16)."[1]

We see, then, that the Synoptic Gospels, the Gospel of John, Acts, Paul, and the Revelation unite in portraying Christ as both Savior and Judge. In other words, the doctrine of judgment cannot be properly understood apart from a Trinitarian context. In fact, this conclusion should not surprise us; we should have anticipated it from the doctrine of the Trinity. Scripture teaches us to distinguish the persons of the Godhead but never to separate them. The Father is the Judge who sends unrepentant sinners to hell—and so is the Son. He works in harmony with the Father both to save and to condemn. I am not presenting salvation and judgment as equals; God delights to save his people from their sins but takes no delight in the death of the wicked. He sent his Son to be the Savior of the world, even of whosoever believes in him.

But Scripture is clear that not all will believe in him. As a result, it abundantly attests to the fact that the same Jesus who ushers his people into eternal bliss will relegate the ungodly to eternal punishment (Matt. 25:34, 41, 46). The once slaughtered but now victorious Lamb redeems his own and punishes the wicked (Rev. 5:9; 6:16–17; 14:10).

The Incarnation especially qualifies the Son to function as Judge of humanity. This is implied in several of the texts previously cited. God "will judge the world with justice by *the man* he has appointed" (Acts 17:31; italics added). The Father gave the Son "authority to judge because he is the Son of Man" (John 5:27). The

[1]Gregory K. Beale, *The Book of Revelation* (NIGTC; Grand Rapids: Eerdmans, 1999), 760.

New Testament's use of "Son of Man" interweaves two Old Testament strands: the Danielic exalted Son of Man and the frail "son of man" of Psalm 8.[2] Christ is both exalted Lord and glorified man who once was a lowly man. His present exalted position as Lord of all qualifies him to be Judge; as God he will judge human beings. In addition, his experiences as a man qualify him to judge justly the sons and daughters of Adam. It is wise, just, and compassionate of the Father to share the work of judgment with his Son, who was "in the likeness of sinful man" (Rom. 8:3) and who knows from experience what it means to live a human life on earth, to learn "obedience from what he suffered" (Heb. 5:8), and to be "tempted in every way . . . yet was without sin" (4:15). As Man he will judge human beings.

What about the Holy Spirit? Does he too play a role in judgment? Scripture only hints at such a role. In his farewell discourse Jesus declares that when he departs, he will send the *paraklētos*. About him Jesus says: "When he comes, he will convict the world of guilt in regard to sin and righteousness and judgment" (John 16:8). Here the Spirit "will prove the world guilty of the 'sin' of which Jesus' opponents want to show him guilty, although they are not capable of doing this, by exposing what sin really is and showing that it is closely associated with the world."[3] This description of convicting work is as close as Scripture comes to ascribing the work of judgment to the Holy Spirit.

But what was said above concerning the Son applies here too. God is a Triunity, and we dare not separate the divine persons from one another. The Apocalypse reminds us of this when it speaks of "him who is, and who was, and who is to come, and from the seven spirits before his throne, and from Jesus Christ" (Rev. 1:4; cf. 4:3, 5; 5:6). Ultimately, then, since the Trinity is indivisible, the work of judgment is the work of the Trinity: Father, Son, and Holy Spirit. Conceiving judgment in these terms helps us to keep the work of the Trinity in harmony in our minds, enables us to honor the three Trinitarian persons as we ought, and provides a good starting place for further reflection on God's work of judgment.

Hell from the Vantage Point of Divine Sovereignty and Human Freedom

One of the most helpful perspectives in biblical and theological studies is that of the tension between God's sovereignty and human freedom. Regularly the Bible joins these seemingly contradictory notions to provide a more comprehensive view than can be afforded by considering either one alone. As others have pointed out, Scripture is replete with examples of God's sovereign providence and human beings' responsibility.[4] I will cite two biblical examples before applying this perspective to the study of hell: the account of Joseph's brothers selling him

---

[2]So D. A. Carson, "Matthew," *EBC*, 8:212–13.
[3]Rudolf Schnackenburg, *The Gospel According to John* (New York: Crossroad, 1987), 3:128.
[4]D. A. Carson has been especially helpful, with both his scholarly book on the subject, *Divine Sovereignty and Human Responsibility* (Grand Rapids: Baker, 1994), and a semipopular one, *How Long, O Lord?* (Grand Rapids: Baker, 1990).

HeLL UNDeR fire

into slavery, and the betrayal and crucifixion of Christ. A study of these examples will acclimate us to the way in which the tension between sovereignty and freedom works and will teach us not to treat that tension in relation to hell as a special case.

Joseph's Being Sold into Slavery

Genesis records a cruel crime of betrayal: Joseph's brothers selling him into slavery. They were offended at Joseph's wild dreams and sold him to Ishmaelite merchants for twenty shekels of silver (Gen. 37:26–28). The merchants in turn sold him to Potiphar, and eventually Joseph rose to the position of second-in-command over all Egypt (41:41). While Joseph was in that position but without his brothers' being aware of it, they came to Egypt to buy food from him because of the severe worldwide famine. Joseph's words shocked them: "I am your brother Joseph, the one you sold into Egypt! And now, do not be distressed and do not be angry with yourselves for selling me here, because it was to save lives that God sent me ahead of you. . . . So, then it was not you who sent me here, but God" (45:4–5, 8).

The reader's first response is, "But of course Joseph's brothers sent him to Egypt!" Joseph is not denying that fact; he has just said that they sold him into Egypt. Rather, he is appealing to a higher cause of his coming to Egypt—God's sovereign hand. Scripture here teaches a dual causality of the same event. Joseph's brothers *and* God sent him into Egypt. Their sinful act and God's sovereign plan were both realized in the same deed.

This is the mysterious but true teaching here and throughout Scripture. We must be careful to evaluate the dual causality as Scripture does. God's sovereign control does not turn the brothers' sin into something good nor does it implicate God in their sin. They sinned against God and their brother when they sold him into slavery. Neither does the brothers' sin frustrate God's plan. This is what Joseph means when he says, "So, then it was not you who sent me here, but God." Ultimately it was not the brothers but God who brought Joseph to Egypt because God stands behind all events, even sin, though not so as to make him guilty of sin.

After their father Jacob dies, Joseph's brothers fear for their lives, reasoning that with paternal restraint removed, Joseph may take revenge. His response to their fear overflows with grace: "Don't be afraid. Am I in the place of God? You intended to harm me, but God intended it for good. . . . So then, don't be afraid" (Gen. 50:19–21). Here Scripture teaches that the same event had two different motives. The brothers intended harm but God intended good. God is, therefore, not chargeable with the harm the brothers' sin caused. But he is to be credited with the good that came from his overriding of their sinful action and bringing good out of evil.

Christ's Betrayal and Crucifixion

This mystery of God's sovereignty and human freedom is nowhere more evident than in the betrayal and crucifixion of Christ. Notice how Jesus brings sovereignty and freedom together when he speaks of Judas' betrayal: "The Son of Man will go as it has been decreed, but woe to that man who betrays him" (Luke 22:22). Christ's betrayal and crucifixion had been ordained by God, and they must surely come to pass. Jesus personally submits to divine providence when he utters these words. At the same time, however, he holds his betrayer, Judas Iscariot, culpable. Judas is guilty of betraying Christ, and he will pay the consequences. In fact, Matthew's Gospel adds a sentence to Jesus' saying of woe above: "It would be better for him if he had not been born" (Matt. 26:24). Woe to Judas for betraying Christ!

Does Judas's betrayal of Christ cause God to adjust his plan to the circumstances to make the most out of a bad situation? Not at all. Listen to Peter's powerful words assigning the crucifixion to the sovereign will of God:

> This man was handed over to you by God's set purpose and foreknowledge; and you, with the help of wicked men, put him to death by nailing him to the cross. But God raised him from the dead, freeing him from the agony of death, because it was impossible for death to keep its hold on him. (Acts 2:23–24)

> Indeed Herod and Pontius Pilate met together with the Gentiles and the people of Israel in this city to conspire against your holy servant Jesus, whom you anointed. They did what your power and will had decided beforehand should happen. (Acts 4:27–28)

Note first that the betrayal and crucifixion of Christ were accomplished "by God's set purpose and foreknowledge" (Acts 2:23). That is, when sinners did the worst they could do against Jesus, they only did what God's "power and will had decided beforehand should happen" (4:28). The crucifixion of Christ was the act of God. In fact, other Scripture indicates that Christ is "the Lamb that was slain from the creation of the world" (Rev. 13:8; cf. 1 Peter 1:20). His saving death was included in God's plan before creation. So, as surely as God is sovereign, it was certain that Jesus would be crucified.

But note as well that the crucifixion was a terrible crime perpetrated by "wicked men," both Jews and Gentiles who "conspired against" God's "holy servant Jesus." Is a greater crime imaginable than crucifying "the Lord of glory" (1 Cor. 2:8), than killing "the author of life" (Acts 3:15)? Because this foul deed was committed against the Son of God, it is unspeakably horrible.

At one and the same time Jesus' crucifixion filled God's plan and was the greatest crime ever perpetrated! The tension between God's sovereignty and human freedom displayed in the Cross is indeed mysterious. To tamper with either aspect produces terrible results. To deny human responsibility transforms the perpetrators into God's servants who do good when they crucify the Son of God. To minimize divine sovereignty transforms the Cross into an emergency measure of God. Such transformations are wrong in the extreme. Inscrutably the Cross is both God's will, without tarnishing him with evil, and the culpable deed of evildoers, without making them puppets whose strings are pulled by God.

HeLL UNDeR fiRe

Hell, God's Sovereignty and Human Freedom

The mysterious tension between God's sovereignty and humanity's freedom evident in the Joseph narrative and in the crucifixion is also evident in God's sending of guilty sinners to hell. Studying the judgment passages leads to the conclusion that at the Last Judgment, Almighty God the Judge will mete out to sinners what they deserve for their sins. Scripture declares that God himself is both Lord (Rom. 14:9) and Judge of the living and the dead (Acts 10:42; 2 Tim. 4:1; 1 Peter 4:5). As we saw previously, the Holy Trinity, especially the Father and Son, is the executor of the Last Judgment.

God's sovereignty in judgment is also expressed by his throwing people into hell. Jesus warns, "But I will show you whom you should fear: Fear him who, after the killing of the body, has power to throw you into hell. Yes, I tell you, fear him" (Luke 12:5). This theme occurs a number of times in the Gospels and the Revelation.[5] It shows that the power of God over the wicked extends beyond the grave.

God's lordship in judgment means not only that he pronounces the sentence, but also that he rules over hell. Unfortunately, some have erred at this point. John Gerstner is an example when he writes, "Hell is where Satan rules . . . where his complete fury is unleashed."[6] Gerstner does not deny that God rules in hell but affirms that Satan also reigns there, under God. But this is erroneous, for hell is where God alone rules and where *his* complete fury is unleashed against Satan, his angels, and wicked human beings. For this reason Jesus banishes evildoers "into the eternal fire prepared for the devil and his angels" (Matt. 25:41). John agrees: "And the devil . . . was thrown into the lake of burning sulfur. . . . [and] will be tormented day and night for ever and ever" (Rev. 20:10). Rather than being hell's master, Satan suffers eternally with other wicked angels (20:10) and human beings (20:15) at the hands of Almighty God.[7]

The biblical witness to God's sovereignty, then, extends beyond this life to hell itself. But it would be incorrect to conclude from this that Scripture chiefly assigns the reason people perish to God's sovereign will. Instead, the accent is on misused human freedom, as both Old and New Testaments consistently proclaim that God will judge sinners according to their deeds:

Surely you will reward each person according to what he has done. (Ps. 62:12)

I will deal with them according to their conduct, and by their own standards I will judge them. Then they will know that I am the LORD. (Ezek. 7:27)

And it will be: Like people, like priests. I will punish both of them for their ways and repay them for their deeds." (Hos. 4:9)

---

[5]It is expressed by the divine passive (Matt. 18:8–9; Rev. 19:20; 20:10, 15) and by the Son's using of angels to accomplish his will (Matt. 13:41–42, 49–50).

[6]John H. Gerstner, *Repent or Perish: With a Special Reference to the Conservative Attack on Hell* (Ligonier, Pa.: Soli Deo Gloria, 1990), 189–90.

[7]Sydney H. T. Page concurs in *Powers of Darkness: A Biblical Study of Satan and Demons* (Grand Rapids: Baker, 1995).

The Lord Almighty has done to us what our ways and practices deserve, just as he determined to do. (Zech. 1:6)

For the Son of Man is going to come ... and then he will reward each person according to what he has done. (Matt. 16:27)

But for those who are self-seeking and who reject the truth and follow evil, there will be wrath and anger. There will be trouble and distress for every human being who does evil: first for the Jew, then for the Gentile. (Rom. 2:8–9)

Do not be deceived: God cannot be mocked. A man reaps what he sows. The one who sows to please his sinful nature, from that nature will reap destruction. (Gal. 6:7–8)

The sea gave up the dead that were in it, and death and Hades gave up the dead that were in them, and each person was judged according to what he had done. (Rev. 20:13)

Passage after passage points to a holy and just God who gives sinners what they deserve. Judgment is according to deeds, or more precisely, according to thoughts (1 Cor. 4:5), words (Matt. 12:36), and deeds (Rev. 20:12–13). Those whose lives are characterized by evil thoughts, words, and deeds reap God's wrath. When one inquires of the judgment passages why sinners end up in hell, Scripture repeatedly shouts the answer: corrupted human freedom and evil deeds.

There is another sense in which God is sovereign over hell, a sense that is whispered in a quiet voice in the judgment passages. This voice is easily drowned out by the stronger emphasis on human culpability but is audible if one listens attentively. A few of the judgment passages teach that God is sovereign over the fate of the lost. At the Last Judgment Jesus will say these startling words to false disciples: "I never knew you. Away from me, you evildoers!" (Matt. 7:23). What does he mean when he tells the lost that he never knew them? This does not refer to his omniscience for Jesus knows all persons. Rather, he does not know the lost with the intimate knowledge that accompanies salvation. Jesus speaks of this kind of knowledge in the good shepherd discourse: "I know my sheep and my sheep know me" (John 10:14). Jesus knows his sheep with a personal knowledge, the knowledge of salvation, and as a result they know him too.

Paul speaks of the same type of knowledge: "Formerly, when you did not know God, you were slaves to those who by nature are not gods. But now that you know God—or rather are known by God—how is it that you are turning back to those weak and miserable principles?" (Gal. 4:8–9). Observe that the apostle clarifies to prevent misunderstanding: "But now that you know God—*or rather are known by God*" (italics added). As soon as Paul states that his readers have come to know God, he more searchingly attributes their knowledge of God to his knowledge of them. That is, the Galatians came to know God as a reflex action to his knowing them personally and savingly.

Similarly, when Jesus (in Matt. 7:23) tells the false disciples that he never knew them, he means that he never knew them with the same intimate knowledge that

hell under fire

accompanies salvation. That is why he rejected them. It is important to correlate this truth with the predominant one discussed earlier—people are condemned for their sinful lifestyles. The fact that Christ never knew some does not nullify their responsibility before God, because he still holds them accountable for their sins. He does not regard his sovereignty over the fate of the lost as canceling their personal culpability—and neither should we.

John also affirms that God stands behind the fate of the wicked:

> Then I saw a great white throne and him who was seated on it. Earth and sky fled from his presence, and there was no place for them. And I saw the dead, great and small, standing before the throne, and books were opened. Another book was opened, which is the book of life. The dead were judged according to what they had done as recorded in the books. The sea gave up the dead that were in it, and death and Hades gave up the dead that were in them, and each person was judged according to what he had done. Then death and Hades were thrown into the lake of fire. The lake of fire is the second death. If anyone's name was not found written in the book of life, he was thrown into the lake of fire. (Rev. 20:11–15)

This passage is noteworthy because it presents the fates of human beings in terms of both divine sovereignty and human responsibility. The major accent here (as in all of Scripture) is on human culpability: God condemns the unsaved because of their sinful deeds. The dead are judged according to their actions, as those actions were recorded in God's books of judgment (Rev. 20:12, 13).

The passage also speaks of another book opened at the Judgment—the book of life. This is a picture of God's sovereignty in salvation and, by implication, in judgment. "The book of life" (Rev. 3:5; 17:8; 20:12, 15) or "the Lamb's book of life" (13:8; 21:27) is mentioned frequently in the Revelation. Because only those whose names are written in "the Lamb's book of life" will enter the new Jerusalem (21:27), this book serves as the census register of that city, the city of God. Furthermore, the names of the saints were enrolled "in the book of life *from the creation of the world*" (17:8; italics added).

Those whose names were written in the book of life from creation (Rev. 17:8) will be spared the lake of fire (20:15) and will enter the new Jerusalem (21:27).[8] When John says, therefore, "If anyone's name was not found written in the book of life, he was thrown into the lake of fire" (20:15), he speaks of God's sovereignty over the fate of the lost. To have one's name recorded in the book of life from creation is to belong to the people of God, the redeemed. Not to have one's name written in the book of life is to be rejected by God, to be lost. God enrolls people in the book of life by his mysterious election; he chooses who will be registered in it. When John speaks of the books that recorded people's deeds and of the book of life, he speaks of human freedom and God's sovereignty, respectively. Thus, both human freedom and divine sovereignty are true. Sinners get what they deserve from the hand of a holy God at the Last Judgment. At the same time God stands behind the fate of every person, the unsaved included.

---

[8] See Beale, *Revelation*, 281–82.

Revelation 20:11–15, therefore, summarizes the conclusions reached so far—there are at least two reasons why people perish: because of their actual sins (the predominant reason presented) and because of God's sovereign will. It is helpful at this point to add a third reason. The Bible also teaches that people end up in hell because of Adam's original sin. Paul sets this forth in no uncertain terms in Romans 5:

The many died by the trespass of the one man....

The judgment followed one sin and brought condemnation....

By the trespass of the one man, death reigned through that one man....

Just as the result of one trespass was condemnation for all men....

Just as through the disobedience of the one man the many were made sinners.... (5:15, 16, 17, 18, 19)

When Scripture highlights human responsibility, it teaches that people perish because of both original sin and actual sins. Obviously, original sin is more ultimate than actual sins, because it is the reason why actual sins occur; when Adam fell, "sin entered the world through one man" (5:12). But notice that Scripture does not regard original sin as nullifying sinners' culpability for their actual sins. This is easily demonstrated by the fact that before Romans discusses original sin (in 5:12–19) it has much to say about actual sins (in 1:18–3:20). Original sin is more ultimate than actual sin, but both are genuine reasons why people go to hell.

Scripture gives an even more ultimate reason why people perish—the sovereign will of God in reprobation. Reprobation refers to God's passing over those whom he allows to pay the penalty for their sins.[9] We saw this truth in Revelation 20:15: "If anyone's name was not found written in the book of life, he was thrown into the lake of fire." Other passages of Scripture also imply it.[10]

We must be careful to allow Scripture to give us a sense of proper proportion when considering these three reasons why people are condemned. The order of least to greatest ultimacy is: actual sin, original sin, and reprobation. Sinners actually sin during their lifetimes. More ultimate is the fact that Adam sinned in the Garden of Eden after God created all things. And God's sovereign decision to pass by many sinners and allow them to suffer the consequences for their sins is most ultimate because it occurred before the creation of the world.

It is critical to note that Scripture teaches all three reasons why people perish and does not regard any one of them as canceling the others. We are not able to explain this any more than we can explain the tension between divine providence and human freedom in regard to Joseph's brothers selling him into slavery or in regard to Christ's betrayal and crucifixion. But God declares the mystery of divine sovereignty and human responsibility, and we are obligated to believe it on the authority of his Word.

---

[9]The technical term for God's passing them by is preterition; see Louis Berkhof, *Systematic Theology* (Grand Rapids: Eerdmans, 1939, 1941), 116.
[10]These include John 10:26; Rom. 9:22; 11:7; 1 Peter 2:8.

A summary is in order. Scripture presents God as the sovereign Judge before whom sinners stand on Judgment Day. It gives three reasons why they are condemned. The predominant note sounded by the judgment passages is human freedom abused by sinners in rebellion against their Maker. But this does not tell the whole story. Behind actual sin stands Adam's original sin. It is Scripture's explanation for the existence of actual sins in God's good world. But this in no way nullifies the fact that sinners are deserving of God's condemnation.

If we press as far as Scripture allows concerning the reasons people perish, we come to the further fact that God has sovereignly chosen multitudes for salvation before the creation of the world and has passed over others, allowing them to reap condemnation for their sins. With Scripture we confess that God stands behind the destiny of every human being. But with Scripture we also confess that he does so asymmetrically with respect to the elect and the reprobate. He is proactive in election; he grants grace to those who would perish without it. But he is passive in reprobation, allowing sinners to receive what their sins deserve. Once again we must underscore a significant point: God's reprobation does not make invalid either original or actual sin. Although we cannot explain how this is so, we confess its truth, even as we confess the mysteries of the Holy Trinity and the two natures in the person of Christ.

Hell from the Vantage Point of the "Already" and the "Not Yet"

The most important contribution of twentieth-century New Testament studies to eschatology is the insight concerning the "already" and the "not yet."[11] The "already" refers to the fact that the great eschatological event predicted in the Old Testament has been fulfilled—the Christ has come. The "not yet" refers to the fact that the New Testament itself indicates that there are still prophecies to be fulfilled, such as the Second Coming. Although these concepts have been studied chiefly with reference to the New Testament, they are not absent from the Old Testament. Throughout much of their history, the Israelites lived in the tension created by the "already" of the deliverance from Egypt and the "not yet" of the future Day of the Lord.

While the roots of the "already/not yet" distinction sink deep into Old Testament soil, the distinction does not come to full flower until the New Testament. Every major aspect of New Testament theology is affected by the "already/not yet" tension. These include the signs of the times (Matt. 24:14), adoption (Gal. 4:7; Rom. 8:23), the Antichrist (1 John 2:19), the resurrection of the dead (John 5:24–29), and even glorification (John 17:22, 24). So it is that although salvation and judgment properly and technically pertain to the Last

[11]See Herman Ridderbos, *The Coming of the Kingdom*, trans. H. de Jongste (Philadelphia: Presbyterian & Reformed, 1962), 36–56; Oscar Cullman, *Salvation in History*, trans. S. G. Sowers (New York: Harper & Row, 1967), 32, 172–85; G. C. Berkouwer, *The Return of Christ*, trans. James Van Oosterom (Grand Rapids: Eerdmans, 1972), 20–23, 110–15, 121–22, 138–39; Anthony Hoekema, *The Bible and the Future* (Grand Rapids: Eerdmans, 1979), 14–15, 68–75.

Day—they are "not yet"—they are also realized in the present in anticipation of that day—they are "already."

As beautifully as anywhere in Scripture, 1 John 3:1–3 combines the realized and unrealized aspects of salvation:

> How great is the love the Father has lavished on us, that we should be called children of God! And that is what we are! . . . Dear friends, now we are children of God, and what we will be has not yet been made known. But we know that when he appears, we shall be like him, for we shall see him as he is. Everyone who has this hope in him purifies himself, just as he is pure.

John combines the "already" ("now we are children of God") with the "not yet" ("what we will be has not yet been made known") in order to extol the Father's great love and to motivate Christians to purity.

Judgment too is fulfilled in one sense and unfulfilled in another. We see the "already" aspect of salvation and judgment clearly portrayed in the fourth Gospel:

> For God so loved the world that he gave his one and only Son, that whoever believes in him shall not perish but have eternal life. For God did not send his Son into the world to condemn the world, but to save the world through him. Whoever believes in him is not condemned, but whoever does not believe stands condemned already because he has not believed in the name of God's one and only Son. (John 3:16–18)

God loved a world that hated him and sent his Son into it on a rescue mission. Although the purpose of the Son's coming is to save and not to condemn, condemnation is a by-product of the Son's saving mission. For every believer in Christ the verdict of the last day is announced ahead of time—he or she is "not condemned." And for everyone who rejects the Son the final verdict is also announced—he or she is "condemned already." The final verdicts of justification or condemnation (the "not yet") are proclaimed in the "already" based on a person's relationship to Christ. If we ask what has brought about this state of affairs, what has created the tension between the "already" and the "not yet," the answer lies close at hand. It is the coming of Christ, God's sending of his Son, that has brought the eternal destinies to light with a clarity previously unseen in the history of special revelation (cf. 2 Tim. 1:9).

Similarly, John speaks of eternal life as the present possession of believers and of God's wrath presently abiding on unbelievers: "Whoever believes in the Son has eternal life, but whoever rejects the Son will not see life, for God's wrath remains on him" (John 3:36). Eternal life is already God's gift to believers; they possess now what will not be revealed fully until the last day. God's wrath already remains on unbelievers; their judgment begins now in their separation from the life of God. And as long as they persist in unbelief, they "will not see life"—now or forever (v. 36).

Although the New Testament affirms present aspects of both salvation and judgment, it is incorrect to say that heaven and hell are what one makes of this life.

It is erroneous to reduce the eternal destinies to the "already" because Scripture's main focus when speaking of them is on the "not yet." But before we discuss the final aspect of salvation and judgment, we must treat a strange topic—the intermediate state. It is strange because it does not fit neatly into the "already" or the "not yet"; it occupies a twilight zone between the two. It does not belong entirely to either but shares features of each.

Before summarizing the biblical teaching concerning the intermediate state for believers and unbelievers, I hasten to add that, from the perspective of biblical theology, that state is temporary and even abnormal. God created humans as holistic beings consisting of body and soul united. That is how we are now, and that is how we will be as resurrected beings on the new earth. Nevertheless, Scripure affirms the existence of the intermediate state, and so must we.

The intermediate state of believers involves a disembodied spiritual existence in Christ's immediate presence in heaven. Jesus spoke of it when he promised the repentant thief on the cross, "Today you will be with me in paradise" (Luke 23:43). Paul longed for it because he regarded it as "better by far" to "depart and be with Christ" (Phil. 1:23). He says that believers "would prefer to be away from the body and at home with the Lord" (2 Cor. 5:8).[12]

What does Scripture teach concerning the intermediate state of the lost? Judgment chiefly concerns the Last Day, but it also has intermediate ramifications, according to a couple of biblical passages. As we have seen, there is a sense in which judgment begins in this life. There is also a sense in which it occurs at death. The parable of the rich man and Lazarus speaks of human beings continuing to exist after death and before the resurrection of the dead. Lazarus, the penitent poor man, died and went to "Abraham's side," where he was "comforted" (Luke 16:22, 25). "Abraham's side" was a Jewish expression, arising in the intertestamental period, that referred to the intermediate "heaven" or "paradise." By contrast, the impenitent rich man died and went to "hell, where he was in torment . . . in agony in . . . fire." He was "in agony" in a "place of torment" (Luke 16:23, 24, 25, 28). At death, Lazarus and the unsaved rich man left their bodies and went to places of bliss and woe, respectively. The parable points to the intermediate rather than the final state, because the rich man in hell pled with Father Abraham to send someone to warn his five unrepentant brothers lest they too come to share his fate. Such a request would have been impossible following the resurrection of the dead and Last Judgment.

The only other text that possibly teaches the conscious suffering of the wicked in the intermediate state is 2 Peter 2:9: "The Lord knows how to rescue godly men from trials and to hold the unrighteous for the day of judgment, *while continuing their punishment*" (italics added). Peter says this after he has taught that God punishes certain evil angels by sending "them to hell, putting them into gloomy dungeons to be held for judgment" (2:4). There is thus a penultimate judgment for certain wicked angels. Similarly, Peter could be saying in 2:9 that there is a penultimate (intermediate) judgment and existence for all wicked human

---

[12]Other texts can be adduced, such as Acts 7:59; Heb. 12:23; Rev. 6:9–10.

beings who die. This is the opinion of some commentators, although the majority translate the participle *kolazomenous* as "to be punished" and interpret 2:9 as referring to the Judgment Day.[13]

Although there are present and intermediate ramifications to the Last Judgment, the most important things are still to come. Christ will return in glory. As Matthew writes, "When the Son of Man comes in his glory, and all the angels with him, he will sit on his throne in heavenly glory" (Matt. 25:31). At his word all of the dead will rise: "All who are in their graves will hear his voice and come out" (John 5:28–29). Then, he will make the final separation between the saved and unsaved. Indeed, "all the nations will be gathered before him, and he will separate the people one from another as a shepherd separates the sheep from the goats" (Matt. 25:32). King Jesus will invite God's children to enter into their inheritance but will banish unbelievers "into the eternal fire, prepared for the devil and his angels" (Matt. 25:34, 41). As succinctly as any verse in Scripture, Matthew 25:46 describes the final destinies of the lost and saved: "Then they will go away to eternal punishment, but the righteous to eternal life."

This final dimension of judgment and hell is anticipated in the Old Testament (Dan. 12:1–2; Isa. 66:24) and taught in every section of the New: the Gospels (Matt. 5:22, 29–30; 7:13, 23; 8:12, 29; 10:28; 13:42, 49–50; 18:6–9; 22:13; 23:33; 24:51; 25:30, 41, 46; 26:24; Mark 1:24; 5:7; 9:43, 45, 47–48; Luke 3:17; 4:34; 12:5; 13:3, 5; 16:23–25, 28; John 3:16–18, 36; 5:28–29; 8:21, 24); Acts (10:42; 17:31); the New Testament letters (Rom. 2:5, 8–9, 12; 6:23; 9:3, 22; 1 Cor. 11:32; 2 Cor. 2:15–16; 4:3; Gal. 1:8–9; 6:8; Eph. 5:6; Phil. 1:28; 3:19; Col. 3:6; 1 Thess. 1:10; 5:3, 9; 2 Thess. 1:8–9; 2:10; Heb. 6:2; 9:27; 10:27, 39; James 4:12; 2 Peter 2:1, 3, 4, 9, 12, 17; 3:7; Jude 4, 6, 7, 13); and the Apocalypse (Rev. 2:11; 6:16–17; 11:18; 14:10–11, 19; 16:19; 17:8, 11; 18: 8, 9, 18; 19:3, 15, 20; 20:10, 14–15; 21:8; 22:15). Plainly, the New Testament has much to say about the final destiny of the unsaved.

To summarize: Judgment, like salvation, is "already" and "not yet." Already believers are justified before God and unbelievers are condemned. At death the souls of the saved go immediately into the joyous presence of Christ in heaven, while the souls of the lost go immediately into an intermediate hell. At Christ's return, the dead will be resurrected to stand before the Trinity at the Last Judgment, which will result in eternal bliss for the righteous on the new earth and eternal punishment for the wicked in the lake of fire. These truths should drive unsaved persons to Christ for eternal life and God's people to their knees in worship. These truths should motivate us who know the Lord to love, pray for, and speak with unsaved persons concerning eternal destinies.

---

[13]See Richard J. Bauckham, *2 Peter, Jude* (WBC 50; Waco, Tex.: Word, 1983), 254.

HELL UNDER FIRE

Chapter 8

Universalism: Will everyone Ultimately Be Saved?

J. I. Packer

Definition of Universalism

A *universalist* is someone who believes that every human being whom God has created or will create will finally come to enjoy the everlasting salvation into which Christians enter here and now. *Universalism* is the recognized name for this belief. The universalist contention is a far-reaching belief that cannot but make waves. Among the competing worldviews and ideologies of humankind it appears as an extreme optimism about the future of our race: Each and every one of us, it declares, and all of us together, will end up beyond this nightmarish world in a state of supreme God-given and God-centered bliss. Among the world's religions it appears as an imperial kind of paternalism, assuring each person that whatever final destiny they anticipate at this moment, hopefully or fearfully as the case may be, and whatever their present pattern of life, religious or not, moral or not, nothing less than the full felicity of the Christian, Christ-centered salvation will be theirs.

Among Christian theological options it appears as an extreme optimism of grace, or perhaps of nature, and sometimes, it seems, of both. But in itself it is a revisionist challenge to orthodoxy, whether Roman Catholic, Eastern Orthodox, or Protestant evangelical; for the church has officially rated universalism a heresy ever since the second Council of Constantinople (the fifth ecumenical council, A.D. 553), when the doctrine of *apokatastasis* (the universal return to God and restoration of all souls) that Origen taught was anathematized.[1]

In recent years universalism has made a remarkable comeback among mainstream Christian thinkers, and it cannot now be dismissed out of hand as a foolish fantasy in the way it once could. It is, as we will see, the most audacious of modern views about human destiny, yet it is almost certainly the one most widely held among Christian people in the West, at both popular and academic levels.

Applied to our six-billion global-village world, multicultural, multifaith, and endlessly diversified as it is, the scope of universalism is breathtaking. It covers all the dead from earliest times as well as all the living, both present and future. It embraces all the adherents of all the religions and cults that ever have been or

---

[1]On Origen's universalism, see Frederick W. Norris, "Universal Salvation in Origen and Maximus," in Nigel M. de S. Cameron, ed., *Universalism and the Doctrine of Hell* (Carlisle: Paternoster; Grand Rapids: Baker, 1992), 35–72; also John Sanders, *No Other Name* (Grand Rapids: Eerdmans, 1992), 98–101; Larry Dixon, *The Other Side of the Good News* (Tain, U.K.: Christian Focus, 2003), 33–38. There is some uncertainty as to whether Origen was named as a heretic by the Council of Constantinople, as he had been by the 543 Synod of Constantinople, but the condemnation of his doctrine, as stated in his *De Principiis*, is explicit. The Council's first canon was: "If anyone teaches the mythical doctrine of the pre-existence of the soul and the *apokatastasis* that follows from it, let him be anathema."

HeLL UNDeR fire

shall be—theistic, deistic, pantheistic, polytheistic, atheistic, trinitarian, unitarian, syncretist, Satanist, animist, shamanist, white- or black-magic oriented, earth- or self-centered, tribal or ethnic, primitive or sophisticated. It extends to the many millions who have no religion and no interest in religion, including those who, like Bertrand Russell, believe that "when I die I shall rot, and nothing of my ego will survive."[2] Bloody-handed practitioners of treachery, genocide, and torture, and bloody-minded devotees of personal cruelty and child abuse are included; no one is left out. Universalism thus asserts the final salvation of, for instance, Judas, Hitler, Genghis Khan, Stalin, and Saddam Hussein, to name a few. These are test cases to have in mind when assessing the universalist claim.

Motivation

Most universalists (granted, not all) concede that universalism is not clearly taught in the Bible; what then is the warrant for the universalist confidence? It seems plain that the deepest motivation in their minds has always been revolt against mainstream belief in endless punishment in hell for some people. It is argued that the biblical revelation of God's love to his world entails a universal salvific intention, that is, a purpose of saving everybody, and that sooner or later God must achieve that purpose. Madeleine L'Engle, the gifted Christian fantasy novelist, puts it like this:

> I know a number of highly sensitive and intelligent people in my own communion [i.e., Anglicanism] who consider as a heresy my faith that God's loving concern for his creation will outlast all our willfulness and pride. No matter how many eons it takes, he will not rest until all of creation, including Satan, is reconciled to him, until there is no creature who cannot return his look of love with a joyful response of love. . . . I cannot believe that God wants punishment to go on interminably any more than does a loving parent. The entire purpose of loving punishment is to teach, and it lasts only as long as is needed for the lesson. And the lesson is always love.[3]

Overtones of Origen sound out here, but knowing where such ideas as Satan's salvation come from is of academic interest only and should not delay us. What matters for us now is to see what drives this kind of thinking, whether in Origen or L'Engle, or in her literary predecessor George MacDonald;[4] or in liberal Protestants like eighteenth-century Charles Chauncy, chief critic of the Great Awakening;[5] or nineteenth-century Friedrich Schleiermacher,[6] the epoch-making

---

[2]Bertrand Russell, *Why I Am Not a Christian* (London: Unwin, 1967), 47.
[3]Madeleine L'Engle, *The Irrational Season* (New York: Seabury, 1977), 97.
[4]See quotes in Dixon, *The Other Side*, 69f.
[5]Charles Chauncy, *The Mystery Hid from Ages and Generations . . . the Salvation of All Men the Great Thing Aimed at in the Scheme of God. . . .* (1784), is discussed in Sanders, *No Other Name*, 101–3.
[6]"Schleiermacher argued for a single predestination by which all people would be saved through God's omnipotent grace," ibid., 91. See Schleiermacher, *The Christian Faith*, ed. and trans. H. R. Mackintosh and J. S. Stewart (Edinburgh: T. & T. Clark, 1928), secs. 117–20, 163 (pp. 536–60, 717–22).

J. I. PACKER

Protestant revisionist; or the twentieth-century Bible scholar C. H. Dodd;[7] and theologians J. A. T. Robinson,[8] Nels Ferré,[9] the early John Hick,[10] and most recently Thomas Talbott.[11] The answer is clear: As L'Engle's words testify, it is a vision of God as universal sovereign love toward his rational creatures—of all those creatures, however rebellious, as his children—and of a coming consummation in which God's fatherly desire for a perfectly reconciled and responsive family—from which no one is excluded—finds fulfillment.

Rejecting all thought of an endless hell for some is prompted partly, to be sure, by direct compassion for one's fellow humans, but mainly by the thought that inflicting eternal punishment is unworthy of God, since it would negate his love. This is apparent throughout the story scholars tell of medievals and some individual Anabaptists in the sixteenth century; of the influence of Bohemist belief in final restoration in the seventeenth; of the personal impact in America of George DeBenneville, John Murray (the excommunicated Irish Methodist), and Hosea Ballou; of the ramifications of Enlightenment optimism about divine benevolence and human possibilities; and of the growing resolve of latter-day liberal Protestants to find a way of seeing all religions as one and of affirming salvation through them all. This vision of God's loving nature and purpose has been the constant motivational taproot, the control belief that shapes everything else to itself.

Variety

Motivationally, then, universalists are at one, but not in substantive theology. Far from it! On closer inspection, universalism dissolves into a cluster of distinct universalisms. That is, universalism appears as "a variegated species some types of which root and grow in theological soils where others would only wither and die."[12] As Richard Bauckham primly puts it: "Only the belief that all men will ultimately be saved is common to all universalists. The rationale for that belief and the total theological context in which it belongs vary considerably."[13]

Robinson and Ferré, for instance, among the dogmatic universalists, present universal salvation as a certainty; others, such as Karl Barth, Emil Brunner, Hans Küng, and John MacQuarrie, class it rather as a theological possibility that is

---

[7]"As every human being lies under God's judgment, so every human being is destined, in His mercy, to eternal life," C. H. Dodd, *The Bible Today* (Cambridge: Cambridge Univ. Press, 1960), 118. When the present writer was a theological student, Dodd was the dean of English-language New Testament study, and the *bon mot* was, "Thou shalt love the Lord, thy Dodd, with all thy heart (and thy Niebuhr as thyself)."

[8]J. A. T. Robinson, *In the End, God* (London: James Clarke, 1950).

[9]See Nels Ferré, *Evil and the Christian Faith* (New York: Harper, 1947); idem, *The Christian Understanding of God* (London: SCM, 1951); idem, *Christ and the Christian* (New York: Harper, 1958).

[10]John Hick, *Evil and the God of Love* (London: Macmillan, 1966); idem, *Death and Eternal Life* (New York: Harper & Row, 1976).

[11]Thomas Talbott, *The Inescapable Love of God* (n.p.: Universal Publishers, 1999).

[12]Trevor Hart, "Universalism: Two Distinct Types," in *Universalism and the Doctrine of Hell*, ed. Nigel M. de S. Cameron (Grand Rapids: Baker, 1992), 2.

[13]Richard Bauckham, "Universalism: A Historical Survey," *Themelios* 4/2 (January 1979): 49.

Hell under fire

beyond us to verify, and so they embrace it simply as a pious hope.[14] Some envisage it as the fruit of postmortem evangelism, succeeding in every case. (Others who envisage postmortem evangelism limit it to persons not confronted with the gospel of Christ in this life and do not anticipate so much success from it.) Some universalists, as we will see, expect God's postmortem address to be backed by a chastening experience of the pains of hell. Hell exists and will have a vast number of occupants for a longer or shorter period, but it is guaranteed to end up empty.

By contrast, the so-called "death-and-glory" message of Hosea Ballou (who taught that death as such brings the unregenerate to repentance) and many pagan fantasies of our time in fiction and on film seem to merit R. C. Sproul's lighthearted if heavy-handed lampoon:

A prevailing notion is that all we have to do to enter the kingdom of God is to die. God is viewed as being so "loving" that he really doesn't care too much if we don't keep his law. The law is there to guide us, but if we stumble and fall, our celestial grandfather will surely wink and say, "Boys will be boys."[15]

---

[14]Barth holds that through and in Jesus Christ all humankind has been and now actually is redeemed, and faith is simply believing this to be the truth about oneself. But, fearing it would infringe upon God's freedom should he speak of the destiny of unbelievers, Barth takes "no position for or against" universalism—no dogmatic position, that is (*The Humanity of God* [Richmond, Va.: John Knox, 1960], 61). Wishfully, however, he says: "Universal salvation remains an open possibility for which we may hope" (*Church Dogmatics* IV.3 [Edinburgh: T. & T. Clark, 1961], 478). His unwillingness to embrace dogmatic universalism is deeply problematical, for his insistence on the factuality of every person's actual redemption makes it seem as if the divine freedom he wants to safeguard is simply God's freedom to not take his own achievement in Christ seriously—which is, of course, unthinkable.

Brunner says: "We teach ... the Last Judgment ... and universal salvation" (understanding biblical statements about both as having an invitational rather than informational logic, and insisting that so understood the former does not cancel out the latter). "We must hearken to the voice that speaks of world judgment as God's voice, that we may fear Him, and we must hearken to the voice that speaks of the reconciliation of all as God's voice, that we may love him" (*The Christian Doctrine of the Church, Faith, and the Consummation: Dogmatics*, vol. 3 [Philadelphia: Westminster, 1962], 421–22, 424). Brunner is ruling out any Bible-based denial of universalism as exegetically wrong-headed, in accordance with his control belief that truth from God is met as we move dialectically between mutually exclusive poles of thought that Scripture sets before us. Brunner's control belief, however, seems to have died with him.

Küng sounds like Barth as he declares: "Christian faith represents radical universalism, but one grounded and made concrete in, and centered upon, Jesus Christ.... Every human being can be saved, and we may hope that everyone is...." And then, not so Barth-like: "Every religion can be a way of salvation, and we may hope that every one is" ("The Freedom of Religions" [1964] in Owen C. Thomas, ed., *Attitudes Toward Other Religions* [London: SCM, 1969], 216). Küng here develops further Vatican II's development of a qualified affirmation of non-Christian religions.

MacQuarrie writes: "A doctrine of conditional immortality is at least preferable to the barbarous doctrine of an eternal hell.... But perhaps the Christian hope can carry us further even than a belief in conditional immortality ... we prefer a doctrine of 'universalism' to one of 'conditional immortality.' ..." (*Principles of Christian Theology*, 2d ed. [New York: Scribner's, 1977], 361). Whether questions of objective divine fact should be decided by subjective personal preference is, of course, a question in itself.

[15]R. C. Sproul, *Reason to Believe* (Grand Rapids: Zondervan, 1982), 99–100; cited from John Blanchard, *Whatever Happened to Hell?* (Darlington, U.K.: Evangelical Press, 1993), 189.

HeLL under fiRe   173

Is it then that God is too good finally to damn anyone, or that man is too good ever to merit final damnation? Or should we affirm both together? Whatever the answer from this quarter, it sets one in a different world from that of those who think that persons dying without faith in Christ will not get to glory without experiencing hell first.

Most universalists have affirmed explicitly that all will eventually be found acknowledging Christ's dominion as Lord (see Phil. 2:9–11). They will praise and adore him, fellowship with him, and find their salvation and joy in so doing. Some have based this confidence in their belief that, after death as before, God is sovereign in effectual calling; others have rooted it in a glowing vision—a somewhat incoherent vision, it must be said—of God persuasively wearing down free human agents till, in some sense against their will, unbelievers bow to his will. (Clearly, this is not meant to sound like brainwashing, though it does.)

But the latter-day John Hick, for one, now predicates his universalism on the idea that all religions are essentially the same, an idea he reaches by resolving the Trinity into a unitarian belief in a nonpersonal Real, and dissolving salvation syncretistically and theosophically into a shift from self-centeredness to Real-centeredness, in which the Real is never directly known and nothing that can be called fellowship with the Father and the Son (see 1 John 1:3) ever takes place.[16] Hick made this move in order to construct an account of religion that, by taking in all religions, would rise above the exclusiveness that has historically marked Christianity. But in seeking to rise above historic Christian faith, he has actually fallen below it; he has lost the Christian understanding of salvation and of God, and his universalistic religious pluralism must be judged a post-Christian reversion to sub-Christianity.

What our survey of the variety of universalisms (which is by no means exhaustive) points to is the fact that (1) the various universalisms are corollaries or spin-offs of other beliefs about God and/or man, and that (2) universalism in all its forms is a human wish seeking a divine warrant. What holds universalists together is a shared sense of embarrassment, indeed outrage, at the thought of a loving God ever excluding anyone from final happiness, rather than any common mind as to what that happiness includes and how today's unbelievers worldwide will reach it. Pain at the prospect of souls being lost is not, of course, improper; the improper thing, rather, would be the absence of such pain. Surely C. S. Lewis speaks for us all when he says, "I would pay any price to be able to say truthfully: 'All will be saved.'"[17] But the crucial word is *truthfully*. Do any of the speculations we have reviewed, marginal as they are to the main flow of Christianity over two thousand years, strike us as having the ring of truth? We must keep that question in mind as we proceed.

---

[16]Hick's journey from a profession of evangelical faith to the universalist Real-centeredness suggested to him by the Tibetan *Book of the Dead* is conveniently surveyed by Ronald Nash, *Is Jesus the Only Savior?* (Grand Rapids: Zondervan, 1994), 29–100.

[17]C. S. Lewis, *The Problem of Pain* (London: Bles, 1940), 107. The passage continues: "But my reason retorts, 'Without their will, or with it?' If I say, 'Without their will,' I at once perceive a contradiction; how can the supreme voluntary act of self-surrender be involuntary? If I say, 'With their will,' my reason replies, 'How if they *will not* give in?'"

Importance

Universalism is making great strides today, both among the church's leaders and among its rank and file. There are several discernible reasons for this. First, living in what have become multireligious communities and rubbing shoulders regularly at work, in school, in sports, and in social life with people of many faiths, we would like to be able to tell ourselves that their religions are as good for them as ours is for us—which means that, whatever salvation is, it will finally be theirs as we hope it will finally be ours. Second, linked with this is another reason: Few today are as clear as they need to be on the specifics of the Christian view and way of salvation and on how it differs from what is prescribed and hoped for in Hinduism, Buddhism, Islam, and other world faiths. So no problem is seen in treating all religions as one and on that basis taking universalism for granted. Third, with Christianity losing ground so fast in the West, it is reassuring to think that God will finally save all those who now shrug off Christianity as an irrelevance, and reassurance in the face of troubling facts is always welcome, at least to most people. Finally, establishing affirmative rapport with non-Christian faiths remains a main agenda item for liberal theologians, and that is a frame into which universalism naturally fits. Thus it seems likely that universalism, which has certainly come to stay, will generate more interest in the future than it does now, and this makes it increasingly important that we should properly understand it and soberly assess it by the light of the Bible.

In any case, we must face up to the two far-reaching claims that all forms of universalism make. The first claim is made constantly and with emphasis: Universalism alone does justice to the biblical revelation of the love of God—that is, of God as love—and, in connection with that, to the victory of Jesus Christ the Savior over sin and death and to the overall thrust of the Bible, with its expectation that one day God will be all in all—all of life, that is, to all his people, both corporately and individually. While sitting loose to some of the specifics of biblical teaching, modern universalists insist that the overall trajectory of Holy Scripture is as stated and must be adhered to. By contrast, so they claim, any belief in the eternal loss and unending torment of any of God's rational creatures makes God out to be a failure and something of a devil (the rhetoric is frequently unbridled here). This is a bold claim, implying as it does that most Christians' belief in God has grossly misrepresented and dishonored him. We must ask ourselves whether this contention is really true.

The second claim is not always verbalized but is constantly implicit in the strategies that pastors and church leaders follow and is a direct corollary of the conviction stated above: Evangelism is not the prime task in the Christian mission, whatever the Great Commission of our Lord in Matthew 28:19–20 might seem to indicate. When the Faith and Order Commission of the World Council of Churches, meeting at Bangkok in 1979, redefined the Christian mission in terms of seeking the socio-politico-economic well-being of the nations, with evangelism and church planting added in if circumstances and resources allowed, I was so shocked that I wished the World Council goodbye on the spot, and I have,

I confess, kept at a distance from its activities ever since. But had I been a universalist, as I suspect most of the architects of the Bangkok theology were, I should have taken in stride this politicized adjustment of Christian missionary priorities, for I would have realized that if all are, as the title of a nineteenth-century tract put it, "Doomed to be Saved," evangelizing them here and now may be less urgent. If everyone's final salvation is guaranteed anyhow, whether or not people become Christians in this life is no longer crucial. In that case, other ways of loving my neighbor can take priority over seeking by word and prayer to win him or her to Christ.

It is noticeable that for more than a century—from Frederick Denison Maurice (who in 1853 lost his job at King's College, London, for dropping hints against hell and for openness to universalism) to dogmatic universalist John A. T. Robinson and hopeful universalist Karl Barth—a socialist agenda as a life task and universalist inclinations of theological thought have frequently gone together. After all, if universalism is true, public Samaritanship (which is how Christian socialism sees itself) may serve my neighbors better than evangelizing them. Many nonsocialist pastors seem to think similarly; they preach and teach and practice goodwill as if everyone is heading for heaven and no danger of eternal hell exists. One supposes that it was this behavior as much as anything that in 1914 led Hugh Ross Mackintosh to opine that a "frank and confidential" plebiscite (i.e., a full vote) of pastors would show that a "considerable majority ... adhere to universalism. They may no doubt shrink from it as a dogma but they would cherish it privately as at least a hope."[18]

Nothing seems to have changed here during the past ninety years, save in the extent to which mainstream leaders are now ready to reveal their real thoughts. Generally speaking, whereas up to the end of the nineteenth century, with exceptions, universalism was execrated within the denominations as a pastorally disastrous falsehood, and straightforward acknowledgement of the reality of eternal punishment was generally held to be necessary and healthy, today the crypto-universalists are out in the open and the boot is definitely on the other foot. Universalism has become thoroughly respectable, while assertion of hell for the most part, at least in the Western Protestant world, is felt to be disreputable to a degree.

So here is a second major claim, namely, that the Christian mission should be radically reconceived and its priorities altered in light of universalist eschatology. A view that has these claims as its practical implications is clearly important and needs to be critically examined.

Examining Universalism I: The Method of Assessment

We must test the theory of universalism by the teaching of the Bible; and because the Bible has been pressed into service in various ways already in expounding the theory in its various forms, it will be helpful to state at the outset how the Bible will be used here.

---

[18]Quoted from Bauckham, "Universalism: A Historical Survey," 47 n. 3.

In most versions of universalist theory, it is common ground that biblical teaching is from God and is to be taken as true and trustworthy; interpretation and application are singled out as the areas of dispute. Now the proper key principles here are, and always will be, that interpretation must be context-specific, author-specific, and focus-specific. That means, first, that passages must be exegeted in terms of the thought-flow of which they are part and not have their meaning extrapolated beyond the manifest perspectives, limits, and boundaries of that thought-flow; otherwise, we will be reading into them what cannot truly be read out of them. (2) It also means that writers must not be assumed to contradict themselves, but must be respected as knowing their own minds; thus, what they write in one place must be treated as cohering with what they write elsewhere. And it means, finally, that in seeking the writer's meaning, we must never lose sight of the immediate point he is making, the persuasive strategy of which that point is part, and the effect that he shows himself wanting to produce on his readers. The way into the mind, meaning, and message of God the Holy Spirit in the biblical text is always through the mind, meaning, and message of its human writers. Though many passages in their canonical context carry a greater weight of meaning than their divinely led human writers knew, none carries less meaning than its human writer actually expressed, and none should ever be treated as if the three guidelines set out above do not apply to it.

Therefore, all impressionistic selectivity that discounts some things Scripture specifically says while claiming to detect and affirm the Bible's general thrust, overall view, basic perspective, sustained trajectory, or whatnot—as if the Bible is partly out of sync with itself, and its writers sometimes vacillate and speak out of both sides of their mouths—are false trails. To follow any of them is a mistake of mental method. It fortifies us against such lapses to remember that all biblical teaching yields information, directly or indirectly, one way or another, about past, present, or future states of affairs that are under God's control and in which he is somehow active. The information about God in action may be explicit, as in the four Gospels, or implicit, as in the book of Esther, where God is not mentioned, or in the Song of Solomon, where Yahweh appears only once in passing. But we miss part of the writer's message if we do not look for the direct God-relatedness of all that he tells us, and we surely err if we fancy that at any point false witness of God is being borne.

A further principle, equally important, is that all the things that the Bible says about God, including all that it reports him as saying about himself, his world, and his servants, involve an *analogical* use of human language. That is, the meaning of all the verbs, nouns, and adjectives that Scripture applies to God, and that we ourselves use when we echo Scripture in our prayers, hymns, and theology, is adjusted in its details from the meaning that we express when we use these words. The central meaning is substantially as before, but the changes round the edges, if we may put it so, give the word a new "feel" and alter some of its implications.

Why must this adjusting be done? Because of the many ways in which God the Creator differs from his human creatures. Since God made us in his own image and likeness—personal, rational, moral, and relational beings with our own real though limited powers of creating and controlling—and gave us the gift of language for two-way communication with him as well as with each other, one stock of words suffices for both purposes. The *anthropomorphism* of language used by and of God is warranted by the *theomorphism* of humankind: We can speak of God, and God can speak of himself, as if he is really in key respects like us because we have been made in key respects really like him.

But we are finite and sinful, while God is neither; and God is perfect, infinite, and self-sustaining, while we are none of these things. So the peripheral adjustments referred to above are always necessary. When we speak of God, all implications of finitude and imperfection must be dropped out of our meaning and the known excellencies of God (omnipresence, omniscience, omnipotence, eternity, holiness, love, justice, truthfulness, etc.) must be brought in. In biblical usage these analogical adjustments are consistently made, and we must learn to recognize them and make them, too. Oxford professor Basil Mitchell outlined the rule for doing this as follows:

A word should be presumed to carry with it as many of the original [ordinary-use] entailments as the new [biblical or theological] context allows, and this is determined by their compatibility with the other descriptions which there is reason to believe also apply to God. That God is incorporeal dictates that "father" does not mean "physical progenitor," but the word continues to bear the connotation of tender protective care. Similarly God's "wisdom" is qualified by the totality of other descriptions which are applicable to him; it does not, for example, have to be learned, since he is omniscient and eternal.[19]

Thus, when (for instance) Scripture speaks of God's "wrath" against persons who sin or tells us that God "loves," "hates," and "repents," we must remember that the language is analogical and must be interpreted within the frame of the rest of what is said about him. Otherwise, we will lapse into false inferences of our own, based on overlooking the analogical quality of the discourse—as when it is said (e.g., by liberals, skeptics, and revisionists) that a good father would never expose his son to such suffering as Jesus underwent on the cross, or that for God to appoint the cross for his Son was child abuse, or that God's repenting of things he did shows that he did not foresee the consequences when he did them.[20]

The relevance of this will appear shortly. At present, suffice it to say that in assessing universalism we will seek only to read out of Scripture what is demonstrably there, letting the inspired writer himself show us what he meant and always construing the analogical aspects of Bible teaching by the light of Professor Mitchell's rule. Now let us proceed.

---

[19]Basil Mitchell, *The Justification of Religious Belief* (London: Macmillan, 1973), 19.
[20]Exponents of "open theism" lay great weight on this inference; it is the point on which the entire pyramid of their thought seems to be balanced. It is remarkable how little awareness they show of the analogical nature of biblical language.

HeLL UNDeR fire

Examining Universalism II: The Meaning of Salvation

Salvation in Scripture

When universalists affirm the salvation of all, they are clearly intending to use the word in its full Christian sense. So let us remind ourselves of what that is. Salvation, in Scripture as in life, is the process, or outcome, of being saved: that is, being rescued from jeopardy and misery, preserved and kept safe from evil and disaster, protected against hostile forces, and thus firmly established in a state of security. The Bible focuses throughout on God as the One who saves, and on needy humans as beneficiaries of his saving action.

Thus, we read of God's saving Israel from Egyptian captivity, Jonah from the fish's belly, the psalmist from death, and the crew of the ship taking Paul to Rome from drowning (see Ex. 15:2; Ps. 116:6; Jonah 2:9; Acts 27:31, 44). But the master theme of the New Testament is God's work and gift of spiritual, eternal salvation through Jesus Christ the Lord, a work whereby guilty, vile, and helpless humans are delivered from sin, God's wrath, death, and hell. They are reconciled to God, justified, and adopted into his family as they rest their faith on Christ; they enter a new life in Christ, and they are finally brought to fullness of Christlike glory with Christ for Christ, that is, for his everlasting praise (see Rom. 10:11–13; 11:36; Eph. 2:5–7; Col. 1:16; Heb. 2:10; etc.)

This Christian salvation has three tenses—past, present, and future. Believers have been saved from *sin's penalty*, are being saved from *its power*, and will one day be saved from *its presence*, for when we are glorified there will be no sin either in us or in our environment. At each stage, salvation centers on, and is mediated through, a personal relation that constitutes its very heart, namely: (1) faith-and-love fellowship with the Father and his Son, Jesus Christ, in adoring gratitude for what has been given so far and in expectant hope for more to come; and (2) a relation supernaturally created and sustained in the present by the Holy Spirit, one that it seems will last forever. And as it will not be an isolated experience but a continuous one, so it will not be an experience in isolation but a communal involvement with a countless host, enjoying their togetherness as they enjoy their communion with the Savior, who loves each of them separately (cf. Gal. 2:20) within his love for his church as a whole (cf. Eph. 5:25).

Universalists and Salvation

The first critical question in our assessment is this: Do universalists really understand salvation in these terms? To answer it, we must distinguish three different sorts of universalism that modern minds entertain. We label them secular salvationism, postmortem salvationism, and pluralist salvationism.

Secular salvationism contends that the destination everyone will share after he or she has died is not conceived in a way that includes the elements in the biblical gift of salvation as specified above. This corresponds with Hollywood's fantasy-laden dreams of happy futures for all departed ones. Note also Hosea Ballou (1771–1852), who taught that everyone dies into some sort of happiness. Under his leadership "the Universalist Church threw out the doctrines of the Trinity, the deity of Christ, original sin and the need for conversion."[21]

"Is it not of the very nature of biblical salvation," asks Trevor Hart, "that it consists in a conscious personal sharing in sonship; in embracing joyfully the knowledge of who God is, the Father who willingly delivers up the Son in the Spirit that we might share in the Spirit of sonship; in having one's life transformed by a thankful *metanoia* rooted firmly in this knowledge, and by the ongoing sharing in that trinitarian *koinōnia* which is its ultimate end?"[22] The answer is yes, and any idea of a final salvation into which these cognitive and relational realities do not enter must be dismissed as inaccurate. All constructions in which loving communion with the Father and the Son by the Spirit and unending praise and gratitude for redemption are not central are mere pagan fantasies. So we label them *secular* and strike them out of our reckoning.

Postmortem salvationism is the belief that after death God will deal savingly with all who, for whatever reason, left this world without faith in Christ. Their Creator will carry out a procedure that has been described as eschatological evangelization.[23] He will confront them with their sin and set before them the Christ of the gospel, and he will continue to do this till they turn to Christ in repentance and faith and so qualify to join the great company of saints and angels who are already worshiping on the true Mount Zion (Heb. 12:22–24). How exactly God will achieve that effect is variously explained, and the speculations raise problems, as we are soon to see; but our present point is simply that postmortem salvationists are sure that he will do it somehow. In contrast to the secular salvationists, they work with a fully Christian idea of final salvation, and that is what concerns us at this moment.

By contrast, *pluralist salvationism* is deeply problematical with regard to the meaning of salvation. To pinpoint this we focus on its best-known Western exponent, John Hick.

What is pluralism? As the word is currently used, it is the venturesome assertion that plurality—that is, a range and variety of thoughts, beliefs, ideals, convictions, hypotheses, and points of view on a subject, or of cultural and religious life-patterns and value-systems overlapping or in parallel—is good, because all these different views have real validity and so the mix of them is enriching. Instead of contrasting them and grading them, therefore, the natural course is to equate and blend them as fully as one can, on the basis that they are in reality equally good.

The fact on which we focus here is that partway through his career as a philosophy teacher, having already committed himself to universalism for purposes of theodicy within a broadly Christian frame,[24] John Hick embraced religious pluralism—that is, the view that, so far from Christianity being the one true faith,

---

[21]Blanchard, *Whatever Happened to Hell*, 191.
[22]Hart, "Universalism," 11–12.
[23]Sanders, *No Other Name*, 177–214.
[24]Hick, *Evil and the God of Love*.

all major religions are essentially on a par, sharing a generic transcendent unity, which now Hick set himself to identify.[25] This move, for Hick as for all pluralists, involved "rejecting the premise that God has revealed himself in any unique or definitive sense in Jesus Christ. . . . He is simply one of many great religious leaders who have been used by God to provide salvation for humankind."[26] All "authentic" religions, says Hick, diagnose the present human condition as in some radical way imperfect and offer a path via their teaching to "salvation/liberation/ultimate fulfillment."[27] The surface differences between Christianity and other faiths are simply

> variations within different conceptual schemes on a single fundamental theme: the sudden or gradual change of the individual from an absorbing self-concern to a new centering in the supposed unity-of-reality-and-value that is thought of as God, Brahman, the Dharma, Sunyata, or the Tao.[28]

We need not follow Hick's speculations further. It is already clear that he is not affirming, nor can affirm, the specifically Christian salvation in which all the redeemed find their ultimate delight in worshiping Jesus Christ, the Lamb on the throne, the Alpha and Omega of God's purposes, their loving and beloved Savior, Friend, Lord, and God. For Hick, as a pluralist, this Jesus is a myth, not a fact, and final salvation, whatever its nature, is as accessible through other faiths with other

---

[25]See Hick, *God and the Universe of Faiths* (London: Macmillan; New York: St. Martin's, 1973); idem, *God Has Many Names* (London: Macmillan, 1980; Philadelphia: Westminster, 1982); idem, *An Interpretation of Religion* (London: Macmillan; New Haven, Conn.: Yale Univ. Press, 1989). Sanders notes that "a considerable number of universalists have moved in this direction [pluralism] during the twentieth century, developing syncretistic theologies. They typically begin by abandoning the singular importance of Christ, then the finality of the Christian faith, and sometimes even the worship of God" (*No Other Name*, 116, referring to Ernest Cassara, ed., *Universalism in America* [Boston: Beacon, 1971], 39–42, for details). For fuller treatments of Hick's universalism, see Ronald H. Nash, *Is Jesus the Only Savior?*; Robert A. Peterson, *Hell on Trial* (Phillipsburg N.J.: Presbyterian and Reformed, 1995), 139–59.

[26]Harold A. Netland, *Dissonant Voices: Religious Pluralism and the Question of Truth* (Grand Rapids: Eerdmans, 1991), 10. Netland refers to *The Myth of God Incarnate*, a provocatively titled conference volume edited by John Hick and Paul F. Knitter (Maryknoll, N.Y.: Orbis, 1987) "that was intended by the contributors to serve as a kind of 'crossing of a theological Rubicon,' or a public rejection of both exclusivism and inclusivism and acceptance of a genuinely pluralistic view of religions." (Exclusivism is the Christian claim that faith in Christ here and now is needed for final salvation; inclusivism is the Christian theory that people with a fit attitude of mind "can receive the gift of salvation without knowing the giver or the precise nature of the gift" [Sanders, *No Other Name*, 215].) Contributors to *The Myth of God Incarnate* included, besides the editors, Gordon Kaufman, Langdon Gilkey, Wilfred Cantwell Smith, Rosemary Radford Ruether, and Raimundo Pannikar—a nice mix of liberal Protestants and liberal Roman Catholics. See Netland, *Dissonant Voices*, 26–27, with his comment: "Pluralists include some of the most influential theologians and philosophers of religion today."

[27]This cumbersome phrase comes from Hick (*An Interpretation of Religion* [New Haven, Conn.: Yale Univ. Press, 1989], 240), as he seeks to square the circle of the ultimately incompatible understandings of the Real (God) and the human religious ideal in the world's major faiths (Hinduism-Buddhism-Christianity-Islam-Shinto).

[28]Ibid., 36. Brahman and the Dharma are Hindu; Sunyata is Buddhist; the Tao is Chinese.

myths as it is through historic Christianity. Hick's formula was that all will ultimately achieve the ideal of Real-centeredness

> through a gradual, and at times painful, therapeutic and purgatorial process continuing beyond this life (according to Hick's later work, perhaps through several others), and leading eventually to the conformity of the person to what Christian tradition has called the "divine likeness." The suffering and pain of this present existence is thus justified on the grounds not only that each individual will ultimately be received into a glorious salvation, but also that this same darkness and pain is a necessary part of the road which leads to salvation.[29]

Hick brought this universalism with him when he moved into pluralism, but the jettisoning of his Christian ontology—a real incarnate personal Savior, a real triune *koinōnia* as the reality of God, a real atonement, reconciliation, justification and adoption through Christ, and a real new creation in union with Christ—leaves his salvation talk without any clear content at all. If it ever was the Christian salvation that he had in view, it is not so now. So at this point we rule pluralist salvationism out of our reckoning, just as a moment ago we ruled out secular salvationism. Both are charitable but unbiblical and indeed antibiblical dreams, nothing more.

A distinction needs to be drawn here between the agnosticism of the dogmatic pluralist about the nature of the salvation/liberation/ultimate fulfillment to which all of us are supposedly heading (whether we know it or not), and the agnosticism of the self-styled inclusivist about the way in which good pagans—leaving this world in a spirit of humble trust in an unknown God and thus as possessors (though they do not yet know it) of a saving relation to their Maker—will learn about the Christ who has brought about their salvation. Inclusivists do not know how after death this information will be conveyed to these people, but they are sure it will be. Nor do pluralists know how Christians who live and die believing that the so-called "myth" of God incarnate is a divine revelation of reality and that fellowship with Christ is already the rock-bottom fact of their life will be disabused of their mistake, but they are sure such Christians will be. Two entirely different agnosticisms are at work here, and they must not be confused.

Examining Universalism III: The Meaning of Eternal Punishment

Our survey of universalist ideas about salvation has shown the speculative character of this theory in all its forms and has uncovered in passing one of the motives that drives it today, namely, a generous desire to affirm all major religions as highways to the highest human happiness, so that no adherent of a different faith need ever convert to Christianity. Evident here is a wish to explode the thought, widespread in contemporary Hinduism and Islam, that Christianity is

---

[29]Hart, "Universalism," with reference to Hick, *Death and Eternal Life* (New York: Harper & Row, 1976), 7.

religious imperialism from the arrogant West, lingering on after political imperialism has become a thing of the past.

We did not dwell on how this universalist attitude negates the Christian mission as defined by Jesus and modeled by the apostles and the early church, though we might have done so had our space not been limited; all we did was note that fanciful ideas about final salvation enter into every form of universalism and then set aside those versions of the theory that clearly and inescapably involve sub-Christian soteriology. Now we will focus on the other main motivations that sustain this speculation: compassionate opposition to the belief that in a good God's ordering of things agony without end could ever be anyone's final destiny; and insistent certainty that the God of the Bible has a universal salvific purpose, revealed and ratified by the words and work of Jesus Christ, a purpose to which only the universalist hypothesis does justice. First we look at the question of eternal punishment; the following section will explore the love of God as revealed in Jesus.

The Biblical Teaching

The phrase "eternal punishment" comes from Jesus' parabolic prophecy of the separation of the sheep from the goats (Matt. 25:31–46). As on other occasions, Jesus here speaks of himself in the third person as the messianic Son of Man and as executing the purpose of "my Father" (v. 34). In this prophecy, the Son of Man has returned to the world as its King (vv. 34, 40) and is now judging "all the nations" (v. 32). Those who, by serving others, have actually served him inherit "the kingdom prepared for you since the creation of the world" (v. 34); those who, by not serving others, have failed to serve him are banished to "the eternal fire prepared for the devil and his angels" (v. 41).

The evident lesson here is that one's profession of faith is validated by the quality of one's life. So the wicked "will go away to eternal punishment, but the righteous to eternal life" (Matt. 25:46). "Eternal" (*aiōnios*) means belonging to the age to come, which in contrast to the present world order will not end. "Punishment" (*kolasis*) means retributive, as distinct from causeless, infliction of pain by or on behalf of whoever's authority has been flouted, as an expression of that person's displeasure. So eternal punishment means a divine penal infliction that is ultimate in the same sense in which eternal life is ultimate—prima facie, therefore, everlasting and unending.

Matthew 25:46, said O. C. Quick, Regius Professor of Theology at Oxford, is one of the two most explicit New Testament texts affirming permanent penal pain for some after death. Quick's other passage is Revelation 20:10, 15, where a "lake of fire" appears as the place of torment for the devil, the beast, and the false prophet "forever and ever," and with them for any whose names are not found written in the "book of life." Quick observes, sharply enough: "The strain of anti-universalist teaching in the New Testament can hardly be regarded by an impartial mind as other than conclusive."[30]

---

[30]O. C. Quick, *The Gospel of the New World* (London: Nisbet, 1944), 116.

Eternal punishment is not merely a matter of these two texts, however. Jesus declared, "Anyone who speaks against the Holy Spirit [rejecting his outward and inward witness to Jesus' own identity and role] will not be forgiven, either in this age or in the age to come" (Matt. 12:32). In his teaching on discipleship, Jesus said that it was better to get rid of a hand, foot, or eye that triggers sin than "to be thrown into hell [Gehenna, the spot outside Jerusalem where rubbish was burned], 'where their worm does not die and the fire is not quenched'" (Mark 9:43–48). In his teaching on neighbor love, Jesus envisages a hardhearted rich man describing his after-death state as "agony in this fire" (Luke 16:24). Cries of agony and gnashing of teeth in outer darkness and in a fiery furnace also appear in Jesus' utterances (Matt. 8:12; 13:42; 24:51; Luke 13:28).

In such passages Jesus is using, and thereby endorsing, the lurid penal imagery of the Jewish popular imagination and apocalyptic writing known in his time. In view of Jesus' personal divine teaching authority, however, one can see why the nineteenth-century Presbyterian theologian W. G. T. Shedd wrote: "Jesus Christ is the person who is responsible for the doctrine of eternal perdition."[31] From the standpoint of its status as an item of Christian belief, indeed he is.

Nor is it just Jesus and John in Revelation who talk in this fashion. Paul speaks of Christ's return "in blazing fire. He will punish those who do not know God and do not obey the gospel of our Lord Jesus. They will be punished with everlasting destruction" (2 Thess. 1:8–9; cf. Rom. 2:5–9, where the words wrath, fury, tribulation, and distress are used for what awaits the disobedient and defiant). The writer of Hebrews tells us of "eternal judgment" (Heb. 6:2), stating that "man is destined to die once, and after that to face judgment" (9:27), and declaring that apostasy brings "a fearful expectation of judgment and of raging fire that will consume the enemies of God. . . . It is a dreadful thing to fall into the hands of the living God" (10:27, 31). The point is that anticipation of eternal punishment for the impenitent pervades the whole New Testament.[32]

We can make four comments on this material:

As to the exegesis of passages threatening eternal punishment, it has been suggested that they are not informational at all, but that Christ and the apostles spoke them as in effect a horrific bluff, invoking their hearers' and readers' prejudices in order to drive them into faith and faithfulness out of fright. But this cynical and unpastoral idea fits neither the context in which these statements were made (i.e., to committed believers; Thessalonians, Romans, and, as the writer to the Hebrews trusts [see 6:9], his ex-Judaic addressees) nor their actual logical form, in which revelations or reminders of grim facts are clearly basic to whatever admonition, exhortation, or encouragement is being expressed.

(2) As to the meaning of these passages, anyone who, for whatever reason, thinks these passages inconclusive regarding eternal punishment for the impenitent must answer the question: How could our Lord and his apostles have made this belief any clearer? What more could they have said that they did not say had

[31]W. G. T. Shedd, *Dogmatic Theology* (Edinburgh: T. & T. Clark, 1889), 2:680.
[32]See chapter 9, "Annihilationism: Will the Unsaved Be Punished Forever," 195–218.

HeLL UNDeR fire

they wanted to put everyone out of doubt that this was indeed their meaning? To recognize the reality of eternal punishment is, to be sure, awesome, jolting, and traumatic, but surely there is no room for doubt that this was exactly what Jesus and his apostles wanted their hearers to recognize.

(3) As to the theory of annihilation (i.e., the idea that the fiery destruction that unbelievers will undergo ultimately will end in their nonexistence), this idea has to be read into the texts; it cannot be read out of them, since the fire is a picture not of destruction but of ongoing pain, as Luke 16:24 makes unambiguously clear. Also the Greek words that express destruction (verb, *apollymi*; nouns, *apōleia* and *olethros*; adjective, *olethrios*) signify functional ruination (as when one totals a car, thereby reducing it to a heap of wreckage) rather than ontological abolition (reducing something to a state of complete nonexistence). This popular theory could be called universalism in reverse, since universalism anticipates all persons who exist being saved while annihilationism anticipates that those who are saved are the only persons who exist. Both views are speculations, seemingly driven by the same conviction that the idea of endless punishment is not acceptable, and hence by the same desire that hell should one way or another be emptied.[33]

(4) As to theodicy (the discipline that seeks to safeguard God's praiseworthiness by showing that when he does what he does he is in the right and is doing or sanctioning something significantly good), so far from seeing endless retribution as creating a moral problem, as if it were really divine cruelty on those persons who do not deserve it, the New Testament sees it as resolving a moral problem, namely, the problem created by the way in which rebellious evil and human cruelty have constantly been allowed to run loose and unchecked in God's world. As in the Old Testament, so in the New: The vindicating of God's justice and the manifesting of his righteousness in merited retribution are treated as matters for praise (note, though, how the judgment on spiritual "Babylon" is viewed in Rev. 18:20; 19:2). Joy flows, and will forever flow, from the knowledge that God has finally taken action, and his righteous judgment (Rom. 2:5) has ended the running sore of global moral disorder at last.

The Universalist Thesis

The task for the universalist, as we can now see, is to circumvent the seemingly clear New Testament witness to the eternal destiny of those who live and die without Christ, under the self-serving sway of the anti-God allergy in human nature that constitutes our original corruption. Christless living is existence under sin, God's law, God's wrath, and death, as Paul analyzes our plight (see Rom. 1:18; 3:9, 19; 5:17). Today's universalists for the most part posit that the unconverted will spend time in hell exposed to postmortem evangelism as previously described, along with steady divine pressure on their spirits to change from what they were,

---

[33]Annihilationism is put under the microscope in my articles "The Problem of Eternal Punishment"(*Crux* 26/3 [September 1990]: 18–25), and "Evangelical Annihilationism in Review" (*Reformation and Revival* 6/2 [Spring 1997]: 37–51); also Peterson, *Hell on Trial*, 161–82.

J. I. PACKER

until the moment comes when they emerge, transformed, to join in the ongoing praises of the Lamb. Hell thus becomes, in the words of Emil Brunner, "a pedagogic cleansing process."[34] Thus, as Nels Ferré strikingly put it, "we must preach hell as having also a school and a door in it."[35]

Ferré was the most exuberant expositor of this line of thought that the twentieth century produced, and he is worth our attention.[36] He started, forthrightly enough, by declaring *agapē*—"unconditional, uncaused, unmotivated, groundless, uncalculating, spontaneous Love"—to be a complete account of God's moral character as expressed in his actions. "Love for enemies, if need be," he added, "is an intrinsic, inseparable part of Agape, universally, unconditionally and eternally."[37] This means, at least, that "if eternal hell is real, love is eternally frustrated and heaven is a place of [not only the church's, but also God's!] mourning and concern for the lost. . . . That is the reason that heaven can be heaven only when it has emptied hell, as surely as love is love and God is God."[38]

"The final victory of final love is universal salvation" and the Christian message (Ferré actually wrote Christology) "is deceit except it end in a hallelujah chorus."[39] The process may be slow. In an extraordinary flight of fancy, Ferré writes:

There may be many hells. There may be enough freedom even in the life of hell for man to keep rejecting God for a very long time. Hell may be not only unto the end of the age, but also unto the end of several ages. It cannot be eternal, but it can be longer than we think, depending upon the depth and stubbornness of our actual freedom now and whether or not God will give us fuller freedom in the life to come, and how much.[40]

But, Ferré notes, "God has no permanent problem children,"[41] and in hell he will "put on the screws tighter and tighter until we come to ourselves and are willing to consider the good he has prepared for us."[42]

This is typical mainstream universalist thinking, as is Ferré's confidence (Hick's, too) that here we have the one and only pathway to a credible theodicy. Says Ferré: "Without the ultimate salvation of all creatures, men and, we think, animals [and birds? and insects? and fish? and reptiles? presumably so], in God's time and way, it is easy to see that there can be no full solution of the problem of evil."[43] Not all universalists would involve pets and wildlife and mosquitoes in their eschatological hope, but most of them, it seems, would agree that the hurt and badness of human life are such that only by rating the evils as integral to the

[34]Emil Brunner, *Eternal Hope* (London: Lutterworth, 1954), 183.
[35]Ferré, *The Christian Understanding of God*, 241.
[36]A fuller discussion of Ferré's views will be found in Dixon, *The Other Side*, 55–67, 79–82.
[37]Ferré, *Christ and the Christian*, 63–64.
[38]Ferré, *The Christian Understanding of God*, 237.
[39]Ferré, *Christ and the Christian*, 63–64.
[40]Ferré, *The Christian Understanding of God*, 230.
[41]Ferré, *Evil and the Christian Faith*, 120.
[42]Ferré, *The Christian Understanding of God*, 240.
[43]Ferré, *Evil and the Christian Faith*, 117.

hell under fire

educational process that leads everyone to full final happiness can we, so to speak, save God's face regarding the way he orders his world.

So hell, the condition that Jesus called "eternal punishment," must be seen as really a means of grace. It is a rough reality, a house of correction as well as a place of conversion; it is the milieu in which the perverse and deluded come to their senses, and to that end it needs to be dreadful, as Jesus in particular stressed that it is. It is a kind of purgatory for those—that is, the totally Christless ones—whom official Roman Catholicism would not admit to purgatory. (Rome reserves purgatory for Christians only.) We have here a doctrine of salvation through, and out of, the state that the New Testament labels "perdition" and "eternal destruction." Universalism is indeed an unqualified and unlimited optimism of grace. Sin and hell, it tells us, are most certainly grim and grievous realities, just as we thought; but in the end God will save everyone out of both, and that will be the final triumph of his love. In these terms universalists seek to turn the flank of the historic Christian understanding of the Bible's witness to eternal punishment.

How do the universalists justify their hypothesis about hell? Some have claimed specific exegetical justification, citing as their front line three linked classes of texts: six allegedly predicting the actual salvation of all (John 12:32; Acts 3:21; Rom. 5:18; 11:32; 1 Cor. 15:22–28; Phil. 2:9–11); two supposedly announcing God's intention to save all (1 Tim. 2:4; 2 Peter 3:9); and five held to affirm that through Christ's redemptive death on the cross, followed by his resurrection and dominion, God must and will eventually save all (2 Cor. 5:19; Gal. 1:20; Titus 2:11; Heb. 2:9; 1 John 2:2). What these texts affirm, it is argued, by their use of the key words "all" and "world," is the proper frame within which to contextualize, relativize, and in effect scale down what the New Testament says about eternal punishment.

But this argumentation is, to say the least, forlorn. First, the universal terms in these texts (forms of *pas*, "all," and *kosmos*, "world") are all limited or generalized by their context in such a way that it is nowhere possible to maintain that every human being everywhere, past, present, and future, is being clearly, specifically, and inescapably spoken of as destined for salvation. The most that standard commentaries find in these passages is that God will save his elect and restore his world, and that the summons and invitation of the gospel of Jesus Christ is equally applicable to, and valid for, everyone to whom it comes. What more universalists read into the texts cannot be read out of them.[44]

Second, all except one of the New Testament books quoted also contain statements that on any natural view anticipate the final rejection and destruction of some because of their unbelief (see John 3:18, 36; 5:29; 12:25, 48; Acts 13:46; 28:24–27; Rom. 2:5–12; 6:23; 1 Cor. 6:9–10; cf. Gal. 6:7–8; 2 Cor. 4:3–4; Eph. 5:6; Col. 3:6, 25; Phil. 1:28; 3:19; 1 Tim. 4:16; 5:24; 6:9; Heb. 3:14–19; 6:4–8; 10:26–31, 39; 2 Peter 2:3, 6, 9–10, 17, 20–22; 3:7, 16; 1 John 2:19; 3:10, 15; 5:16). Unless we are to assume that the biblical writers involved did not know their own minds

---

[44]See Moo's "Paul on Hell," in this book, 91–110; an effective popular treatment of many of these texts is found in Blanchard, *Whatever Happened to Hell?* 189–208.

or could not recognize that they were contradicting themselves, we must conclude that they cannot have meant to affirm universal final salvation in these texts.

Third, it must be said with all possible emphasis that there is no scriptural support for any form of this postmortem evangelism, probation, or conversion theorizing.[45] What appears instead is a drumbeat insistence on the decisiveness of this life's decisions (see esp. Matt. 12:32; 25:41, 46; 26:24; Luke 16:26; John 8:21; Rom. 2:1–16; 2 Cor. 5:10; Gal. 6:7). As long ago as 1908, Robert Mackintosh, himself a wishful universalist, wrote: "The question is generally argued as one of New Testament interpretation, but the present writer does not think that hopeful. He sees no ground for challenging the old doctrine on exegetical lines."[46]

Most universalists, seeing this, fall back on generalized theological justification for their speculation about eternal punishment. Thus, Ferré uses his mantra of God-as-totally-*agapē* to become a biblical critic. He thinks it "likely that eternal damnation was actually intended by some of the writers of the Bible," though "whether Jesus taught eternal hell or not is uncertain."[47] In any case, "it is not the biblical Christ of the past that is the standard but the living Christ who bids us look less back to Jesus than up to God,"[48] and it is "the full picture of the universal love of God the Father in the face of Jesus Christ that is the authority of the Bible."[49]

The same control belief (i.e., that God is all *agapē*) prompts John A. T. Robinson to argue that God's retributive justice must be a function of his love and so must have a restorative purpose, whether the texts state that clearly or not. He rejects the idea that God's loving purpose could triumph if even one rational soul was lost on the grounds that such thinking "cannot preserve the absolute identity of divine love and justice."[50]

> Christ, in Origen's old words, remains on the cross so long as one sinner remains in hell. That is not speculation: it is a statement grounded in the very necessity of God's nature. In a universe of love there can be no heaven which tolerates a chamber of horrors, no hell for any which does not at the same time make it hell for God.[51]

---

[45]The puzzling text, 1 Peter 3:19, which says that in the reality and power of the Spirit Christ went and preached to the spirits now in prison (hell, undoubtedly) "who disobeyed ... in the days of Noah," cannot be pressed into service of the universalist cause. Whether it refers to Christ's visiting the underworld to announce the victory of the cross, either before or after his bodily resurrection, or to Christ's preaching repentance in the preaching of Noah himself (the better view, I think; see Wayne Grudem, *1 Peter* [TNTC; Grand Rapids: Eerdmans, 1988], 157–62, 203–39), it speaks of a message to a particular group, not to all the dead as such.

[46]See J. Hastings, ed., *Dictionary of Christ and the Gospels* (Edinburgh: T. & T. Clark, 1908), 2:785.

[47]Ferré, *The Christian Understanding of God*, 245.

[48]Ferré, *Know Your Faith* (New York: Harper & Brothers, 1959), 23.

[49]Ibid.

[50]Robinson, *In the End, God*, 104.

[51]J. A. T. Robinson, "Universalism: Is It Heretical?" *SJT* 2 (June 1949): 155; also Robinson, *In the End, God*, 123.

HeLL UNDeR fire

Does this match the biblical presentation of the goodness and severity of our holy Creator? If not, it is speculation, whatever Robinson may say.

Meanwhile, we should note that universalist speculation about God and eternal punishment is more than a little incoherent. The basic assertion is that God in love purposes everyone's salvation and will somehow make it happen. But how can it happen if, as most universalists believe, human freedom excludes full divine control? If the Creator is thought so to have limited his power when he made us that it is now beyond him to convert all those to whom his gospel comes in this world, however much he wants to, then how can we be sure that he will be able to do it hereafter? Picturesque fancies about schools and discipline and problem children do not resolve that question. Sanders writes:

> Ferré, Hick and Robinson all *claim* God can bring about the reconciliation of all free creatures, but they never plausibly demonstrate *how* this can be if the creatures remain forever free. And if, as they suggest, human freedom entails the possibility that individuals will continue to fall from grace and return to hell in the afterlife, how can it be guaranteed that there will ever come a time when all people will cease to turn away from God and hell will be done away with?[52]

Universalists cannot answer this question unless they are crypto-Calvinists after all. For the moment, we let the matter rest there.

From all standpoints, the theorizing about eternal punishment that most universalists lay before us must be judged unsuccessful. It is intrinsically speculative, internally incoherent, and wholly out of line with what the Bible actually teaches. The attempt to turn the flank of the doctrine of eternal punishment fails. So we leave it and move to the final part of our discussion.

Examining Universalism IV: The Meaning of the Love of God

It has already become clear that several motivating concerns together drive universalism. One is theodicy, the unending task of showing that God is in the right and is worthy of praise for all he does. Another is compassion. "Schleiermacher argued that if eternal damnation existed, eternal bliss could not, since the awareness of those suffering in hell would ruin the blessedness of those in heaven"[53]— and many since Schleiermacher have pressed the same point. But the main driving force is undoubtedly the belief that universalism grasps God's loving purpose for our race better than other viewpoints do. God's character and plan are for universalists the true central battlefield. Thus Robinson writes of "war to the death.... We are here in the presence of two doctrines of God, and between them there can be no peace."[54] And Ferré proclaims, "Traditional orthodoxy has to be challenged, fought and slain."[55]

---

[52]Sanders, *No Other Name*, 113.
[53]Ibid., 97, with reference to Schleiermacher, *The Christian Faith*, 721.
[54]Robinson, *In the End, God*, 102.
[55]Nels Ferré, *The Sun and the Umbrella* (New York: Harper & Brothers, 1953), 79.

What is at issue here? The question is whether God has a universal saving purpose that he guarantees, by hook or by crook as we would say, to fulfill in every respect in every case—that is, whether our theology is going to embody the salvation of everyone as the full truth about God's sovereign love to man. Some ascribe to God a salvific purpose that is universal but will not be fully achieved; others ascribe to him a purpose of saving sinners that is guaranteed to be accomplished as planned but does not include all the sinners there are. Both beliefs (Arminian and Calvinist, as we may for convenience label them, though labels are prejudicial and dangerous) leave some souls in hell forever. Universalism now steps forward to declare both views wrong at this point—wrong in ways which, though different, are equally insulting to God—and to announce itself as the only view that gives full honor to our Maker for his love. That, in essence and at heart, is what the battle between universalism and orthodoxy is all about.

Biblical Teaching on God's Love

How is the biblical truth about God's love to be ascertained? By contextual, analogical, author-specific, focus-specific exegesis of Holy Scripture, as we indicated earlier. "Love" is a much-abused word in our culture, having been cheapened to mean liking and wanting things for oneself ("I love ice cream/music/ skiing/sex," etc.), or liking and indulging particular people ("I love my son so I give him everything he wants"). The Bible's presentation of God's love for his creatures is, however, quite different from all of that.

In Scripture, God's love appears framed by three realities. The first is his ownership of, and dominion over, all that he has made—that is, *his universal lordship*. He is always God on the throne and in control. Second is *his holiness*, the quality whereby he requires virtue and purity of us, recoils from our vices and rebellion against him, visits the vicious with just judgment for what they have done, and vindicates himself by establishing righteousness in his world. The third reality is *everybody's actual sinfulness* and constant failure to match God's standards and obey his Word. It is within this framework that the divine way of acting—which the Old Testament usually calls goodness and loving-kindness (covenant love) and the New Testament calls *agapē* and *charis* (grace)—finds expression. Its relational form is always that of being mercy from the holy Lord to persons who do not deserve any good gift from his hand.

Thus, the love of God set forth in Scripture may be described as an action by God that expresses his goodwill, generosity, and kindness towards the personal subjects who are its direct objects. God's acts of love aim to enrich the loved ones and are calculated to draw out of them the appropriate response of gratitude, devotion, and abandonment of all wrong ways (cf. Rom. 2:3–4). By God's own standards, the loved ones, fallen and sinful as by nature they are, always and at every stage lack merit and are thus unfit for reward, but God pities their need, and despite their deserving of rejection, he expresses love to them by his actual blessing of them. God's love is always mercy contrary to merit, well-wishing, and good-giving in face of ill desert. Though his love embraces vast numbers of people simultaneously, it focuses personally on each individual whom it benefits, individualizing them more deeply than was the case before through their awareness of God encountering them in mercy. God loves all members of the human family in some ways (cf. Ps. 145:9) and a great number of them in all ways, for, taking the initiative in love, he draws out of these latter, spiritually dead (lifeless and unresponsive) as they are, true trust in Christ and raises them to new life with Christ in Christ to serve Christ, so that "in the coming ages he might show the incomparable riches of his grace, expressed in his kindness to us in Christ Jesus" (Eph. 2:7; see the entire paragraph, vv. 1–10).

"I am confident of one thing—God loves me in all ways" was the headline quote from the printed testimony of a recent convert. These words, the natural and spontaneous expression of Christian assurance, are also the perfect theological formulation for the love God has revealed toward all who believe. And one further point must be made: In all God's purposes of saving sinners through his love, the exalting of the Lord Jesus Christ—Son of God and Savior, our Mediator and Redeemer—is centrally significant, and the supreme privilege of those who experience God's saving love is to know that they are the appointed and predestined means to that end (Eph. 1:3–14; Col. 1:13–20, 27–28; 2:6–7; 3:1–4; Rev. 5; 19:6–16). Every aspect of salvation is the fruit of God's free, sovereign, holy, Christ-exalting love.

Twice John declares that God is *agapē* (1 John 4:8, 16). The logic of the phrase is parallel to that of "God is light" (1 John 1:5) and "our God is a consuming fire" (Heb. 12:29; cf. 12:18; also 6:8; 10:27). "Is" in each of these texts points to the consistent expression of a particular characteristic in God's behavior toward human beings. Here the characteristic is love, *agapē*. John does not mean that God's character consists of, and his activity expresses, only *agapē* to the exclusion of all else, but that all his acts in relation to those who become, and are, Christians ("us," 1 John 4:9–10) are acts of *agapē*, one way or another, whatever other aspects of his character they show forth as well.

John continues by saying that God's supreme demonstration of this *agapē* was sending his Son to be the propitiatory (wrath-quenching) sacrifice for our sins (cf. 2:2), and to become the sustaining source of our new life as God's supernaturally-born children. The particularizing nuance in all this is well caught in some words from James Montgomery's hymn, "Hail to the Lord's Anointed":

The tide of time shall never
His covenant remove;
His Name shall stand forever—
That Name *to us*[56] is Love.

It is what God is to Christians specifically that John is highlighting here.

It is true, indeed, that love marks all the inward, relational, perichoretic (interwoven and interpenetrating) life of the triune Lord. The Trinity is a society, a fellowship of mutual love, as the New Testament clearly shows. When theologians

---

[56]Our italics.

say that "God is love," this is usually what they mean. But though it may be implicit in John's thought here, as it is certainly explicit in his Gospel, that is not what John is actually speaking of at this point.

What then is God's revealed plan of love? It is a *restorative* plan for a fallen world. The entire human race is guilty and corrupt (Rom. 1:18–3:20), and God has chosen to create a new humanity through, in, and for Christ, his incarnate Son. For this he has chosen, redeemed, and now calls into faith and newness of life a multitude of Jews and non-Jews, from every tribe and language and people and nation (Rom. 8:29–9:29; Eph. 1–3; 5:25–27; Rev. 5:9–14; 7:9–17). Paul pictures them as a body of which Christ is the Head (leader, command center, and life-imparting authority) and in which all Christians are functioning units (Rom. 12:4–8; 1 Cor. 12; Eph. 4:11–16). With, through, and under Christ, these persons will finally constitute God's new Jerusalem, from which the vicious and ungodly will be excluded (Rev. 21:1–22:5; note esp. 21:8, 27).

Such is God's strategy of love, from which Christian believers, looking back, draw the assurance of their faith in Christ and, looking forward, draw the confidence of their hope in Christ. They are "in the know" as to what God has done, is doing, and will do, and because of this knowledge, unthinkable evils and hostilities find them unsinkable in their faith, hope, and love Christward and Godward, as the book of Revelation celebrates.

That this plan of love contains elements of mystery—that is, divine fact beyond our full understanding—is not a new discovery. The question "Why has God chosen to show his sovereign mercy in saving this sinner and not that one?" is as old as Augustine, and probably as old as the apostle Paul (see Rom. 9). We do not know why, and it looks as if we will never be told; our part is not to ask or try to guess why, but to praise God for his love to us whom he has called. We must also prayerfully invite others, as Jesus and the apostles did, to turn to the Lord and so enter the new life—and to do this in the confidence that Christ himself is always present, when his gospel is preached to change and save everyone whom the Father draws to him.

What we know is that everyone, including ourselves, deserves condemnation, rejection, and eternal punishment in hell, so that it is supreme *agapē* that God should go into the business of saving sinners at the cost of the humiliation and death of his Son. It is surpassingly marvelous that God should save many; it is, indeed, a wonder that he should save any, and it was certainly "Amazing grace! . . . that saved a wretch like me." Knowing these things must and will keep us in endless praise, both here and hereafter, and praise will preempt any puzzlement about God's revealed and unrevealed ways.

Universalist Teaching on God's Love

What we offer under this heading is an attempt at a generic statement, based on the generalizations, insinuations, and deprecations of universalist spokesmen, who too often behave as if assaulting what we have just affirmed suffices to make their own case. We now state what they seem to us to mean positively by what they say.

The word that best describes the universalists' idea of God's plan of love is *progressive* rather than restorative. They reason as if God owes it, if not to sinful humans, at least to himself, to take human and perhaps angelic sin in stride, so to speak, maintaining his creational purpose that all rational souls without exception should come to share the life of love and joy to which Christians are already consciously en route. God's election for final salvation does not, therefore, separate some from others; all are elect, as Schleiermacher insisted, and all will finally be saved in and through Christ. God's universal salvific purpose thus includes a resolve to work in hell with all who go there until they attain the sanity of repentance and faith in Christ and so are ready to leave for heaven. The controlling analogy, more basic than that of the school, evidently is of therapy in a sanitarium: God, it seems, made hell to be a help to health and uses it that way in every case. This is why hell will be empty in the end. In its own way the idea is noble and compassionate; but not only is it wholly unscriptural, it is incoherent and unrealistic, as we will now show.

Universalists seem not to understand sin. Leaving Scripture behind, they second-guess God's plan by contending that he uses hell to get sinners on track at last, and in so doing they fail to take the measure of the tragic twisting and shattering and consequent perversity of our souls through the Fall, and of the tragic irrationality and inaneness of sin as the now radical ruling force in humanity's spiritual system. So here is a further reason why their account of God's love seems simplistic and shallow when assessed by the scriptural standard.

Typically, as we saw, universalists think that God created and established our free will as an ultimate fact, so that he never does more than persuade, never finally determining our choices. They see this as God's affirming human dignity; they do not see that, since the addictive grip of sin holds us fast, leaving us to choose in spiritual matters would make our salvation an impossibility. "Hell at any time can be turned into purgatory if it is accepted and used," writes Michael Paternoster.[57] But over and above the unbiblical and indeed antibiblical nature of this notion, are these words not facile? unrealistic? indeed, fatuous? "The fact that [sin] is essentially irrational opens the door to the possibility that even God must suffer with it, that he may not be able to guarantee that all people will finally accept his love."[58] When rational persuasion is the ace, inbred irrationality trumps it. Bodily addictions such as pill-popping and heroin-shooting can, we know, defy all attempts at therapy; is there any reason to suppose that the habit of sin will be easier to talk its addicts out of, even when our loving God is doing the talking?

There is a lack of realism here, just as there is a lack of biblical faithfulness. The universalists' dream—fantasy, rather—about God's universal salvific purpose is in truth a kite that will not fly in an Arminian breeze. And should they, facing this fact, shift to belief in universal effectual calling in hell through the regeneration there of sin-dominated human hearts, they would still have to face the questions: Why, in that case, does God leave multitudes who know the gospel to go

---

[57]Michael Paternoster, *Thou Art There Also: God, Death and Hell* (London: SPCK, 1967), 155.
[58]Sanders, *No Other Name*, 113.

to hell as unbelievers before he calls them to faith? And, more searchingly, why do Christ and the apostles give no hint that God intends to lead every member of this fallen human race from the cradle to the crown, via hell if need be? And why do they speak instead, with such strong emphasis, as if each person's decisions made here determine their state hereafter, so that unbelievers face irremediable eternal loss? Is not the New Testament viewpoint on this issue clearly expressed, consistently maintained, and constantly enforced? Is there not then something heretical about the universalist account of God's plan of love, which parts company with the Bible so radically?

Conclusion

To critique a speculative hypothesis that, however well meant, seeks with real if unacknowledged and unrecognized arrogance to be wiser than the Word of God gives no pleasure. We have, however, done it, and this is what we have found: Universalism does not stand up to biblical examination. Its sunny optimism may be reassuring and comfortable, but it wholly misses the tragic quality of human sin, human unbelief, and human death as set forth in the Scriptures, while its inevitable weakening of the motives for evangelistic prayer and action is subversive of the church's mission as Christ and the apostles defined it. Universalism reinvents, and thereby distorts and disfigures, biblical teaching about God and salvation, and it needs to be actively opposed, so that the world may know the truth about the holiness, the judgment, the plan, the love, the Christ, and the salvation of our God.

Chapter 9

aNNihiLationism:
WiLL the Unsaved
Be Punished forever?

Christopher W. Morgan

Well, emotionally I find the concept [i.e., the historic view of an endless hell] intolerable and do not understand how people can live with it without either cauterizing their feelings or cracking under the strain.... We need to survey the biblical material afresh and to open our minds (not just our hearts) to the possibility that Scripture points in the direction of annihilationism, and that "eternal conscious torment" is a tradition which has to yield to the supreme authority of Scripture.[1]

These words from John Stott ignited the worldwide debate about hell in contemporary evangelicalism. Stott's reputation as an evangelical statesman brought instant credibility to this nontraditional view called *annihilationism* (sometimes known as *conditionalism*).

What Is Annihilationism?

Annihilationism is the belief that those who die apart from saving faith in Jesus Christ will be ultimately destroyed. Thus, annihilationists reject the historic view of hell as conscious, endless punishment. According to some annihilationists, this occurs at death. Most of its proponents associated with evangelicalism, however, hold that this destruction will take place after a period of punishment in hell, which will pass away at the new creation.[2]

The most popular version of annihilationism in evangelical thought today is conditionalism (often called "conditional immortality"). Conditionalism is the belief that God has created all human beings only potentially immortal. Upon being united to Christ, believers participate in the divine nature and receive immortality. Unbelievers never receive this capacity to live forever and ultimately cease to exist. Partly because annihilationism has historical connections to Socinianism, materialism, and the teachings of the Jehovah's Witnesses, most annihilationists in contemporary evangelicalism prefer to be known as conditionalists.[3]

---

[1]David L. Edwards and John R. W. Stott, *Evangelical Essentials: A Liberal-Evangelical Dialogue* (Downers Grove, Ill.: InterVarsity Press, 1988), 314–15.
[2]*The Nature of Hell: A Report by the Evangelical Alliance Commission on Unity and Truth Among Evangelicals* (Carlisle, UK: ACUTE/Paternoster, 2000), 4–6 (acronym ACUTE).
[3]Kendall S. Harmon, "The Case against Conditionalism: A Response to Edward William Fudge," in *Universalism and the Doctrine of Hell: Papers Presented at the Fourth Edinburgh Conference on Christian Dogmatics, 1991*, ed. Nigel M. de S. Cameron (Grand Rapids: Baker, 1992), 195–99.

Is Annihilationism New?

Annihilationism is not new. Its advocates existed in the patristic, post-Reformation, and modern periods.[4] The first appearance of annihilationism in Christian writing seems to have been from a fourth-century apologist named Arnobius of Sicca (died c. 330). In his book *Adversus Nationes*, Arnobius criticized Plato's teaching concerning the natural immortality of the soul. Discussing the final punishment of unbelievers, Arnobius wrote:

> That which is immortal, which is simple, cannot be subject to any pain; that, on the contrary, cannot be immortal which does not suffer pain. . . . For they are cast in, and being annihilated, pass away vainly in everlasting destruction. . . . For that which is seen by the eyes is only a separation of the soul from the body, not the last end—annihilation: this, I say, is man's real death, when souls which know not God shall be consumed in long-protracted torment with raging fire.[5]

Some scholars have argued that others in this period were annihilationists, but those proposed are highly debatable. There has been a tendency to read annihilationism into certain early church fathers. If these historical figures embraced a certain view of human mortality, it is often assumed or inferred that they can be labeled annihilationists. This common fallacy has made it difficult to ascertain the truth about their views on the duration of hell.[6]

Condemned by the Second Council of Constantinople (553) and the Fifth Lateran Council (1513), annihilationism reappeared in the works of Socinians like John Biddle (1615–62) and eighteenth-century Arians like William Whiston. In the 1800s, the United States saw a minimal emergence of annihilationism, primarily in new fringe groups like the Jehovah's Witnesses and Seventh-Day Adventists. But during that century England saw the rise of several books defending this doctrine, such as Archbishop of Durham Richard Whately's *A View of the Scripture Revelations Concerning a Future State* (1829), Congregationalist Edward White's *Life in Christ* (1846), English Baptist Henry Dobney's *The Scripture Doctrine of Future Punishment* (1858), and Anglican priest Henry Constable's *Duration and Nature of Future Punishment* (1868).[7]

In the twentieth century, Church Missionary Society missionary Harold Guillebaud defended annihilationism in *The Righteous Judge* in 1941, which was

---

[4]I could not find a clear defense of annihilationism in the medieval, scholastic, or Reformation periods.

[5]Cited in Hamilton Bryce and High Campbell, eds., *The Seven Books of Arnobius against the Heathen*, *ANF*, 2:14, 441–42. See also David Brattson, "Hades, Hell, and Purgatory in Ante-Nicene Christianity," *Churchman* 108 (1994): 69–79.

[6]This tendency is especially obvious in LeRoy Edwin Froom, *The Conditionalist Faith of Our Fathers*, 2 vols. (Washington, D.C.: Review & Herald, 1965). See also Edward William Fudge, *The Fire That Consumes: A Biblical and Historical Study of Final Punishment* (Houston: Providential, 1982).

[7]Geoffrey Rowell, *Hell and the Victorians: A Study of the Nineteenth-Century Theological Controversies Concerning Eternal Punishment and the Future Life* (Oxford: Clarendon, 1974), 180–207.

privately printed in 1961. Basil F. C. Atkinson, a prominent evangelical apologist and leader in Cambridge University's Inter-Collegiate Christian Union and Inter-Varsity Fellowship, taught annihilationism to his students and later had his book *Life and Immortality* privately printed (1962). His leadership influenced several up-and-coming evangelical annihilationists (e.g., John Wenham, Robert Brow, and possibly others).[8]

But the year 1974 serves as a benchmark in the debate over annihilationism in evangelical history. That year evangelical publisher InterVarsity Press published John Wenham's *The Goodness of God* (later titled *The Enigma of Evil*), in which Wenham questioned the historic view of endless punishment and proposed annihilationism.[9] Also in 1974, InterVarsity Press published Stephen Travis's *The Jesus Hope*, in which he questioned whether annihilationism might be the better alternative.[10] Two years later *Christianity Today* included an article by Edward Fudge defending annihilationism called "Putting Hell in Its Place." Fudge's thorough book on the subject came out in 1982 and was an alternate selection of the Evangelical Book Club.[11] In 1987, *Christianity Today* allowed Clark Pinnock to declare his belief in annihilationism in a short article entitled "Fire, Then Nothing."[12]

Then in 1988, the issue received heightened awareness as John Stott acknowledged his openness to and tentative acceptance of annihilationism. In *Evangelical Essentials*, Stott admitted his reluctance to publish his views on the duration of hell:

[8]Edward William Fudge, *The Fire That Consumes: The Biblical Case for Conditional Immortality*, ed. Peter Cousins, rev. ed. (Carlisle, U.K.: Paternoster, 1994), 8–10. For a brief history, see *The Nature of Hell*, 60–67. See also Robert A. Peterson, "Basil Atkinson: A Key Figure for Twentieth-Century Evangelical Annihilationism," *Churchman* 111 (1997): 198–217.

[9]John Wenham, *The Goodness of God* (Downers Grove, Ill.: InterVarsity Press, 1974). See also its reprint, *The Enigma of Evil* (Grand Rapids: Zondervan, 1985). Wenham developed his views in "The Case for Conditional Immortality," in *Universalism and the Doctrine of Hell*, 161–91. Note also Wenham's personal reflections on this issue in his autobiography, *Facing Hell: An Autobiography 1913–1996* (Carlisle: Paternoster, 1998), 229–57.

[10]Stephen H. Travis, *The Jesus Hope* (Downers Grove, Ill.: InterVarsity Press, 1974). See also how Travis developed his views in *Christian Hope and the Future* (Issues in Contemporary Theology 3; Downers Grove, Ill.: InterVarsity Press, 1980); idem, *I Believe in the Second Coming of Jesus* (Grand Rapids: Eerdmans, 1982); idem, *Christ and the Judgment of God: Divine Retribution in the New Testament* (Basingstoke, U.K.: Marshall Pickering, 1986); idem, "The Problem of Judgment," *Themelios* 11 (January 1986): 52–61; idem, "Judgment," in *Dictionary of Paul and His Letters*, ed. Gerald F. Hawthorne and Ralph P. Martin (Downers Grove, Ill.: InterVarsity Press, 1993); idem, "Eschatology," and "Judgment of God," in *New Dictionary of Theology*, ed. Sinclair B. Ferguson, David F. Wright, and James I. Packer (Downers Grove, Ill.: InterVarsity Press, 1988).

[11]Edward William Fudge, "Putting Hell in Its Place," *ChrT* 20 (August 6, 1976): 14–17. For more detail on Fudge's views, see "The Eschatology of Ignatius of Antioch: Christocentric and Historical," *JETS* 15 (September 1972): 23–37; idem, *The Fire That Consumes* (1982; rev. ed. 1994); idem, "The Final End of the Wicked," *JETS* 27 (September 1984): 325–34.

[12]Clark H. Pinnock, "Fire, Then Nothing," *ChrT* 31 (March 20, 1987): 40–41. See also Clark H. Pinnock and Delwin Brown, *Theological Crossfire: An Evangelical-Liberal Dialogue* (Grand Rapids: Zondervan, 1990), 226–27; Clark H. Pinnock, "The Destruction of the Finally Impenitent," *CTR* 4 (Spring 1990): 243–60; idem, "The Conditional View," in *Four Views on Hell*, ed. William Crockett (Grand Rapids: Zondervan, 1992), 135–66.

I am hesitant to have written these things, partly because I have a great respect for the longstanding tradition which claims to be a true interpretation of Scripture, and do not lightly set it aside, and partly because the unity of the world-wide Evangelical constituency has always meant much to me. But the issue is too important to suppress, and I am grateful to you for challenging me to declare my present mind. I do not dogmatize about the position to which I have come. I hold it tentatively. But I do plead for frank dialogue among Evangelicals on the basis of Scripture. I also believe that the ultimate annihilation of the wicked should at least be accepted as a legitimate, biblically founded alternative to their eternal conscious torment.[13]

Other distinguished evangelicals continued this trend. In 1989 Philip Hughes resigned from Westminster Theological Seminary and espoused similar views in *The True Image*. In 1990 Michael Green adamantly opposed the historic view of hell in his *Evangelism through the Local Church*. Robert Brow followed suit in 1994, Nigel Wright in 1996, and Earle Ellis in 1997.[14]

Recently two works have stood out in offering a rationale for conditionalism. The first is David Powys's massive monograph *'Hell': A Hard Look at a Hard Question*. Tony Gray commended it as "the strongest and most articulate defense of the conditionalist position written thus far."[15] Published in Paternoster Biblical and Theological Monographs, this slightly revised version of Powys's doctoral

---

[13]Edwards and Stott, *Evangelical Essentials*, 319–20. See also John R. W. Stott, "The Logic of Hell: A Brief Rejoinder," *Evangelical Review of Theology* 18 (January 1994): 33–34.

[14]Philip E. Hughes, *The True Image: The Origin and Destiny of Man in Christ* (Grand Rapids: Eerdmans, 1989), 398–407; idem, *Evangel: The British Evangelical Review* 10 (Summer 1992): 10–12; E. Michael B. Green, *Evangelism through the Local Church* (London: Hodder & Stoughton, 1990; reprint, Nashville: Thomas Nelson, 1992), 71–74; Clark H. Pinnock and Robert C. Brow, *Unbounded Love: A Good News Theology for the Twenty-First Century* (Downers Grove, Ill.: InterVarsity Press, 1994); Nigel Wright, *The Radical Evangelical: Seeking a Place to Stand* (London: SPCK, 1996), 87–102; E. Earle Ellis, "New Testament Teaching on Hell," in *Eschatology in Bible and Theology: Evangelical Essays at the Dawn of a New Millennium*, ed. Kent E. Brower and Mark W. Elliott (Downers Grove, Ill.: InterVarsity Press, 1997), 199–205.

[15]Tony Gray, review of *'Hell': A Hard Look at a Hard Question: The Fate of the Unrighteous in New Testament Thought*, by David Powys, in *Churchman* 114 (2000): 280–82. This claim is far too generous, however. Powys helpfully lists and addresses the major biblical texts concerning hell, but his exegesis is regularly skewed by his desire to reject retributive justice and by his hermeneutic. Similar to Edward Fudge, his tendency is to interpret the New Testament passages according to his presuppositions of life, death, and judgment in the Old Testament, rather than allowing the context of the passage to be primary in determining its meaning. In his attempt to stress the rhetorical effect of various passages (esp. concerning Jesus' teaching on hell) Powys (quite unlike Fudge) occasionally undermines biblical authority. For example, in his attempt to make Matt. 25:41–46 fit his conditionalist interpretation (an impossibility in my mind), Powys maintains, "This all suggests that this teaching was aimed at motivation, not revelation. Its purpose was not to reveal information concerning the fate of the unrighteous, but rather to warn and disturb those who claimed to be followers of Jesus" (290). While it is obviously valid to interpret a passage according to its intention (and thus its intended rhetorical effect), it is dangerous to assume that the passage has no revelatory or doctrinal value. In fact, the rhetorical effect actually depends on the truthfulness of Jesus' teaching concerning eternal punishment.

dissertation strives to interpret all relevant New Testament passages on hell according to their thought worlds. Particular attention is given to Old Testament passages and traditions, the culture and thought of Palestine, and to some extent the culture of the wider Greco-Roman world.[16] Powys's goal is to focus on the biblical teaching because he recognizes that "the great majority of modern positions on the fate of the unrighteous may be classified and largely explicated in terms of presuppositionally-determined reactions against 'traditional orthodoxy.'"[17] Powys's primary contribution lies in his breadth of coverage and his attempt at serious biblical exegesis.

Surpassing Powys's considerable book in precision and clarity is *The Nature of Hell*, published in 2000. This work is a report resulting from a two-year study on hell by a working group of ACUTE, the Evangelical Alliance Commission on Unity and Truth Among Evangelicals. The working group included the following scholars: David Hilbourn, Faith Forster, Tony Gray, Philip Johnston, and Tony Lane. The Evangelical Alliance is an umbrella organization that serves as an association of British-based evangelicals. ACUTE is composed of three evangelical groups: the Evangelical Alliance, the British Evangelical Council, and the Evangelical Movement of Wales.

Anglican evangelicals have had serious disagreement with one another on the nature and duration of hell. So ACUTE studied the doctrine of hell with hopes of bringing evangelicals together in a united front against universalism while simultaneously promoting a cooperative spirit among fellow evangelicals concerning the nature of hell. Robert Peterson aptly summarized this work as "an attempt at damage control."[18] *The Nature of Hell* introduces historical, biblical, theological, and practical issues related to the debates over hell. It is a helpful, careful, judicious, and first-rate summary of the positions and arguments of "traditionalists" (the common but poorly chosen term to designate those holding to the historic view of endless punishment) and conditionalists. Its chief contributions lie in the clarity it brings to several of the important questions concerning the duration of hell as well as in thoroughly addressing the most important issues surrounding the nature of hell.

Why Do Annihilationists Reject an Endless Hell?

Because both ACUTE's *The Nature of Hell* and Powys's *'Hell': A Hard Look* are such recent and important challenges to the historic view of endless punishment, they will be addressed regularly in this essay (ACUTE's *The Nature of Hell* throughout and Powys in the exegetical section). But because other capable conditionalists have wielded tough arguments against an endless hell, their challenges will also be addressed. While each conditionalist scholar nuances the arguments

---

[16]David Powys, *'Hell': A Hard Look at a Hard Question* (Paternoster Biblical and Theological Monographs; Carlisle: Paternoster, 1998), xix.

[17]Ibid., 40–41.

[18]Robert A. Peterson, "Undying Worm, Unquenchable Fire," *ChrT* 44 (October 23, 2000): 30–37.

HeLL UNDER fire

a little differently from the others, a careful reading of all of them uncovers a discernible string of objections to the historic view of the conscious, endless punishment of non-Christians in hell.[19] The best expressions of these conditionalist objections will be considered and evaluated.

These objections are primarily theological, while some are exegetical/linguistic. Each was considered central in ACUTE's *The Nature of Hell*. The first objection is concerned with the interpretation of the biblical terms "eternal" and "destruction." The second objection focuses on the nature of human mortality/immortality. The next three are actually the most foundational in the debate; they center on God's justice, love, and ultimate victory. Even those who stress a biblical rationale for conditionalism usually unveil emotional and theological presuppositions that shape their interpretation of hell. Clark Pinnock openly admits this of himself (and similar conclusions could be drawn from reading Wenham, Travis, Fudge, Stott, and Green):

> Obviously, I am rejecting the traditional view of hell in part out of a sense of moral and theological revulsion to it. The idea that a conscious creature should have to undergo physical and mental torture through unending time is profoundly disturbing, and the thought that this is inflicted upon them by divine decree offends my conviction about God's love. This is probably the primary reason why people question the tradition so vehemently in the first place. They are not first of all impressed by its lack of a good scriptural basis (that comes later) but are appalled by its awful moral implications.[20]

For the sake of clarity and to produce a heightened sense of the conditionalist case, each objection will be placed in question form. This chapter will respond to the conditionalists' following objections:

- Can't the Bible be interpreted to teach annihilationism?
- Isn't an endless hell based on a Greek view of the soul?
- Wouldn't an endless hell be unjust?
- Wouldn't an endless hell be unloving?
- Wouldn't an endless hell diminish God's victory over evil?

Can't the Bible Be Interpreted to Teach Annihilationism?

Although it seems that most conditionalists in contemporary evangelicalism are primarily driven to reject the historic position of endless punishment because of their beliefs concerning God's love, justice, and victory, they also stress that the Bible can be interpreted to teach the ultimate annihilation of the wicked. Even from a casual reading of their defenses of conditionalism, no one can doubt that these scholars (note especially Wenham, Fudge, and Ellis) genuinely believe that

---

[19]For the most part, their usage of these objections also comprises their case for conditional immortality. At the risk of oversimplification and with the notable exceptions of Edward Fudge and David Powys, most conditionalists are still reacting to the historic view more than they are constructing their own view.

[20]Pinnock, "The Conditional View," 164–65.

they offer the better interpretation of the biblical teaching on hell. The question used as the heading in this section comes from Clark Pinnock's related assertion, "the Bible can easily be read to teach the final destruction of the wicked."[21]

Since the earlier chapters in the present book have specifically addressed the biblical teaching concerning hell (see the chapters by Daniel Block, Robert Yarbrough, Douglas Moo, and Gregory Beale), I will limit my discussion to the overarching issues raised by conditionalists—the interpretations of the words "eternal" and "destruction" (as mentioned in ACUTE's *The Nature of Hell*).

Eternal. Conditionalists generally set forth two arguments related to the meaning of "eternal" (*aiōnios*). Some maintain that it connotes that which pertains to "the age to come." For example, Michael Green argues, "This does not primarily indicate unending quantity of life or death, but ultimate quality. It means life of the age to come or ruin for the age to come."[22]

Conditionalists also argue that *aiōnios* can refer to a permanent result of the punishment rather than an ongoing process of punishing. Philip Hughes stressed this in his comments on 2 Thessalonians 1:9: "Everlasting life is existence that continues without end, and everlasting death is destruction without end, that is destruction without recall, the destruction of obliteration. Both life and death hereafter will be everlasting in the sense that both will be irreversible."[23] David Powys agrees. In his interpretation of Matthew 25:41–46, Powys contends that *aiōnios* should be taken qualitatively and with the connotation of irreversible rather than everlasting.[24]

But it is Edward Fudge who places the most weight on this argument for conditionalism. Because of this, he also develops it more fully than other conditionalists, devoting an entire chapter to the issue in *The Fire That Consumes*. Fudge contends that *aiōnios* can have a qualitative or a quantitative meaning. He proposes that *aiōnios* can refer to the age to come as a period distinct from the present one (qualitative) or to endlessness (quantitative). Fudge also maintains that *aiōnios* can be used to communicate finality of consequences rather than always conveying an unending process. He argues that this is the case in the New Testament references to "eternal salvation" (Heb. 5:9), "eternal judgment" (6:2), "eternal redemption" (9:12), "eternal punishment" (Matt. 25:46), "eternal sin" (Mark 3:29), and "eternal destruction" (2 Thess. 1:9).[25]

The conditionalists' arguments concerning the word "eternal" are unconvincing. Even if *aiōnios* only refers to the age to come in passages concerning hell (which is highly unlikely), then the question still remains, "How long is the age to come?" Since life in the age to come is ongoing and the extent of the destinies of the righteous and unrighteous are kept parallel in Scripture (e.g., Matt. 25:31–46), then it seems most tenable to conclude that hell is ongoing. So the condi-

---

[21]Ibid., 143.
[22]Green, *Evangelism through the Local Church*, 73.
[23]Hughes, *The True Image*, 405.
[24]Powys, *Hell*, 291–93.
[25]Fudge, *The Fire That Consumes*, rev. ed., 11–20.

HeLL UNDeR fire

tionalists' first argument from *aiōnios* cannot demonstrate conclusively the belief in the annihilation of unbelievers in hell but can only claim its remote possibility. The conditionalists' second argument from *aiōnios*, that it can connote an eternal result of punishment rather than the continual process of punishing, is also not cogent. The biblical portrait of the punishment of the wicked is often connected to their expulsion from the glorious presence of God (2 Thess. 1:5–10). Both punishment and separation from God require conscious existence.

Destruction. Conditionalists also point to a "vocabulary of destruction" that refers to the state of unbelievers in the New Testament. John Stott argues, "It would seem strange, therefore, if people who are said to suffer destruction are in fact not destroyed; and as you put it, it is difficult to imagine a perpetually inconclusive process of perishing."[26] John Wenham further submits that when the Bible speaks of the unrighteous' perishing, destruction, and death, it indicates total extinction, utter loss, or complete ruin.[27] Green, Hughes, Pinnock, and Ellis all set forth this point. But it is David Powys who devotes the most attention to this argument. Interacting with several passages employing the language of destruction, Powys asserts, "Destruction is the most common way of depicting the fate of the unrighteous within the Synoptic Gospels."[28]

The conditionalists correctly remind us that destruction is a central motif in depicting hell in the New Testament. But in their interpretation of the "destruction" passages, they tend to assume a connotation of extinction or annihilation rather than the more probable sense of loss, ruin, or corruption. D. A. Carson shows this in his critique of Stott's previously-quoted objection: "Stott's conclusion ... is memorable, but useless as an argument, because it is merely tautologous: *of course* those who suffer *destruction* are *destroyed*. But it does not follow that those who suffer destruction cease to exist. Stott has assumed his definition of 'destruction' in his epigraph [emphasis his]."[29]

Douglas Moo provides the most penetrating challenge to the conditionalist argument from the vocabulary of destruction. In his chapter in this book, "Paul on Hell," Moo addresses the meaning of Paul's words for destruction—*olethros* and *apollymi/apōleia*—especially as they relate to 2 Thessalonians 1:8–9. He observed:

> Definitive conclusions about the meaning of these words in each case are not easy to attain. But this much can be said: The words need not mean "destruction" in the sense of "extinction." In fact, leaving aside for the moment judgment texts, none of the key terms usually has this meaning in the Old and New Testaments. Rather, they usually refer to the situation of a person or object that has lost the essence of its nature or function.... The key words for "destroy" and "destruction" can also refer to land that has lost its fruitfulness

---

[26]Edwards and Stott, *Evangelical Essentials*, 316.
[27]Wenham, "The Case for Conditional Immortality," 170–78.
[28]Powys, *Hell*, 284.
[29]D. A. Carson, *The Gagging of God: Christianity Confronts Pluralism* (Grand Rapids: Zondervan, 1996), 522.

(*olethros* in Ezek. 6:14; 14:16); to ointment that is poured out wastefully and to no apparent purpose (*apōleia* in Matt. 26:8; Mark 14:4); to wineskins that can no longer function because they have holes in them (*apollymi* in Matt. 9:17; Mark 2:22; Luke 5:37); to a coin that is useless because it is "lost" (*apollymi* in Luke 15:9); or to the entire world that "perishes," as an inhabited world, in the Flood (2 Pet. 3:6). In none of these cases do the objects cease to exist; they cease to be useful or to exist in their original, intended state.[30]

Isn't an Endless Hell Based on a Greek View of the Soul?

ACUTE's *The Nature of Hell* quotes Clark Pinnock and Robert Brow's expression of this issue. Pinnock and Brow maintain:

Why has the annihilationist possibility not been noticed much before? Why would anybody have turned the notion of destruction into everlasting life in hell, creating this monstrous problem? We attribute it to the influence on theology of the Greek idea of the immortality of the soul. With that view entering the picture, the shift is logical and inevitable. If souls are immortal and hell exists, it follows that the wicked will have to suffer consciously forever in it. If the soul is naturally immortal, it has to spend eternity somewhere.... The Bible points to a resurrection of the whole person as a gift of God, not a natural possession. Humans were not created with a natural capacity for everlasting life—Jesus Christ brought immortality to light through the gospel (2 Tim. 1:10).[31]

Earle Ellis finds this objection to be foundational: "Biblical anthropology is an essential presupposition for understanding biblical eschatology." According to him, that starting point is a doctrine of humanity that stresses the individual person as a complex, mortal, and indivisible unity. He also emphasizes the centrality of seeing that God alone has immortality and believers only receive it at Christ's second coming.[32] Conditionalists Wenham, Travis, and Fudge also advance this argument.[33]

Thus, according to conditionalists, an endless hell is the product of a merger between Christian theology and Greek notions of the soul's immortality. Because Robert Yarbrough so ably addresses this in his chapter in this book, I will only interact briefly with this part of the argument.[34] But conditionalists also contend that an endless hell is not a logical necessity if humans are created mortal and do not have immortal souls.

It is important to notice, first of all, that Pinnock recognizes that the rejection of the immortality of the soul is essential for conditionalism. He admits, how-

[30]See Douglas Moo's chapter, "Paul on Hell," 104–5.
[31]Pinnock and Brow, *Unbounded Love*, 92. See also *The Nature of Hell*, 96–102.
[32]Ellis, "New Testament Teaching on Hell," 199, 211–13.
[33]Wenham, "The Case for Conditional Immortality," 174–76; Travis, *Christian Hope and the Future*, 135; Fudge, *The Fire That Consumes*, 51–76.
[34]See Robert Yarbrough's chapter, "Jesus on Hell," 83–87.

HeLL UNDeR fire

ever, that it could be argued that God grants immortality to unbelievers in order to punish them.[35] In other words, the conditional immortality of the soul only makes conditionalism possible and cannot positively establish it. In his response to this argument, Tony Gray points out that the argument from conditional immortality may be a red herring. If Scripture teaches eternal punishment in the form of conscious torment, then other considerations such as immortality are relatively unimportant. Gray concludes: "A person may acknowledge the Platonic influence on Christian theology at this point (if this is a correct analysis, and it is unclear whether Ellis has demonstrated this), yet fail to be a conditionalist because of his interpretation of Scripture."[36]

This argument from conditional immortality is also based in part on a genetic fallacy (i.e., of assuming that explaining the existence of an idea is sufficient to account for it and discount it). It is founded on a misunderstanding of the historic Christian teaching on the immortality of the soul (as well as its relationship to Plato). Orthodox theologians have consistently taught that only God is inherently immortal, rejected all ideas of the preexistence of the soul, and stressed that God grants eternal life (which is the connotation of "immortality" in 2 Tim. 1:10 and 1 Cor. 15:53) only to the redeemed. There is no disagreement on these things between the conditionalists and those holding a historic view of hell. The real issue is whether God grants endless existence to unbelievers for the purpose of punishing them or whether he punishes them into nonexistence.[37]

It seems clear from Revelation 20:10 as well (as will be discussed later) that Satan, the beast, and the false prophet are punished forever. Do they somehow have inherent immortality? Of course not. God will keep them in existence endlessly in order to punish them. Similarly, the wicked will be punished consciously forever in hell, not because they exist as immortal souls but because God will sustain them.

Larry Pettegrew aptly detects that some of the difficulty in the debate over the immortality of the soul is that the term "immortal" has different connotations in philosophy, theology, and Scripture.[38] In Plato "immortality" is tied to the notion of the preexistence of the soul, but historic Christian theologians mean something

---

[35]Pinnock, "The Destruction of the Finally Impenitent," 253.

[36]Tony Gray, "The Nature of Hell: Reflections on the Debate Between Conditionalism and the Traditional View of Hell," in *Eschatology in Bible and Theology: Evangelical Essays at the Dawn of a New Millennium*, ed. Kent E. Brower and Mark W. Elliott (Downers Grove, Ill.: InterVarsity Press, 1997), 238–39.

[37]John Colwell helpfully states, "Edwards's vision of the creation as continually dependent upon God would render any 'independent' or 'necessary' understanding of the soul's immortality quite inconceivable.... The soul's continuing punishment in hell is the outcome, not of God's passive acquiescence, but of God's active determination, continually maintaining the existence of the soul in judgment." See John E. Colwell, "The Glory of God's Justice and the Glory of God's Grace: Contemporary Reflections on the Doctrine of Hell in the Teaching of Jonathan Edwards," *EvQ* 67 (October 1995): 297.

[38]Larry D. Pettegrew, "A Kinder, Gentler Theology of Hell?" *The Master's Seminary Journal* 9 (Fall 1998): 212.

quite different, namely, that the human soul will never cease to exist in the future, but that it has a starting point in the past (although differences of opinion exist concerning the precise beginning).[39] Although not monolithic, the Greek view was that of a natural or inherent immortality. The historic Christian position is that the soul is derived from and continually dependent on God. Because of the biblical understanding of the unity of the human being and because of the contemporary misunderstandings related to the phrase "immortality of the soul," it admittedly might be better to speak of the person's continuity or existence after death.

To make matters more confusing, the meaning of "immortality" in the Bible largely depends on its context. Two Greek words, *athanasia* and *aphtharsia*, are often translated "immortality." When *athanasia* refers to God in 1 Timothy 6:16, Paul seems to be referring to God's independent life or inherent self-existence. When *athanasia* refers to the resurrection of believers in 1 Corinthians 15:53–54, Paul is stressing that through Christ's resurrection, believers will be immune from death forever. *Aphtharsia* (see Rom. 2:7; 1 Cor. 15:42, 52–54; 2 Tim. 1:10) generally connotes immunity from decay and is typically linked with eternal life.[40] Carson brings some clarity to the confusion:

> Doubtless some affirmations of human immortality are misleading since they tend to give the impression of intrinsic indestructibility that not even God could reverse. It is better to think of the sovereign God, through his triumphant Son, upholding all things by his powerful word. In other words, however "immortal" we are, we live and move and have our being because God sanctions it, not because we have achieved some semi-independent status. Within some such framework, I perceive no decisive argument against a properly articulated view of human "immortality," and much to commend the idea.[41]

It appears, then, that the conditionalist argument from conditional immortality should not be given much credence. Though it may make for fruitful discussion concerning the biblical doctrine of humanity, it makes little difference in this debate over the duration of hell. In fact, it often just provides a smokescreen that masks the more important theological and exegetical matters. In any event, it is clear that the argument from conditional immortality cannot itself establish conditionalism.

---

[39]Millard J. Erickson, *How Shall They Be Saved? The Destiny of Those Who Do Not Hear of Jesus* (Grand Rapids: Baker, 1996), 226. Erickson points out these differences in Christian theology: "This is true, whether in the creationist view that God directly and specially creates each soul at the time of conception, or the traducianist theory that God created in seminal form all the souls of the human race at the beginning of the race, which then came into individual existence in the multiplication process of human reproduction" (226).

[40]Murray J. Harris, *Raised Immortal: Resurrection and Immortality in the New Testament* (Grand Rapids: Eerdmans, 1983), 189. See also Eryl Davies, *An Angry God? What the Bible Says about Wrath, Final Judgment, and Hell* (Bridgend, U.K.: Evangelical Press of Wales, 1991), 121–31.

[41]Carson, *The Gagging of God*, 535.

heLL under fire

Wouldn't an Endless Hell Be Unjust?

The ACUTE working group raises the issue:

> This questioning often packs a strong emotional punch.... What useful purpose could be served by God's sustaining the unrighteous in continual torment? This question is regularly cited by conditionalists as a starting point for their own abandonment of the traditional position.... The argument in each case is a forceful one: it asks what love and justice could possibly be manifested in everlasting, unrelenting conscious torment, and responds that there is surely a grave disproportion between crimes committed in a single lifetime, and punishment administered for all eternity.[42]

Of all the conditionalists, Clark Pinnock argues this particular point most persuasively. The full weight of his argument and "emotional punch" bears repeating:

> The need to correct the traditional doctrine of hell also rests on considerations of the divine justice. What purpose of God would be served by the unending torture of the wicked except sheer vengeance and vindictiveness? Such a fate would spell endless and totally unredemptive suffering, punishment just for its own sake.... But unending torment would be the kind of utterly pointless and wasted suffering which could never lead to anything good beyond it. Furthermore, it would amount to inflicting infinite suffering upon those who have committed finite sins. It would go far beyond an eye for an eye and a tooth for a tooth. There would be a serious disproportion between sins committed in time and the suffering experienced forever.[43]

Conditionalists Stott, Wenham, Green, and Travis reason similarly.[44] Notice that this argument actually turns on two points. First, it suggests that endless punishment seems to serve no purpose. Second, it asserts an inequity between sins committed in a limited amount of time and an endless punishment. We now analyze these two issues.

Is it really true that endless punishment would serve no purpose? In his previously quoted objection, Pinnock is clearly looking for a redemptive or remedial purpose. Failing to seriously interact with the historic view, he concludes such a nonredemptive judgment must be purely vindictive, vengeful, utterly pointless, and wasted (also notice his pejorative use of "torture" rather than an appropriate word like "punishment").

---

[42] *The Nature of Hell*, 102–3.

[43] Pinnock, "The Destruction of the Impenitent," 255.

[44] Stott questions whether there would be "a serious disproportion between sins consciously committed in time and torment consciously experienced throughout eternity" (see Edwards and Stott, *Evangelical Essentials*, 318). Wenham ("The Case for Conditional Immortality, 187) maintained, "Unending torment speaks to me of sadism, not justice." Note also Green, *Evangelism through the Local Church*, 72; Travis, *Christian Hope and the Future*, 135.

But this is a far cry from the Scriptures, which assert that God's judgment settles all moral problems, it does not create them.[45] God's judgment is not evil or vindictive, but just, holy, righteous, necessary, and even glorious (Rom. 9:19–23). Part of God's beauty is his just character. The biblical writers were not so concerned with how God could be just if he punished the wicked forever, but rather with how God could be just and not punish evildoers immediately. The people of God in the Scriptures (e.g., Habakkuk and Jonah) struggled regularly with the merciful patience of God, but seldom with his judgment on evildoers (unless, of course, they themselves were the evildoers).

In fact, the central "problem" of the Bible that the gospel solves is centered on how God can be holy and just and still forgive rebellious and guilty sinners who trust him. As a result, even in biblical forgiveness God demands that a penalty due for sin must be paid. The amazing message of the gospel is that through Jesus' substitutionary death on the cross, the Just One becomes the Justifier (Rom. 3:21–31). The just God declares guilty sinners who trust in his Son to be righteous because of the righteousness of Christ imputed to them. So Jesus died not only because God is love but also because he is just.

After all, the world as it stands now is not a thoroughly just place. In the present, justice does not totally prevail. Most criminals seem to be punished here and now, but some go free. Some seem to get what they deserve while others suffer minimally. Mark Talbot is on the mark: "Hitler, as the ultimate perpetrator of the Nazi Holocaust, ought not to be able to escape being brought to account for his crimes against humanity by just blowing out his brains. . . . Indeed, something would be profoundly wrong with a world where its Hitlers could, when the time of reckoning drew near, just step off into nescience."[46]

Interestingly, the doctrines of judgment and hell were an important part of the moral reasoning of the New Testament writers and first-century believers. Unlike contemporary evangelicals, though, for the biblical authors hell *answered* (not raised) the ultimate questions related to the justice of God. In fact, the apostles even used the doctrine of hell as strong encouragement to believers who were suffering at the hands of evil and persecution (e.g., Paul in 2 Thess. 1:5–11, Peter in 2 Peter 2, and John in Rev. 6:10).

Indeed, through the Final Judgment and hell, God will set the record straight. God will call every human being to give a full account for his life (Matt. 12:36; 25:31–46; cf. Ps. 31:23). Notice that no one will escape this judgment (Acts 17:30–31; Rev. 20:10–15). When God exposes the hidden and secret motives of everyone's heart, unbelievers will finally realize the incredible depth of their sin and believers will better appreciate the infinite price of Christ's death (Rom. 2:16; 1 Cor. 4:5; 2 Thess. 1:6; Heb. 4:12–13).[47]

---

[45]See the superb, albeit brief, article: David F. Wells, "Everlasting Punishment," *ChrT* 31 (March 20, 1987): 41–42.
[46]Mark Talbot, "The Morality of Everlasting Punishment," *Reformation and Revival Journal* 5 (Fall 1996): 117–34.
[47]Ibid.

Annihilationlism: Will the Unsaved Be Punished Forever?

In the end, justice will prevail. The wicked will be punished and the redeemed and angels burst into praise (e.g., Rev. 6:10; 11:15–18; 14:14–15:4; 19:1–8).[48] In doing so, God will vindicate his character for all to see. What purpose could an endless hell possibly serve? To glorify God by the execution of divine justice—retributive justice.[49]

Is there really a disparity between sins executed in time and everlasting punishment? Stott, Pinnock, and others argue that the Bible commands us to punish in accordance with the offense (e.g., "an eye for an eye and a tooth for a tooth").[50] Although at first glance this objection seems substantial, it actually flows primarily from a misunderstanding of the nature of sin and a sentimental view of God's justice. Jonathan Edwards challenged a similar tendency of annihilationists in his day. He criticized their approach to God's justice and their corresponding view of the problem of evil:

> There are innumerable calamities that come to pass in this world through the permission of Divine Providence, against which (were it not that they are what we see with our eyes, and which are universally known and incontestable facts) this caviling, unbelieving spirit would strongly object; and which, if they were only proposed in theory as matters of faith, would be opposed as exceedingly inconsistent with the moral perfections of God.[51]

In other words, the annihilationists' view of divine justice (as stated in their objections) would not only be incompatible with an endless hell, but also would ultimately lead them to deny many realities of evil in existence today (e.g., deranged mothers taking unwanted babies and throwing them into a garbage can to be killed). "God would not allow that!" they might object. Yet these tragedies do occur because of the horrible reality and awfulness of sin.

Interestingly, John Wenham even suggested, "The ultimate horror of God's universe is hell."[52] While hell indeed may in some sense rightly be seen as an awful

---

[48]Note that this also undercuts the oft-repeated argument that an endless hell would tarnish the joy of the redeemed in heaven.

[49]It is important to note that Stephen Travis views salvation, condemnation, and judgment basically in terms of relationship and non-relationship to God (which is certainly a biblical metaphor, but dozens of others should be brought in to balance the picture). In doing so, he rejects retributive punishment and suggests that hell is not as much a punishment by God as it is just where the road leads. According to Travis, divine judgment is intrinsic and works out what is already inherent in the act itself. In a sense, it is divine confirmation of human choice. See Stephen H. Travis, "The Problem of Judgment," *Themelios* 11 (January 1986): 52–61; idem, *Christ and the Judgment of God: Divine Retribution in the New Testament.* Notice the odd choice of subtitle on this book for one who dislikes retributive judgment.

[50]For a philosophical attempt at this "eye for an eye" argument from a universalist perspective, see Marilyn McCord Adams, "Hell and the God of Justice," *RelS* 11 (December 1975): 433–47.

[51]Jonathan Edwards, "Concerning the Endless Punishment of Those Who Die Impenitent," in *The Wrath of Almighty God: Jonathan Edwards on God's Judgment against Sinners*, ed. Don Kistler (Morgan, Pa.: Soli Deo Gloria, 1996), 335–36.

[52]Wenham, *The Goodness of God*, 27.

HeLL UNDeR fiRe   209

reality, sin is actually the ultimate horror of God's universe. Hell is merely the punishment. Sin is the crime. Which is worse, murder or the life sentence? Obviously, the crime is worse than the punishment. So often the contemporary conditionalists minimize the biblical teaching concerning retributive punishment, however, and replace it with a human-centered view. Yet the Bible is clear: Sin is inherently *against* God, who is infinite in all his perfections. Thus, sin is an infinite evil and merits endless punishment. So it is better to view hell not as a horror in God's universe but as a demonstration of final and decisive justice in a universe once marred by sin.

Pinnock and others have objected to this understanding of the enormity of sin, considering it a throwback to the feudalism of Anselm's era. But that simply will not do. If an angry teenage boy punched his mother, he would deserve more punishment than if he punched his older brother. The relationship and the offended party do matter. It is also important to remember that God is not only different from human beings in degree; he is also different in being. If in a robbery, the gunman shoots and kills the owner of the house, he should receive a greater punishment than if he killed the family cat (as much as this writer loves cats!). Thus, because sin is against God, and God is infinitely worthy of obedience, sin merits an infinite punishment.[53]

This God-centered view of divine justice and human sin stands in stark contrast to that of the contemporary conditionalists. They seem to measure the appropriate punishment for sin as it relates to humanity rather than evaluating it in light of God's holiness. Another analogy might prove helpful here. What would be the best way to evaluate the horror of murder? Would it be to survey hundreds of murderers on death row to inquire their opinions as to the proper extent of their punishment? Of course not. On the whole, the penalty would be minimized by them. Why? Because they are the offenders, not the offended parties. It would be a much better approach to interview hundreds of mothers, fathers, wives, husbands, friends, sons, and daughters of the murder victims. They would be able to provide a much more reliable account of the horror of murder. They would also be able to give a better understanding of its corresponding penalty. Why? Because they are the ones affected by this evil.

In the same way, it seems that we humans will always tend to underestimate the sinfulness of sin. We will have a propensity to view our sin as an accident, blunder, or mistake. But unless sin is viewed in light of God's holiness (and that will only occur through divine self-revelation), it will never be seen as evil, wicked, hateful, and worthy of damnation as it really is (cf. Isa. 6). We offenders will fail to measure it aright. Only the offended God knows the full extent of its awfulness.

Endless punishment is also appropriate for humans who are totally depraved. Personal identity with Adam would be sufficient grounds for eternal condemnation. Yet sinners continually sin. Jonathan Edwards appropriately charged:

---

[53]Jonathan Edwards, "The Eternity of Hell Torments," in *The Wrath of Almighty God*, 91–92.

HeLL UNDeR fiRe

Their heads and their hearts are totally depraved; all the members of their bodies are only instruments of sin, and all their senses (seeing, hearing, tasting) are only inlets and outlets of sin, channels of corruption. There is nothing but sin, no good at all.... There are breaches of every command in thought, word, and deed; a life full of sin; days and nights filled up with sin ... [while] mercy and justice, and all the divine perfections [are] trampled on.[54]

The extent of the penalty due sin might also be better understood when the perpetual sinning of sinners is realized. If the highest of all commands is to love God with all of our heart, mind, and strength, then none of us except Christ himself has ever kept the highest command for even ten seconds. The second highest of all commands is to love our neighbor as ourselves. Yet all of us love ourselves more than God or others. If all of us continually break the two highest commandments, then our guilt must be enormous—especially if we add to the equation the guilt of every other sin we have ever committed (Rom. 2:5).

The Scriptures also make clear that even the most seemingly minor infractions of God's commands are taken with inestimable seriousness. Whereas we might be inclined to overlook one violation of God's law as trivial, the Bible portrays it in a way that is truly frightening. James asserts, "For whoever keeps the whole law and yet stumbles at just one point is guilty of breaking all of it" (James 2:10). Everyone will give an account for every careless word ever uttered (Matt. 12:33–37). God will reveal and judge every thought, attitude, and intention (Heb. 4:12–13).

While acknowledging that none of his examples directly address eternal punishment, Robert Peterson skillfully exposes the gravity of sin:

Measured by biblical standards, few of us take sin seriously. As evidence of this, consider God's judgments against what might be called "little sins." An impressive list can be drawn up. For example, because Lot's wife looked back at Sodom and Gomorrah, "She became a pillar of salt" (Gen. 19:26)—the death penalty for a glance! Because of irregularities in their priestly service in the tabernacle, Nadab and Abihu "fell dead before the LORD" (Num. 3:4; cf. Lev. 10:1–2)—capital punishment for faulty worship! ... Because Uzzah steadied the ark with his hand, "The LORD's anger burned against Uzzah ... God struck him down and he died" (2 Sam. 6:6–7)—punishment of death for trying to keep the ark from falling! Because Ananias and Sapphira lied to the apostles, God struck them dead (Acts 5:1–10)—capital punishment for lying! ... If people lied to us or disobeyed us, would they deserve death? Of course not. If they do these things against God, do they deserve capital punishment? The Bible's consistent answer is yes.[55]

Peterson then adds one more biblical example. In Romans 5:12–21, Paul teaches that because Adam ate of the forbidden fruit, he plunged the human race

---

[54]Ibid.

[55]Robert A. Peterson, *Hell on Trial: The Case for Eternal Punishment* (Phillipsburg, N.J.: Presbyterian and Reformed, 1995), 170–71.

into sin and its horrible consequences. Physical death, spiritual death, and eternal death all come to humanity through this one sin. Someone might be tempted to ask, "Damnation of the world for one man's eating a piece of fruit?" Peterson reminds us that this disobedience was fueled by pride and unfaithfulness and merited divine judgment.[56]

Note also in the conditionalist objection the mistaken assumption that the time used to commit a sin plays a chief role in determining its appropriate punishment. Yet this does not hold true. It may only take a moment to pull a trigger and kill a dozen people, but the punishment will (hopefully) not be merely momentary. It is not the amount of time that determines the punishment, the crime itself does. Sin is an infinite and cosmic treason. Sin is a horrible crime because it screams, "I hate you," to the true and living God, who deserves and demands our total love. In sin, human beings turn their back on the end for which God has created them and become worthless (Rom. 3:12).[57]

It also seems likely that those in hell remain in their sinful state, at least in the sense of their privation of love for God (see Rev. 16:11; 22:11). If they indeed remain unregenerate, they would likely be continuing in sin and therefore stockpiling more and more guilt and its consequent punishment. Carson agrees, "What is hard to prove, but seems to me probable, is that one reason why the conscious punishment of hell is ongoing is because sin is ongoing."[58]

Therefore, an endless punishment would be the only means by which finite sinners could approach paying the infinite penalty due sin. Even an endless hell, however, will never fully satisfy the justice of God because there will never be a time when it could be said that now justice is satisfied.[59] David Wells wisely concludes:

> If God is as good as the Bible says he is, if his character is as pure, if his life is as infinite, then sin is infinitely unpardonable and not merely momentarily mischievous. To be commensurate with the offense, God's response must be correspondingly infinite. Annihilationism looks instead for a finished, finite, temporal response. An infinite response, however, is what we see occurring at the Cross. Christ stood in the place of those whom he represented, and bore their punishment. In doing so, was he annihilated? Of course not. What we see is Christ bearing their actual punishment, and he

---

[56]Ibid., 172.

[57]See Jonathan Edwards, "Wicked Men Useful in Their Destruction Only," in *The Wrath of Almighty God: Jonathan Edwards on God's Judgment against Sinners*, ed. Don Kistler (Morgan, Pa.: Soli Deo Gloria, 1996), 232–53.

[58]Carson, *The Gagging of God*, 533. A. H. Strong asserted, "However long the sinner may be punished, he never ceases to be ill-deserving. Justice, therefore, which gives to all according to their deserts, cannot cease to punish. Since the reason for punishment is endless, the punishment itself must be endless." A. H. Strong, *Systematic Theology*, 8th ed. (Valley Forge, Pa.: Judson, 1907), 1048.

[59]Jonathan Edwards, "Dissertation on the End for Which God Created the World," *The Works of Jonathan Edwards*, ed. Edward Hickman (Carlisle, Pa.: Banner of Truth, 1974; reprint, 1992), 1:120–21.

HeLL UNDeR fiRe

could exhaust it because he himself was the eternal and infinite God. He did not bear a punishment merely like that which sinners deserved, one that was merely analogous to theirs. A gospel, then, that trades on a diminished view of sin, a modified notion of divine righteousness, and a restructured Atonement is not one that is more appealing, as Pinnock thinks, but one that is less. It is a gospel that has lost its nerve because it has lost its majesty.[60]

Wouldn't an Endless Hell Be Unloving?

In their treatment of this objection, ACUTE's *The Nature of Hell* quotes Nigel Wright as offering a significant critique of the historic view. Wright asserts:

> If the only God who exists is the Christlike God who loves his enemies, the Father of Jesus Christ, it becomes impossible to believe in an inscrutable, hidden God who is other than what we see in Christ Jesus. Jesus did not deny the human sense of love and justice and its potential as an analogy for imaging God.[61]

But it is Clark Pinnock again who has most graphically shown the weight of this moral argument.[62] He charges, "Everlasting torment is intolerable from a moral point of view because it makes God into a bloodthirsty monster who maintains an everlasting Auschwitz for victims whom he does not even allow to die. How is one to worship such a cruel and merciless God?"[63] Without employing such extreme rhetoric, conditionalists Wenham, Green, and Travis each make use of essentially the same argument.[64]

This objection has two components. The first is that Jesus depicts God as primarily loving, not in a way compatible with an endless hell. The second part of the objection suggests that God's mercy is inconsistent with endless punishment. **Is Jesus' teaching about God's love incompatible with the historic view of hell?** This is one of the weakest of the conditionalist objections. In this

---

[60]Wells, "Everlasting Punishment," 42. Timothy Phillips also points out, "It is no accident that, historically, annihilationism has gone hand in hand with a denial of Jesus' deity." Annihilationism has been a popular choice among Arians and Socinians. See Timothy R. Phillips, "Hell: A Christological Reflection," in *Through No Fault of Their Own? The Fate of Those Who Have Never Heard*, ed. William V. Crockett and James G. Sigountos (Grand Rapids: Baker, 1991), 47–59.

[61]Wright, *Radical Evangelical*, 91. See also *The Nature of Hell*, 102–6.

[62]Interestingly, Pinnock's case for conditionalism is not nearly as strong as some of the others. Yet more than the others he is able to capture the heart of the conditionalist argument and present it persuasively (although at times manipulatively).

[63]Pinnock, "The Destruction of the Impenitent," 253.

[64]Wenham maintained, "I cannot see that endless punishment is either loving or just.... It is a doctrine which I do not know how to preach without negating the loveliness and glory of God" (see his "The Case for Conditional Immortality," 185–87). Green asked, "What sort of God would He be who could rejoice eternally in heaven with the saved while downstairs the cries of the lost make an agonizing cacophony" (see his *Evangelism through the Local Church*, 72). Travis considered an endless hell "vindictive" and "incompatible with the love of God in Christ" (see his *Christian Hope and the Future*, 135).

quotation, Wright seems to imply a theological method that is inconsistent with evangelicalism. In function, it would constrain the doctrine of God to the teachings of Jesus in the Gospels. Yet all the Scriptures are God's self-revelation, unveiling his nature and attributes. To limit our view of God to the Gospels alone is a grievous mistake. It would be akin to the common fallacy that the Old Testament portrays a God of wrath and the New Testament pictures a God of love. It is more likely that Wright intended his statement to mean that one's view of God's love must be consistent with that revealed by Jesus. If so, no one disagrees with that. But caution is still needed. Too often people presuppose a certain image of Jesus and his teachings and then use that as an interpretive guide for the rest of their theology. In the modern academic studies on Jesus, it seems clear that the picture of Jesus drawn by many scholars resembles the wishes of the scholar more than the historical Jesus. Everyone seems to claim Jesus for his cause.[65]

Wright's Jesus lays stress on love and justice, even promoting the human sense of love and justice and its potential for imaging God. And Wright's Christlike God is not hidden or inscrutable. Does this hold up to Scripture? At best, it shows only part of the picture of God. At worst, it could be a sentimental, democratic, and humanitarian view of God masquerading as a Christlike picture.[66] Scripture no doubt presents God as loving and seeking justice. But in addition to revealing God as loving, compassionate, merciful, and good, the Scriptures also portray God as holy, just, Lord, Judge, King, Lawgiver, sovereign, wrathful upon sin and sinners, and yes, even inscrutable.

For example, contrary to Wright, the apostle Paul uses "unsearchable" to describe God's ways in Romans 11:33–36. Further, Jesus' words to the Pharisees seem less than loving to many ears. When Jesus overturned the moneychangers' tables, he does not initially come across as kind. Most importantly, Jesus' teaching on the doctrine of hell will certainly offend some universalists' view of divine love (e.g., Matt. 5:22–30; 7:13–27; 8:12; 10:28; 13:30–50; 18:6–9; 23:15, 33; 24:51; 25:31–46; Mark 9:42–49; Luke 16:19–31; John 3:16–21, 36; 5:28–29; Rev. 21:8).[67] So our understanding of God's love must be weighed against the whole fabric of Scripture, not just a small fraction of it.

Against such objections, Carson offers an important reminder: "Should it not be pointed out that it is the Lord Jesus, of all persons in the Bible, who consis-

---

[65]Scot McKnight, "Who Is Jesus? An Introduction to Jesus Studies," in *Jesus under Fire*, ed. Michael J. Wilkins and J. P. Moreland (Grand Rapids: Zondervan, 1995), 53–56.

[66]For a more careful and biblical perspective on God's love, see D. A. Carson, *The Difficult Doctrine of the Love of God* (Wheaton, Ill.: Crossway, 2000), 9–11. Carson proposes, "For this widely disseminated belief in the love of God is set with increasing frequency in some matrix other than biblical theology.... I do not think that what the Bible says about the love of God can long survive at the forefront of our thinking if it is abstracted from the sovereignty of God, the holiness of God, the wrath of God, the providence of God, or the personhood of God—to mention only a few non-negotiable elements of basic Christianity. The result, of course, is that the love of God in our culture has been purged of anything the culture finds uncomfortable. The love of God has been sanitized, democratized, and above all sentimentalized."

[67]For more on Jesus' view of hell, see Robert Yarbrough's chapter "Jesus on Hell," 67–90.

HeLL UNDeR fIRe

tently and repeatedly uses the most graphic images of hell?"[68] Leon Morris help-fully concludes, "Why does anyone believe in hell in these enlightened days? Because Jesus plainly taught its existence. . . . He said plainly that some people will spend eternity in hell. . . . He spoke plainly about hell as well as about heaven, about damnation as well as salvation."[69]

Is God too merciful to punish sinners eternally? There is a tendency for certain conditionalists (e.g., Pinnock, Brow, and Wright) to stress God's mercy to the point of departure from Christian orthodoxy. As proponents of not only con-ditionalism but also inclusivism and the openness of God theology, Pinnock and Brow assert that God's "unbounded love" is their control belief: "Jesus' metaphor of the Father who loves us unconditionally is the central image in creative love theism rather than Judge or Sovereign, and it controls the meaning of these other metaphors."[70]

John Piper and David Wells offer valuable correctives to this unbalanced view of God. Piper reminds us that "the statement 'God is love' does not imply that God relates to individuals only in terms of love."[71] Wells warns, "Of course the Bible tells us that God is love, but the Christians of modernity seem to think that this constitutes an adequate theology in itself, that God is fundamentally if not exclusively love."[72]

Thankfully, most conditionalists do not push the argument as far as Pinnock and Brow. Instead, when these conditionalists consider the possibility of an end-less hell they wonder how God's mercy would allow such punishment. But like Pinnock and Brow, they often fail to balance God's mercy with his holiness, jus-tice, and wrath. Jonathan Edwards is again helpful:

---

[68]Carson, *The Gagging of God*, 530.
[69]Leon Morris, "The Dreadful Harvest," *ChrT* 35 (May 27 1991): 34.
[70]Pinnock and Brow, *Unbounded Love*, 29. Conditionalist, inclusivist, and openness the-ologian Richard Rice similarly maintains, "Love, therefore, is the very essence of the divine nature. Love is what it means to be God. . . . The assertion 'God is love' incorporates all there is to say about God" (Richard Rice, "Biblical Support for a New Perspective," in *The Openness of God: A Biblical Challenge to the Traditional Understanding of God*, ed. Clark Pinnock et al. [Downers Grove, Ill.: InterVarsity Press, 1994], 18). On page 21, Rice later cites Karl Barth, Emil Brunner, and Wolfhart Pannenberg in support of his thesis that the only way in which God will relate to the world is through love. For a helpful critique of this point, see Todd S. Buck, "A Critical Analysis of Inclusivism Among Evangelical Writers" (Ph.D. dissertation, Mid-America Baptist Theological Seminary, 1999), 49–51.
[71]John Piper, "How Does a Sovereign God Love?" *Reformed Journal* 33 (April 1983): 11.
[72]David F. Wells, *God in the Wasteland: The Reality of Truth in a World of Fading Dreams* (Grand Rapids: Eerdmans, 1994), 135. Wells also observes a trend in contemporary evangeli-calism to soften the doctrine of God: "We have turned to a God that we can use rather than to a God we must obey; we have turned to a God who will fulfill our needs rather than to a God before whom we must surrender our rights to ourselves. . . . And so we transform the God of mercy into a God who is at our mercy. We imagine that he is benign. . . . And if the sunshine of his benign grace fails to warm us as we expect, if he fails to shower prosperity and success on us, we will find ourselves unable to believe in him anymore. . . . It is our fallenness fleshed out in our modernity that makes God smooth, that imagines he will accommodate our instincts, shabby and self-centered as they so often are, because he is love. . . . We need to recover a sense of God's transcendence" (114–16).

It is an unreasonable and unscriptural notion of the mercy of God that He is merciful in such a sense that He cannot bear that penal justice should be executed. This is to conceive of the mercy of God as a passion to which His nature is so subject that God is liable to be moved, affected, and overcome by seeing a creature in misery so that He cannot bear to see justice executed.... The Scriptures everywhere present the mercy of God as free and sovereign, and not that the exercises of it are necessary.[73]

Because of the unity of the divine attributes, all attempts to separate God's love from his justice should be rejected. God's love does not drive his justice. The implementation of God's justice does not undermine his love. God's love and justice cohere. John Frame explains this historic understanding of God:

None of his attributes can be removed from him, and no new attribute can be added to him. Not one attribute exists without the others. So each attribute had divine attributes; each is qualified by the others. God's wisdom is an eternal wisdom; his goodness is a wise goodness and a just goodness.... The essential attributes of God are "perspectival." That is, each of them describes everything that God is, from a different perspective. In one sense, any attribute may be taken as central, and the others seen in relation to it. But in that sense, the doctrine of God has many centers, not just one.... Whatever they [open theists like Pinnock] may think about the relative importance of love, they are nevertheless responsible to do full justice to everything else that the Bible says about God. To do that, it is important to look at him from many perspectives.[74]

Approaching God's attributes in this way is much wiser because it balances our doctrine of God according to the whole of Scripture. It also demonstrates that God's mercy is not inconsistent with endless punishment.

Wouldn't an Endless Hell Diminish God's Victory over Evil?

Here conditionalists assert that the historic view of hell fails to allow for a complete victory over evil. Pinnock best articulated this point:

History ends so badly under the old scenario. In what is supposed to be the victory of Christ, evil and rebellion continue in hell under the conditions of burning and torturing. In what is supposed to be a resolution, heaven and hell go on existing alongside each other forever in everlasting cosmological dualism.... In the new order how can there be still a segment of unrenewed being, i.e., two kingdoms, one belonging to God and the other to Satan, who

---

[73]Edwards, "The Eternity of Hell Torments," 339–40. Notice how different this is from Pinnock's desire for complete "fairness" in God's mercy. Pinnock maintains, "It is being taken for granted" that God treats everyone alike in mercy (Clark H. Pinnock, "An Inclusivist View," in *More Than One Way? Four Views on Salvation in a Pluralistic World*, ed. Dennis L. Okholm and Timothy R. Phillips [Grand Rapids: Zondervan, 1995], 97).

[74]John M. Frame, *No Other God: A Response to Open Theism* (Phillipsburg, N.J.: Presbyterian and Reformed, 2001), 53–54.

reigns at least in hell? It just doesn't sound right. Surely God abolishes all that in the new creation.... Victory means that evil is removed and nothing remains but light and love.[75]

The Nature of Hell recounts John Stott's version of this objection. Stott suggests that the eternal existence of the unrepentant in hell is hard to reconcile with the biblical promises of God's final victory over evil. Stott also thinks that endless punishment seems inconsistent with the "apparently universalistic texts" (e.g., John 12:32; 1 Cor. 15:28; Eph. 1:10; Phil. 2:10–11; Col. 1:20). While rejecting universalism, Stott admits, "But [these passages] do lead me to ask how God can in any meaningful sense be called 'everything to everybody' while an unspecified number of people still continue in rebellion against him and under his judgment. It would be easier to hold together the awful reality of hell and the universal reign of God if hell means destruction and the impenitent are no more."[76]

At first glance, this argument seems persuasive. The ultimate eradication of the wicked seems to be a better victory than endless punishment. One passage Stott refers to in proffering this objection is 1 Corinthians 15:24–28 (a favorite passage of universalists):

Then the end will come, when he hands over the kingdom to God the Father after he has destroyed all dominion, authority and power. For he must reign until he has put all his enemies under his feet. The last enemy to be destroyed is death.... When he has done this, then the Son himself will be made subject to him who put everything under him, so that God may be all in all.

Paul is not teaching universalism here, Stott asserts, because many other biblical texts speak of "the terrible and eternal reality of hell."[77] Yet, Stott falls into the same trap by presupposing a certain understanding of what God's being "all in all" means.[78]

But a better approach is to ask: What do the Scriptures teach about the final victory of God? The Bible seems to teach that God's ultimate victory is compatible with the endless punishment of the wicked. The final chapters of Revelation contrast the final state of the redeemed with that of the wicked. Revelation 20:10 even states, "And the devil, who deceived them, was thrown into the lake of burning sulfur, where the beast and the false prophet had been thrown. They will be tormented day and night forever and ever." This may not "sound right" to Pinnock, Stott, or the other conditionalists, but it is unmistakable that at least Satan, the beast, and the false prophet will be in hell forever. It seems hard to imagine a more graphic way of teaching the endless punishment of these evil

---

[75]Clark H. Pinnock, "The Conditional View," in *Four Views of Hell*, ed. William Crockett (Grand Rapids: Zondervan, 1992), 151, 154–55.

[76]Edwards and Stott, *Evangelical Essentials*, 319.

[77]Ibid.

[78]Peterson, *Hell on Trial*, 175–76. After surveying Rev. 20–22 Peterson asserts, "God's being 'all in all' means that he reigns over the just and the unjust; it does not mean that only the former remain."

enemies than the apostle John's expression, "tormented day and night for ever and ever."[79]

After depicting God's three opponents being cast into hell forever, John goes on to discuss the Final Judgment. The glorious God is seated on the great white throne. All of the dead, great and small, stand before him for their judgment. In Revelation 20:15 the apostle details the momentous verdict: "If anyone's name was not found written in the book of life, he was thrown into the lake of fire." Thus, the fate of the wicked parallels the fate of the three enemies of God mentioned earlier in 20:10. Confirming this interpretation are the words of Jesus himself. He likens the fate of the wicked to the fate of the devil and his angels in Matthew 25:41, 46: "Then he will say to those on his left, 'Depart from me, you who are cursed, into the eternal fire prepared for the devil and his angels. . . .' Then they will go away to eternal punishment, but the righteous to eternal life."

Certainly, heaven is a place where only light, love, and holiness exist—uncontaminated by sin, suffering, death, or evil. Heaven is marked by the manifest glory of God and newness of his creation. Revelation 21 and 22 make that clear. The redeemed will worship the Lord "for ever and ever" (22:5). But hell will also continue forever.

But the coexistence of heaven and hell does not hinder the glorious victory of God or the utter happiness of the redeemed. Through punishing non-Christians eternally in hell, God will vindicate his majesty, display his power, glorify his justice, and indirectly magnify his grace.[80] It is an unbiblical and sentimental conception of God that somehow the execution of this justice will hurt the Judge as much as the sinner.

Through the Final Judgment and hell, God will set the record straight. No evil will go unpunished. All who have trampled God's grace and holiness will pay the due penalty of their sin. God's archenemy Satan will be completely subdued and punished. Satan will not reign as Pinnock charged. Instead, even Satan himself will feel the full force of God's justice (Rev. 20:10). This is not some sort of cosmological dualism as the conditionalists allege. How could there be dualism when God reigns supreme and all his enemies are vanquished? No, there will be no hint of dualism. Instead, God's victory will be glorious, his reign will be absolute, and justice will prevail.

---

[79]See Gregory Beale's chapter, "The Revelation on Hell," 111–34.

[80]Jonathan Edwards, "The Eternity of Hell Torments," 339–57. See also James I. Packer, "The Problem of Eternal Punishment," *Evangel: The British Evangelical Review 10* (Summer 1992), 13–19.

HeLL UNDeR fiRe

Chapter 10

Pastoral Theology:
the Preacher
and Hell

Sinclair B. Ferguson

To speak of hell is to speak of things so overwhelming that it cannot be done with ease. While the exegetical case for annihilation, made by some significant evangelical leaders, seems to me to be inadequate, every right-minded Christian should surely have a deep sympathy with John R.W. Stott's comment on everlasting punishment: "Emotionally, I find the concept intolerable."[1] There is, surely, a profound sense in which this ought to be the reaction of all of us. For hell is viewed by our Lord Jesus not as "made for man" but "made for the devil and his angels." Humans as such were made for fellowship with God and for eternal glory. That such creatures should be banished forever into the outer darkness, with no escape exit, should fill us with a sense of horror. This was not the destiny for which we were created; emotionally, therefore, it should be an intolerable contradiction. Hell is not the fruit of God's good creation for humanity but the consequence of humankind's rebellion and perversion.

The thought of hell, then, can carry no inherent attraction to the balanced and coherent human mind. When, in the Upper Room and in the Garden of Gethsemane, our Lord contemplated his own predestined taste of it, only the strongest of language served the Gospel writers in describing his experience: "deeply distressed," "troubled," "overwhelmed with sorrow" (Mark 14:33–34). The verb "to be troubled" (*adēmoneō*) is used in the New Testament only here (as well as in the parallel Matt. 26:37) and in Philippians 2:26. It "describes the confused, restless, half-distracted state, which is produced by physical derangement, or by mental distress, as grief, shame, disappointment."[2] The contemplation of hell prostrated holy humanity. Our Lord never spoke of it with relish.

Yet hell exists; this is the testimony of the Scriptures, of the apostles, and of the Lord Jesus himself. The emotionally intolerable is also the truth—and therein lies its awfulness. Moreover, given the broad spectrum of biblical testimony to the reality of hell, and especially our Lord's own teaching, it is incumbent on the Christian pastor to be familiar with it, to feel the weight of it, to preach it, and to counsel his flock in connection with its meaning and personal implications.

Pastors are teachers. One of the virtues of a teaching ministry of any systematic kind is that, whatever our distinctive personalities and spiritual burdens, we can avoid no biblical subject. That should be true whatever the specific model of preaching we use, be it consecutive exposition of whole books (the *lectio continua* approach), a focus on specific passages (the employment of what our forefathers called an "ordinary," i.e., a small portion of Scripture expounded in detail over a

---

[1]David L. Edwards and John R.W. Stott, *Evangelical Essentials: A Liberal-Evangelical Dialogue* (Downers Grove, Ill.: InterVarsity Press, 1988), 314.
[2]J. B. Lightfoot, *St. Paul's Epistle to the Philippians* (London: MacMillan, 1913), 123.

heLL unDeR fire

period of weeks), a series topically arranged, or even "random" textual preaching (which over the years constitutes an exposition of "the whole counsel of God").

It may seem cautious to say "should be true," but even in systematic exposition it is possible for us so to slant our preaching that passages majoring on a theme like hell are muted under the guise of the compassion of the preacher. But here for "compassion" we need to read "muddle-headedness at best, cowardice at worst." That is why teachers and preachers from time to time ought to read through the New Testament quickly, pen in hand, noting the frequency with which this aspect of eschatological reality occurs. While by no means the central theme of the New Testament, it receives considerable emphasis as the context in which the gospel is set and the destiny from which it delivers us. It is written into the warp and woof of the tapestry of God's revelation in Jesus Christ. It is that from which salvation delivers us.

The Bible is not a detailed manual on preaching. There is no chapter division, for example, in Paul's letters entitled "Preaching," far less "Preaching on Hell." But in a remarkable section in 2 Corinthians Paul reflects on and defends his ministry, and in that context he sheds much light on our topic. Conscious of the pressures on him to distort the gospel by manipulating or adulterating it, Paul affirms that the preacher's task is "setting forth the truth plainly . . . to every man's conscience in the sight of God" (2 Cor. 4:1–2). Even if this unveiling of the gospel remains veiled to some, Paul notes, it is veiled "to those who are perishing (*apollymenois*)." Against this background he describes what undergirds his preaching about Christ the Savior.

Here we may note, in the order Paul mentions them, the important principles that governed his ministry (2 Cor. 5:10–15):

- the appearance of all before the judgment seat of Christ and the implications of that for people
- the wonder of the love of Christ for sinners who will appear there and the implications of that for the preaching of the gospel

The Judgment Seat of Christ

The preacher speaks as one who is conscious that he himself must stand before the judgment seat of Christ: "We must all appear before the judgment seat of Christ, that each one may receive what is due him for the things done in the body, whether good or bad" (2 Cor. 5:10). Perhaps more than anything else, this must become the atmosphere from which God's servants approach their tasks as preachers and pastors. We—not just you—must appear there. Only those who are consciously aware that they will come before the judgment seat can speak with any sense of the weightiness of the issues of life and death, heaven and hell.

The first task of the pastor, then, in relationship to hell is to keep watch over himself (Acts 20:28). This means that consciously and deliberately we live before the judgment seat of Christ.[3] It is here that we learn for ourselves the dreadful

---

[3]Note that Paul does not distinguish between the judgment seat of Christ and the judgment seat of God. The former is the vehicle by which the latter is enacted, since God has entrusted all judgment to his Son (cf. John 5:22).

unveiling of our sinfulness, and this, in turn, enables us to stress three things essential for our preaching:

- the righteousness of God
- the sinfulness of our sin
- the absolute justice of God's condemnation of us

Unless we have established these coordinated principles and impressed them on the minds and consciences of our hearers, there is little likelihood that we can make much impression by preaching on hell.

Paul does this in a searching way in Romans 2:1–16. In response to those who seem to agree with his assessment of the pagan world in 1:18–32, he spells out the character of God's judgment. There is no escape from it. He outlines a number of important elements in God's justice that ought to be demonstrated if our preaching on hell is to fulfill its biblical function.

(1) *God's judgments are absolutely righteous, perfectly just, and unerringly accurate.* Human beings are forever remaking God in their own image, foolishly assuming that God's judgments are approximate to our own. But our judgments are at best partial, at worst horribly wrong. We judge by appearance; God looks on the heart (1 Sam. 16:7). Paul presses this home in four different ways.

(a) The judgment of God is based on truth (*kata alētheian*, Rom. 2:2). "According to truth" here means "consistent with the facts of the case, true to reality." The God who judges is alone able to sift through the evidence and to weigh the motives of the heart. Nothing is hidden from his sight. When he passes judgment, it mirrors reality.

Moreover, by judgment here is implied condemnation, as Paul's conclusion shows (Rom. 3:20). At no point will we be able to produce last minute, hidden, or unconsidered evidence to defend ourselves from a guilty verdict. The sense of being shut into a cul-de-sac by God's holy gaze so that there is nowhere to turn from the divine scrutiny—the experience of David in Psalm 139 or Isaiah in Isaiah 6—is expressed here in propositional form. The judgment of God turns inside-out the reality of our lives, hearts, minds, and motives, sifts them before his all-seeing eye, and brings in a verdict of guilty so powerful that before God every mouth is stunned into silence and all the world held guilty before him (Rom. 3:19).

(b) The judgment of God "does not show favoritism" (Rom. 2:11). With him there is absolute equity. The language here is picturesque, drawn from the ancient Near Eastern custom of lowering the face to the ground when showing respect. The person greeted would then raise the face of the individual as a sign of recognition and esteem. This is to show "respect of person" to someone, to show him or her favor. Paul is underlining that no matter who I am or what I may think myself to be, God never favors me on account of position, lineage, or possessions. This is devastating to our egocentricity, for by nature we assume that God views us the way we view ourselves: each as a special case.

(c) The judgment of God is "righteous" (Rom. 2:5). Righteousness is not a well-understood concept. In the Hebrew world it indicated conformity to a norm. Here God himself is the norm. In this sense, God's judgment perfectly expresses his identity and holy character. But it also matches the truth about us. Thus, his judgment perfectly matches the reality of our lives.

Scripture frequently illustrates that the punishment "fits"—that is, it is utterly consistent with—the crime. Paul gave striking illustration of that in Romans 1:21–32. Those who claimed to be wise became fools and exchanged God's truth for the lie. Even while flouting themselves against God's law and believing his wrath to be powerless, they "receive in themselves the due penalty for their perversion" (1:27). As a result, God "gave them over" to reap the whirlwind from the wind they have sown—all the while blind to the fact that their being given up to their lusts is itself the righteous judgment of God.

(d) The judgment of God leads justly to condemnation. God reveals his wrath by handing us over to the present consequences and the eternal implications of what we have been and done. Paul's repeated verb "gave them over" (Rom. 1:24, 26, 28, *paradidomai*) refers to a judicial handing over. If even now our consciences bear witness (2:14–15) to accuse as well as excuse, how much more will they bear witness to the absolute accuracy of God's final judgment? The frightening reality is this: The Judge of all the earth will do right.

(2) *God's judgment will be intensely personal and individual.* God will accurately weigh each person's individual responsibility. He will "give *to each person* according to what he has done" (Rom. 2:6, italics added).

This individualizing is frequently reiterated in Scripture (e.g., Ps. 62:12; Prov. 24:12; Rom. 14:12; 2 Cor. 5:10) and constitutes an element of God's judgment that unnerves us. It is true that at the last judgment the nations are envisaged as gathered (Matt. 25:32), and doubtless individuals will be judged within the national, social, cultural, and temporal context in which they have lived. How otherwise would God's judgment be "according to truth"? Yet we are each to stand before God as individuals with individual responsibility for the decisions, thoughts, and actions that are unique to us.

Paul spells out clearly the basis on which this will take place. It will be in the context of what we have known. "All who sin apart from the law will perish apart from the law, and all who sin under the law will be judged by the law" (Rom. 2:12). This is justice. In Paul's eyes, however, it carries with it not the possibility of acquittal but the certainty of condemnation. For he has already argued that those without the special revelation of the law have sinned and stand under the wrath of God. He is now (or, on some interpretations of Rom. 1–3, soon will be) dealing with those who have the special revelation of Torah; they too stand condemned.

The precise point toward which Paul drives his argument is that none of us has lived according to the revelation we have received, whether general or special, common or redemptive. And we are not judged on the basis of what we have known but on the basis of how we have responded to what we have known and what we have done or left undone (cf. Matt. 25:31–46).

Furthermore, what has been hidden or kept secret will then be brought before the court. Here Paul exposes the folly and superficiality of our externalism and deception (whether of others or of self). God will on that day "bring to light what is hidden in darkness and will expose the motives of men's hearts" (1 Cor. 4:5). In terms of the picture-language of Revelation, "the books [will be] opened," and an account will be given for every thought, word, and deed (Rev. 20:11–12). The hard drive of our lives, from which nothing can be erased, on which every motive, attitude, disposition, and act is indelibly recorded, will be accessed and scrutinized in one great moment by the Judge. What hubris on our part to think that what we are capable of creating in a machine—a permanent record—is beyond the wit and power of the Creator of the universe!

(3) *God's judgment leaves men and women "without excuse" (Rom. 1:20)*. What is the point of emphasizing these things? Paul himself provides the answer within the context of the lawsuit he presents against the whole of humanity in Romans 1:18–3:20. The whole purpose of this section is to convict of guilt and condemnation, in the process of which Paul argues that each individual is *anapologētos*—without excuse, self-justification, or mitigating plea (2:1). His terrible indictment against humanity and his graphic description of God's impending wrath leads to the final moments of a trial scene of apocalyptic and eternal proportions. He portrays the entire mass of humanity standing before his judgment seat—every person's mouth shut and the whole world declared guilty and condemned by God (Rom. 3:19–20).

Paul, a seasoned evangelist, is well aware of the fact that every member of fallen humanity needs to have thrust in front of him the radical and total inexcusability of sin and the absolute justice of God's condemnation. Only then will he, can he, take hell seriously. The preaching of these truths is intended to tear away the blindness, to arouse and pierce the slumbering conscience. Otherwise, we persist in our assumption that whatever fate befalls others (a Nero, a Hitler, an Idi Amin), we ourselves at least are safe from divine condemnation.

In particular, the preacher needs to unmask the specific conscience-easing lies we speak to ourselves through an open manifestation of the truth, in which—in terms of Paul's preaching grid in 2 Timothy 3:16 and 4:2—we correct and rebuke. Several particularly self-vindicatory thoughts are destroyed by this apostolic emphasis.

(a) "I have nothing to hide." On the contrary, each of us hides from God's gaze, Adam-like, clutching our pathetic reassurances. But the preaching of universal and individual guilt, universal and individual judgment, serves to dispel our self-delusions. The person who claims he or she has "nothing to hide" from God displays only ignorance of both God and self. Paul's teaching underlines that such a person has everything to hide but is no more adequate to cover his or her nakedness and manifest guilt than the leaf Adam pathetically tore off the fig tree to try to cover his nakedness from the Lord.

There is a well-known story in this connection about Sir Arthur Conan Doyle (author of the great Sherlock Holmes books). He sent a telegram to twelve respectable people in London, simply worded: "Flee—all is revealed." By the following night six of them had left the country! If God marked our iniquities, which of us could stand (Ps. 130:4)?

(b) "I have been better than most." God's judgment is not an assessment of our ranking in the league table of humanity; it is an evaluation of individuals against

HeLL UNDeR fire

his own perfect standard of justice—himself—in the light of his perfect knowledge of persons. The point of Paul's argument is that one could be better than everyone else and nevertheless fall under the just condemnation of God, whose standard of righteousness involves comparing our lives not with the patterns of others' behavior but with God's own holy character.

(c) "God would never condemn me if he really understood my difficulties." On the contrary, Paul notes that it is through Jesus Christ that God exercises his perfectly righteous judgment (Rom. 2:16). The Father has entrusted all judgment to his Son (John 5:27). That Son now judges as one who has lived from within the confines of frail humanity. He knows the human condition; he has faced the fiercest of temptations; he has gone to the extremity of death. He who is both standard and judge understands perfectly our difficulties—and measures our failure, sin, and guilt with perfect knowledge and precision.

(d) "The loving Jesus of the Gospels would never condemn someone like me. My goodness, I've been a church member all my life!" On the contrary, in the Sermon on the Mount our Lord spells out the fact that even our good and impressive religious activities are no safeguard against the judgment that is according to truth. The following words are not those of Moses, or Jonathan Edwards, or Billy Sunday, but of Jesus:

> Not everyone who says to me, "Lord, Lord," will enter the kingdom of heaven, but only he who does the will of my Father who is in heaven. Many will say to me on that day, "Lord, Lord, did we not prophesy in your name, and in your name drive out demons and perform many miracles?" Then I will tell them plainly, "I never knew you. Away from me, you evildoers!" (Matt. 7:22–23)

(e) "I admit I am not perfect, but I scarcely deserve the effects of divine condemnation described in Scripture." In fact, Paul lists these effects in strong language in Romans 2: wrath (2:5, 8), anger (2:8), trouble, distress (2:9), and perishing (2:12). Here we must respond in at least two ways. The first is to stress that this is the teaching of Jesus in the Gospels. Indeed, this teaching is woven deeply into the cloth of the Synoptic Gospels. Pull this single thread away and the whole garment will be destroyed. W. G. T. Shedd was right to argue: "The strongest support of the doctrine of Endless Punishment is the teaching of Christ, the Redeemer of man."[4] It is Jesus who speaks of the darkness outside (Matt. 22:13; 25:30), the fiery furnace (13:42, 50), weeping and gnashing of teeth (8:12; 13:42, 50; 22:13; 24:51; 25:30), everlasting punishment (25:46), and being condemned to hell and its fire (5:22, 29–30; 10:28; 18:9; 23:33).

Furthermore, thus to assess our merits—albeit in a different context—we have the famous words of Anselm of Canterbury to Boso: "You have not yet considered

---

[4]William G. T. Shedd, *The Doctrine of Endless Punishment* (New York: Scribner's, 1886; reprint, Carlisle, Pa.: Banner of Truth Trust, 1986), 12. The identical material on endless punishment was inserted by Shedd into his *Dogmatic Theology* (New York: Scribner's, 1889–94; reprint, Nashville: Thomas Nelson, 1980), 2:675.

how great the weight of sin is."[5] In fact, here lies the nub of the problem: A truncated view of who God is, combined with a minimalist view of what we have become in our sinfulness, inevitably leads to a myopic view of the Last Judgment. Until I sense how great, glorious, and holy God is and therefore how horrific my sin is, the absolute justice of God's condemnation will remain a mystery.

The implication of this for our ministry is important. For it becomes clear, therefore, that narrowly focused preaching on the theme of hell is inadequate. Rather, it must be done in tandem with preaching on the character of God, his loving creation of man, the radical character of the Fall, and consequent nature of sin. Then the judgment that leads to hell can be expounded coherently, rightly, and ultimately even compassionately.

What then shall we preach on hell? There are several things we need to affirm.

(1) *Hell is real.* There is, of course a principle of progressive revelation in the Bible. Revelation in the Old Testament was partial and fragmentary, including the relative opaqueness in its description of the nature of the afterlife. But the revelation of God in Christ brings with it a fuller unveiling of the nature of the afterlife and of human destiny. Consistent with this is the fact that it is the Lord Christ himself who most frequently warns against the danger of hell (see, e.g., Matt. 5:22, 29–30; 7:13; 8:10–12; 10:26–28; 13:40–42, 47–50; 18:8–9; 23:33; 25:41, 45–46).

It is as characteristic of Jesus' teaching to warn against the prospect of hell as it is for him to describe the high privileges of heaven. For him, at least, hell is just as real as heaven. In addition, if we take seriously the significance of his death on the cross as a sacrifice of atonement (Rom. 3:25), what, short of the reality of hell, explains the necessity for and nature of his sufferings? It would be folly to think that all he went through was merely exemplary or, for that matter, unnecessary. His cry of dereliction is an enigma whose only solution is Christ's enduring of hell—his separation from and sense of the absence of God in order to save us from it.

It is said that on one occasion a member of the British Royal Family, now deceased, inquired of the dean in one of the great Anglican cathedrals whether or not there was a hell. On giving the careful, if impersonal, answer, "Ma'am, our Lord and his Apostles taught so, the Creeds affirm so, and the Church believes so," the dean in turn received her reply: "Why, then, in God's Name, do you not tell us so?"

(2) *Hell is vividly described in the pages of the New Testament.* Over the centuries theologians have discussed whether the biblical vocabulary for hell is to be taken literally or metaphorically. Great names fall on each side of that question. My own view is that in any aspect of biblical teaching where various descriptions contain elements in tension with each other, those descriptions are in all likelihood metaphorical. We are not under constraint to resolve how utter darkness can also have perpetually burning flames. These, I take it, are metaphors.

---

[5]Anselm, *Cur Deus Homo*, xxi.

But, having said this—and here is a vital point—metaphors are used precisely in order to describe realities greater than themselves. Hell itself is not metaphorical but real; these vivid metaphors point to a reality more awful than themselves, indeed, terrible beyond mere words (hence metaphor rather than prosaic language is required).

Hell is a sphere of separation and deprivation, of pain and punishment, of darkness and destruction, and of disintegration and perishing. The vocabulary of the New Testament in regard to includes: darkness outside, weeping and grinding of teeth, destruction of body and soul, eternal fire, fire of hell, condemned to hell, forfeiting eternal life, the wrath of God, everlasting destruction away from the presence of the Lord, perishing, separation, blackest darkness.

What is the preacher to do with this language? Exactly what one does with other biblical language: use it to the limits of its significance within the text, no more, no less. In particular, the word "eternal" underscores the magnitude of what is in view. This condition is not only one of separation from God and disintegration of all that is pleasing; it is perpetually and permanently so. We would be foolish to pretend that we either felt or understood all that this implies; we would be unfaithful if we did not spell out in our exposition of these significant passages that this is the truth Scripture teaches. It is this that made the great seventeenth-century preacher Thomas Brooks cry out, in words found also on the lips of his contemporaries:

> Oh, but this word eternity, eternity, eternity; this word everlasting, everlasting, everlasting; this word for ever, for ever, for ever, will even break the hearts of the damned in ten thousand pieces.... Impenitent sinners in Hell shall have end without end, death without death, night without day, mourning without mirth, sorrow without solace, and bondage without liberty. The damned shall live as long in Hell as God himself shall live in Heaven.[6]

(3) *Hell, though prepared for the devil and his angels, is shared by real human beings.* The Greek word *geenna*, used frequently for hell in the New Testament, is derived from the Hebrew *ge hinnom*, the Valley of Hinnom, where child sacrifices were once made to Molech (2 Chron. 28:3). It developed into a prophetic symbol of judgment.

The transferred use of this place name for the final state of the lost employs it as a symbol of judgment. It is the wasteland of humanity, inhabited by all those who reject Christ and his revelation. Those who do not belong to the kingdom of God are there: "Outside are the dogs, those who practice magic arts, the sexually immoral, the murderers, the idolaters and everyone who loves and practices falsehood" (Rev. 22:15; cf. 1 Cor. 6:9). The rich man is there (Luke 16:19–31); those who did not love Christ's brothers are there (Matt. 25:41–46); some who prophesied, cast out demons, and worked miracles in Christ's name are there

---

[6]Thomas Brooks, *The Golden Key to Open Hidden Treasures* (London: Printed for Dorman Newman, 1675) in A. B. Grosart, ed., *The Works of Thomas Brooks* (Edinburgh: J. Nichol, 1861–67), 5:130.

(7:21–23); "those who do not know God and do not obey the gospel of our Lord Jesus Christ" are there (2 Thess. 1:8–9); Judas Iscariot is there (Acts 1:25), for it were better for him that he had never been born (Matt. 26:24); the devil and his angels, the beast, and the false prophet are there, "tormented for ever and ever"; anyone whose name is not found in the Lamb's book of life will be there (Rev. 19:19–20; 20:10, 15).

So awful is the prospect of this judgment that when it is revealed,

the kings of the earth, the princes, the generals, the rich, the mighty, and every slave and every free man hid in caves and among the rocks of the mountains. They called on the mountains and the rocks, "Fall on us and hide us from the face of him who sits on the throne and from the wrath of the Lamb! For the great day of their wrath has come, and who can stand?" (Rev. 6:15–17)

It is, indeed, too terrible to contemplate—more terrible than the vocabulary used to describe it, just as heaven is more glorious than our words can possibly describe.

Like millions of others, on September 11, 2001, in horror and foreboding I watched, in real time, on television in the United Kingdom, the second jet crash into the New York Twin Towers and then saw the buildings collapse in rubble as people fled for their lives. It was the most horrific event most of us will ever witness "live." As I watched, I also asked: "What kind of cataclysmic horror would make strong men run into that falling rubble to find protection, preferring such a holocaust to the wrath of the Lamb?" It is indeed unimaginable. But if the gospel is true at all, if Christ's cry of dereliction has real substance, if what is portrayed by the book of Revelation is gospel truth, then the unimaginable is the real. That from which he came to save us is indeed terrible beyond words, and both Scripture and we ourselves must employ words to describe it.

(4) *Most important, in expounding and applying the biblical teaching on hell, we must emphasize that there is a way of salvation.* There is somewhere to hide from the wrath of the Lamb. This point, thus baldly stated, leads us directly into a second major consideration.

The Compulsion of the Love of Christ

Paul combines a second driving force in his ministry along with his expectation of God's judgment. It is the impact on him of the love of Christ (2 Cor. 5:14). He finds it compelling. The love of Christ "compels" Paul because of the way in which he understands the significance of Christ's death. The word he uses for "compels" (*synechō*) expresses the idea of constraint, restraint, or holding in custody. He has a sense that the love of Christ (Christ's love for him, primarily, although by implication perhaps including his responsive love to Christ) does not leave him any choice in the matter—preach he must.

What is the relevance of Christ's love to this discussion? Simply this: That love led to Christ's death, and Paul views that death, implicitly, as a hell-bearing-in-love experience undergone by Christ on our behalf.

This suggests a vital principle for our ministry. The gospel is not a message about hell. We ought to be on our guard against the mentality that sees the preaching of hell as the sure sign of "faithfulness." That, indeed, would be, what John Stott describes as an evangelical form of *Schadenfreude*—delight in the misfortune of others. The fact that a preacher speaks of hell is not in and of itself identical to faithfulness to Scripture, unless it is preached in the context and with the balance, spirit, and intent of Scripture. Yet one cannot be faithful to Scripture without preaching about it for the simple reason that, as we have seen, the gospel itself cannot be understood apart from its reality.

Paul spells out the implications of this by explaining the significance of Christ's death. His death constitutes a substitutionary act ("for all," 2 Cor. 5:14–15) in which God was reconciling the world to himself in a manner involving the nonimputation to us of our sins and their consequences (5:19). But this nonimputation to us does not mean that sins are not imputed. It means that, rather than being imputed to us, they were imputed to God's Son: "God made him who had no sin to be sin for us" (5:21). In a nutshell, the gospel is this: Christ took our place, bearing our sin, tasting our judgment, dying our death—so that we might share his place, be made his righteousness, taste his vindication, and experience his life.

But to be made sin implies liability to the condemnation of God and the righteous judgment of the punishment of hell. This, in effect, is how the New Testament (always in the light of the Old) sees the inner significance of Jesus' death. To the fact of it the Bible adds the interpretation. To say that Jesus died is fact; to say that being made our sin he died for us, reconciling us to God, is the interpretation. And it is the fact thus interpreted that constitutes the gospel.

What, then, did Jesus experience as One who was "made sin [or a sin offering] for us"? Commentators are divided over the precise nuance of *hamartia* ("sin") in this context. Does it refer to Christ as being made a "sin offering" or "sin"?[7] The strength of the latter view lies both in the antithetical parallelism of 2 Corinthians 5:21 (sin/righteousness is a more coherent antithesis than sin offering/righteousness) and in the fact that it requires a strong case to make the same word ("sin") used twice in the same context carry two different nuances.

That notwithstanding, implied in Christ's being made sin is the fact that he became an offering for that sin. It follows that the death of Christ was itself a form of enduring the judgment of God, and therefore of the hell-condemnation that the sin he bore justly deserves.

(1) *Christ became a curse for us.* In being made sin for us, Christ was cursed for us in order that divine blessing might flow to us. Paul spells this out in Galatians 3:13, which operates with the same pattern of exchange as 2 Corinthians 5:21: Christ takes our curse, and we receive his blessing.

But there is biblical depth to the language Paul uses, although it is often overlooked. For "curse" and "blessing" belong integrally to the covenant vocabulary

---

[7]Ambrose, Augustine, Cyril of Alexandria, F. F. Bruce, and R. P. Martin take it as the former; John Calvin, Philip Hughes, and Paul Barnett as the latter.

of Scripture. In view here is that the work of Christ reverses the work of Adam, the representative man to whom God gave blessing but whose sin brought a curse (Gen. 3:14, 17). That language then pervades the Mosaic covenant. Through sacrifices (whose inner meaning is grasped by faith) God provides the way in which he himself takes the curse and provides blessing in its place (cf. Deut. 27–30). The whole sacrificial system is redolent of all it means to fall under the curse of God and for God to provide a substitute for us in our predicament. This pattern Jesus fulfilled in his death on the cross.

(2) *In doing so, Christ took the cup of God's wrath.* To become a curse is to become liable to God's wrath. Jesus did that the moment he assumed our humanity as the Second Man and Last Adam. But by the time of the crucifixion, that liability had become a reality. This is vividly expressed in the Passion narrative of the Synoptic Gospels, which contains a kind of subplot involving two cups—the first a cup of blessing (which Jesus gave to his disciples in the Last Supper) and the second a cup of cursing (which he took from his Father in the Garden of Gethsemane: Matt. 26:17–46; Mark 14:12–52; Luke 22:1–53). "This cup" (Mark 14:36) is not to be interpreted merely as Jesus' general providential lot; it is specifically the cup of which the prophets had spoken:

"You who have drunk from the hand of the LORD
    the cup of his wrath,
you who have drained to its dregs
    the goblet that makes men stagger....
"See, I have taken out of your hand
    the cup that made you stagger;
from that cup, the goblet of my wrath,
    you will never drink again.
I will put it into the hands of your tormentors,
    who said to you,
'Fall prostrate that we may walk over you.'
And you made your back like the ground,
    like a street to be walked over." (Isa. 51:17, 22–23)[8]

(3) *True, the New Testament nowhere explicitly says that our Lord endured the holy wrath of God; but it is equally true that no other conclusion can be drawn from viewing Calvary in the light of Gethsemane and Gethsemane in the light of Old Testament prophecy.*
All this is given pointed expression in the way in which darkness covered the land during the final three hours of the crucifixion—symbolic of the fact that Jesus was entering the darkness outside. When it came time to bear "our sins in his body on the tree" (1 Peter 2:24), he also bore "the disgrace" (itself an illuminating term) "outside" (Heb. 13:11–13). "Outside the camp" on this true Day of Atonement, he became the fulfillment of the scapegoat let loose to wander in the solitary desert place, bearing the sins of the people (Lev. 16:6–10, 20–22) and

---

[8]Cf. Jer. 25:15, 17; Ezek. 23:31–33; Hab. 2:16.

heLL unDeR fire

experiencing the ultimate combination of human and divine alienation at the nadir of his suffering as he cried out, "My God, my God, why have you forsaken me?" That was the darkness outside.

Darkness in Scripture is the place of chaos, where the blessing of creation becomes an accursed disintegration. It is the formlessness and void, the *tohû wabohû*, the deep-and-dark that requires the divine light and the divine word to form and fill it (Gen. 1:2–5). This is the darkness in which God came to "cut" his covenant with Abraham, moving as a light through dismembered animals. This was how it would be when the covenant promises would be fulfilled in reality, when the "light of the world" passed through an even deeper darkness on the cross, as God taking to himself the consequences of a violated bond of fellowship with him.

It is also the darkness foreshadowed in Egypt, the darkness that the angel of death penetrated to slay the firstborn in those covenant-less homes where no lamb's blood of sacrifice had been applied. So the angel of death moved over the Roman gibbet where Christ, our Passover Lamb, was sacrificed (1 Cor. 5:7): "At the sixth hour darkness came over the whole land until the ninth hour. And at the ninth hour Jesus cried out in a loud voice, '*Eloi, Eloi, lama sabachthani?*'"

Forsaken. He entered territory unimaginable for a Jew—exiled to a far country where the covenant of God no longer functions, where all appears to relapse into inexplicable chaos, a world of deep, unfathomable, unanswering disintegration. It was the consummation of Gethsemane's cup: "He began to be deeply distressed and troubled. 'My soul is overwhelmed with sorrow to the point of death'" (Mark 14:33–34). Here, as we have seen, is the language of distress of mind, distraction of spirit, unbearable restlessness, the final shocking derangement of one's being.

Mark's verb (*adēmoneō*) is derived from the idea of being away from home. Certainly Jesus' experience gives expression to his desperate but unanswered homesickness as God the Son in our flesh is distanced on the cross from God the Father in his infinite holiness. The One who abandons and forsakes him is the Father, who has covenanted with his children: "Never will I leave you, never will I forsake you" (Heb. 13:5). As Ceslas Spicq notes in this context:

> The fivefold pleonastic repetition of negation . . . reinforces the absoluteness of the thought and thus the certainty of the divine help: "never, never, never, in any circumstance whatsoever, God will not fail" . . . a statement of the unchangeableness of providence, one of the most essential items of Israel's faith.[9]

Here, then, on the cross, is all that makes hell into hell: darkness, pain, isolation, sin-bearing, divine judgment, curse, alienation, utter darkness, separation from God. If we need to be convinced of the reality of hell, all we need to do is to consider the cross. It is all there.

---

[9]Ceslas Spicq, *Theological Lexicon of the New Testament*, trans. and ed. J. D. Ernest (Peabody, Mass.: Hendrickson, 1994), 1:400–401.

It may be asked, however, how the sacrifice of one can atone for many, and more particularly in this context, how the anguish of one day can substitute for the anguish of eternity. With that question theologians have long wrestled. The view of historic orthodoxy is this: Christ bore the sins of a finite number of people and the just condemnation of eternal duration because in all he did, he acted as their representative in their humanity, the Last Adam. In that capacity he was also the Son of God. Sin against an eternal Person brings eternal judgment; that eternal judgment was accepted, received, and experienced by Christ who is an eternal Person capable of bearing it until he has exhausted it in death and rises again in the new order of the Last Man.

Why is this apparent digression from the topic of hell important? Because it underlines hell's reality—Jesus experienced it. It is at the same time the clearest indication of hell's awfulness. Yet, simultaneously and gloriously, it is the divine provision to enable us to escape. It is in this context that preaching on hell belongs to the preaching of the gospel. When we understand that this is what the death of Christ means, when this grips our soul, we will begin to find the apostolic model of preaching reduplicated in our own ministry. For constrained thus by the love of Christ, several things follow.

(a) *Courage and commitment:* "If we are out of our mind it is for the sake of God; if we are in our right mind, it is for you" (2 Cor. 5:13). Unless one is an individual of warped and masochistic mind, with a callous pleasure in the destruction of the wicked and therefore devoid of the emotions of Christ (Luke 19:41), it takes courage and commitment to preach hell.

Courage is needed because in many contemporary contexts one mention of hell is enough to guarantee the accusation of a harsh spirit and a bigoted mind. *Commitment* is required because such ministry demands a desire to live for Christ (2 Cor. 5:15) and to see men and women brought to Christ, which is greater than our native desire for security and popularity. It is not possible to be liked for preaching the truth about hell (although it is, paradoxically but thankfully, possible to be loved for having done it). So Paul discovered. "Out of his mind," they said of him; but he knew he was in his right mind for the sake of those to whom he preached.

(b) *A truly biblical perspective:* "So from now on we regard no one from a worldly point of view" (2 Cor. 5:16). Throughout this whole section of 2 Corinthians Paul has been underlining the way in which the gospel restores a true perspective on the whole of life: "We fix our eyes not on what is seen but what is unseen. For what is seen is temporary, what is unseen is eternal" (2 Cor. 4:18). Sinful humanity naturally looks at life through the wrong end of the telescope. For them time is long and eternity is short; this life is large, the afterlife is small; this world is real, the world to come unreal. This is what it means to live *kata sarka* ("according to the sinful nature") rather than *kata pneuma* ("according to the Spirit"; Rom. 8:4). But the Christian's eyes have been opened, and they are fixed on Christ, on eternity.

A Christian, then, looks at life in the light of the destination to which it leads, and sees every person within that framework. Famous words penned around 1843 by the still young but soon-to-die Robert Murray M'Cheyne express well this view and its implications: "As I was walking in the fields, the thought came over me with almost overwhelming power, that every one of my flock must soon be in heaven or hell. Oh, how I wished that I had a tongue like thunder, that I might make all hear; or that I had a frame like iron, that I might visit every one, and say, 'Escape for thy life!' "[10] Behind everyone we know and meet stands the shadow of judgment. They themselves do not see it; we know they may have spent all their lives denying it or hiding from it. But one day the account will be presented, the verdict will be past, the judgment given.

Knowing this, how can we remain silent—or cowardly? We can only do so if we ourselves live in denial of the reality that we know has been revealed in the gospel.

(c) *A deep awareness of our calling:* "God . . . reconciled us to himself through Christ and gave us the ministry of reconciliation . . . he has committed to us the message of reconciliation. We are therefore Christ's ambassadors, as though God were making his appeal through us . . . Be reconciled to God" (2 Cor. 5:18–20).

The Christian preacher is a debtor because through Christ he has himself been delivered from future judgment. He is a steward, because the message of reconciliation has been committed to him. He is to employ the resources provided by his Lord, not to diminish, add to, or transform them. He is also an ambassador, whose task is always to represent his Master and faithfully to deliver his message. On every side he is hemmed in, constrained not merely by a powerful sense of duty and obligation but by an overwhelming sense of the privilege of bringing the message of grace to those who are destined for darkness.

This is why our own excuses must never prevail ("I am not that kind of preacher"; "the congregation would not receive it well"; "people do not take these things seriously any longer"; "we are living in a day when that kind of emphasis does not draw people to Christ"). We should no more give credence to these voices than we should leave undisturbed the self-justifying excuses that people foolishly believe will shield them from God's wrath. The more profoundly aware we are of the issues, the more rigorous we will be with ourselves and the more tender toward the lost.

In his book *Whatever Happened to Hell?* John Blanchard includes a dramatic description of a multi-auto pile-up in dense fog on a major highway outside of London, England:

The hazard warning lights were on, but were ignored by most drivers. At 6.15 a.m. a lorry carrying huge rolls of paper was involved in an accident, and within minutes the carriageway was engulfed in carnage. Dozens of cars were wrecked. Ten people were killed. A police patrol car was soon on the scene, and two policemen ran back up the motorway to stop oncoming traffic. They waved their arms and shouted as loud as they could, but most drivers took

---

[10]Andrew A. Bonar, ed., *Robert Murray M'Cheyne: Memoirs and Remains* (London: Banner of Truth Trust, 1966), 148.

no notice and raced on towards the disaster that awaited them. The policemen then picked up traffic cones and flung them at the cars' windscreens in a desperate attempt to warn drivers of their danger; one told how tears streamed down his face as car after car went by and he waited for the sickening sound of impact as they hit the growing mass of wreckage farther down the road.[11]

Should we be any less burdened about the future shock of those who will find hell waiting for them? When Robert M'Cheyne met his dearest friend Andrew Bonar one Monday and inquired what Bonar had preached on the previous day, only to receive the answer "Hell," he asked: "Did you preach it with tears?" That we cannot do until we have come to recognize our own great need of grace to save us from the wrath to come, the terrible nature of that judgment, the provision that God has made for us in Christ, and the calling he has given us to take the gospel to every creature in the name of the One who did not come into the world to condemn it but to save it.

So we are called to preach as his representatives: with biblical balance, with a Christocentric focus, with the humility of those who realize their own need of grace before the judgment seat of Christ, with a willingness to suffer in the light of the coming glory, with love and compassion in our hearts, and in a way that commends and adorns the doctrine of God our Savior.

Questions

It is inevitable as a result of such preaching in a pastoral context that questions, difficulties, and stumbling blocks of various kinds will arise in the minds and the emotions of our people. Four of these may be mentioned briefly here.

(1) *Is hell fair?* This is really part of a larger question: Is God fair? The answer given by most unbelievers is likely to be: "No, not if he condemns *me*." Yet, deep down, as Paul affirms, the unbeliever knows that sinners deserve condemnation (Rom. 1:32).

God is the righteous Judge, and we may be confident that he does what is right. But therein lies the problem: Is the manner and duration of the punishment of hell as conceived in orthodox theology appropriate to the crime? Driving the resurgence of annihilationism among evangelicals today seems to be a negative answer to this question. That is, the nature of hell-as-eternal-punishment far outweighs the nature of the crime committed against God.

How can a *lifetime* of sin merit an *eternity* of condemnation? The standard answer to this question is that it does so because the nature and gravity of sin are determined not merely by the character of the agent (the sinner) but by the identity and nature of the Person against whom that sin is committed. In the case of sin against God himself, who is an infinite and eternally good Person, the sin takes on an eternal dimension that merits eternal punishment.

---

[11]John Blanchard, *Whatever Happened to Hell?* (Durham, England: Evangelical Press, 1993), 297.

To this, however, an important consideration needs to be added: In Scripture the sinfulness of the godly will be brought to an end; the sinfulness of the wicked is viewed as continuing. It might seem tenuous to base this on Revelation 22:11 ("Let him who does wrong continue to do wrong; let him who is vile continue to be vile"), but the refusal to repent in the face of the eschatological judgments of God (16:8–11) implies that the consummation of those judgments in hell does not and will not produce a penitential spirit. Herein, then, is the darkness of the outer darkness: There is no repentance. Hatred of God has no time limitation to it. Ongoing condemnation is met by ongoing alienation in a cyclical fashion. We see enough of this in the present age to understand that it may be so also in the age to come. However incredible it may seem to us that the damned *will not* repent, it is a reality to which both present experience and Scripture witness. Of that we should have no doubts.

(2) *What of those who have never heard the gospel? May we entertain a "larger hope" that many who have never heard the gospel will be saved?* The church's theologians have been divided in their response to this question, and it is important for us to be clear about the biblical parameters to the answer.

As impeccably orthodox a document as the Westminster Confession of Faith indicates that God may and does save people who are incapable of understanding the gospel. Thus in emphasizing that effectual calling leads to conscious faith, the Divines nevertheless also noted that "elect infants, dying in infancy, are regenerated, and saved by Christ, through the Spirit, who worketh when, and where, and how He pleaseth: so also are all other elect persons who are uncapable of being outwardly called by the ministry of the Word."[12] In view in this last statement, however, are not those who have never heard the gospel (they are not "uncapable of being outwardly called"), but those with congenital disorders rendering them "uncapable" of understanding and responding to the message of Christ. This does not bar God from working sovereignly in their lives.

In an analogous way, it is argued, God can surely work in the lives of those who have never heard, regenerate them, and save them by Christ, perhaps in ways similar to the salvation of Old Testament believers but on the basis of even less knowledge.

It is particularly important to come to this question from the appropriate biblical direction. The Confession essentially assumes that neither infants nor those incapable of receiving the outward call of the Word are saved merely because they are infants and incapable. Nor are they disqualified from salvation by being such. They may be saved—and it is assumed some are saved—by the same Christ, the same work of the Spirit in regeneration, as are believers. That regeneration, however, does not press itself into their consciousness in the same way, by the Word (cf. James 1:28; 1 Peter 1:23). May we not, therefore, *mutatis mutandis*,[13] assume that there may be regenerate among those who have never heard the gospel? This

---

[12]Westminster Confession of Faith, 10.4.

[13]That is, with the respective differences between infants and those who have never heard the gospel having been considered.

view has been held throughout the history of the church by figures so diverse as John Wesley in the eighteenth century, W. G. T. Shedd in the nineteenth century, and D. Martyn Lloyd-Jones in the twentieth century.

But in fact all Scripture allows us to say is that we cannot assume that any who have never heard the gospel will be saved. We must recognize that what God may do is not limited to what he has revealed to us that he will do. But by the same token we may not presume that he will do what he has not specifically revealed that he will do. To return to the argument in Romans 1:18–3:20, Paul's basic position is that all human beings are guilty before God, condemned, and liable to his eternal judgment. That is why, having heard the gospel, they are debtors until they have passed it on. We have no reason to believe in the salvation of any specific individual apart from faith in Christ. This appears to be the logic within which Paul operates in Romans 10:13–15: "'Everyone who calls on the name of the Lord will be saved.' How, then, can they call on the one they have not believed in? And how can they believe in the one of whom they have not heard? And how can they hear without someone preaching to them?"

But if this is our conviction, it is empty and we ourselves rendered doubly inexcusable if we do not shift heaven and earth for the purpose of bringing the gospel to every creature in the missionary enterprise.

(3) *What are we to say at the funerals of unbelievers and to their relatives?* This, again, is a sensitive and delicate question. Not all ministers will be asked to conduct the funeral service of those who made no profession of Christ; but many will be, in the context of parish ministry, local residence, or family connections.

Here are several things that should be said. The first is that we are not omniscient about the spiritual condition of any individual and are not capable of making infallible personal judgments. In addition, our task at a funeral is not to speak to the dead but to the living. Christ as Savior of all and any who will come to him is our theme.

We cannot offer false hope, but we are ministers of a gospel that offers comfort in Jesus Christ—though it does not offer us all the comfort we might like, nor does it deny the reality of ungodliness and its consequences. But Christ the Savior does not break bruised reeds or quench dimly burning wicks (Isa. 42:3; cf. Matt. 12:17–21), and it is surely vital to remember that.

We also must remember to hold out the gospel to mourning hearts in its proper order and proportion. Jesus seems to have spoken about hell largely within the context of warning and rebuking hypocrisy, religious self-sufficiency, and opposition to his divine claims.

There are times when we may be asked the most pointed of questions. We cannot speak with certainty about individuals, but we can be sure that the Judge of all the earth will do right. Nevertheless, we must also make known those Scriptures that point to an eternal destiny so terrible that we will say, however tenderly: "Flee from the wrath to come."

(4) *How can I ever be happy in heaven if I know that there are people in hell—including people I have loved?* Again, Christian orthodoxy since at least the time of

Augustine has had a standard answer to this question. Just as the saints rejoice in holy fashion at the destruction of Babylon in the book of Revelation, so perfected believers will be able to rejoice in the revelation of the justice and righteousness of God in the destruction of the wicked. The argument here is that so startling and glorious will God's character appear that what seems to us now to be emotionally impossible will then be possible.

Perhaps this is the case, although it involves certain extrapolations that are not clearly stated in Scripture. We should not think that our understanding of heaven is as yet perfect or that our knowledge of it is comprehensive. There are unanswered questions now, and we must learn to live with them. It should be axiomatic to the biblical Christian who realizes the infinite greatness of God and his holy character that there are many things about his ways we cannot fathom. Indeed, it may be that the best we can say as creatures, both now and in the hereafter, is that the only answer to such questions will be to keep gazing on the glory of God's righteousness and the wonder of the Lamb's sacrifice.

Hell is at the end of the day the darkness outside; dense like a black hole, it is the place of cosmic waste. Who can contemplate this for long? Who, indeed, is sufficient for these things? The question is surely rhetorical. None of us is sufficient. But our sufficiency is to be found in Christ, the Savior, the perfect Man, the Redeemer, the Judge. We must constantly remind ourselves that it is the Savior who spoke clearly of the dark side of eternity. To be faithful to him, so must we.

CONCLUSION

CHRISTOPHER W. MORGAN AND ROBERT A. PETERSON

Hell is under fire—even in evangelicalism. This doctrine that God punishes eternally in hell all sinners who do not trust Christ is certainly not in vogue. Because of this, it would be a lot easier for all of us to downplay this doctrine. After all, the doctrine of hell will regularly repel moderns and postmoderns alike. It will tend to imply that Christians are narrow-minded and intolerant. In a sense, hell stands for everything the contemporary culture rejects—that God's love is not sentimental but interconnected to his justice, that humans are wicked by fallen nature and choice, that Jesus is the only substitute for human sin, that explicit faith in Christ is the only means available to receive God's forgiveness, and that all sin will ultimately be punished either via Christ the substitute or by the sinner in hell. So to speak of hell in today's world truly is precarious.

But what is the alternative? Not to embrace or speak of hell? No, that is not an option for Christians because God's Word clearly teaches the reality of hell. *Every* New Testament author speaks of the reality of the future punishment of the wicked. And the Lord Jesus himself stands out as hell's chief defender—neither Thomas Aquinas nor Jonathan Edwards ever spoke as fearsomely about the horrors of hell as Jesus did. Surely those of us who call Jesus "Lord" do not have the privilege of rejecting or neglecting a doctrine so explicit in Scripture and so emphatic in our Lord's teachings.

But Christians also must embrace and teach the doctrine of hell because of its prominent place in the biblical worldview. Although hell is not a doctrine on which the church stands or falls, it is inexorably linked to the doctrines of God, sin, and the atonement.

Hell emerges from a biblical understanding of God. It reminds us that though God's love is central in Scripture, it should not be viewed independently of God's other attributes. His love is in unity with his justice and holiness. God's love is not sentimentality, but a holy love and a just love. Therefore, God's love should not be viewed as suggesting that he cannot bear to see justice executed.

Hell is also connected to a biblical understanding of humanity and sin. Hell reminds us that being human comes with awesome privileges as well as awesome responsibilities. To choose sin rather than God is a high crime indeed. Anselm's familiar reply to his pupil Boso's question is on the mark: "You have not yet considered the gravity of your sin." So most fundamentally, hell is correctly understood as God's just punishment on sin.

239

Yet hell is also appropriately viewed as a tragedy. It is tragic that sin entered the world through Adam, that humans still perpetuate rebellion against God, and especially that sinners persistently reject the Savior. In this sense, the horror of hell *should* offend our modern moral sensibilities. Even more so, the suffering of those in hell should even break our hearts—not only because of the dreadfulness of the punishment in hell but also because of the awfulness of sin, the crime that demands such a penalty. But the problem is not hell, and the problem is not God. Sin is the problem, and it is what should repulse us.

The biblical doctrine of hell is also linked to Christian convictions concerning Jesus' death. Fully God and fully human, Jesus the Mediator died on the cross as the only substitute for our sin. He bore the infinite penalty of sin for every believer. But those who fail to come to Christ in faith and repentance will have to pay that penalty themselves. In other words, just as there are only two options available for sinners (to receive forgiveness from Christ or to be punished eternally for their sins), there are only two ways to gauge the horror of sin—by reflecting on the cross and by considering hell. Both of these vantage points are key components in the biblical story.

Further, these aspects of the doctrines of God, sin, and the atonement are themselves also interwoven and can only be understood fully in light of hell. Let us explain. First, only when we recognize God's holiness will we be able to appraise the horror of sin. Second, only when we become aware of the awfulness of our sin will we sense the dreadfulness of hell and the price of Christ's death. Third, only when we grapple with the punishment of hell and the extent of Christ's atoning death can we begin to grasp God's amazing grace. Clearly, then, hell is an integral part of Christian theology.

As such, hell must be on the lips of those who want to be faithful to Jesus and his Word. To speak of hell is precarious. But not to speak of hell is more precarious. God our Judge requires us to proclaim his whole counsel, and we owe it to fellow sinners to teach them a full version of the grand biblical story of how God forgives sin, so that they too can better understand their desperate need for forgiveness and experience the joy found only in knowing Christ. Our prayer is that you will join us and the countless Christians throughout history and around the world today who seek to proclaim the whole counsel of God—yes, including hell—to Christians and non-Christians alike. Together may we do it with a passionate love for the Lord Jesus, abiding conviction in the truthfulness of God's Word, and authentic compassion for the lost.

SELECTED BIBLIOGRAPHY

Almond, Philip C. *Heaven and Hell in Enlightenment England*. Cambridge: Cambridge Univ. Press, 1994.

Atkinson, Basil F. C. *Life and Immortality: An Examination of the Nature and Meaning of Life and Death as They Are Revealed in the Scriptures*. Taunton, U.K./: Goodman, 1962.

Bernstein, Alan E. *The Formation of Hell: Death and Retribution in the Ancient and Early Christian Worlds*. Ithaca, N.Y.: Cornell Univ. Press, 1993.

Blanchard, John. *Whatever Happened to Hell?* Durham, U.K.: Evangelical Press, 1993.

Bonda, Jan. *The One Purpose of God: An Answer to the Doctrine of Eternal Punishment*. Grand Rapids: Eerdmans, 1997.

Bowles, Ralph G. "Does Revelation 14:11 Teach Eternal Torment? Examining a Proof-Text on Hell." *EvQ* 73 (January 2001): 21–36.

Bray, Gerald. "Hell: Eternal Punishment or Total Annihilation?" *Evangel: The British Evangelical Review* 10 (Summer 1992): 19–24.

Brower, Kent E., and Mark W. Elliott, eds. *Eschatology in Bible and Theology: Evangelical Essays at the Dawn of a New Millennium*. Downers Grove, Ill.: InterVarsity Press, 1997.

Brown, Harold O. J. "Will the Lost Suffer Forever?" *CTR* 4 (Spring 1990): 261–78.

Buis, Harry M. *The Doctrine of Eternal Punishment*. Grand Rapids: Baker, 1957.

Butler, Jonathan M. *Softly and Tenderly Jesus Is Calling: Heaven and Hell in American Revivalism, 1870–1920*. Chicago Studies in the History of American Religion. Ed. Jerald C. Brauer and Martin E. Marty. Vol. 3. Brooklyn, N.Y.: Carlson, 1991.

Cameron, Nigel M. de S., ed. *Universalism and the Doctrine of Hell: Papers Presented at the Fourth Edinburgh Conference on Christian Dogmatics, 1991*. Grand Rapids: Baker, 1992.

Camporesi, Piero. *The Fear of Hell: Images of Damnation and Salvation in Early Modern Europe*. Trans. Lucinda Byatt. University Park: Pennsylvania State Univ. Press, 1991.

Carson, D. A. *The Gagging of God: Christianity Confronts Pluralism*. Grand Rapids: Zondervan, 1996.

Cassara, Ernest, ed. *Universalism in America: A Documentary History*. Boston: Beacon, 1971.

Chan, Simon. "The Logic of Hell: A Response to Annihilationism." *ERT* 18 (January 1994): 20–32.

Constable, Henry. *The Duration and Nature of Future Punishment.* New Haven, Conn.: Charles C. Chatfield, 1871.

Crockett, William, ed. *Four Views on Hell.* Grand Rapids: Zondervan, 1992.

_____ and James Sigountos, eds. *Through No Fault of Their Own? The Fate of Those Who Have Never Heard.* Grand Rapids: Baker, 1991.

Davidson, Bruce W. "Reasonable Damnation: How Jonathan Edwards Argued for the Rationality of Hell." *JETS* 38 (March 1995): 47–56.

Davies, Eryl. *An Angry God? What the Bible Says about Wrath, Final Judgment, and Hell.* Bridgend, U.K.: Evangelical Press of Wales, 1991.

Davies, Paul C. "The Debate on Eternal Punishment in Late Seventeenth– and Early Eighteenth-Century English Literature." *Eighteenth Century Studies* 4 (1970–71): 257–76.

Dixon, Larry. *The Other Side of Good News: Confronting the Contemporary Challenges to Jesus' Teaching on Hell.* Geanies House, U.K.: Christian Focus, 2003.

Edwards, David L., and John R. W. Stott. *Evangelical Essentials: A Liberal-Evangelical Dialogue.* Downers Grove, Ill.: InterVarsity Press, 1988.

Erickson, Millard J. *How Shall They Be Saved? The Destiny of Those Who Do Not Hear of Jesus.* Grand Rapids: Baker, 1996.

_____. "Principles, Permanence, and Future Divine Judgment: A Case Study in Theological Method." *JETS* 29 (September 1985): 317–25.

Evangelical Alliance Commission on Unity and Truth Among Evangelicals (ACUTE). *The Nature of Hell.* London: ACUTE/Paternoster, 2000.

Fernando, Ajith. *Crucial Questions about Hell.* Wheaton, Ill.: Crossway, 1994.

Froom, LeRoy Edwin. *The Conditionalist Faith of Our Fathers.* 2 vols. Washington, D.C.: Review & Herald, 1965.

Fudge, Edward William. "The Final End of the Wicked." *JETS* 27 (Spring 1984): 325–34.

_____. *The Fire That Consumes: A Biblical and Historical Study of Final Punishment.* Houston: Providential, 1982.

_____. *The Fire That Consumes: The Biblical Case for Conditional Immortality.* 2d ed. rev. Peter Cousins. Carlisle, U.K.: Paternoster, 1994.

_____ and Robert A. Peterson. *Two Views of Hell: A Biblical and Theological Dialogue.* Downers Grove, Ill: InterVarsity Press, 2000.

Gerstner, John H. *Jonathan Edwards on Heaven and Hell.* Grand Rapids: Baker, 1980.

_____. *Repent or Perish: With Special Reference to the Conservative Attack on Hell.* Morgan, Pa.: Soli Deo Gloria, 1990; reprint 1996.

Gomes, Alan W. "Evangelicals and the Annihilation of Hell, Part 1." *Christian Research Journal* 13 (Spring 1991): 15–19.

_____. "Evangelicals and the Annihilation of Hell, Part 2." *Christian Research Journal* 13 (Summer 1991): 9–13.

Gray, Tony. "Destroyed Forever: An Examination of the Debates Concerning Annihilation and Conditional Immortality." *Themelios* 21 (January 1996): 14–18.

Guillebaud, Harold E. *The Righteous Judge.* N.p., 1941.

Helm, Paul. "Universalism and the Threat of Hell." *TrinJ* 4 (Spring 1983): 35–43.

Hick, John H. *Death and Eternal Life*. New York: Harper & Row, 1976.

Hoekema, Anthony A. *The Bible and the Future*. Grand Rapids: Eerdmans, 1979.

Hughes, Philip Edgcumbe. *The True Image: The Origin and Destiny of Man in Christ*. Grand Rapids: Eerdmans, 1989.

Hunsinger, George. "Hellfire and Damnation: Four Ancient and Modern Views." *SJT* 41 (1998): 406–34.

Kantzer, Kenneth S., and Carl F. H. Henry, eds. *Evangelical Affirmations*. Grand Rapids: Zondervan, 1990.

Kistler, Don, ed. *The Wrath of Almighty God: Jonathan Edwards on God's Judgment against Sinners*. Morgan, Pa.: Soli Deo Gloria, 1996.

Kvanvig, Jonathan L. *The Problem of Hell*. New York: Oxford Univ. Press, 1993.

Linfield, Alan M. "Sheep and Goats: Current Evangelical Thought on the Nature of Hell and the Scope of Salvation." *VE* 24 (June 1994): 63–75.

Master's Seminary Journal 9 (Fall 1998) is devoted to the doctrine of hell.

Martin, James P. *The Last Judgment in Protestant Theology from Orthodoxy to Ritschl*. Grand Rapids: Eerdmans, 1963.

Milne, Bruce. *The Message of Heaven and Hell: Grace and Destiny*. BST. Downers Grove, Ill.: InterVarsity Press, 2002.

Moore, David George. *The Battle for Hell: A Survey and Evaluation of Evangelicals' Growing Attraction to the Doctrine of Annihilationism*. Lanham, Md.: Univ. Press of America, 1995.

Morgan, Christopher W. *Jonathan Edwards and Hell*. Geanies House, U.K.: Christian Focus, 2004.

Morris, Leon. *The Biblical Doctrine of Judgment*. Grand Rapids: Eerdmans, 1960.

The Mystery of Salvation, The Story of God's Gift: A Report by the Doctrine Commission of the General Synod of the Church of England. London: Church House Publishing, 1995.

Nash, Ronald H. *Is Jesus the Only Savior?* Grand Rapids: Zondervan, 1994.

Okholm, Dennis L., and Timothy R. Phillips, eds. *Four Views of Salvation in a Pluralistic World*. Grand Rapids: Zondervan, 1995.

Packer, James I. "The Problem of Eternal Punishment." *Evangel: The British Evangelical Review* 10 (Summer 1992): 13–19.

Peterson, Robert A. *Hell on Trial: The Case for Eternal Punishment*. Phillipsburg, N.J.: Presbyterian & Reformed, 1995.

_____. "The Hermeneutics of Annihilationism: The Theological Method of Edward Fudge." *Presb* 21 (Spring 1995): 13–28.

_____. *See* Fudge, Edward William, and Robert A. Peterson, *Two Views of Hell*.

_____. "Undying Worm, Unquenchable Fire." *ChrT* 44 (October 23, 2000), 30–37.

Pinnock, Clark H. "The Destruction of the Finally Impenitent." *CTR* 4 (Spring 1990): 243–60.

_____. *A Wideness in God's Mercy: The Finality of Jesus Christ in a World of Religions*. Grand Rapids: Zondervan, 1992.

Powys, David J. *'Hell': A Hard Look at a Hard Question: The Fate of the Unrighteous in New Testament Thought*. Paternoster Biblical and Theological Monographs. Carlisle, U.K.: Paternoster, 1998.

Ramesh, Richard P. *The Population of Heaven*. Chicago: Moody Press, 1994.

Robinson, John A. T. *In the End, God*. London: James Clark, 1950.

Rowell, Geoffrey. *Hell and the Victorians: A Study of the Nineteenth-Century Theological Controversies Concerning Eternal Punishment and the Future Life*. Oxford: Clarendon, 1974.

Sanders, John, ed. *What About Those Who Have Never Heard? Three Views on the Destiny of the Unevangelized*. Downers Grove, Ill.: InterVarsity Press, 1995.

_____. *No Other Name: An Investigation into the Destiny of the Unevangelized*. Grand Rapids: Eerdmans, 1992.

Scharen, Hans. "Gehenna in the Synoptics, Part 1." *BSac* 149 (July–September 1992): 324–37.

_____. "Gehenna in the Synoptics, Part 2." *BSac* 149 (October–December 1992): 454–70.

Shedd, William G. T. *The Doctrine of Endless Punishment*. New York: Scribner's, 1886; reprint, Minneapolis: Klock & Klock, 1980.

Stott, John R. W. *See* Edwards, David L. and John R. W. Stott. *Evangelical Essentials*.

Talbot, Thomas. "The Doctrine of Everlasting Punishment." *Faith and Philosophy* 7 (January 1990): 19–42.

Toon, Peter. *Heaven and Hell: A Biblical and Theological Overview*. Nashville: Nelson, 1986.

Travis, Stephen H. *Christ and the Judgment of God: Divine Retribution in the New Testament*. Basingstoke, U.K.: Marshall Pickering, 1986.

Walker, D. P. *The Decline of Hell: Seventeenth-Century Discussions of Eternal Torment*. Chicago: Univ. of Chicago Press, 1964.

Walls, Jerry L. *Hell: The Logic of Damnation*. Library of Religious Philosophy 9. Notre Dame: Univ. of Notre Dame Press, 1992.

Wenham, John W. *The Enigma of Evil*. Grand Rapids: Zondervan, 1985.

Wheeler, Michael. *Heaven, Hell, and the Victorians*. Cambridge: Cambridge Univ. Press, 1994.

HeLL UNDeR fire

SCRIPTURE INDEX

Roman type indicates reference(s) or passing reference(s) to a particular verse or verses, whether in the text or in footnotes. *Italic* type indicates a brief discussion of the referenced verses. **Bold** type indicates a major discussion.

Genesis
1:1 45
1:2–5 231
2:7 59
3 . . . . 94, 150
3:14, 17 230
3:19 . . . . 59, 63
4:16 150
6:4 50
14:5 46
15:20 46
17 49
18:25 78
19:24 114
19:26 211
19:28 . . . . 114, 115
21:19, 25 45
23 44
25:8, 17 44
35:29 44
37:24 45
37:26–28 159
41:41 159
45:4–5, 8 159
49:29, 33 44
50:19–21 159

Exodus
12:29 45
15:2 179

Leviticus
10:1–2 211
16:6–10 230
16:20–22 230

Numbers
3:4 211
27:13 44
31:2 44

Deuteronomy
2:11, 20a. b 46
3:11, 13 46
18:11 . . . . 45, 46
27–30 230
28:25–26 49
29:23 114
30:15–20 102
32:21 99
32:33 45
32:50 44
33:6 131

Joshua
7:25 100
12:4 46
13:12 46
15:8 46
17:15 46
18:16 46

Judges
2:10 44
8:32 44
16:31 44

1 Samuel
16:7 222
28:6 45

2 Samuel
2:32 44
5:18, 22 46
6:6–7 211
17:23 44
19:38 44
21:14 44
22:9 114
23:13 46

1 Kings
11:21, 43 53
13:22 44
13:77 49
14:10–11 49
14:20, 31 53
15:8, 24 53
16:6 53
16:28 53
17:17–24 59
22:40, 50 53

2 Kings
4:18–37 59
8:24 53
10:35 53
13:9, 13 53
13:20–21 59
14:22, 29 53
15:7, 22, 28 53
16:20 53
16:3 61
20:21 53
21:6 61
21:18 53
22:20 44
23:6 44
23:10 61
24:6 53

1 Chronicles
10:13 45
11:15 46
14:9 46
20:4, 6, 8 46

2 Chronicles
9:31 53
12:16 53
14:1 53
16:13 53
21:1 53
26:2, 23 53
27:9 53
28:3 227
28:27 53
28:33 61
32:33 53
33:6 61
33:20 53
34:28 44
35:24 44

Nehemiah
2:3–5 44

Job
3:11–19 55
3:13, 18 58
7:9 58

10:9 53
10:18–22. 55
12:10 53
14:12 54
18:13–14 46
18:15–17 114
21:20 113
26:6 46
27:3 53
28:13 45
28:22 46
31:12 46
32:8 53
33:4 53
33:22, 24, 28 45
34:14–15 59
34:15 53
38:17 . . . . 46, 53

Psalms
6:5 46
7:15 45
8 158
9:14 . . . . 46, 53
11:6 114
13:3 54
16:10 45
16:11–12 59
22:30 45
27:13 45
28:1 . . . . 45, 49
30:3 . . . . 45, 49
30:10 45
31:23 208
40:2 45
49:9 45
49:15–16 59
49:15 46
52:7 45
55:24 45
60:3 113
62:12 . . . . 161, 223
63:9 45
75:8 113
76:5–6 54
88 47
88:4 . . . . 45, 49, 50
88:5 46
88:6 45
88:10 46
88:11–12 56
88:12 46
90:2 64
90:5 54
103:19 13
104:29 . . . . 53, 59
106:28 46
107:18 . . . . 46, 53
115:16–18. 50
115:17 46
116:6 179
116:9 45
127:3–5 64
130:4 224
139 222
139:15 45

141:7 46
142:6 45
143:3 . . . . 46, 49, 56
143:7 . . . . 45, 49
145:9 191

Proverbs
1:12 . . . . 45, 46, 49, 52
2:18–19 48
7:27 46
9:18 48
15:11 46
21:16 48
23:14 44
24:12 223
27:20 46
30:15–16 . . . . 46, 52

Ecclesiastes
3:18–21 59
4:2 46
9:3, 5 46
12:5 . . . . 50, 64
12:7 . . . . 53, 59

Song of Songs
8:6 46

Isaiah
1:22 113
2:10–21 107
5:14 46
6 . . . . 210, 222
8:19 46
14:4–21 56
14:9 47
14:15 . . . . 45, 50
14:19 58
17:5 46
19:3 48
21:1 132
22:2 49
22:14 131
25:8 129
26:13–14 47
26:14 46
26:19 . . . . 45, 46, 59
28:15, 18 46
30:27–33 114
34 . . . . 115, 117
34:9–10 . . . . 114, 115, 118, 121
38:1 45
38:10 . . . . 46, 53
38:17–18 45
42:3 236
44:23 45
51:4 45
51:17 . . . . 113, 230
51:21–23 113
51:22–23 230
53:18 45
59:10 46
60:11, 15 118
62:6 118
63:6 113
65:14–18 131
65:17 132
66 . . . . 60, 87
66:15–16 105
66:16 . . . . 60, 61, 63
66:22–24 . . . . 114, 131
66:22 132
66:24 . . . . 59, 62, 64, 65, 74, 82,
83, 95, 120, 137, 168
66:24b 132

Jeremiah
7:31 61
9:24–25 49
11:19 45
14:17 118
14:18 49
16:4 49
19:4–5 61
25:15–18 113
25:15 . . . . 113, 230
25:17 230
25:27–33 113
26:23 44
32:35 61
37:16 45
38:6 45
51:7 113
51:39, 57 . . . . 54, 131

Lamentations
2:18 118
3:6 . . . . 46, 49, 56
3:55 45
4:9 49

Ezekiel
1 119
6:14 . . . . 105, 146, 204
7:27 161
8:3 45
14:16 . . . . 105, 146, 204
19:4, 8 45
23:31–33 230
24:17 46
26:2 45
26:20 . . . . 45, 49, 53
26:21 . . . . 49, 55
27:36 55
28:8 45
28:19 55
31:14 . . . . 45, 49
31:15 49
31:16 . . . . 45, 49
31:17 49
31:18 . . . . 45, 49
31:32 49
32:17–32 . . . . 49, 58
32:18 . . . . 45, 49
32:19 49
32:20 116
32:21 . . . . 49, 50, 58
32:22–23 53
32:23 . . . . 45, 49, 50, 53
32:24 . . . . 45, 49, 58, 116
32:25 . . . . 45, 49, 58
32:26 45
32:27 . . . . 45, 49, 50, 58
32:28 . . . . 49, 58
32:29 . . . . 49, 58
32:30, 31 . . . . 49, 58, 116
32:32 . . . . 45, 49, 58
35:8 49
37:1–14 . . . . 47, 59
37:12–14 63
37:26–28 118
38:22 114
39:11, 14 50

Daniel
7 134
7:17, 23 134
11:35, 36–40 62
12:1–3 . . . . 61, 62
12:1–2 . . . . 62, 131, 168

12:2 . . . . 58, 59, 62, 65, 74, 83,
95, 131

Hosea
4:9 161
6:1–3 59
13:14 46

Amos
4:13 56

Obadiah
16 113

Jonah
2:6 45
2:9 179

Habakkuk
2:5 46
2:16 230

Zechariah
1:6 162

Malachi
1:2–4 122

Matthew
3:1–12 147
3:7–12 . . . . 137, 139
3:7, 10 137
3:10–12 138
3:11–12 137
3:12 144
4:24 116
5–7 . . . . 72, 137
5:20–30 . . . . 137, 143
5:20 137
5:22–30 214
5:22 . . . . 60, 72, 79, 80, 81, 137,
168, 225, 226
5:24–25 143
5:29–30 . . . . . . 72, 80, 137, 144, 168,
225, 226
5:29, 30 137
7:13–27 . . . . 137, 214
7:13–14 145
7:13 . . . . 137, 168, 226
7:14, 19 137
7:21–23 . . . . . 137, 138, 147, 150, 228
7:22–23 225
7:23 . . . . 138, 155, 162, 168
7:24–27 . . . . 138, 145
8:6 116
8:10–12 . . . . 138, 226
8:12 . . . . 138, 144, 147, 168, 184,
214, 225
8:29 . . . . 81, 116, 168
9:17 . . . . 105, 146, 204
9:24 58
9:34 73
10 80
10:17 80
10:24–25 72
10:26–28 226
10:28 . . . . 30, 72, 73, 80, 81, 138,
139, 140, 168, 214, 225
10:28b 19
12:17–21 236
12:24 73
12:32 . . . . 184, 188
12:33–37 211
12:36 . . . . 162, 208

13:30–50 214
13:36–43 138
13:38 73
13:40–42 226
13:40–41 138
13:41–42 .... 155, 161
13:42 ... 138, 144, 147, 168, 184, 225
13:47–50 .... 138, 226
13:49–50 .... 138, 161, 168
13:50 .... 138, 144, 147, 225
14:24 116
16:18 13
16:27 .... 155, 162
18:6–9 .... 138, 168, 214
18:8–9 .... 81, 82, 161, 226
18:8 .... 72, 138
18:9 .... 72, 82, 225
18:34 116
22:1–14 138
22:13 .... 138, 144, 168, 225
22:31 77
23:13 73
23:15 .... 73, 214
23:33 ... 138, 143, 168, 214, 225, 226
24:5–31 62
24:12 89
24:14 165
24:45–25:46 .... 143, 149
24:45–51 138
24:51 ..... 138, 144, 145, 149, 168,
.... 184, 214, 225
25 155
25:1–13 138
25:10–12 .... 138, 147, 149
25:14–30 138
25:30 ... 138, 144, 147, 149, 168, 225
25:31–46 .... 82, 138, 143, 145,
151, 183, 202, 208, 214, 223
25:31 .... 155, 168
25:32 .... 155, 168, 183, 223
25:34 .... 151, 155, 157, 168, 183
25:41–46 .... 199, 202, 227
25:41 ..... 120, 128, 138, 144, 147,
149, 155, 157, 161, 168, 183,
188, 218, 226
25:45–46 226
25:46 ..... 17, 76, 120, 138, 144,
148, 149, 155, 157, 168, 183,
188, 202, 218, 225
26:8 .... 105, 146, 204
26:24 .... 160, 168, 188, 228
26:37 220
26:42 150
27:17–46 230
27:46 150
28:19–20 175
28:20 88

Mark
1:24 .... 81, 145, 155, 168
2:22 .... 105, 146, 204
3:17 73
3:29 .... 106, 202
4:13–19 73
5:5 115
5:7 .... 81, 116, 155, 168
6:48 116
9 .... 74, 137
9:42–49 214
9:42–48 ..... 136, 137, 138, 143, 147
9:42 .... 136, 144

9:43–48 184
9:43 .. 60, 74, 136, 137, 138, 144, 168
9:45 .... 74, 137, 168
9:47–48 .... 74, 82, 120, 168
9:47 137
9:48 .... 83, 137, 141
9:50 74
13:5–27 62
14:4 .... 105, 146, 204
14:12–52 230
14:33–34 .... 220, 231
14:36 230

Luke
3:7–12 139
3:17 168
4:34 .... 81, 168
5:37 .... 105, 146, 204
8:28 .... 81, 116
9:54 73
12:5 .... 60, 73, 139, 161, 168
13:1–5 139
13:3–5 145
13:3, 5 168
13:22–30 148
13:28 184
15:9 .... 105, 146, 204
15:24, 32 131
16:19–31 .... 139, 143, 147, 214, 227
16:22 167
16:23–25 .... 139, 168
16:23 .... 74, 116, 167
16:24 .... 139, 167, 184, 185
16:25–26 139
16:25 167
16:26 188
16:27 139
16:28 .... 116, 167, 168
18:7 115
19:41 232
21:8–28 62
22:1–53 230
22:22 160
23:43 167

John
3:3–5 141
3:14 121
3:16–36 .... 141, 150
3:16–21 214
3:16–18 .... 166, 168
3:16 .... 75, 141, 145
3:17–21 141
3:18 .... 75, 187
3:36 ..... 74, 141, 166, 168, 187, 214
4:13 77
5:22–23 155
5:22 .... 75, 221
5:24–29 .... 141, 165
5:24–28 150
5:24 .... 75, 141, 155
5:27 .... 155, 157, 225
5:28–29 .... 76, 124, 144, 156,
168, 214
5:28 75
5:29 .... 97, 108, 141, 187
5:30 .... 75, 156
5:39, 46 77
6:27, 50, 56 75
8:21 .... 168, 188
8:24 168
8:35 75
8:56 77
10:14 162

10:26 164
10:28 .... 75, 141
11:11 58
12:25 187
12:31 73
12:32 .... 187, 217
12:34 75
12:41 77
12:48 187
14:2–3 77
14:30 73
15:1–8 141
15:1–7 147
15:1, 6–7 141
16:8 158
16:11 73
17:22, 24 165

Acts
1:25 228
2:23–24 160
3:15 160
3:21 .... 101, 187
4:27–28 160
4:28 160
5:1–10 211
7:59 167
9:24 115
10:42 .... 156, 161, 168
13:46 187
17:30–31 208
17:31 .... 156, 157, 168
17:32 84
20:28 221
23:6 96
24:15 96
26:5 96
27:31, 44 179
28:24–27 187

Romans
1–3 223
1:8–2:8 150
1:16–17 98
1:16 96
1:18–3:20 .... 143, 164, 192,
224, 236
1:18–2:11 .... 93, 109
1:18–32 .... 100, 139, 222
1:18 .... 92, 93, 94, 185
1:19–23 104
1:20 224
1:21–32 223
1:23 108
1:24 .... 94, 148, 223
1:26 .... 94, 148, 223
1:27 223
1:28 .... 94, 148, 223
1:32 .... 92, 139, 234
2:1–16 .... 188, 222
2:1–11 139
2:1–5 94
2:1 93
2:2 .... 93, 222
2:3–4 190
2:5–12 187
2:5–9 184
2:5–8 .... 139, 144
2:5 .... 92, 93, 94, 168, 185, 211,
222, 225
2:6 223
2:7 206
2:8–11 139
2:8–9 .... 94, 162, 168

2:8 . . . 92, 225
2:9 . . . 93, 225
2:11 . . . 222
2:12 . . . 92, 93, 94, 104, 139, 168, 223, 225
2:14–15 . . . 223
2:16 . . . 95, 208, 225
3:5–6 . . . 78
3:5 . . . 92, 139
3:7–8 . . . 93, 139
3:9 . . . 185
3:12 . . . 212
3:19–20 . . . 224
3:19 . . . 185, 222
3:20 . . . 222
3:21–31 . . . 150, 208
3:21–22 . . . 98
3:25 . . . 226
5–8 . . . 94
5:6–11 . . . 150
5:9–21 . . . 139
5:9–10 . . . 99
5:9 . . . 92, 94
5:10 . . . 94, 100
5:11 . . . 100
5:12–21 . . . 94, 99, 139, 150, 211
5:12–19 . . . 164
5:12 . . . 92, 94, 98, 164
5:14 . . . 92, 94
5:15 . . . 92, 164
5:16 . . . 93, 164
5:17 . . . 92, 98, 164, 185
5:18–19 . . . 11
5:18 . . . 93, 94, 98, 102, 164, 187
5:19 . . . 164
5:21 . . . 92, 98
6:16–23 . . . 139
6:16, 21 . . . 92
6:23 . . . 92, 93, 139, 145, 168, 187
7:5 . . . 92, 139
7:9, 10, 11, 13 . . . 92
7:24 . . . 92
8:1 . . . 93
8:2 . . . 92
8:3 . . . 158
8:4 . . . 232
8:6 . . . 92
8:10 . . . 95
8:12–13 . . . 109
8:13 . . . 92, 140
8:23 . . . 165
8:29–9:29 . . . 192
8:38 . . . 92
9–11 . . . 99
9 . . . 192
9:3 . . . 93, 96, 140, 168
9:19–23 . . . 208
9:22–24 . . . 102
9:22 . . . 92, 93, 104, 139, 140, 145, 164, 168
10:1 . . . 96
10:8–17 . . . 35
10:9–10 . . . 96
10:11–13 . . . 179
10:13–15 . . . 236
10:16 . . . 103

10:19 . . . 99
10:21 . . . 103
11:7 . . . 164
11:11, 12, 14 . . . 99
11:15 . . . 100
11:18, 25 . . . 99
11:26 . . . 99, 100
11:30–31 . . . 103
11:32 . . . 31, 99, 100, 101, 102, 104, 187
11:33–36 . . . 214
11:36 . . . 179
12:4–8 . . . 192
14 . . . 71
14:9 . . . 161
14:12 . . . 223
14:15, 20 . . . 92, 104
15:19, 30 . . . 77

1 Corinthians
1:18 . . . 92, 93, 104
2:8 . . . 160
2:9 . . . 80
2:10–14 . . . 77
4:5 . . . 162, 208, 223
5:5 . . . 104
5:7 . . . 231
6:9–10 . . . 187
6:9 . . . 227
7:40 . . . 77
10:9, 10 . . . 105
11:23 . . . 77
11:30 . . . 58
11:32 . . . 93, 168
12 . . . 192
12:3 . . . 93
15:12–19 . . . 97
15:18 . . . 92, 104
15:20–28 . . . 97, 102
15:21 . . . 92
15:22–28 . . . 187
15:22 . . . 31, 92, 97, 98, 99
15:23 . . . 97
15:24–28 . . . 217
15:26 . . . 95
15:28 . . . 217
15:42 . . . 206
15:51 . . . 58
15:52–54 . . . 206
15:52 . . . 108
15:53–54 . . . 206
15:53 . . . 205
15:54–55 . . . 129
16:22 . . . 93

2 Corinthians
2:15–16 . . . 168
2:15 . . . 92, 93, 104
2:16 . . . 92
3:6, 7, 9 . . . 92, 94
4:1–2 . . . 221
4:3–4 . . . 187
4:3 . . . 92, 104, 168
4:18 . . . 232
5:8 . . . 167
5:10–15 . . . 221
5:10 . . . 95, 98, 188, 221, 223
5:13 . . . 232
5:14–15 . . . 229
5:14 . . . 228
5:15, 16 . . . 232
5:18–20 . . . 100, 233
5:19 . . . 187, 229
5:21 . . . 229

7:10 . . . 92
11:22–29 . . . 96
Galatians
1:8–9 . . . 93, 168
1:20 . . . 187
2:20 . . . 179
3:10 . . . 93
3:13–14 . . . 121
3:13 . . . 93, 229
3:22 . . . 100
4:7 . . . 165
4:8–9 . . . 162
6:7–8 . . . 162, 187
6:7 . . . 188
6:8 . . . 92, 104, 145, 168
Ephesians
1–3 . . . 192
1:3–14 . . . 191
1:10 . . . 100, 217
2 . . . 150
2:1 . . . 92, 95, 131
2:3 . . . 92, 93
2:5–7 . . . 179
2:7 . . . 191
2:12 . . . 131
2:16 . . . 100
3:5 . . . 77
4:11–16 . . . 192
5:6 . . . 92, 168, 187
5:25–27 . . . 192
5:25 . . . 179
Philippians
1:23 . . . 167
1:28 . . . 92, 104, 140, 145, 168, 187
2:9–11 . . . 174, 187
2:10–11 . . . 101, 217
2:26 . . . 220
3:5 . . . 96
3:19 . . . 92, 104, 140, 145, 168, 187
Colossians
1:13–20 . . . 191
1:15–20 . . . 100
1:16 . . . 101, 179
1:20 . . . 100, 217
1:22 . . . 100
1:27–28 . . . 191
2:6–7 . . . 191
2:13 . . . 131
3:1–4 . . . 191
3:6 . . . 92, 168, 187
3:25 . . . 187
1 Thessalonians
1:5 . . . 77
1:10 . . . 92, 168
2:9 . . . 115
2:16 . . . 92
3:10 . . . 115
4:6 . . . 93
4:14 . . . 58
4:15 . . . 103
5:3 . . . 92, 104, 140, 168
5:5 . . . 73
5:9 . . . 92, 168
5:10 . . . 58
5:13 . . . 145
2 Thessalonians
1:5–11 . . . 208
1:5–10 . . . 140, 143, 145, 147, 149, 203
1:6–10 . . . 156
1:6–9 . . . 150

1:6–7 156
1:6 . . . . 104, 140, 143, 149, 208
1:7b–10a 156
1:8–10 94
1:8–9 . . . . . . 103, 108, 109, 168, 184,
. . . . 203, 228
1:8 . . . . 93, 104, 140, 149, 156
1:9 . . . . . . 92, 93, 106, 108, 140, 145,
. . . . 148, 149, 150, 202
2:3–4 134
2:3 . . . . 104, 140
2:7 134
2:8 140
2:9–10 94
2:10 . . . . 92, 104, 140, 168
2:12 . . . . 93, 140
3:8 115

1 Timothy
1:16 101
2:1 101
2:4 . . . . 101, 187
3:16 101
4:1 77
4:10 101
4:16 187
5:5 115
5:24 . . . . 93, 187
6:9 . . . . 92, 104, 140, 145, 187
6:15–17 108
6:16 206

2 Timothy
1:3 . . . . 115, 118
1:9 166
1:10 . . . . 204, 205, 206
3:16 224
4:1 161
4:2 224

Titus
2:11 187

Hebrews
2:9 187
2:10 179
3:14–19 187
4:12–13 . . . . 208, 211
4:15 158
5:8 158
5:9 . . . . 106, 202
6:1–3 140
6:2 . . . . 106, 140, 168, 184, 202
6:4–8 187
6:8 191
6:9 184
9–10 150
9:12 . . . . 106, 202
9:27 . . . . 168, 184
10:26–31 187
10:27–31 . . . . 143, 144
10:27–30 140
10:27 . . . . 140, 145, 168, 184, 191
10:31 . . . . 140, 184
10:39 . . . . 168, 187
12:18 191
12:22–24 180
12:23 167
12:29 191
13:5 231
13:11–13 230

James
1:11, 15 . . . . 140, 145
1:28 235
2:10 211
4:12 . . . . 140, 143, 145, 168

5:1–5 . . . . 140, 143, 144
5:3–5 145
5:20 . . . . 140, 145

1 Peter
1:17 154
1:20 160
1:23 235
2:8 164
2:24 230
3:18 150
3:19 . . . . 140, 188
4:5 161

2 Peter
2 . . . . 140, 208
2:1 . . . . 141, 168
2:3 . . . . 141, 168, 187
2:4–17 143
2:4 . . . . 141, 167, 168
2:6 . . . . 141, 145, 187
2:8 116
2:9–10 187
2:9 . . . . 141, 167, 168
2:12 . . . . 141, 168
2:13 141
2:17 . . . . 141, 143, 168, 187
2:20–22 187
3:6 . . . . 105, 146, 204
3:7 . . . . 141, 168, 187
3:9 . . . . 141, 187
3:16 187

1 John
1:3 174
1:5 . . . . 73, 191
2 134
2:2 187
2:18 134
2:19 . . . . 165, 187
2:22–23 134
3:1–3 166
3:10, 15 187
4:1–3 134
4:8, 9–10, 16 191
5:16 187

Jude
4 . . . . 141, 168
5 141
6–23 143
6 . . . . 141, 168
7 . . . . 106, 115, 141, 144, 168
10 141
11 141
13–23 143
13 . . . . 141, 168
15, 23 141

Revelation
1:4 158
1:6 . . . . 118, 129
1:14 113
1:16 123
1:18 . . . . 118, 129, 130
2:11 . . . . 132, 168
2:12, 16 123
2:18 113
3:5 163
3:18 113
4:1–22:5 112
4:3 158
4:5 . . . . 114, 133, 158
4:8 . . . . 118, 119
4:9–10 . . . . 118, 119, 129

5 191
5:5 157
5:6 . . . . 156, 158
5:8 156
5:9–14 192
5:9 . . . . 156, 157
5:12–14 156
5:13 . . . . 118, 129
6:1 157
6:8 130
6:9–11 126
6:9–10 167
6:10 . . . . 126, 208, 209
6:11 119
6:12–17 . . . . 119, 123
6:15–17 228
6:16–17 . . . . 157, 168
6:16 . . . . 114, 157
7:9–17 192
7:10 156
7:12 . . . . 118, 129
7:15 118
8:4 117
8:5 . . . . 114, 133
8:7–8 114
9:5–6 114
9:5 116
9:11 46
9:17–18 114
10:6 . . . . 118, 129
11:5 114
11:10 . . . . 114, 116
11:15–18 209
11:15 . . . . 118, 129
11:18 . . . . 119, 123, 168
11:19 133
12:2 116
13 132
13:8 . . . . 160, 163
13:11–18 126
13:11 157
13:15 112
14 . . . . . 115, 117, 120, 127, 133, 134
14:6–11 126
14:6–8 113
14:6–7 126
14:6 115
14:8 . . . . 113, 115, 126
14:9–12 112
14:9–11 . . . . 117, 124, 125, 126,
. . . . 132, 141
14:10–11 . . . . 112, 113, 114, 115,
. . . . 16, 119, 123, 127
14:10 . . . . . . 113, 114, 115, 125, 127,
. . . . 133, 141, 144, 154, 157
14:11 . . . . 78, 81, 113, 115, 116,
. . . . 117, 118, 119, 120, 121, 123,
. . . . 124, 125, 126, 128, 133,
. . . . 134, 141, 144
14:11a 114, 117, 126
14:11b 125, 126
14:12–13 126
14:13 . . . . 118, 119, 126
14:14–15:4 209
14:14–20 . . . . 119, 123
14:18 126
14:19 168
15:2 114
15:3 156

Index

15:7 . . . . 118, 129
16:8–11 235
16:8–9 114
16:11 212
16:17–21 . . . . 119, 123
16:18 133
16:19 . . . . 113, 168
17:8 . . . . 163, 168
17:11 168
17:14 156
17:16 . . . . 114, 122
18 . . . . . 114, 116, 119, 120, 121, 122
18:4–24 123
18:6–24 122
18:6–9 113
18:7 . . . . 114, 116
18:8 . . . . 114, 168
18:9 . . . . 122, 168
18:10 . . . . 114, 116
18:11–14 122
18:15 . . . . 114, 116, 122
18:17 122
18:18 . . . . 120, 121, 168
18:20 185
18:22–23 122
19 . . . . 122, 123, 127
19:1–8 209
19:2 . . . . 119, 185
19:3 . . . . 78, 118, 120, 121, 122,
123, 124, 168
19:6–16 191
19:11–21 119
19:12 114
19:15 . . . . 113, 123, 168
19:17–21 . . . . 123, 127
19:19–21 123
19:19–20 228
19:20 . . . . . . 114, 116, 124, 129, 132,
133, 161, 168
20–22 . . . . 142, 147, 217
20 . . . . 127, 134
20:4–6 131
20:6 132
20:7–10 127
20:9–10 114
20:10–22:15 149
20:10–15 . . . . 123, 129, 134, 141,
143, 145, 149, 150, 208
20:10 . . 112, 114, 116, 118, 121, 123,
124, 127, 128, 129, 130, 131,
132, 133, 134, 141, 144, 161,
168, 183, 205, 217, 218, 228
20:11–15 . . . . 123, 124, 163, 164
20:11–12 224
20:11 154
20:12–13 . . . . 131, 162
20:12 . . . . 124, 163
20:13–15 124
20:13 . . . . 162, 163
20:14–15 . . . . 30, 114, 129, 132, 141,
. . . . 168
20:14 . . . . . . 112, 116, 129, 130, 131,
. . . . 132, 145, 149

20:15 . . . . . . 116, 128, 130, 132, 133,
142, 161, 163, 164, 183,
218, 228
21:1–22:5 192
21 218
21:1–8 129
21:2–4 128
21:4 . . . . 78, 129, 131, 132
21:6–8 142
21:8 . . . . 114, 124, 129, 131, 132,
133, 141, 142, 145, 149,
168, 192, 214
21:21 80
21:27 . . . . 131, 163, 192
22 218
22:2 80
22:5 . . . . 118, 129, 218
22:11 . . . . 212, 235
22:14–15 . . . . 116, 131, 147
22:15 . . . . . . 131, 141, 142, 168, 227
22:19 131

Index of Other Ancient Texts

Apocalypse of Peter
6–13 (Ethiopic) 117
32 (Akmim) 117

Barnabas
5:6 84

2 Baruch
30:2–5 96
42:8 96
44:12–15 120
49:1–51:10 96
51:2 120
51:5–6 114
51:6 120

b. Sanh.
92a 131

1 Enoch
10:6–22 120
21 114
22:10–13 120
27:2–3 114
39:12–40:5 119
48:9 114
61:10–12 119
62:12 114
63:1–6 119
91:9 . . . . 114, 120
102:3, 8 119
103:4, 8 120
108:14–15 114

4 Ezra
7:32 96
7:35–44 120
7:36–38 130
7:37 . . . . 96, 130
7:75–87 120
7:85 114
7:93–94 120
7:93 114

8:52, 53, 54 130

Jubilees
30:4 117
36:9–11 117

Judith
7:17 83
11:15 105

3 Maccabees
2:5 114

4 Maccabees
9:9 117
10:11 117
12:12, 19 117
13:15 117

Midr. Pss.
11.5 113
15:6 131
18.11 115
23.7 114
75.4 113

Midr. Rab. Eccl.
VII.14 114

Midr. Rab. Exod.
9.13 115

Midr. Rab. Gen.
XVI.4 113
LXXXVIII.5 113

Midr. Rab. Lev.
XXXII.1 114

Pirke Rab. Eliezer
XXXIV 131

1 QS
II, 6–18 . . . . 114, 120
IV, 12–14 . . . . 114, 120

Septuagint (LXX)
Ps. 21:2 115
Ps. 31:4 115
Ps. 41:3 115
Ps. 54:10 115
Isa. 34:9 115
Isa. 60:11 115
Jer. 9:1 115
Jer. 14:17 115
Lam. 2:18 115

Sibylline Oracles
2:284–310 120

T. Ben.
10:8 96

Targum of Isaiah
33:17 114
34:9 115
65:5–6, 15 132
66:24 132

Testament of Judah
25:3 127

Wisdom of Solomon
1:14 105
5:1–14 114
5:1–5 114
10:6–7 115

Author Index

Ambrose, 229n7
Anselm, 210, 225, 239
Aquinas, Thomas. *See* Thomas Aquinas.
Aristotle, 87, 87n80
Arnobius of Sicca, 85, 197
Athenagoras, 85
Augustine (Bishop of Hippo), 17, 20, 34, 83, 84, 87, 148, 192, 229n7, 237

Ballou, Hosea, 172, 173, 179
Balthasar, Hans Urs von. *See* von Balthasar, Hans Urs
Barth, Karl, 26, 172, 173n14, 176, 215n70
Bayle, Pierre, 19
Berger, Peter, 36
Blanchard, John, 187n44, 233
Bonda, Jan, 11, 12
Boring, M.E., 96n11
Bowles, Ralph G., 116n14, 120, 121, 121n25, 122, 123, 124, 125n36
Brooks, Thomas, 227
Brow, Robert, 35, 198, 199, 204, 215
Bruce, F. F., 31, 31n61, 100n22, 229n7
Brunner, Emil, 172, 173n14, 186, 215n70
Bultmann, Rudolf, 25, 26

Carroll, Lewis. *See* Dodgson, Charles Lutwidge.
Carson, D. A., 75n27, 76, 76n29, 146, 158n4, 203, 206, 212, 214, 214n66
Celsus, 17, 86, 86n72, 86n73, 87n80
Chauncy, Charles, 171, 171n5
Chrysostom, John. *See* John Chrysostom
Colenso, J. W., 24
Constable, Henry, 197
Cooper, John W., 95n7, 109n49
Crockett, William V., 98n14, 104, 104n34, 213n60
Cyril of Alexandria, 229n7

Dodd, C. H., 172, 172n7
Dodgson, Charles Lutwidge, 22

Edwards, David L., 30, 207n44
Edwards, Jonathan, 18, 34, 38, 205n37, 209, 210–211, 215–216, 216n73, 225, 239
Ellis, Earle, 199, 201, 203, 204, 205
Erickson, Millard J., 54n42, 206n39
Eusebius, 84
Farrar, F. W., 23–24, 25
Ferré, Nels, 172, 186
Frame, John M., 216
Fudge, Edward W., 33, 34n74, 77–83, 78n38, 79n40, 79n43, 93n3, 108n46, 116, 116n14, 117, 118, 127, 127n42, 128, 133, 133n59, 143n5, 146n17, 148, 196n3, 197n6, 198, 198n11, 199n15, 201, 201n19, 202, 204

Gerstner, John H., 161
Gray, Tony, 86, 88n83, 199, 199n15, 200, 205

Green, Michael, 199, 201, 202, 203, 207, 207n44, 213, 213n64
Guillebaud, Harold A., 197

Harmon, Kendall S., 143n5, 145n11, 147, 148, 149n22
Harris, Murray J., 76, 76n29, 96n9, 108–109
Hart, Trevor, 180
Head, Peter, 79n42, 82
Henry, Carl F.H., 31
Hexham, Irving, 69
Hick, John, 102, 172, 174, 174n16, 180, 181, 181n25, 181n26, 181n27, 182, 182n29, 186, 189
Hobbes, Thomas, 20
Hughes, Philip E., 31n62, 32, 108n46, 199, 202, 203, 229n7
Hutchinson, William R., 25

Irenaeus, 85, 86

John Chrysostom, 104
John Paul II (pope), 27
Josephus, 49n24, 96n10
Justin Martyr, 84, 85, 86–87, 87n78

Kantzer, Kenneth S., 31
Küng, Hans, 172, 173n14

L'Engle, Madeleine, 171, 172
Lewis, C. S., 38, 143n5, 145n11, 174, 174n17
Lloyd-Jones, D. Martyn, 236

MacDonald, George, 171
Mackintosh, Hugh Ross, 176
MacQuarrie, John, 172, 173n14
Maurice, F. D., 23, 25, 176
M'Cheyne, Robert Murray, 233, 234
McKnight, Scot, 71, 76, 79n39
Mill, John Stuart, 38
Mitchell, Basil, 178
Moo, Douglas J., 100n20, 143n7, 146, 146n16, 150n24, 203, 204n30
Moltmann, Jürgen, 27
Morris, Leon, 106n39, 215
Motyer, J. Alec, 83
Murray, John, 172

Niebuhr, Reinhold, 26, 172n7

O'Brien, Peter, 101
Oden, Thomas, 17
Origen, 17, 18, 86, 86n77, 87, 101, 170, 170n1, 171, 188

Pannenberg, Wolfhart, 215n70
Papias of Hierapolis, 70
Pelikan, Jaroslav, 21
Peterson, Robert A., 200, 211–212, 217n78

Index

Pinnock, Clark, 32, 33, 35, 38, 198, 201, 202, 203, 204–205, 207, 209, 210, 213, 213n62, 215, 216, 216n73, 217, 218
Piper, John, 215
Powys, David, 12, 17n6, 69, 70, 70n12, 94n5, 127n42, 133n59, 143n5, 145n17, 146, 199–200, 199n15, 201n19, 202, 203

Rahner, Karl, 27
Reid, Daniel G., 105, 106, 150n23
Robinson, J. A. T., 172, 176, 188, 189
Robinson, John. *See* Robinson, J. A. T.
Rowell, Geoffrey, 22, 24
Russell, Bertrand, 171

Sanders, E. P., 96n10
Sanders, John, 171n5, 181n25, 181n26, 189
Sasse, H., 76, 76n29
Schleiermacher, Friedrich, 37, 171, 171n6, 189, 189n53, 193
Shedd, W. G. T., 184, 225, 225n4, 236
Spicq, Ceslas, 231
Sproul, R.C., 173
Spurgeon, Charles H., 21, 28, 38
Stott, John R. W., 30–31, 31n61, 31n62, 32, 88, 90, 145, 146, 196–197, 198, 201, 203, 207, 207n44, 209, 217, 220, 229

Strong, A. H., 212n58

Talbot, Mark, 208
Talbott, Thomas, 172
Tatian (emperor of Rome), 84
Tertullian, 30, 85
Theophilus, 85
Thomas Aquinas, 87, 87n80, 239
Travis, Stephen H., 198, 198n10, 201, 204, 207, 209n49, 213, 213n64

Voltaire, 20
von Balthasar, Hans Urs, 27
Vos, Geerhardus, 37

Walker, D. P., 19
Weldon, John, 32
Wells, David F., 36, 208n45, 212, 215, 215n72
Wenham, John, 29–30, 29n54, 32, 74n26, 108n46, 146, 198, 198n9, 201, 203, 204, 207, 207n44, 209, 213, 213n64
Wesley, John, 236
Whately, Richard, 197
Whiston, William, 197
White, Edward, 197
Wilson, A.N, 21, 21n22
Wright, Nigel, 199, 213, 214, 215

SUBJECT INDEX

Abaddon, 46, 48.
"abode of the dead," 44, 45, 46, 50, 53, 56, 56n45. *See also Gehenna*; "grave"; *Hades*; hell; netherworld; *sheol*
ACUTE. *See* Alliance Commission on Unity and Truth Among Evangelicals (ACUTE)
aiōnios, 183, 202, 203. *See also* "eternal"
Alliance Commission on Unity and Truth Among Evangelicals (ACUTE) 33, 68, 200, 201, 202, 204, 207, 213. *See also Nature of Hell, The*
"already/not yet," 154, 165–68. *See also* eschatology: inaugurated eschatology
angel, angels, 25, 46, 103, 112, 114, 119, 125, 128, 131, 133, 134, 138,141, 147, 149, 155, 156, 157, 161, 161n5, 167, 168, 180, 183, 209 218, 220, 227, 228
Anglican, Anglicanism, 22, 23, 30, 31, 39, 171, 197, 200, 226. *See also* Church of England Doctrine Commission; hell: Anglican views of; *Mystery of Salvation, The*
annihilation, annihilationism, annihilationist, 29, 36, 37, 65, 79, 81, 83, 87, 92, 112, 145, 146, 195–218, 220, 234; and God's justice, 207–12; and God's love, 213–18; definitions of, 11, 12, 13, 77, 185, 196; early Christian writers on, 85; history of, 19, 197–200; rejection of traditional view of hell, 30–31, 33–35, 102, 200–206; supposed evidence for in Paul, 103–9; supposed evidence for in Revelation, 115–34. *See also* conditional immortality
Antichrist, the; antichrists, 62, 63, 132, 134, 165
apocalyptic, apocalypticism, 47, 97, 114n9, 184, 224
apokatastasis, 17, 18, 101, 170, 170n1. *See also* universalism
apollymi, 30, 81, 92, 104, 105, 146, 185, 203, 204. *See also* destroy, destruction; *olethros*
Arian, Arianism, 19, 197, 213n60
athanasia, 206. *See also* immortality; resurrection of the dead
atonement, 34, 35, 149, 150, 182, 213, 226, 230, 239, 240

Babylon, fall of (as OT model of destruction), 47, 54, 56, 58, 113, 116, 120–23, 122n28, 127, 185, 237
banishment, 13, 80, 136, 138, 142, 145, 147–48, 149, 150, 151, 161, 168, 183, 220. *See also* hell: descriptions of
beast, the, 112, 113, 115, 116, 117, 118, 119, 123, 125, 126, 127, 127n44, 128, 129, 130, 132, 133, 134, 141, 183, 205, 217, 228. *See also* devil; false prophet, the; Satan
Book of Life, 61, 62, 141–42, 163, 164 183, 218, 228

Catholicism. *See* hell: Roman Catholic views of
Church of England Doctrine Commission, 32. *See also* Anglican, Anglicanism; hell: Anglican views of; *Mystery of Salvation, The*
conditional immortality, 23, 29, 32, 36, 77, 92, 103, 108, 109, 173n14, 196, 201n19, 205, 206. *See also* annihilation, annihilationism, annihilationist
conditionalism, conditionalist. *See* annihilation, annihilationism, annihilationist; conditional immortality
Constantinople, Second Council of (A.D. 553), 18, 85, 170, 197, 170n1
conversion, 180, 187, 188
"curse(d)," 64, 93, 119, 128, 140, 149, 155, 218, 229, 230, 231

dark, darkness, 48, 49, 51, 55, 56, 56n44, 56n45, 84, 119, 120, 138, 141, 142, 147, 149, 150, 161n7, 182, 184, 220, 223, 225, 226, 227, 230, 231, 233, 235, 237
"day and night," 30, 47, 112, 115, 116, 117, 118, 119, 121, 125, 127, 128, 129, 132, 133, 141, 144, 161, 217, 218
Day of Judgment, 89, 94, 120, 131n52, 141, 167
dead, death, die, 11, 12, 17, 20, 33, 34, 35, 44, 44n1, 45, 45n12, 46, 46n15, 46n17, 47, 47n17, 48, 49, 49n20, 50, 51, 51n29, 52, 53, 53n37, 54, 54n40, 54n42, 55, 56, 56n45, 57, 58, 59, 60, 61, 63, 64, 64n59, 65, 68, 72, 74, 75, 76, 77, 78, 80, 81, 82, 83, 84, 85, 89, 92, 93, 94, 95, 95n7, 96, 97, 98, 99, 101, 102, 105, 106, 109, 112, 113, 116, 117, 119, 120, 121, 122, 122n28, 123, 124, 125n37, 128, 129, 130, 130n47, 131, 132, 132n55, 133, 136, 139, 140, 141, 142, 144, 145, 145, 149, 150, 150n24, 151, 155, 156, 157, 159, 160, 161, 162, 163, 164, 167, 168, 170, 171, 172, 173, 173n14, 174, 174n16, 175, 179, 180, 182, 183, 184, 185, 187, 188n45, 189, 191, 192, 194, 196, 197, 199n15, 202, 203, 206, 208, 211, 212, 213, 218, 221, 225, 226, 227, 228, 229, 230, 231, 232, 233, 236, 240
destroy, destruction, 13, 17, 19, 20, 30, 31, 46, 47, 57, 70, 72, 73, 75, 79, 80, 81, 82, 92, 93n3, 94, 103, 104, 105, 106, 107, 108, 113, 115, 116, 119, 120, 121, 121n25, 122, 123, 124, 125n37, 129, 136, 137, 138, 139, 140, 141, 142, 142n5, 144–46, 145n11, 146n17, 148, 149, 150, 151, 155, 156, 162, 184, 185, 187, 196, 197, 201, 202, 203, 204, 217, 227, 232, 237. *See also apollymi*; hell: descriptions of
devil, 81, 116, 118, 127, 128, 129, 133, 134, 138, 141, 147, 149, 155, 161, 168, 175, 183, 217, 218, 220, 227, 228. *See also* beast, the; false prophet, the; Satan

Index

Enlightenment, 11, 20, 36, 68, 172. *See also* hell: Enlightenment views of; skepticism

election, 102, 163, 165, 193

eschatology, 27, 33, 62, 84, 96, 165, 176, 204; inaugurated eschatology, 93, 94, 150, 150n24. *See also* "already/not yet"

"eternal," 17, 50, 64, 72, 75–76, 77, 80, 81, 103, 106, 108, 117, 118, 126, 144, 183, 201, 202–3, 227, 232. *See also aiōnios*; hell: descriptions of

eternal fire, 81, 84, 115, 117, 128, 138, 141, 144, 147, 149, 155, 161, 168, 183, 218, 227. *See also* hell: descriptions of

eternal life, 11, 29, 63, 64, 74, 75, 76, 77, 82, 92, 93, 95, 97, 98, 99, 108, 109, 123, 143, 144, 145, 151, 155, 166,168, 183, 205, 206, 218, 227. *See also* immortality

eternal punishment. *See* hell: eternal nature of; punishment: eternal nature of

eternal torment. *See* hell: eternal nature of; punishment: eternal nature of

"Evangelical Affirmations," 31. *See also* National Association of Evangelicals

Evangelical Alliance. *See* Alliance Commission on Unity and Truth Among Evangelicals (ACUTE)

evangelical, evangelicalism, 11, 12, 13, 19, 21, 28, 29, 30, 31, 32, 33, 33n72, 33n73, 35, 36, 37, 39, 40, 41, 68, 69, 69n7, 78n38, 88, 103n29, 105, 147, 148, 170, 174n16, 185n33, 196, 198, 199, 200, 201, 208, 214, 215n72, 220, 229, 234, 239. *See also* hell: evangelical views of

evangelism, 175, 199; eschatological evangelization, 180; postmortem evangelism, 36, 173, 185, 188

evil, 17, 24, 25, 26, 31, 37, 38, 49, 54n42, 57, 60, 64n59, 73, 89, 93, 117, 138, 155, 159, 160, 161, 162, 167, 179, 185, 186, 192, 198, 208, 209,210, 216, 217, 218, 225. *See also* God: victory of (over evil); sin

exclusivism, 33, 181n26

Fall, the, 86, 94, 150, 193, 226. *See also* sin: original sin

false prophet, the, 112, 116, 118, 123, 127, 127n44, 128, 129, 130, 132, 133, 134, 137, 141, 183, 205, 217, 228. *See also* beast, the; devil; Satan

freedom (human), 13, 33, 33n72, 37, 154, 158–65, 186, 189. *See also* election; God: sovereignty of; reprobation

free will. *See* freedom (human)

Gehenna, 44, 60, 60n30, 61n52, 72, 79, 81, 82, 92, 120, 130, 132n54, 146n17, 184, 227. *See also* "abode of the dead"; "grave"; *Hades*; hell; netherworld; *sheol*

general epistles. *See* hell: NT general epistles' teaching on

God: analogical language and, 177–78; as "eternal torturer," 30, 78, 108; attributes of, 178, 216, 239; character of, 19, 186, 189, 191, 208–9, 237; doctrine of, 25, 38, 213, 234, 239, 240; eternal nature of, 23, 64, 118, 119, 128; faithfulness of, 47, 99; fatherhood of, 34, 160; fear of, 72, 78, 80; foreknowledge of, 34, 160; glory of, 30, 40, 75, 128; goodness of, 22; grace of, 60, 92, 93, 98, 104, 109, 240; holiness of, 17, 39, 73, 109, 162, 163, 190, 210, 214, 215; image of, 63, 177–78; judgment/justice of, 17, 17n6, 18, 24, 27, 31, 32, 65, 75, 88, 94n5, 95, 103, 105, 109, 113, 114, 115, 119, 124, 139, 140, 143, 145, 147, 148, 149, 156, 157–58, 162, 185, 188, 201, 208, 209, 210, 211, 212, 214, 215, 218, 221–26, 221n3, 231, 232, 235, 237, 239 (*see also* judgment); kingdom of, 74, 82, 136, 137, 138, 141, 147, 148, 151, 173; knowledge of, 103–4, 140, 148, 162, 179; law of, 11, 140, 185, 217; love of, 11, 32, 33, 37, 88, 145, 154, 171, 172, 174, 175, 186, 188, 189–94, 201, 208, 213, 214, 215, 216, 239; mercy of, 23, 119, 192, 214, 215–16; omniscience of, 37; peace of, 21; presence of, 12, 64, 74, 102, 108, 136, 143, 147, 148, 151, 166; punishment of, 24, 79, 92, 93, 95, 117, 140, 149, 156, 167, 184, 239 (*see also* punishment); reconciliation with, 99, 100, 101, 179, 189, 229; rejection of traditional view of, 34, 35, 37, 38, 39, 40, 71, 78, 89, 172, 173, 174, 175, 181–82, 183, 186–87, 213; righteousness of, 94, 126, 202, 234, 237; separation from, 27, 108, 109, 121, 131, 136, 138, 140, 147, 148, 150, 203, 226, 227, 231 (*see also* "separation"); sovereignty of, 13, 28, 31, 37, 97, 98, 158–65, 174, 175, 177, 206, 214, 218, 235; victory of (over evil), 17, 26, 31, 201, 216–18; will of, 19, 34, 90, 101, 160, 164; Word of, 36, 71, 177, 239, 240; wrath of 35, 42, 58, 61, 74, 75, 78, 83, 92, 93, 94, 109, 112, 113, 117, 125, 126, 137, 139, 141, 143, 150, 154, 157, 162, 166, 179, 185, 214, 215, 223, 227, 228, 230, 233, 234, 236

Gospels. *See* hell: Jesus' teaching on

"grave," 44, 46, 47, 48, 49, 50n25, 53, 54n42, 55, 57, 63, 64, 131, 155, 161, 168. *See also* "abode of the dead"; *Gehenna*; *Hades*; hell; netherworld, *sheol*

Greek thought, 17, 83–87, 96n10, 201, 204–6. *See also* Hellenism, Hellenistic; Platonism

guilt, guilty. 37, 40, 57, 94, 145, 150, 158, 159, 160, 161, 179, 192, 208, 211, 212, 222, 224, 225, 236. *See also* shame

Hades, 30, 44, 106, 129, 130, 130n47, 132, 147, 162, 163. *See also* "abode of the dead"; *Gehenna*; "grave"; hell; netherworld; *sheol*

heaven, heavens, 11, 13, 18, 21, 25, 26, 27, 29, 32, 33, 45, 50n29, 51, 52, 54, 57, 60, 64, 72, 73, 75, 76, 77, 78, 82, 93, 94, 100, 101, 103, 131, 137, 139, 142, 147, 148, 149, 150, 151, 156, 166, 167, 168, 176, 186, 188, 189, 193, 209n48, 213n64, 216, 218, 221, 225, 226, 227, 228, 233, 236, 237

hell: Anglican views of, 32–33; as "myth," 25–26; changing cultural influences and, 36–41, 88–90; descriptions of, 47, 142–48 (*see also*

254

banishment; destroy, destruction; "eternal"; eternal fire; "lake of fire"; "Pit"; "second death"; "separation"; "weeping and gnashing of teeth"); "disappearance" of, 16, 18, 19; doctrine of, 11, 12, 13, 16, 22, 41, 44, 58, 65, 68, 87, 92, 95, 97, 103, 109, 136, 137, 138, 140, 141, 142, 154, 200, 208, 214, 239, 240; emotional responses to, 30, 88, 89, 90, 196, 207n44, 213, 220; Enlightenment views of, 19–20; eternal nature of, 17, 18, 20, 23, 24, 28, 32, 35, 40, 69, 71, 81, 82, 84, 87, 89, 90, 92, 96–102, 106–8, 112, 115, 132–34, 148, 176, 186, 202–3, 217, 239; evangelical views of, 28–36, 88, 147, 148; Jesus' teaching on, 17, 19, 28, 60, 61, 62, 67–90, 96, 136–39, 143–44, 145, 147, 149, 183, 184, 218, 220, 225–26, 239 (see also Greek thought; Hellenism, Hellenistic; Platonism); liberal views of, 32–33; medieval views of, 18; modern views of, 25–27; NT general epistles' teaching on, 140–42 (see also judgment; punishment); OT teaching on, 43–65 (see also judgment; punishment); patristic views of, 16, 17, 18, 84–87; Paul's teaching on, 92–109, 139–40; preaching/pastoral theology and, 220–37; punitive nature of (see God: judgment/justice of; God: punishment of; judgment; punishment); reality of, 11, 17, 72, 92–96, 185, 186, 217, 220, 226, 231, 232; Reformation views of, 18–19; rejection of traditional doctrine of, 12, 13, 16, 17, 19, 20, 21, 23, 24, 26, 27, 28, 29–41, 68, 69–71, 78, 88, 154, 196, 207; Revelation's teaching on, 111–34, 141–42; Roman Catholic views of, 16, 27, 28, 37, 39, 40, 170, 181n26, 187 (see also purgatory); Victorian views of, 20–25; traditional view of, 16, 68. See also "abode of the dead"; Gehenna; God: judgment/justice of; God: punishment of; "grave"; Hades; judgment: role of Trinity in; netherworld; punishment: eternal nature of; sheol

Hellenism, Hellenistic, 84, 85, 86, 87n78. See also Greek thought; Platonism

Holy Spirit, 154, 158, 177, 179, 184. See also judgment: role of Trinity in; Trinity

immortality, 23, 29, 81, 85, 87, 103, 108, 109, 109n49, 196, 198, 201, 204, 205, 206. See also eternal life; soul: immortality of

inclusivism, 25, 33, 34, 36, 181n26, 215, 215n70. See also salvation: universal salvationism; universalism

intermediate state, 120n23, 167

Jehovah's Witnesses, 196, 197

Jesus: as destroyer, 145 (see also destroy, destruction); as Judge, 138, 143,155–58, 161, 162, 163, 183, 221–28, 234; as King, 138, 155, 156, 168, 183; as Lamb, 156, 157, 160, 181; as Son of God, 79, 85, 101, 155, 156, 157, 158, 160, 166, 178, 179, 183, 191, 229, 232; death of (as sin offering), 229, 232, 239, 240 (see also atonement); love of, 213–15, 228–34 (see also

God: love of); on God's sovereignty, 159–60, 161; rejection of traditional view of, 40, 68, 69–71, 181, 183, 188; resurrection of, 85. See also hell: Jesus' teaching on; Trinity

Jesus Seminar, the, 68, 68n4

judgment: and eschatology, 165–68; and God's sovereignty, 161–65 (see also God: sovereignty of); and preaching, 227–28, 234; Catholic teaching on, 27; early Christian teaching on, 16, 18; eternal nature of, 114–20, 132–34, 184, 202, 205n37; in Daniel, 65; in Isaiah, 61; in Jesus' teaching, 75, 77, 136–39, 141–42 (see also hell: Jesus' teaching on); in Paul's teaching, 93–98, 102, 104, 105, 109, 139–40; in Revelation, 112, 113, 114n7, 117n16, 121n25, 122–32, 125n37; other NT teaching on, 140–41, 143, 144, 146, 147; rejection of traditional view of, 29, 88n85, 96n11, 199n15, 209n49; role of Trinity in, 154–58; "vindictive" nature of, 207–8. See also Day of Judgment; God: judgment/justice of; God: punishment of; hell; punishment

Judgment Day. See Day of Judgment

justice, 30, 38, 39, 89, 90, 103, 134, 137, 139, 143, 156, 157, 199n15, 207, 207n44, 208, 209, 210, 211, 212, 212n58, 213, 214, 216, 218, 223, 225, 239. See also God: judgment/justice of; God: punishment of; judgment

"lake of fire," 30, 116, 124, 127, 128, 129–32, 132n55, 141, 163, 164, 168, 183, 218. See also hell: descriptions of; "second death"

love. See God: love of; Jesus: love of

Mystery of Salvation, The, 32. See also Anglican, Anglicanism; Church of England Doctrine Commission; hell: Anglican views of

National Association of Evangelicals, 31. See also "Evangelical Affirmations"

Nature of Hell, The, 33, 33n73, 68n2, 70n18, 71n19, 72n22, 77n34, 85n68, 103n29, 196n2, 198n8, 200, 201, 202, 204, 204n31, 207n42, 213, 213n61, 217. See also Alliance Commission on Unity and Truth Among Evangelicals (ACUTE)

netherworld, 45n10, 46n17, 48n20, 53n38, 59, 60, 61, 61n52; nature of, 50–58; occupants of, 46–50; vocabulary of, 44–46. See also "abode of the dead"; Gehenna; "grave"; Hades; hell; sheol

Old Testament. See hell: OT teaching on

olethros, 92, 104, 105, 106, 146, 185, 203, 204. See also apollymi; destroy, destruction

"outer darkness." See dark, darkness

pastoral theology. See hell: preaching/pastoral theology and Paul (apostle). See hell: Paul's teaching on

"perish," 46, 63, 75, 92, 93, 94, 105, 120, 136, 139, 141, 142, 145, 146, 161, 164, 165, 166, 203, 204, 221, 223, 225, 227. See also destroy, destruction

"Pit," 45, 48, 49, 50, 52, 52n34, 53, 57, 120, 130.
   See also hell: descriptions of
Platonism, 19, 81, 83, 84, 85, 86, 86n72, 86n73,
   87, 108, 205. See also Greek thought;
   Hellenism, Hellenistic
pluralism, 40, 174, 180, 181n25, 182
pluralist salvationism. See salvation: pluralist
   salvationism
postmodernism, 37, 69, 69n8, 88, 97, 239
postmortem evangelism. See evangelism:
   postmortem evangelism
postmortem salvationism. See salvation:
   postmortem salvationism
preaching on hell. See hell: preaching/pastoral
   theology and
punishment: annihilationist views of, 195–218;
   conscious nature of, 68, 74, 75, 83, 87, 88, 89,
   90, 106–8, 117, 120, 131, 133, 196; eternal
   nature of 11, 13, 17, 18, 19, 20, 22, 23, 24, 25,
   27, 28, 30, 31, 32, 33, 37, 38, 39, 44, 59, 61, 65,
   69, 70–79, 83, 84, 85, 87, 88, 89, 90, 92, 95,
   96, 102, 109, 112, 113, 116, 117, 118, 120–34,
   138, 143, 144, 148, 149, 151, 155, 157, 168,
   172, 176, 182, 183, 184, 187, 188, 192, 196,
   205, 211, 217, 218, 232, 234, 239, 240;
   universalist views on, 182–83, 185–89. See also
   God: judgment/justice of; God: punishment of;
   hell; judgment; justice
purgatory, 39, 187, 193. See also hell: Roman
   Catholic views of

reprobation, 164, 165. See also election; freedom
   (human); God: sovereignty of
resurrection of the dead, 20, 54n42, 58, 59, 59n48,
   62, 65, 76, 84, 85, 86, 86n73, 96, 97, 98, 108,
   124, 130, 131, 131n52, 156, 165, 167, 187,
   188n45, 204, 206. See also athanasia; immortality
Revelation, Book of. See hell: Revelation's teaching
   on

salvation, 11, 25, 27, 28, 31, 31n61, 32, 34, 39, 40,
   47, 68, 75, 85, 88, 96, 97, 98, 99, 101, 104, 140,
   145, 149, 170, 171, 172, 173n14, 174, 175, 176,
   179–82, 181n26, 183, 187, 191, 193, 194, 202,
   209n49, 215, 221, 228, 235, 236; pluralist
   salvationism, 180, 182; postmortem
   salvationism, 180; secular salvationism, 179,
   182; universal salvationism 32, 97, 186, 188,
   189 (see also universalism)
Satan, 34, 38, 83n59, 127, 128, 129, 130, 131, 161,
   171, 205, 216, 217, 218. See also beast, the;
   devil; false prophet, the
"second death," 80, 116, 123, 129, 130, 131, 132,
   132n55, 133, 136, 142, 145, 149, 150, 163. See
   also hell: descriptions of; "lake of fire"
secular salvationism. See salvation: secular
   salvationism
"separation," 95, 107, 137, 138, 139, 140, 142,
   147, 148, 150, 156, 166, 168, 183, 197, 203,
   226, 227. See also God: separation from; hell:
   descriptions of

Seventh-day Adventists, 54
shame, 40, 61, 63, 220. See also guilt
sheol, 44, 45–46, 47, 48, 49, 49n21, 50, 51, 52n34,
   53, 54, 56, 56n45, 57, 58, 59, 61, 62n55, 63, 64,
   65. See also "abode of the dead"; Gehenna;
   "grave"; hell; netherworld
sin, sinner, sinfulness, 17, 29, 31, 39, 40, 51,
   78n37, 89, 92, 98, 99, 102, 106, 136, 138, 139,
   140, 145, 150, 156, 158, 159, 164, 165, 175,
   179, 184, 187, 193, 194, 202, 207, 208, 214,
   215, 218, 221, 222, 223, 225, 226, 239, 240;
   Christ's atonement for, 229–32 (see also Jesus:
   death of [as sin offering]); eternal consequences
   of, 102, 106, 207, 207n44, 209–13, 212n58,
   226, 227, 234–35; habitual nature of, 193, 210,
   212; original sin,150, 164, 165, 180, 211–12,
   240 (see also Fall, the). See also God:
   punishment of; God: victory of (over evil);
   God: wrath of; Jesus: love of
skepticism, 20, 68, 71, 178. See also Enlightenment
"smoke of their torment," 112, 114–15, 116, 117,
   118, 120, 125, 141, 144. See also hell:
   Revelation's teaching on; judgment;
   punishment
soul, 19, 23, 34, 48, 56n45, 72, 80, 85, 123, 138,
   167, 168, 170, 174, 188, 190, 193, 227, 231,
   232; Greek view of, 81, 83, 86, 86n73, 87,
   87n80, 95n7, 109n49, 170n1, 197, 201, 204–6,
   205n27, 205n38. See also Greek thought;
   Hellenism, Hellenistic; Platonism
"soul sleep," 54

theodicy, 37, 40, 180, 185, 186, 189
Trinity, 13, 19, 154, 158, 161, 165, 168, 174, 180,
   191. See also judgment: role of Trinity in

unevangelized, fate of. See inclusivism
universal salvationism. See salvation: universal
   salvationism; universalism
universalism, 11, 12, 13, 17, 25, 29, 30, 32, 33, 34,
   36, 92, 96, 97, 98, 99, 100, 101, 102, 169–94,
   200, 214, 217; and eternal punishment, 182–
   89; and love of God, 189–94; and salvation,
   179–82; definition of, 170–71; significance of
   and problems with, 175–78; varieties of, 172–
   74. See also apokatastasis; inclusivism; salvation:
   universal salvationism

Valley of Hinnom. See Gehenna
Vatican II (Council), 27, 173n14. See also hell:
   Roman Catholic views of; purgatory
victory. See God: victory of (over evil); Jesus: death
   of (as sin offering)

"weeping and gnashing of teeth," 138, 144, 155,
   225, 227. See also hell: descriptions of
Westminster Confession of Faith, 235
World Council of Churches, 175
"wrath," 56, 92, 93, 94, 102, 106, 139, 140, 142,
   184, 191, 225. See also God: judgment/justice
   of; God: punishment of; God: wrath of